Golden Hands

*A Comprehensive Guide to Knitting,
Dressmaking, and Needlecraft*

EDITOR

Beverley Hilton

VOLUME 6

MARSHALL CAVENDISH CORPORATION / NEW YORK

Contents

Crafts/millinery

For anyone who makes her own clothes, millinery is a most satisfying skill to develop. It is much quicker to make a new hat than a new dress and, as a hat requires less than a yard of material, expensive fabrics can be indulged in. Some hats are made from "hoods" of felt or straw which are dampened with steam and then blocked into shape. For the milliner working at home, wooden blocks are an expensive investment and hoods are not always easily available.

However, with fabrics similar to those used in dressmaking and paper patterns, a number of stitched and draped styles can be achieved quite easily.

All the hats illustrated in this chapter were made from one basic pattern shape—the base plate of an electric iron. By making adjustments to the shape of the base plate, patterns for full crowned hats, such as the beret, and high crowned, such as the brimmed hat,

are simply made. Try out one or two of the hats and you will realize that this basic pattern can be used to make endless variations.

Basic equipment

Your dressmaking equipment includes nearly everything you need for home millinery, but there are additional items which are necessary for ease of working and satisfactory results. Besides a sewing machine, you will need two mirrors—a full length one for checking that your hat is in proportion to the rest of your ensemble, and a hand mirror for checking side and back views.

To make the hats in this chapter you will also need:

☐ An electric iron (not a steam iron)
☐ Newspaper
☐ 1 13/16 inch steel pins
☐ Tape measure
☐ Fabric and paper scissors
☐ Silk-covered millinery wire No. 90 for headwires
☐ Wire cutters
☐ Millinery needles (straw needles) No. 6
☐ No. 40 mercerized sewing thread to match fabric
☐ Hand and standing mirrors

Fabrics

The material for a hat doesn't have to be expensive—the most important thing is that it should be easy to handle and have plenty of bias give. Don't choose very slippery nylon jersey or very stiff cotton or taffeta. Ideal fabrics are soft, pliable, and lightweight.

Interfacing

Most stitched styles need an interfacing to give body and shape to the top material. The exception, in this chapter, is the suede cap, where the peak only is stiffened with lightweight buckram. The kind of interfacing needed depends on the style of hat. Permanently stiffened cotton is the most versatile of interfacings and has the added advantage of being easy to obtain. It is, therefore, used for all the hats in this chapter.

The non-woven type of interfacing is not suitable for hats as it has no grain or bias give.

The golden rule of hatmaking is that *all* materials, including interfacing, must be cut on the bias. Shaped pieces are cut with center or center front on the bias.

Making the basic pattern

The sole plate of your electric iron gives you the shape of one section of the basic pattern. Stand the iron flat on a sheet of 1 inch squared paper and, using a felt pen, draw around the outline of the sole plate. Decide on the number of sections you need for the hat, 8 sections make the full, velvet beret, 6 make the suede cap and the brimmed hat, 6 make the base of the draped turban. Measure around your head at the point where the hat will fit comfortably. Hats always get tighter as they are being made so add ½ inch of ease to your head measurement. Divide this measurement by the number of sections and adjust the bottom of the 1502

shape accordingly (figure **1, 2** and **3**). You will also need to adjust the height and the width of the section shape, as shown in the diagrams for different hat styles.

Cut out the section shape and then fold it down the center to make sure adjustments are the same on both sides.

Cut out the section, allowing ⅝ inch seam allowance all around.

Once you have made a basic section pattern, you can use it to make hats out of newspaper to try out various styles. Newspaper is surprisingly malleable, and ideal for the purpose.

Suede peaked cap

You will need:
One small suede skin
⅝yd lightweight taffeta for lining
Small piece of lightweight buckram
Milliner's grosgrain ribbon
Adjust the basic shape as shown in figure **2**.
Cut six sections from the skin for the

crown. Cut out a headband and two brim shapes from the graph on page 1505. Pin headband around head loosely. Pin the sections to this for fitting and make any adjustments necessary to get the style to suit you. A slight alteration to all six seams will make quite a difference to the fullness of the shape. When you are satisfied with the style, mark the pinned seams lightly on the wrong side with a pencil. Baste, and then machine stitch the six crown sections together, stitching from the points down to the headline (figure **4**). If the points do not come together perfectly, they can be finished off with a few hand stitches. A neat effect can be achieved by joining the six sections together in two groups, trimming the turnings at the points and then stitching the two halves together with one seam right over the top. Join the headband at the back, open and trim the seam. The headband fits over the crown sections (figure **5**). If the sectioned crown is slightly fuller than the headband, there will be an attractive pouch of extra

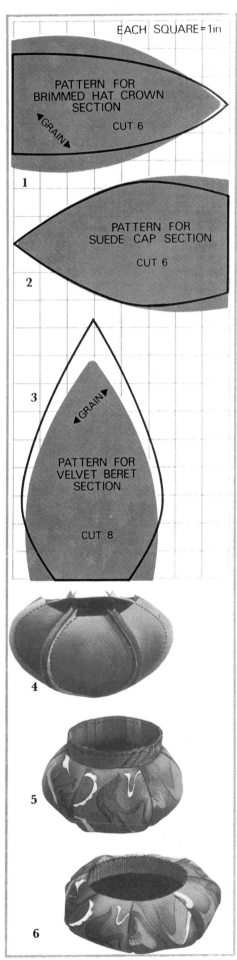

PATTERN FOR
BRIMMED HAT CROWN
SECTION

CUT 6

GRAIN

1

PATTERN FOR
SUEDE CAP SECTION

CUT 6

2

3

GRAIN

PATTERN FOR
VELVET BERET
SECTION

CUT 8

4

5

6

fullness around the head. Machine stitch the headband to the hat crown, and fold it back so that all the raw edges lie inside the hat.

Make the peak as you would make a collar, with the two layers of suede right sides facing and the buckram on top. Then layer and clip the brim edge so that the top fabric lies smoothly when the peak is turned right side out. Top-stitch the edge of the brim and join it to the hat, either hand-stitching as shown in figure **10**, or machine stitching. The brim can be left off this cap for a more formal shape.

Finishing off

Cut a piece of 1 inch wide milliner's grosgrain ribbon to the head measurement plus $\frac{3}{4}$ inch for overlap. Curve the ribbon by pulling it under a hot iron and a damp cloth. Hem the long curved edge of the ribbon to the inside of the headband and the ribbon will set neatly into place without fluting (figure **6**). For the lining,

cut out the six sections from taffeta and seam. Slip stitch the lining behind the head ribbon for a professional finish.

Soft velvet beret

You will need:
$\frac{7}{8}$yd velvet
$\frac{7}{8}$yd permanently stiffened cotton
Milliner's grosgrain ribbon
$\frac{5}{8}$yd lightweight taffeta for lining
Lightweight buckram

Adjust the basic shape as shown in diagram **3**. Cut out eight pieces in the interfacing and in the velvet. Baste the interfacing sections to adjust the fit and style. Then mount the interfacing sections on the velvet sections and make them as one, using the same method as given for the suede cap.

A soft beret will sit on the head better if a narrow bias strip of lightweight buckram is stitched in behind the turnings at the headline. Finish off with grosgrain ribbon and lining as for the suede cap.

Brimmed hat

You will need:
☐ 1yd linen-type fabric
☐ 1yd permanently stiffened cotton
☐ Silk-covered milliner's wire No. 90
☐ Milliner's grosgrain ribbon
☐ 2 spools mercerized thread No. 4

The headwire

This style of hat requires a headwire to support the brim while it is being planned, and also prevents the hat from becoming too tight when it is being made. Cut a length of silk-covered milliner's wire to the head measurement, plus $\frac{1}{2}$ inch of ease (using wire cutters to obtain neat ends). Remove the spring in the wire by pulling it steadily between finger and thumb. Try it around the head and then bind the overlapped join firmly with thread (diagram **8**). Since the head is oval, press the sides of the ring into an oval-shaped headwire.

Fitting the hat

Adjust the basic section shape and cut out six sections. The squared chart gives a pattern for a fairly large brim. Copy this onto 1 inch squared paper. It is important when making a brimmed hat to make sure that the height of the crown and the width of the brim suit your particular face and build. Make a paper and cotton hat first and try it on in front of a mirror. Cut out the brim in double thickness of newspaper and pin it to the headwire. Cut out the six crown sections in stiffened cotton. Pin the crown over the brim and check the effect. If the brim seems too large for you, trim the newspaper. Reduce the height of the crown if necessary by turning under more than $\frac{5}{8}$ inch at the headline, where it meets the brim. When the hat shape is satisfactory, use the newspaper brim as a pattern to cut out two brims in top material, following the straight of grain as shown on the chart. Cut one or two layers of cotton interfacing, using the same newspaper pattern, according to the amount of stiffness required.
NB Turnings have been allowed on the headline and for the center back seam on the brim, but $\frac{5}{8}$ inch must be allowed all around the outer edge of the shape.

Making the hat

The brim is made rather like a collar, with the right sides of the top fabric facing and the stiffening laid on top. Machine stitch around the outer edge of the brim and then layer the turnings, trimming the interfacing as close as possible to the stitching. Join the back seam and
1504

open and trim the seam. Turn the brim right sides out. Baste the brim edge and then make basting stitches all over the brim through all layers to keep them firm during top-stitching. Before you begin top-stitching, check the machine stitch on spare pieces of fabric because the stitching has to look good on both sides. Start stitching at the headline just before the back seam and about $\frac{13}{16}$ inch from the edge. Work top-stitching as shown in figure **9**. After the first four rows have been worked, the remainder of the brim is stitched in a spiral. When the machine stitching has been completed, remove the basting stitches and sew the headwire into place where the headline will be. Snip into the turnings every $\frac{3}{4}$ inch and try the brim on to see that it still fits, fairly loosely.
Seam the 6 crown sections, two layers together (top fabric and cotton) as for the suede cap. Pin the crown in place over the headwire, turning in the seam allow-

ance. Join the crown to the brim by hand-sewing. Use double thread in a straw needle and make invisible slip stitches (see method in figure **10**). When the brim and crown have been joined, snip the stitches holding the headwire and pull it out. Finish off with grosgrain ribbon and lining as for the velvet beret.
This style looks elegant without trimming, but for a special occasion artificial flowers can be stitched to a length of ribbon tied around the crown with a bow at the back, or, of course, stitched on permanently.

Draped turban

The secret of a successful draped turban lies mainly in the choice of fabric. When the fabric is cut on the bias it should drape easily into folds, without being limp. Chiffons, organzas, silk and wool jerseys are the easiest to use. Velvet can be used, but it tends to be too thick to make more than one or two folds.

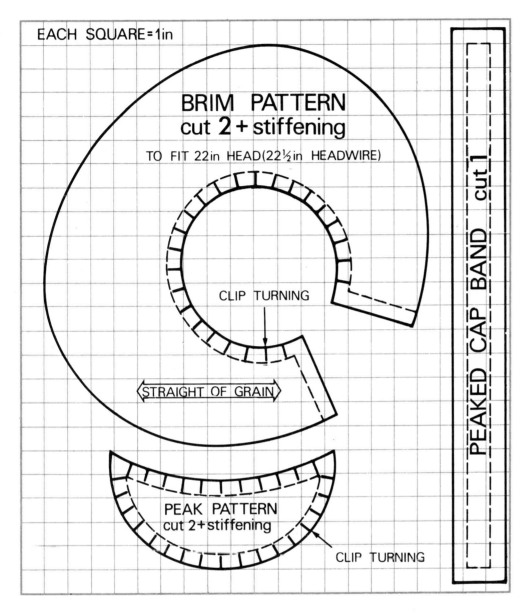

EACH SQUARE=1in

BRIM PATTERN
cut 2 + stiffening

TO FIT 22in HEAD (22½in HEADWIRE)

CLIP TURNING

STRAIGHT OF GRAIN

PEAK PATTERN
cut 2 + stiffening

CLIP TURNING

PEAKED CAP BAND cut 1

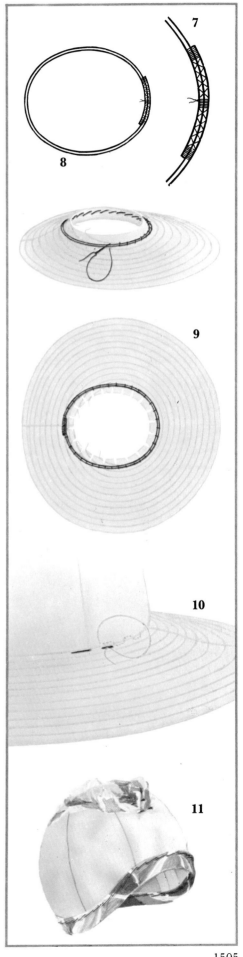

7

8

9

10

11

You will need:
- ☐ 2yds of semi-transparent fabric 40 inches wide, or
- ☐ ⅝yd 36 inches wide in heavier fabric
- ☐ ½yd stiffened cotton for base
- ☐ Silk-covered milliner's wire No.90

Remove all the creases in the fabric and cut bias strips, between 8 and 16 inches wide, according to the weight of the fabric being used. Semi-transparent fabrics are cut into strips 16 inches wide, heavier fabrics into strips 8 inches wide.

The turban base is made up of six sections, cut from stiffened cotton. The basic section shape should be adjusted so that it is slightly fuller and deeper than for the suede cap. Make a headwire to support the shape while it is being draped and make it slightly looser than for the brimmed hat. Shape the oval into a flattering curved line that goes up over the forehead, down over the temples and slightly up at the nape of the neck (figure 11). Baste the headwire to the cotton

crown, and cut away the lower edges of the crown to fit the curves of the headwire but leaving ⅝ inch turnings. Cut a bias strip from the top fabric and cover the lower edge of the crown, backstitching it in place above and below the wired headline (figure 11).

Gathering and stitching

The triangle of fabric left after cutting the first strip is gathered across the middle and pinned to the top of the crown (figure 11). You will find that the long glass headed pins are good for this job. Stitch wherever you pin, placing tiny stitches among the folds, and add more draped pieces to each side of the first drape. It requires some practice to conceal the ends of the final drapes but your skill will increase with every style you create, and each one will be an exclusive model. You might like to try leaving one long drape end and wearing it under the chin and across the shoulder.

Knitting design/working from measurements

Once you know how to make and measure a gauge swatch and how to increase and decrease, you are ready to learn how to design your own knitted and crocheted garments and make them without detailed directions. The basic principles of designing are simple and you can make all the attractive clothes shown in these knitting design chapters by following the easy, step-by-step directions.

This first chapter deals with taking the necessary measurements correctly and converting them into stitches and rows, to make the skirt shown. The top is featured in the following chapter.

Preparation

Designing knitting or crochet, whether it is worked out in words or in symbols on graph paper, is planning what has to be done with each stitch to produce a piece of work of a certain shape and size.

To plan a garment successfully two facts must be ascertained.

1. The exact measurements of the person who is going to wear the garment.
2. The exact gauge obtained from the chosen yarn, pattern and needles.

Measurements

You will need to use two different sets of measurements.

1. The actual measurements. These should not be taken too tightly or over outer clothing but next to the body over lingerie.

Keep a note of your own measurements, and from time to time check that they have not changed.

2. The measurements of the finished garment. These have to be calculated from the actual body measurements plus an additional allowance for what is called "tolerance". This is simply the amount necessary to make the garment comfortable. For instance, a bulky jacket for cold weather wear needs to be more loosely fitting than a dress in fine yarn.

Gauge

Knowing the exact number of stitches and rows to the inch is very important. If you measure carelessly, or do not feel that half a stitch to an inch is very important, you will not be able to produce exactly the size you require. In printed patterns the yarn is specified and you are guided to the needle size required. When designing for yourself, you are no longer limited to obtaining the gauge specified by the designer but must decide for yourself what gauge will produce the effect you want.

First, choose the type of garment you

want to make and then decide what kind of yarn is most suitable.

The next step is to try the pattern with the chosen yarn, changing needle sizes if necessary until you have a swatch that gives the gauge required for the finished garment. The swatch should be at least four inches square, and the larger it is the more accurate a guide to gauge it will be.

Flared Skirt

For your first design, try a simple skirt in stockinette stitch. In order to guide you step by step, several decisions have had to be made for you but the same process will be followed when you are making your own choices.

Using Unger Tosca (machine washable), a swatch of thirty stitches was knitted on No.6 needles. This was carefully measured and was found to have a gauge of five stitches and seven rows to one inch.

Taking measurements

For a skirt, five measurements are required.
1. Actual waist measurement.
2. Actual hip measurement.
3. Actual waist to hipline measurement.
4. Actual hipline to hemline measurement.
5. Required hemline width.

Skirts vary in design, the simplest having almost straight sides and curving into the waist from the hipline. The skirt illustrated is more flared but is just as simple to plan. The back and front of the skirt are the same.

Draw a small plan like diagram II. It does not have to be drawn to scale and simply acts as a guide. Mark the lines A—B, C—D and E—F as in the diagram.

A—B is the waistline. This skirt is seamed at either side with elastic casing at the waist and therefore requires one half inch to be added to the front piece and one half inch added to the back piece for the seams. Therefore add one inch to your own waist measurement. Mark exactly half of the total on the line A—B (for example, if your waist measures 27 inches, 27 plus 1 inch=28 inches. Half of this= 14in A—B).

C—D is the hipline. Mark half your hip measurement plus one inch for tolerance on the line C—D.

E—F is the hemline. Mark half the required hemline. For a straight skirt this may be only two, three or four inches more than the C—D measurement, but for a more flared skirt, such as the one illustrated, it will require C—D plus 13½ inches. B—D is the distance between waistline and hipline. Measure this and mark it B—D. D—F is the distance be- tween hipline and hemline. Measure and mark this D—F.

Working out stitches and rows.

The next stage is to calculate the number of stitches and rows from these measurements. For the measurements A—B, C—D, E—F, multiply the total number of inches by the number of stitches to the inch on your gauge swatch. This will give you the total number of stitches required at these three points. Mark them on your chart. Next, calculate the number of rows between points B—D, and between D—F, by multiplying the total number of inches by the number of rows to the inch on your swatch. Mark these figures on the chart, which should now look like diagram II but with your own measurements. For a straight skirt it will be sufficient to decrease the number of stitches at the sides of the work. The flared skirt has rather a lot of stitches to decrease and looks smoother if stitches are decreased in the middle as well as at the side edges.

The skirt illustrated has six stitches decreased on each decrease row— one at each side edge and one at each side of each dotted line on the sketch. In order to decide which decreasing method to use see Knitting Know-how chapters 7, 8 and 9. Work out how many decrease rows are required and then how many rows are required between decrease rows to give the correct length.

Two final points remain to be decided.
1. The type of finishing on waistline.
2. The type of finishing on hemline.
The simplest waist finishing is simply to work casing stitch neatly behind the upper edge (Knitting Know-how chapter 69). You may prefer to work the last half inch or one inch in ribbing and then work casing stitch behind this, or turn under a hem to run elastic through.

The lower edge may require a hem or simply two or four rows of ribbing or garter stitch, being careful not to change the gauge.

Try a small sample if you are in any doubt. Whichever method you choose, plan so that the skirt is the correct length when finished.

When the skirt is completed, refer to Knitting Know-how chapter 15 for finishing so that you have a professional finish to your first creation.

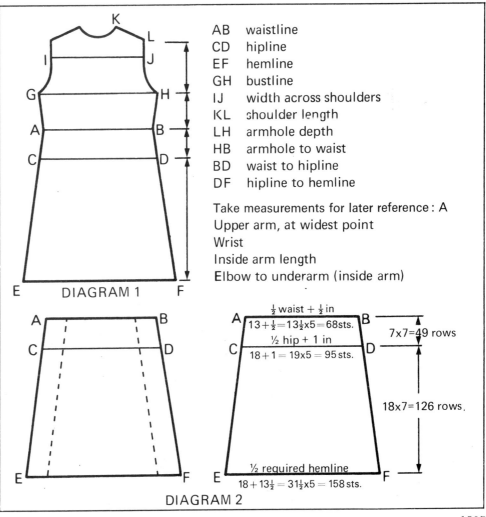

AB	waistline
CD	hipline
EF	hemline
GH	bustline
IJ	width across shoulders
KL	shoulder length
LH	armhole depth
HB	armhole to waist
BD	waist to hipline
DF	hipline to hemline

Take measurements for later reference: A
Upper arm, at widest point
Wrist
Inside arm length
Elbow to underarm (inside arm)

DIAGRAM 1

DIAGRAM 2

½ waist + ½ in
$13\frac{1}{2}=13\frac{1}{2} \times 5 = 68$ sts.
½ hip + 1 in
$18 + 1 = 19 \times 5 = 95$ sts.
$7 \times 7 = 49$ rows
$18 \times 7 = 126$ rows
½ required hemline
$18 + 13\frac{1}{2} = 31\frac{1}{2} \times 5 = 158$ sts.

Crochet pattern/sports coat

This attractive crocheted sports coat has been cleverly designed for the minimum of finishing. The back and front are crocheted in one piece, starting at the neck edge and working down. The sleeves are then worked directly onto the main section so the only seams are on the underarm. One of the advantages of working from the top downward is that the length of the sports coat can easily be adapted, making it possible to make the garment as a short jacket or adapt it to make a full length coat.

Sizes

Directions are for 34in bust. The figures in brackets [] refer to the 37 and 40in sizes respectively.
Length from shoulder, 33in.
Sleeve seam, 17[17½:18]in.

Gauge
4hdc and 3 rows to 1in worked on No.G crochet hook.

Materials

Spinnerin Wintuk Sports 5[6:6] skeins main color, A
4[4:4] skeins contrast, B
One No.F crochet hook;
one No.G crochet hook

Main section

NB The coat is worked from the top downwards, the back and fronts in one, starting at the neck edge. Using No.G hook and A, ch49 loosely.
1st row 1hdc in 3rd ch from hook, 2hdc in each of next 2ch, 4hdc, 2hdc in each of next 2ch, 28hdc, 2hdc in each of next 2ch, 4hdc, 2hdc in each of next 2ch, 2hdc. Place a marker thread between each pair of 2hdc for raglans.
2nd row Ch2 to count as first hdc, hdc in same place, 2hdc, 2hdc in each of next 2hdc (1 inc made at each side of marker thread), 6hdc, 2hdc in each of next 2hdc, 30hdc, 2hdc in each of next 2hdc, 6hdc, 2hdc in each of next 2hdc, 2hdc, 2hdc in last st.
1508

Continue in this way, inc at each side of markers and each end of row for 3 rows more.
6th row Ch12[14:16], 1hdc in 3rd and following 9[11:13] ch, 11hdc, 2hdc in each of next 2hdc, 14hdc, 2hdc in each of next 2hdc, 38hdc, 2hdc in each of next 2hdc, 14hdc, 2hdc in each of next 2hdc, 11hdc. With a separate length of yarn join to top turning ch of 5th row and ch11[13:15] and fasten off, then continuing from 6th row work 1hdc into each of these ch.
7th row Ch2 to count as first hdc, 22[24:26]hdc, 2hdc in each of next 2hdc, 16hdc, 2hdc in each of next 2hdc, 40hdc, 2hdc in each of next 2hdc, 16hdc, 2hdc in each of next 2hdc, 23[25:27]hdc. 134 [138:142] sts.
Continue inc at each side of each marker but not at each end of row for 15[17:19] rows more *at the same time* working in stripe patt rows as follows: (beg at 8th row) 1A, 6B, 8A[1A, 6B, 8A, 2B: 1A, 6B, 8A, 2B, 2A]. 254 [274:294] sts.

Armholes

Next row With B[A:B], ch2, 39[43:47]hdc, ch5, skip next 50[54:58] sts for armhole and continue without breaking yarn, 74[78:82]hdc, ch5, skip next 50[54:58] sts for second armhole, 40[44:48]hdc. 164 [176:188] sts.
Continue without further shaping in hdc working stripe patt rows as follows: 1B, 2A, 2B[1A, 2B:1B], *6A, 4B, 6A, 2B, 2A, 2B*, 8A, 6B, 8A, 2B, 2A, 2B, rep from * to * once more. 100 rows. Fasten off.

Sleeves

Using color to correspond to main section and with RS facing, attach yarn in center of 5ch at underarm.
Ch2, 1hdc in each of next 2ch, 1hdc in each of next 50[54:58] sts of armhole, 1hdc in each of next 2ch at underarm. 55[59:63]hdc.
Continue in stripe patt to correspond to main section dec one st at each end of every 4th row until 12 dec have been worked.
Continue without further shaping until 52[54:56] rows have been worked on sleeve from beg.
Fasten off. Work second sleeve to correspond.

Finishing

Lightly press all pieces on wrong side under a damp cloth using a warm iron. Join sleeve seams.

Edging

Using No.G hook and B, work 2 rows sc around neck edge. Break off yarn. Attach A and work 2 rows more. Break off yarn. Using No.F hook and B, starting at bottom of right front edge work 2 rows sc around all edges, working 3sc into each corner st, Work a 3rd row sc from left to right in crab stitch (see Crochet know-how chapter 23). Fasten off. Work around sleeve edges in same manner. Press all seams.

Jacket made to mid-thigh length ▶
Detail of the second color stripe ▼

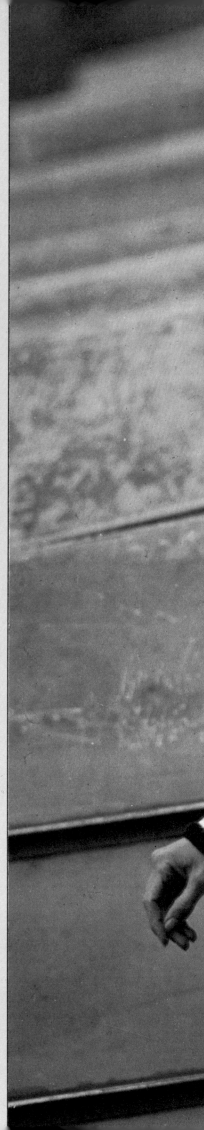

1509

Stitchery design/shape and color

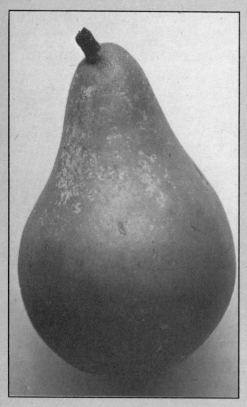

Faced with the idea of creating a design, some embroiderers panic and take refuge in a ready-made embroidery design of some sort. While these are often very good and the results pleasing, all the decisions have been made in advance by someone else, and so the wonderful sense of achievement experienced when one evolves one's own design is lost.

Embroidery is an ideal medium for expressing individuality. With the enormous range of fabrics and threads now available, and a vocabulary of techniques to express the language of design, a whole world of discovery lies at the fingertips of the embroiderer. Once you have mastered a full range of techniques—free-motion embroidery, machine embroidery, black work, needlepoint, counted thread, gold work—and you are familiar with the effects which can be achieved, you are ready to start thinking about designs of your own. This and subsequent chapters will explain the basic principles of designing, using a simple pear shape through-

out for illustration. This chapter covers several methods of how to draw inspiration from objects and how to develop a good color sense.

All good design represents an individual response to four things; the source of the inspiration, the interpretation, the materials used and the use to which the finished design is put.

Sources of inspiration

The world is full of sources of ideas, some of them around your own home. Look at the wood grain on the chopping board in your kitchen for instance, the bubbles in the sink as the light dances through them, or the shadows thrown by the leaves of a potted plant. Look at the fruit bowl and the contents of the vegetable rack—fruits and vegetables come in a variety of interesting shapes. Yet, were two people to be inspired by the same shape, the design produced by each of them would be completely different. It is the individual response to inspiration which produces original design.

For the purpose of this and following chapters, a pear shape has been chosen to illustrate the various aspects of design—the texture of stitches, use of color and the ways in which a basic shape can be repeated to produce a complete design for a piece of embroidery. Trace off the pear shape outline and experiment with embroidery techniques.

The three embroideries shown here are progressions away from a realistic effect. This pear, worked in tent stitch on canvas, with a satin stitch background, uses closely related colors in autumn tones to create the roundness and ripeness of the fruit. The focal point of the sample is achieved by the area of highlight in the foreground.

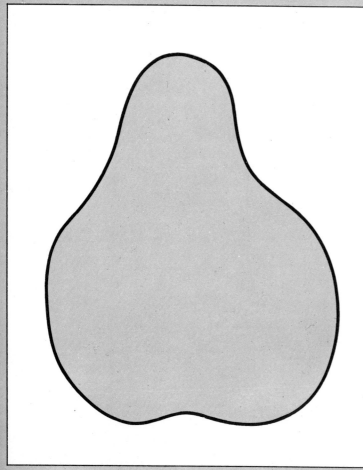

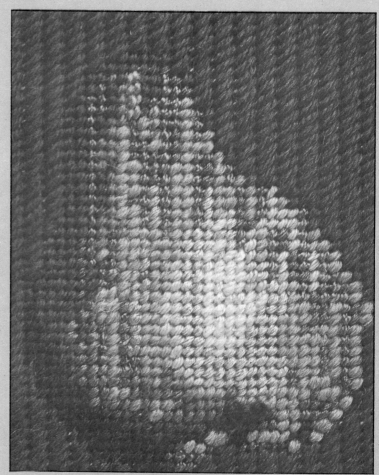

The shapes of things

How does one decide what makes a good shape to begin with. First, it needs to be a simple, open shape to give plenty of scope for experimental stitches. An angular, rigid shape would be boring to work, and a very complicated one would probably take too long to finish. Look at the fruit bowl again and consider the shape of a pear. It is an interesting shape—not too angular, not too regular, it has an adaptable outline and is pleasing to the eye. Many fruit and vegetable shapes would do just as well but for the purpose of this chapter, the pear shape is used.

Color and tone

In embroidery, the opportunities to experiment with color are endless. The pear shape, embroidered in naturalistic colors, yellow, orange and russet, and in stitches chosen to represent the roundness of the fruit, becomes your interpretation of a plump, ripe, juicy fruit. By choosing combinations of colors which are not "pear" colors, a far greater number of designs from the basic shape are possible.

Try experiments with two colors first. Two colors are sufficiently interesting if one color dominates and the other is worked as a small area of true contrast; equal proportions of full strength contrasting colors can appear both harsh and unpleasing. Equal proportions of pale tones, on the other hand, can look monotonous, but if the colors are used in conjunction with stitches, the result can look both subtle and elegant.

It is important to understand that the color of anything is its hue, and the shade of lightness and darkness its tone. A length of fabric, a patch of grass, or a string of beads may all have the same hue, that is, green, but the tone of each will be different. Several colors can have the same tone and one color many tones.

A good arrangement of shapes and interesting textures in embroidery can be upset if the tone values are wrong. You can see this if certain areas of the design seem to jump forward too much or if the eye is continually pulled to one corner of the design. At the same time, two or more colors of the same tone can upset the

balance, producing a flat, unsatisfying effect. It is rather like eating a meal which begins with cream soup, followed by chicken in white sauce, ending with a mousse. The palate craves the sparkle of melon or the bite of a crisp salad. You can check the tone values of a piece of work by looking at it with the eyes half closed, thus reducing sensitivity to color. The tonal values are immediately emphasized.

Learning color sense

A good color sense can be learned by observing and remembering the combinations of colors in nature: the colors on an autumn leaf, for instance, or on a moss-covered stone, and also by looking at paintings in art galleries. Notice how color is used in good modern advertising and in magazine and book production. Get into the habit of making brief written notes when you see a color effect that attracts you. Try out schemes for yourself, pinning small swatches of fabric and short ends of yarn together, before embarking on a piece of embroidery.

To a certain extent, this pear still achieves a realistic look, and once again uses fairly closely related tones to give the fruit a sunlit look, the highlight being the focal point with tones darkening off toward the edges. This sample is worked in chain stitch and whipped chain stitch and is a comparatively free piece of embroidery.

In this interpretation, the designer has opened up the pear to look at the inside, using an appliqué technique, with machine satin stitch and zigzag stitch for contrasting texture. A warm toned tweed is used to indicate the ripeness and texture of the pear's flesh and the bright yellow satin stitch area indicates the shininess of the skin.

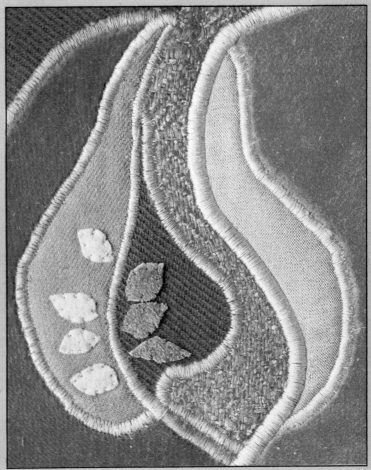

Stitchery pattern/primulas

Simplicity of design is the keynote of this needlepoint panel. It blends equally well with furniture of any period and is shown here applied to the back of a traditionally styled chair. Quickly worked in cross-stitch in unshaded blocks of color, the panel has added straight stitches at the flower centers which are in contrast to the flat remainder. The same design can be made into a handsome small pillow. It could also be mounted as a wall panel. The more advanced embroiderer might experiment with different stitches and a variety of yarns to create more textured effects.

For working the panel 10½ inches by 10½ inches you will need:
- ☐ Double mesh canvas, 10 holes to the inch, 14in by 14in
- ☐ D.M.C. Tapestry yarn 5 skeins of colors **1** and **2**, two skeins of color **3**, and one each of **4** to **9**: **1.** 7469 dark brown; **2.** 7205 clover pink: **3.** 7603 brilliant pink; **4.** 7606 orange; **5.** 7437 yellow/orange; **6.** 7314 blue; **7.** white; **8.** 7548 light green; **9.** 7347 dark green
- ☐ Braid, 42in plus required length for matching trim for the chair
- ☐ Matching sewing thread
- ☐ Tapestry needle No. 20
- ☐ Small, curved upholstery needle
- ☐ Embroidery frame

Working the design
Mark up the centers of the canvas and frame. In cross-stitch, a rhythmical working method makes for an evenly finished texture. Follow the chart and work across in rows one below another. Thread needles with each color. Work the given number of stitches and bring the needle up into position ready for that color when it is next used. Continue working with a second color and needle and complete all the colors and the background stitches across the row. When the canvas is filled,

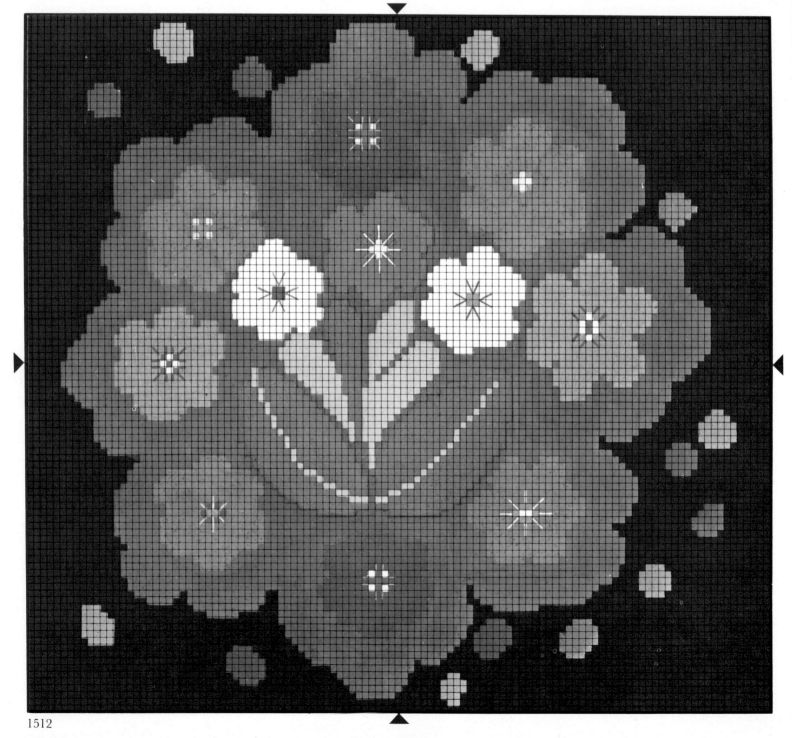

as indicated on the chart, add the straight stitches at the flower centers.

Making the panel

Block the finished canvas. Trim the hem to 1½ inches. Make a single turning, leaving canvas the width of the braid. Herringbone stitch the turning to the back of the needlepoint, stitch the braid to the panel, and mark the centers of the back of the chair. Match with the panel centers and, working from the center outward on each side, pin into position. Stitch with the curved needle, taking the needle down into the panel and up into the chair back. Adjust and smooth as you stitch.

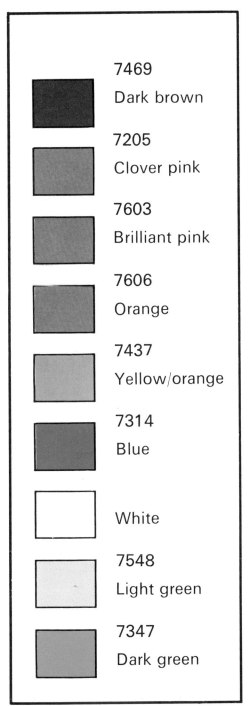

	7469 Dark brown
	7205 Clover pink
	7603 Brilliant pink
	7606 Orange
	7437 Yellow/orange
	7314 Blue
	White
	7548 Light green
	7347 Dark green

Costume design/4 animals

What fun to go to a party dressed as one's favorite animal character! This pattern for a child's costume will adapt to almost any animal and a life-size mask pattern is also given.

There are two approaches to making an animal costume for a child. Either it is going to be worn on a single occasion, in which case one may not want to spend much on materials, or it is to be worn for a play or a parade. Such occasions usually need several rehearsals and it is therefore worth spending more money and time on costumes to make them durable.

For the once-only occasion, Pellon interlinings, which come in a variety of thicknesses, are more than adequate. These bonded non-woven fabrics can be dyed, sprayed, crayonned and decorated with paints for fur effects. For more lasting outfits, fur fabric is ideal of course but stretch terry cloth or other textured fabrics can be used.

The pattern given in this chapter is a basic all-in-one outfit. The bootees are sewn onto the ends of the legs and the mittens have an opening at the wrists to allow the hands to be used. The hood is not attached, but for a more streamlined look it could be fastened on easily with snap fasteners.

Basic suit

To fit a child of about six years old, the suit measures 46 inches from top of head to heel, and chest 25 inches.

You will need:

- ☐ 3¾-4yds of 36in fabric or 2¾-3yds of 54in fabric (fur fabric, stretch terry cloth or Pellon)
- ☐ 16in zipper
- ☐ White knitting yarn for rabbit pompons
- ☐ Kapok stuffing for tail of cat, dog and tiger
- ☐ Pellon interlining to stiffen ears of dog and rabbit
- ☐ Contrasting felt or fabric for ear linings, front of mittens or front patches
- ☐ Cork insoles to foot size
- ☐ Fabric glue

To make the basic suit

When you have measured the child, make a pattern from the graph, adjusting the pattern if necessary.

Cut out the appropriate numbers of pieces. Seam the two back pieces, inserting a tail as required, and join the back to the front pieces along the arm and side seams.

Join the inside leg seams. Insert the front zipper.

Turn back a narrow hem on the straight edge of each of the mitten pieces. Turn a similar hem on the front section sleeve edges. Place the mitten section on the back section "paw", right sides of fabric facing, and machine stitch all around, except the straight edge of the mitten (see diagram). Turn the mitten to the right side and finish the other paw in the same way.

To make the bootees, sew up the front seam (marked x to x) and then stitch on the soles. To prevent the child's feet from slipping on polished floors, glue cork insoles to the sole, cork side down. Pin the completed bootees onto the outfit suit, and check that the leg length is correct before sewing the feet on in case any adjustment is necessary.

Face the neck edge of the suit. Make the hood by stitching the darts to the shape of the head. Place both hood sections together, right sides facing, and complete the seams. Finish off the neck edge and face edge with a neat hem.

For a rabbit costume

Make two large pompons from thick white wool yarn and sew one on the bottom and the other on the hood, just under the chin. Make the rabbit ears with an interlining of Pellon to stiffen them. Pin a fold in the ears before sewing them into the hood.

For a cat costume

The cat costume looks more cat-like if a white patch is made for the front. Cut a patch shape, then cut it down the middle and sew it onto the front pieces before the zipper is inserted. Make the tail and stuff it well. This is stitched into the back seam while the two back pieces are being joined. Tie a bow on the tail or, if you prefer, around the neck, with a small bell suspended. The cat's ears can have contrasting lining to match the front patch.

For a tiger costume

Before the pieces are joined, draw stripes with a felt marker, fabric paint or crayon, depending on the fabric you have chosen. Make the stripes on the tail and ear sections also before sewing on.

For a dog costume

For a patterned dog, such as a Dalmatian, cut out and sew on contrasting patches before joining. Alternatively, the patches can be marked with fabric paint after the costume is finished. The tail can be any length or thickness depending on the type of dog, and the ear shapes are also adjustable. Make a dog collar of felt, using sequins for studs, or purchase a cheap, brightly colored plastic collar.

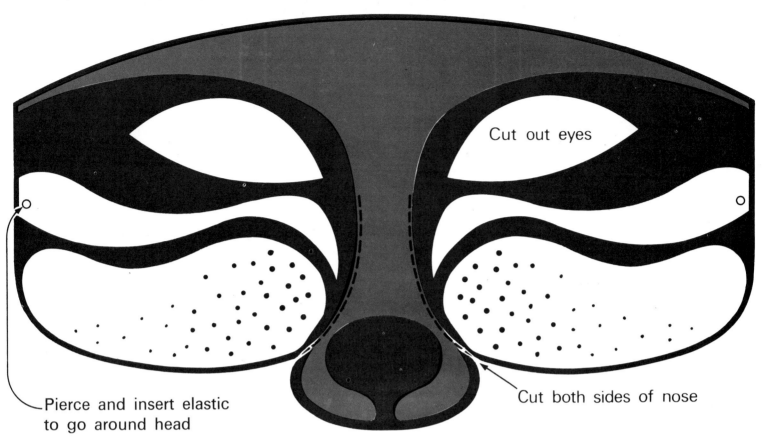

Cut out eyes

Cut both sides of nose

Pierce and insert elastic
to go around head

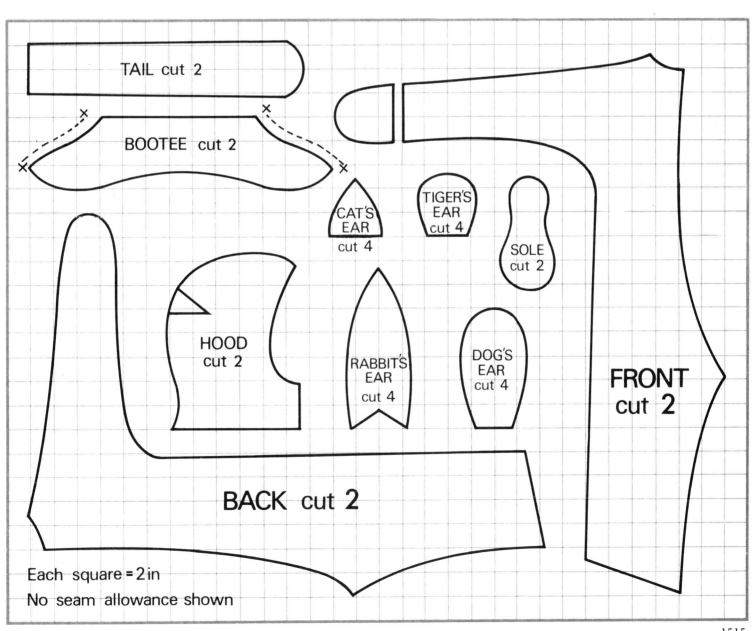

TAIL cut 2

BOOTEE cut 2

CAT'S
EAR
cut 4

TIGER'S
EAR
cut 4

SOLE
cut 2

HOOD
cut 2

RABBIT'S
EAR
cut 4

DOG'S
EAR
cut 4

FRONT
cut 2

BACK cut 2

Each square = 2 in
No seam allowance shown

1515

Design in dressmaking/darts

The first step in designing a dress is to decide which aspect to start with—the fabric, the silhouette, or the decoration; whether to have sleeves, pockets, a collar.

So in this and the following chapters Golden Hands introduces a practical approach to tackling each angle, with design suggestions for varying the collars, necklines and pockets on commercial paper patterns, plus a selection of tracing patterns and a host of ideas for each.

But first of all, what about the cut of the garment and the way it is shaped to your figure?

This shaping is often achieved by means of darts. But most home dressmakers, having selected a commercial pattern with all those other style features in mind, tend to dismiss darts as the necessary shaping of a garment which should be dealt with as neatly, quickly and unobtrusively as possible before getting on to the more exciting and creative bits of the design.

Darts can, however, be one of the most attractive and creative features of a garment. They can be decorative as well as functional, enhancing and improving the appearance of the simplest basic dress by a mere change of position—a simple process known as dart manipulation, or sometimes as "swinging the darts".

The illustrations on these and the following pages show how different a simple commercial pattern looks made up with differently placed darts.

Angled to flatter

Dart manipulation has more than decorative value. Suppose you have chosen a fabric with a large and beautiful pattern which it would be a shame to break up. Obviously the darts should be placed so that no one will notice them—around the corner of the figure, so to speak, and out of sight. On the other hand, an expert dressmaker could place the darts purposely to break up a plain stripe, so adding interest to the design.

Some darts are more flattering to particular figure shapes than others: they can have the effect of slimming the waist; they can make more of a small bust or make a large one look smaller; and they can make the bust look lower or higher. Equally, the wrong dart can be unflattering.

The angle of the darts is also important. Diagonally situated darts, for instance, being more on the bias, are easy to adjust during fitting and so can often help you achieve a better fit or more subtle shaping.

1516

Check your darts

1. Using a closely fitted style, cut out one side only of the front of the chosen bodice pattern in muslin or any piece of cheap cotton fabric you have on hand. Draw the darts and stitching lines in pencil and cut out the fabric with large seam allowances all around. Then pin up the darts on the outside, so that you can get at them easily to make adjustments.

2. Wearing your usual bra or foundation garment, and a closely fitting sweater, pin the half bodice in position down the center front from bustline to waist. Support the rest of the fabric with one or two pins, and put in another pin exactly at the bust point.

Now look at the darts; there are three things to check.

3. First, they should be pointing exactly toward that pin. If they don't, unpin the darts, stroke the fullness into the right position and repin.

Remember, if the side bust has been altered, the waistline must be re-adjusted either up or down to correspond.

4, 5. Second, see that the right amount of fullness has been taken into the darts for your particular figure. If you have a larger than average bust you will need larger darts (**4**); if you have a smaller than average bust you will need smaller darts (**5**). The drawings show you what to look for.

Unpin the darts, stroke away the fullness so that the fabric lies close to the figure, and then repin them.

6, 7. Third, depending on whether you have a rounded or a pointed bust, the points of the darts will be a greater or a lesser distance from the pin at your bust point—further away for a rounded bust (**6**) than for a pointed one (**7**).

8. Draw in the corrected darts in ink, remembering that darts should be stitched in a slight curve rather than a perfectly straight line. In fact, the more rounded your particular figure, the more necessary it is to stitch them carefully in a slight curve.

Swinging the darts

Unpin the darts and stroke all the excess fullness diagonally toward the side seam—you can see now why you needed the extra large seam allowance.

9. Pin the new dart, noticing how, even though it is in a different position, it still points toward your bust point.

10. Try another position. Swing the fullness around and stroke it into a dart which starts from the armhole.

11. And another, starting from the shoulder seam.

12. Yet another, into the neckline.

Vogue pattern 2505—an example of a simple style which lends itself to dart manipulation.

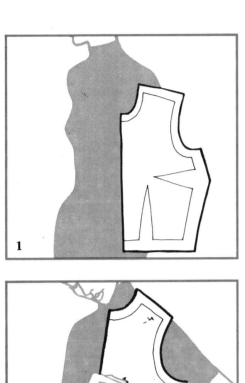

1

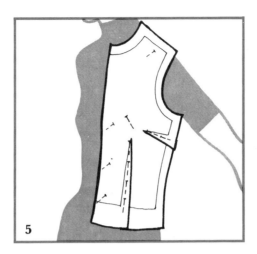

5

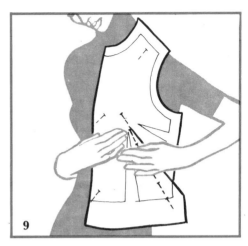

9

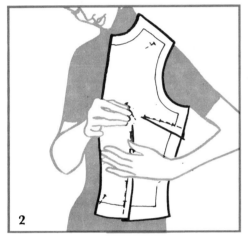

2

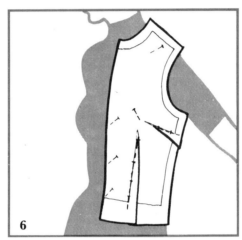

6

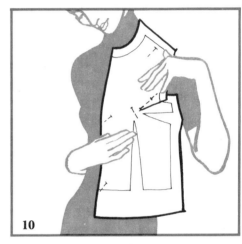

10

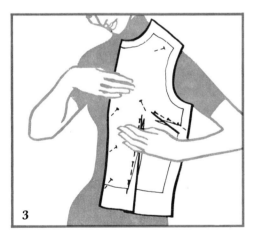

3

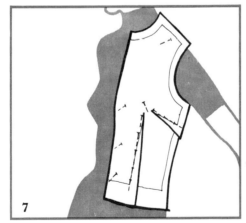

7

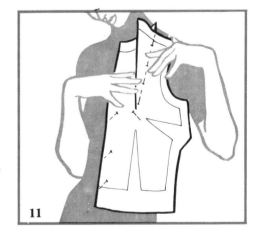

11

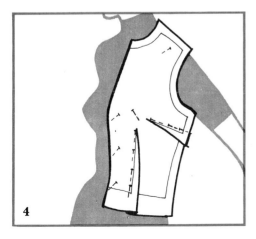

4

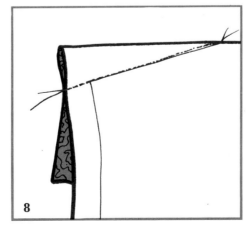

8

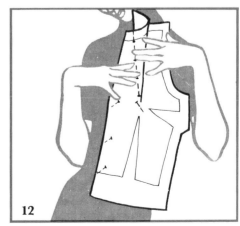

12

13—15. The fullness can also be swung right around so that the darts start from a center seam or dart (**13**), or a lower (**14**) or differently shaped (**15**) neckline.

16, 17. Bust darts can also start from any point along the waistline. But notice how the bust darts always radiate from the bust point, whatever their direction (**17**).

18. Now, although you can see that it is possible to swing darts in any direction, in practice there are some limitations.

Darts and fabric design

19. For instance, it would be bad design to break up a large print by darting it at the most noticeable position of all—at the top or center front of the bodice.

20. A good designer would make sure that the darts were in the least noticeable place possible—probably diagonally into the side seams, thus achieving a completely unbroken expanse of fabric across the top of the front, above the bustline and on down the center front, possibly also taking in the greater part of the skirt.

21. The same principle applies to most printed or patterned fabrics; apart from not wishing to break up the patterns, it is a waste of time putting in decorative darts if they won't even be noticed—except for the wrong reason: that they have broken up the fabric unattractively.

22, 23. It is best to avoid stripes, checks and regular dots for any design where you are intending to swing the darts, unless it is your aim to produce a particularly eye-catching effect and you are 100% confident of your ability to cut and handle such a garment perfectly.

24. If you do want to use a fabric with stripes or checks, the classic four darts, as in this basic design, are the most satisfactory for all but very flat figures because they insure that the fabric lines run closest to the horizontal or vertical. This sort of darting is best for any loosely woven fabric too, where the grain might be tricky to handle; it is best to make sure that it runs as straight as possible, both up and down and straight across the figure.

Making the pattern

Supposing, then, that you have chosen a fabric which is easy to handle such as a firm cotton, jersey or wool crêpe, either plain or with a small, all-over design.

25. Study your commercial pattern and imagine how different it could look with differently placed darts.

26. Compare the corrected dart positions that you've drawn in ink with the darts on the original pattern and redraw those on the paper pattern if necessary.

27. Mark your actual bust point on the pattern and extend darts to that point.

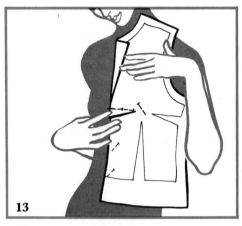

13

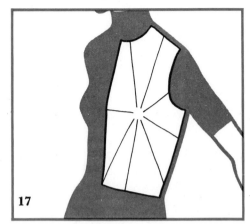

17

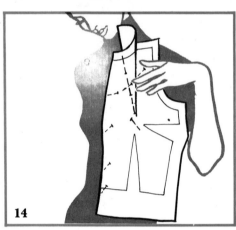

14

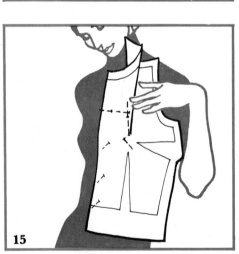

15

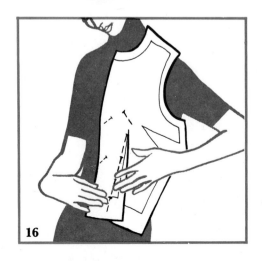

16

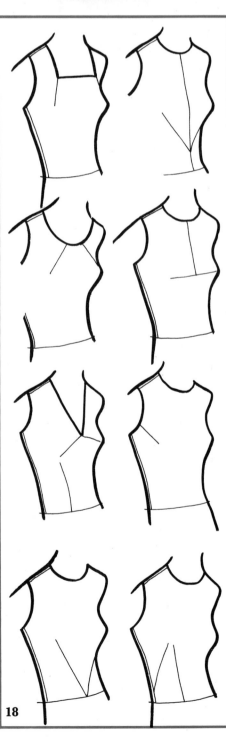

18

19   20   21   22   23   24

25

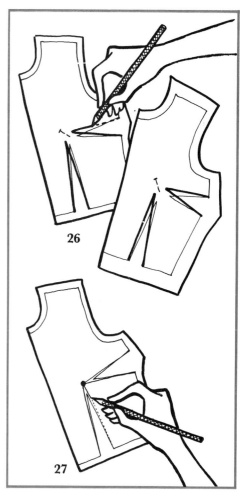

26

27

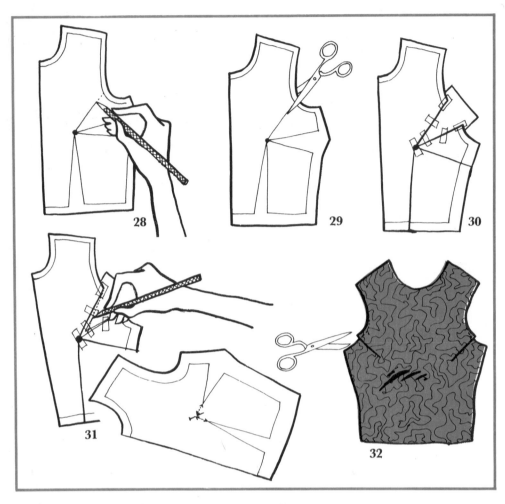

28, 29. Draw in whichever new dart position you want, right to the bust point (**28**), then cut along that line (**29**).

30. Close the original darts and stick a piece of paper behind the new dart that has opened up; then draw it in—remembering that the dart point does not reach as far as the actual bust point.

31. Check back to your muslin pattern to measure this distance.

32. Don't be surprised when making your dress if one side of the dart seems longer than the other; this happens when one side is more on the bias, and consequently stretches more as it is stitched. Simply trim off any surplus along the edge to a smooth line.

33. If you compare these various pattern shapes you'll realize that it is possible to cut bodices with unbroken side seams, waist seams—or any seams you wish—to fit in with a particular style variation, or perhaps a limited amount of fabric. Whether you have two or four, or more, darts on your bodice is up to you entirely.

34. See how the back and fronts of a blouse or jacket can be cut in one piece by swinging the darts into the armhole, shoulder, neck or center front seam—which can, incidentally, be an extremely economical cut. So you see that dart manipulation can have a practical use as well as a decorative one.

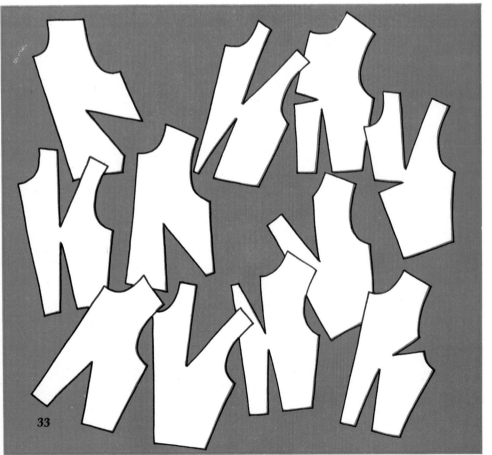

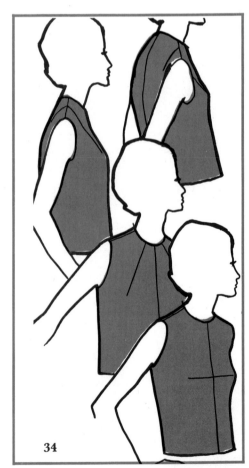

Crafts/batik

Batik is an Indonesian word describing a form of resist printing which is obtained when hot wax, an effective resist to dye, is applied to fabric. When the fabric is dyed, only the unwaxed areas of the cloth take the color. Multicolored patterns are achieved by rewaxing and redyeing different parts of the design, and fine lines are made using a tjanting, which is a tool for applying hot wax. Dyeing is carried out in cool water to prevent the wax from melting. Although batik printing is practiced mainly in Java and in Indonesia, resist printing and dyeing with wax are also known in India, Africa, and parts of Europe. In the western world, batik has become a popular craft and can be done at home using simple domestic equipment, with the exception of the tjanting tool, which can be purchased from specialist craft shops.

Equipment and Materials

For waxing you will need:

A double boiler for melting wax (or a saucepan and a tin to contain the wax, which can be placed in the pan).

A gas ring or electric hotplate—standing on a piece of asbestos if possible, as a safety precaution.

Wax, in the form of domestic candles or blocks of paraffin wax purchased from drug or grocery stores and craft shops. Powdered wax is also available. Beeswax, which is more expensive, provides the most flexible wax.

Artists' brushes for applying wax—medium sized for outlining areas, large sized for filling in large areas.

Tjanting tool. Resin powder.

Old picture frame. Thumbtacks.

A flat table surface.

Quantity of old newspaper.

For dyeing:

A plastic or enamel bowl to hold the dye mixture.

A plastic or glass measure, for water.

Rubber gloves.

Plastic sheeting, to protect table while dyed material dries.

Plastic spoons of various sizes, for spooning out dyes.

Small plastic containers for mixing dyes.

Cold water dyes.

Protective clothing.

Nylon clothes line and clothes pins.

Fabrics for batik

Best results are obtained on cotton, cotton lawn, muslin, silk and linen, also on mixtures of wool and cotton. Man-made fibers and materials with special finishes, such as crease-resistant, non-iron or drip dry fabrics, are not suitable for beginners as the dyes do not penetrate these surfaces easily.

Designs for batik

Some very effective patterns can be made by designs based on the circle, the square or the triangle. Natural objects such as stones, shells, bark, seed, leaves and plants all offer a starting point and the designs will develop almost on their own as the dyeing and waxing progresses.

Museum visits are a good opportunity to study patterns used by primitive peoples on their pottery, weapons and carvings. And photographs of buildings, stacks of building materials, bricks, pavements, drain covers, roofs and stones all provide a basis of pleasing colors, shapes and patterns which can be adapted for use on textiles.

Preparing for waxing

Before dyeing, the cloth must be washed thoroughly to remove all traces of dressing, sizes and natural oils. When the material is ironed free of creases, it is ready for the application of wax resist.

Preparing the wax

Cut up or grate the candles or pieces cut from a block of wax and melt in a double boiler over heat. It should be emphasized that when handling hot wax great care must be taken at all times. A more flexible, less brittle wax is obtained by adding one part of resin to four parts of paraffin wax.

Applying the wax

The wax must be kept hot while you are working and there are two basic methods of applying it. It can be painted on, using a brush, varying the size according to the area to be waxed. For fine lines and for textured effects, a tjanting is used. There are two ways of working when applying wax. The material can be spread out flat on layers of newspaper, and this is the method used when large areas of fabric are being treated. As the wax passes through the fabric, it cools and adheres to the paper beneath. As the fabric is peeled off for dyeing, the wax inevitably cracks and this can cause the color to bleed while dyeing, which may not be part of the design. Beginners will probably find it more satisfactory to work with the fabric pinned to a frame. An old picture frame will do. The tjanting is dipped into the hot wax, filling the reservoir, and is then carried to the prepared fabric. To prevent the wax from dripping hold a piece of paper under the spout. Hold the tjanting in the right hand immediately above the surface of the fabric and move it along the design lines.

1522

Providing the wax is hot enough, a fine trail of wax will flow from the spout. As the wax penetrates the fabric appears to go transparent. Remember, wax is applied only to those areas which are not going to be dyed.

Batik dyeing

The secret of successful batik dyeing is a large enough container, so that the waxed fabric can be moved around without undue crushing.

Follow the manufacturers' instructions for preparing the dye, and make sure that the solution is cool before starting dyeing or the wax will melt and destroy the design. If the wax is cracked the dye will run in, and a fine marbling texture will result. This effect is sometimes used for background to designs. After dyeing is completed, drain the fabric off by laying it flat on several sheets of newspaper spread on a table top. Polythene sheeting under the newspaper will prevent any dye from staining through to the table top. After it has drained, the fabric can be hung up to dry. It is then ready for waxing further areas of the design. After two applications of wax and dye, boil off the wax and start again. This is very important because dye chemicals cause a deterioration in the wax and dye can penetrate the fabric in areas which should be free of dye.

This process of waxing and cold dyeing is repeated until as many colors have been applied as required.

Removing the wax

There are two methods of removing wax. The first is by boiling the wax out of the fabric. Heat water in a large saucepan and while the water is boiling put in the waxed fabric, gently moving it about with a wooden spoon for not more than three minutes. Lift the fabric out and drop it into a bucket of cold water. The wax will solidify immediately. After squeezing out the water, shake off the loose wax. Add half a teaspoonful of detergent to the boiling water and repeat this process twice, or until there is no trace of wax left. Finally, wash and dry the fabric in the usual way. If a small quantity of wax persists in the fabric, professional dry cleaning will remove the residue. The waxy water must never be poured down a sink, as it will cause a blockage. Wait until the water cools, then remove the crust of wax on the surface of the water and pour the clear water away. The wax cannot be used again because the dye chemicals have probably deteriorated it.

Points to watch

The technique of batik printing is straight

forward, but while you are learning you may experience one or two disappointments. Here are some points to watch to help you to achieve the best results.

Bleeding of color under the wax. This can happen if the wax is not hot enough to penetrate the fabric, or if the wax is damaged as the waxed fabric is pulled off the newspaper. It's best to use a frame.

Blurred edges to the design. This will result if the dye solution is warm and the waxed design softened. Make sure the dye is cool.

Blurred designs and muddied colors. This will result if the fabric is left to boil too long when boiling out the wax. The loose dye in the water can be re-absorbed.

Pale colors. If the dye is not sufficiently fixed before the wax is boiled off, the color may wash out and be too pale. Allow the dye to dry thoroughly first. If you are not pleased with the result of waxing and dyeing, the majority of cold dyes can be removed by boiling the fabric in a solution of color remover.

The tjanting, used for applying melted wax, is held just above the surface of the fabric ▼

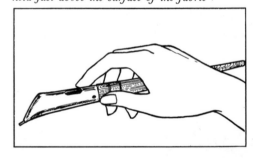

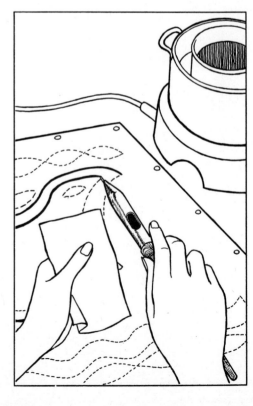

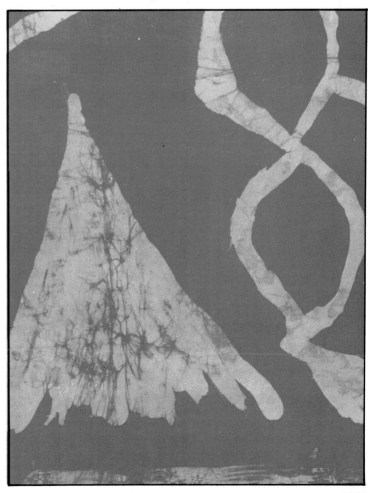

Two yards of white pure silk fabric are required to make this brilliantly colored batik printed lampshade, and four dyeings are needed to produce the effect—brilliant yellow, followed by bright red, bright blue and finally, navy blue. The brilliance and clarity of the colors in this example is achieved by the use of single color in some areas, and this necessitated removing all the wax after each dye process. The wax was then re-applied to the entire surface, except those areas where a pure, single color was required. A certain amount of crackle has been allowed on the background color by immersing the waxed fabric in warm water before the last dyeing. The four stages of dyeing are shown here: top left, the first

color, yellow; top right, red; bottom left, blue; bottom right, navy blue. As a general rule, use the lightest, brightest color for the first dyeing, and the darkest color for the last.

Whether cotton, linen or silk fabric is used, the material must be cleaned of all dressings and oils before batik printing is started. Silk fabric should be soaked in a hot soapless detergent solution for about an hour and cotton should be boiled for about half an hour. Rinse carefully and hang the fabric to dry to minimize creasing. When the material is dry, draw the design out in pencil—the design shown here is based on a simple geometric repeat—and then stretch the fabric across a frame before waxing.

1525

Knitting design/working from charts

This chapter deals with making a sleeveless top to match the skirt, using a graph paper chart and a planned knitting code.

Some knitted garments are so simple to design that a diagram is all that is required. Once a design becomes a little more complex it may be necessary to use a diagram plus a graph paper chart to plan details of shaping.

Sleeveless top

A matching top for the skirt you have already designed involves working with a diagram and graph paper.

1526

Gauge and yarn
The same yarn and needles have been used to make the top as for the skirt (Unger Tosca (machine washable), therefore the number of stitches and rows to the inch are already known. If you change the yarn you must determine the correct gauge and the size of needles to be used before going any further.

Basic measurements
Draw a chart like figure 1.
Start with M—N, which is the total length from center back neck to lower edge. Mark on the line the measurement you want M—N to be. Working from this central line draw in the other lines and

mark the required measurements on each line.
O—P is the lower hemline and is $\frac{1}{2}$ hip measurement plus $\frac{1}{4}$in. V—P is the distance between waistline and hemline. If the hemline is required to be lower, nearer the widest part of the hips, the O—P measurement will have to be increased.
U—V is the waistline and should be $\frac{1}{2}$ the waist measurement plus tolerance. The top illustrated allows 3in tolerance on this measurement, but it is a simple matter to make the tolerance allowance less, depending on how fitted you want the finished garment to be.
Q—R is the bustline and should be $\frac{1}{2}$ the bust measurement plus 1in. The distance between R and P (measured straight as indicated in figure **1**) should be the required length from hem to underarm.
S—T is the shoulderline and should measure your actual shoulder measurement—that is, the distance across your back from sleeve seam to sleeve seam.

Numbers of stitches
You can now calculate the number of stitches required along each of these lines by multiplying the total number of inches on each line by the number of stitches to 1in on your gauge swatch.
You can also calculate the number of rows between one line and the next by multiplying the number of inches by the number of rows to 1 inch, as measured on your gauge swatch.

Graph paper
The diagram you have made gives you the main shape of the top, but for a garment that will fit well it is necessary to add curved armholes, sloping shoulders and, for the front, an attractive curved neckline. Although these shapings can be done simply by increasing or decreasing what you think would be necessary at these points, a detailed plan will save unraveling work if shapings are not correct.
Working out the detailed shapings on graph paper will show you the definite shaping of each section. Remember, your squared plan is NOT a true measurement or paper pattern, and is not therefore to scale. It may look quite out of proportion when completed.
Before you begin, decide on a code so that you can easily read each mark you make. On the following charts \ stands for a stitch knitted, / stands for a stitch purled, O is a stitch cast off, $\wedge$ stands for 2 stitches worked together to decrease 1 stitch, V stands for one stitch worked into twice to increase one stitch. Eventually you will require more symbols but these can be decided on later. Become accustomed to

these simple ones first.

Each row of squares represents one row of knitting. Along the bottom line mark the number of stitches you are going to cast on. On a stockinette stitch garment you only have to mark the first and last stitch of each row. When you begin to work in more intricate patterns, you may need to mark every stitch.

Continue to chart upward, planning all that you have already calculated with the help of your diagram.

Figure **2** shows where shapings need to be worked.

Armholes

The armhole shaping takes place in the first 2½-3 inches of the armhole and curves more sharply at the beginning.

Measure a point 2½ inches along the armhole as a guide. These are points 1 and 1 on Figure **2**. Draw a curve lightly upward from Q and R to the point 1. Decide how you are going to work off the stitches which are to be bound off and decreased, and mark them on your chart.

Figure **3** is the chart for the top illustrated in this chapter.

Shoulders

Measure the shoulder seam length required from each corner (S and T) toward the center line and mark points 2 and 2 as in figure **2**. Points 3 and 3 are measured approximately 1 inch down from S and T. This measurement will vary according to whether your shoulders are straight or sloping. Sloping shoulders will require points 3 to be marked lower down.

Draw a light line between 2 and 3 (figure **4**), marking groups of sts to be bound off on chart. The center neck stitches can be bound off or left on a stitch holder for neckband or collar.

Front

For this top, front and back are alike except for the shaping on the front neck. This can be indicated on the same chart if a different colored pencil is used.

The center front neck is always 2in lower than the back but you may decide you want it lower. Plan the curve after drawing it lightly as in Figure **5**.

All that is left to do now is plan how you are going to finish the neck and armhole edges once the garment is made. Refer to the Knitting Know-how chapters for edgings techniques.

Once your chart is completed, mark needle size, actual garment size, gauge etc on the chart. If you want a similar design again your chart will be ready for you to use, complete with all relevant information.

Remember that for some garments, you will need separate charts for the back and the front.

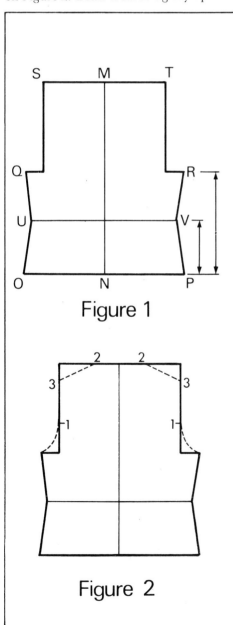

Figure 1

Figure 2

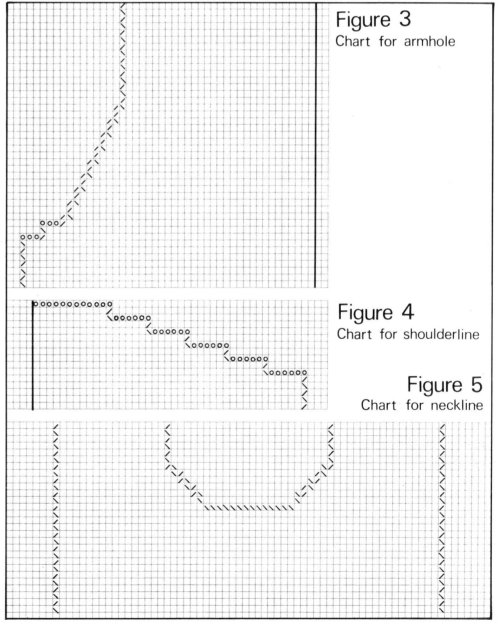

Figure 3
Chart for armhole

Figure 4
Chart for shoulderline

Figure 5
Chart for neckline

Knitting pattern Aran sweater

Warm and practical, this authentic Aran sweater shows how traditional stitches can be combined with more unusual ones to create an interesting effect.

Size

Directions are for 36in chest. The figures in brackets [] refer to the 38, 40, 42, 44 and 46in sizes respectively.
Length at center back, 25[25¼:25½:27½:27¾:28]in.
Sleeve seam, 18[18½:18½:19½:20:20]in.

Gauge
6 sts and 6 rows to 1in over cross st worked on No.6 needles.

Materials

Bear Brand or Fleisher or Botany Shamrock
13[14:15:17:17:18] balls
One pair No.4 needles
One pair No.6 needles
Two cable needles

Back

Using No.4 needles, cast on 97[103:107:113:117:123] sts.
1st row K2, *P1, K1, rep from * to last st, K1.
2nd row K1, *P1, K1, rep from * to end.
Rep these 2 rows 6 times more, then first row once.
Next row (P4, P into the front and then the back of next st—called PFB—,) 2[2:3:3:4:4] times, P4[7:4:7:4:7], K1, *(P1, K into the front and then the back of next st—called KFB—,) 5 times, P1, K1, KFB, K1, (P1, KFB) twice, P1*, K5, (P2, KFB, P2, K2) twice, P2, KFB, P2, K5, rep from * to * once more, K1, P4[7:4:7:4:7], (PFB, P4) 2[2:3:3:4:4] times. 120[126:132:138:144:150] sts.
Change to No.6 needles and commence patt.
1st patt row K1[2:1:2:1:2], (with yarn at back sl 1, K1, psso K st but while it is on the left-hand needle K tbl—called SKPK—,) 7[8:10:11:13:14] times; K1, P1, *(K1, P2) twice, K1, P4, (K1, P2) 5 times, 1528

K1*, P5, (K2, P2) 5 times, K2, P5, rep from * to * once more, P1, K1, SKPK 7[8:10:11:13:14] times, K1[2:1:2:1:2].
2nd patt row P16[19:22:25:28:31], K1, *(P1, K2) 5 times, P1, K4, (P1, K2) twice, P1*, K5, (P2, K2) 5 times, P2, K5, rep from * to * once more, K1, P16[19:22:25:28:31].
3rd patt row K2[1:2:1:2:1], SKPK 7[9:10:12:13:15] times, P1, * (K1, P2) twice, K1, P3, (pass right-hand needle in front of first st on left-hand needle and K second st, then P first st and sl both sts off left-hand needle—called TR—, P1) twice, TR, P2, (K1, P2) twice, K1*, P5, (K2, P2) 5 times, K2, P5, rep from * to * once more, P1, SKPK 7[9:10:12:13:15] times, K2[1:2:1:2:1].
4th patt row P16[19:22:25:28:31], K1, *(P1, K2, P1, K2, P1, K3) twice, (P1, K2) twice, P1*, K5, (P2, K2) 5 times, P2, K5, rep from * to * once more, K1, P16[19:22:25:28:31].
Continue working the 16[19:22:25:28:31] sts at each end of the row in cross st as given in these 4 rows—called CS—.
5th patt row CS16[19:22:25:28:31], P1, *(K1, P2) 3 times, (TR, P1) twice, TR, P3, (K1, P2) twice, K1*, P2, into next st work K1, ytf, K1, ytf, K1, turn, P these 5 sts, turn, K5, turn, P5, turn, sl 2nd, 3rd and 4th sts over first st then K tog rem 2 sts tbl—called MB—, P2, (sl next 2 sts onto cable needle and hold at front, sl next 2 sts onto cable needle and hold at back, K2 from left-hand needle, P2 from back cable needle and K2 from front cable needle—called C6L—, P2) 3 times, MB, P2, rep from * to * once more, P1, CS16[19:22:25:28:31].
6th patt row P16[19:22:25:28:31], K1, *(P1, K2) twice, P1, K4, (P1, K2) 5 times, P1*, K5, (P2, K2) 5 times, P2, K5, rep from * to * once more, K1, P16[19:22:25:28:31].
7th patt row CS16[19:22:25:28:31], P1, *(K1, P2) 5 times, K1, P4, (K1, P2) twice, K1*, P5, (K2, P2) 5 times, K2, P5,

rep from * to * once more, P1, CS16[19:22:25:28:31].
8th patt row. As 6th.
9th patt row CS16[19:22:25:28:31], P1, *(K1, P2) 3 times, (pass right-hand needle behind first st on left-hand needle and pull front loop of second st through to back and P it, then K first st and sl both sts off left-hand needle—called TL—, P1) twice, TL, P3, (K1, P2) twice, K1*, P5, (K2, P2) 5 times, K2, P5, rep from * to * once more, P1, CS16[19:22:25:28:31].
10th patt row As 4th.
11th patt row CS16[19:22:25:28:31], P1, *(K1, P2) twice, K1, P3, (TL, P1) twice, TL, (P2, K1) 3 times*, P2, MB, P2, K2, P2, (sl next 4 sts onto cable needle and hold at back, K2 from left-hand needle, pass 2P sts from other end of cable needle back onto left-hand needle, bring cable needle to front, P2 from left-hand needle and K2 from cable needle—called C6R—, P2) twice, K2, P2, MB, P2, rep from * to * once more, P1, CS16[19:22:25:28:31].
12th patt row As 2nd.
These 12 rows form the patt and are rep throughout.
Continue in patt until work measures 17½[17½:17½:18½:18½:18½]in from beg, ending with a WS row.

Shape armholes
Keeping patt correct, bind off 7[10:10:10:10:10] sts at beg of next 2 rows and 8[8:8:7:9:11] sts at beg of next 2 rows. 90[90:96:104:106:108] sts.
Sizes 36 and 38in only. One st remains from CS at sides which is continued in garter st.
All other sizes. Keep CS correct at sides.
Continue without shaping until work measures 24½[24¾:25:27:27¼:27½]in from beg, ending with a WS row.

Shape neck and shoulders
1st row Patt 38[38:41:44:45:46] sts and slip on spare needle for right Back, bind off 14[14:14:16:16:16] sts in rib patt, patt to end.
Complete left Back on these sts. Patt 1 row.

**Bind off 4[4:4:3:3:3] sts at beg of next row and 3 sts at same edge on next alt row. Then bind off 7 sts for shoulder at beg of next row and 3 sts at neck edge on following row.
Rep last 2 rows 1[1:1:2:2:2] times more.
Bind off rem 11[11:14:8:9:10] sts.******
With WS of work facing, attach yarn to rem sts and complete to correspond to other side, working from ** to **.

Front

Work as given for Back until armhole shaping is completed. Continue without shaping until Front measures 10 rows less than Back to beg of neck shaping ending with a WS row.

Shape neck and shoulders
1st row Patt 41[41:44:47:48:49] sts and slip on spare needle for left Front, bind off 8[8:8:10:10:10] sts in rib patt, patt to end.
Complete right Front on these sts. Patt 1 row.
***Bind off 2[2:2:3:3:3] sts at beg of next row, then dec one st at same edge on next 12 rows.
Bind off 7 sts at beg of next row for shoulder and dec one st at neck edge on following row.
Rep last 2 rows 1[1:1:2:2:2] times more.
Bind off rem 11[11:14:8:9:10] sts.*******
With WS of work facing, attach yarn to rem sts and complete to correspond to other side working from *** to ***.

Sleeves

Using No.4 needles, cast on 45[45:45:51:51:51] sts.
Work 15 rows rib as given for Back.

Sizes 36, 38 and 40in only
Next row K1, P1, KFB, P1, K1, KFB, K1, (P1, KFB) twice, P1, K5, (P2, KFB) 3 times, P2, K5, (P1, KFB) 4 times, P1, K2, P1. 56[56:56] sts.

Sizes 42, 44 and 46in only
Next row (KFB, P1) 3 times,
K1, KFB, K1, (P1, KFB)
twice, P1, K5, P2, K2, P2,
KFB, P2, K2, P2, K5, (P1,
KFB) 5 times, P1, K1, KFB,
K1. 64[64:64] sts.
Change to No. 6 needles.
Commence patt.
1st row P0[0:0:4:4:4], (K1,
P2) 5 times, K1, P5, (K2, P2)
3 times, K2, P5, (K1, P2)
twice, K1, P4, (K1, P2)
1[1:1:2:2:2] times, K1,
P1[1:1:2:2:2].
Continue in patt as established,
inc one st at each end of 5th
and every following 5th[5th:
5th:5th:5th:4th] row until
there are 90[94:96:104:106:
110] sts, working inc sts into
patt as follows:
The first 11[11:11:7:7:7] inc
sts at each side will complete
the panel of straight and wavy
rib, the next st added will be
a P1 rib and the rem 5[7:8:12:
13:15] sts each side are in CS.
Continue without shaping
until sleeve measures 18[18½:
18½:19½:20:20]in from beg,
ending with a WS row.
Place colored markers at each
end of last row, then work
16[19:19:18:20:22] rows
more without shaping.

Shape cap
Bind off 4[6:7:4:5:7] sts at beg
of next 2 rows, 5[5:5:7:7:7]
sts at beg of next 8 rows and
9[9:9:8:8:8] sts at beg of next
2 rows. Bind off rem 24 sts.

Neckband

Using No.6 needles, cast on
113[113:113:121:121:121] sts
and work 8 rows of K1, P1
rib as given for Back.
Change to No.4 needles and
work 16 rows, then change to
No.6 needles and work 8 more
rows. Bind off in rib.

Finishing

Press lightly.
Join shoulder seams. Press
seams on WS under a damp
cloth and using a warm iron.
Sew bound-off edges of sleeves
to sides of armholes and sides
of sleeves above markers to
armhole binding-off. Press

▲ *An Aran sweater to look smart and
keep him warm*
Close-up stitch detail ►

seams. Remove markers.
Join side and sleeve seams and
press.
Join ends of neckband and
press with point of iron. With
RS facing and seam level with
left shoulder seam, sew cast-on
edge to neck edge. Press seam
with point of iron. Fold
neckband in half to WS and
slip stitch bound-off edge
down in place.

Stitchery design/texture

In the first chapter, shape, tone and color were considered, and these aspects of design are as important in embroidery as they are in painting. In embroidery, however, the possibilities for creating visually exciting designs through the use of textures is of particular importance. This chapter deals with the contrasts, balance and textural effects.

Modern embroidery may at first glance look formless, even chaotic. But it's rather like learning a language—once you know the vocabulary it begins to mean something. The last stitchery chapter showed a realistic interpretation of a pear; a design which simplified the play of light over the curving surface; and a design which sliced the pear in half, then cut the shape into sections to make a pattern.

Pears **1-3** in this chapter are like the "sliced" pear—using the flat shape and cutting it up in different ways to produce a decorative pattern as a vehicle for stitches and color.

Designs **4-6** are freer, more abstract. Lines dissolve, flow, shatter. You might see the mellow ripeness of a pear in **4**; or a glistening in sunlight after rain in **5**; or **6** may seem quite abstract, like music.

So before you start to design, decide whether you want a pattern with stitches and colors, or an impressionistic or abstract picture.

The experienced designer feels subconsciously that a shape is right, that an area needs a denser or more open stitch. The embroiderer new to design has consciously to consider basic principles.

If you plan to make your own design it's wise to keep the basic shape simple. If your line work is shaky, make a template of the motif, cut it out of paper, cut it up and move the bits around. Or draw around the template, overlapping the outlines until you have a pleasing design. Now plan the stitch areas, having prepared yourself with a repertoire of techniques, a varied collection of fabrics for backgrounds and applied areas, beads, sequins, and buttons.

Texture versus color. It's risky going to town with every stitch and color in the hope that something "modern" will result —it's liable to produce a chaotic effect. If the aim is to exploit texture, exercise restraint in the range of colors used. If you choose six equally vivid, contrasting colors and six different textures, the vibrations produced by the colors make the texture of secondary importance. Concentrate on ridges and knots, beads, thick and thin threads, slub or nubbly backgrounds, enhanced by closely related colors.

Contrast of texture. Choose stitches that foil each other well, like the curving couched threads with French knots in **4** or the contrast of rough and smooth needlepoint textures in **1**. With counted thread embroidery, bear in mind the relationship between the background fabric and the embroidery thread. Think of the spaces to be filled as well as the areas to be left unfilled.

Placing the texture. The eye tends to go to the area of maximum contrast of tone and texture, so it is usually better to keep heavier texture away from the edges and corners of a design in a rectangle so that the eye remains close to the central area. Of course, these are only suggestions—if you want a riot of color and texture—go ahead and have fun.

The pears illustrated move even further away from the realistic interpretations of the last chapter. The pear is cut in half to show the seeds within the fruit and the texture of the flesh yet, at the same time, the feeling of the whole fruit is retained in abstract outline.

1. The attractive interpretation on the left is worked on canvas using a variety of needlepoint stitches and different textures of thread. 2. The pear below uses a counted thread technique, the background fabric being allowed to contribute to the interesting concept of the design.

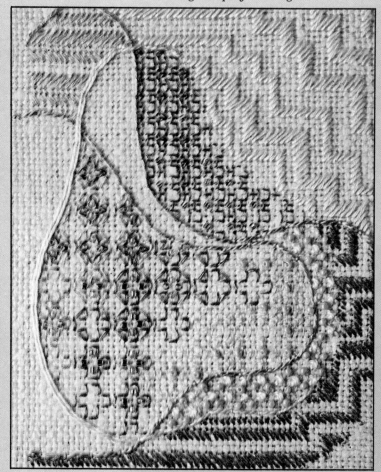

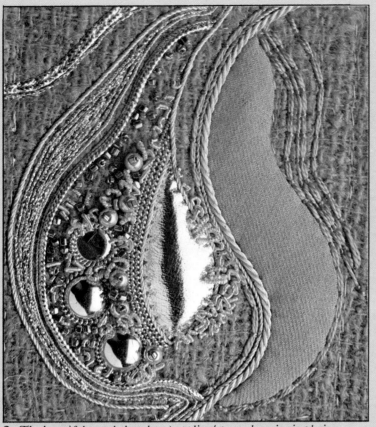

3. *The beautiful metal thread and appliqué pear above is simple in treatment. Color is restricted and the textural contrast is achieved with threads, leather and fabric.* **5.** *The impressionist pear below uses straight stitches, relying on angle and color for the impact of the design.*

4. *The pear above is worked in "free texture", which means the use of line and lumpy texture, the embroidery overcoming a strong fabric background.* **6.** *The pear below is almost pure abstract, the seeds enlarged as a concept of the life within and brought outside the fruit.*

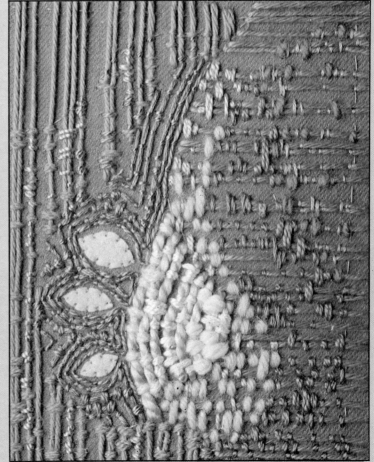

Stitchery pattern/hedgerow

Although only one type of yarn is used to work this design, textural interest is achieved by clever use of stitches. Elegant for a pillow cover, the design also frames well to make a matching picture.

To make a pillow 14 inches square and a picture 14 inches square, excluding frame, you will need:

Pillow
☐ White linen 12in by 12in

☐ Sage green fabric, satin or any close-weave material to complement white linen, 15in by 15in
☐ Sewing thread, sage green
☐ Pillow form 16in by 16in

Picture
☐ White linen 15in by 15in
☐ Sage green fabric 15½in by 15½in
☐ Mat board, two pieces, each measuring 14in by 14in
☐ Fabric adhesive

For both pillow and picture
☐ 1 skein D.M.C. 6-strand floss in each of the following colors:
1. 972 gorse yellow; **2.** 335 rose pink; **3.** 608 orange; **4.** 783 muscat green; **5.** 3052 moss green; **6.** 895 dark moss green; **7.** 3346 grass green; **8.** 729 azure; **9.** 995 periwinkle
☐ Crewel needles Nos. 6 and 7
☐ Sharps needles to use for the plain sewing
☐ Embroidery frame

Working the design

The embroidery method is the same for both the pillow and the picture. Use four strands of thread for color No.1—gorse yellow; one strand for color No.4—muscat green; and two strands for the remaining colors.

Mark the center of the fabric in each direction and transfer the design to the fabric, either by the carbon paper method (Embroidery chapter 4) or by the tissue paper method (Embroidery chapter 66). Frame the fabric.

The stitchery is freely worked and for success in this apparently casual embroidery, stitch with the growing points of the leaves and flowers in mind, shaping the lines and curves as you stitch. The type and direction of the stitch used is indicated on the outline diagram. Work the underlying areas, such as the petals of the large flowers, first.

Making the pillow

Press the finished embroidery. From the 15 inch square sage green fabric cut a 9 inch square from the center. Snip $\frac{1}{2}$ inch into the corners of the remaining fabric frame. Turn in the edge and press. Matching centers, baste the square mount in position over the embroidery and using matching thread, stab stitch the two together. Work a small stitch on the surface and a larger underneath. Couch six strands of oak brown thread where the edge of the mount touches the embroidery. Make the pillow in the usual way.

Preparing the picture for framing

Cut a hole 9 inches square in the center of the $15\frac{1}{2}$ inch square sage green fabric. Cut a hole 10 inches square in the center of one of the pieces of mat board. Snip into the corners of the fabric mount as before and mount the sage green fabric onto the mat board, mitering the corners and securing the fabric on the back of the mount with small spots of glue.

Mount the embroidered linen on the second piece of mat board. Frame in a deep frame.

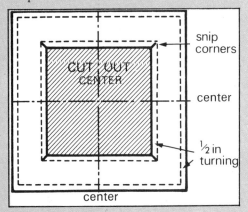

Home crochet/flower pillow

The top of this unusual pillow is covered with three-dimensional flowers in three colors, and the back is a simple circle worked in double crochet using the main color.

Size

About 14in diameter.

Gauge

7dc and 4 rows to 2in worked on No.G crochet hook.

Materials

Coats & Clark's O.N.T. Speed-Cro-Sheen
4 balls main color, A, blue
2 balls B, white
1 ball C, red
One No.D crochet hook
One No.G crochet hook
1 foam pillow form

Flower motif

Using No.D hook and C, ch10, join with a ss into first ch to form a ring.

1st round Ch3 to count as first dc, 17dc into ring. Break off C.

2nd round Attach B, 1sc into first dc, (ch5, skip 2dc, 1sc into next dc) 5 times, ch5, skip 2dc, join with a ss into first sc.

3rd round Into each ch loop work 1sc, 1hdc, 6dc, 1hdc, 1sc.

4th round *Ch7, 1sc into same st as sc on 2nd round, rep from * five times more.

5th round As 3rd.

6th round As 4th.

7th round As 3rd. Break off B.

8th round Attach A and using No.G hook, ch3 to count as first dc, 1dc into each st all around. Fasten off. Make 18 more flowers. Sew together placing one flower in center, 6 around central flower and then 12 on outer circle.

Back

Using No.G hook and A, ch8 and join with a ss to form a ring.

1st round Ch3 to count as first dc, 11dc into ring, join with a ss to 3rd of first 3ch.

2nd round Ch3, *2dc in first st, 1dc in next st, rep from * to end, join with a ss into 3rd of first 3ch. 18 sts.

3rd round Ch3, *2dc into first st, 1dc into each of next 2 sts, rep from * to end, join with a ss into first of 3ch. 24 sts.

4th round As 3rd. 32 sts.

5th round Ch3, *2dc into first st, 1dc into each of next 3 sts, rep from * to end, join with a ss into first of 3ch. 40 sts.

6th round Ch3, *2dc into first st, 1dc into each of next 4 sts, rep from * to end, join with a ss into first of 3ch. 48 sts.

7th round Ch3, *2dc into first st, 1dc into each of next 5 sts, rep from * to end, join with a ss into first of 3ch. 56 sts.

8th round As 5th. 70 sts.

9th round As 6th. 84 sts.

10th round As 5th. 105 sts.

11th round Ch3, *2dc into first st, 1dc into each of next 6 sts, rep from * to end, join with a ss into first of 3ch. 120 sts.

Fasten off.

Finishing

Press work with a warm iron over a damp cloth.
Join Back to Front, leaving an opening to insert the pillow form. Push inner ring of petals into position.

Worked in pretty pastels or bright contrasting colors, the flowerets can be used for a wide variety of decorations for home furnishings. From the top: encircling a lampshade, two on an oven mitt, for an unusual tie-back for curtains, to decorate a crib cover, for an egg cozy, along the edge of a window shade and on a tea set.

Design in dressmaking/more darts, and seams

This chapter continues with dart manipulation covering curved and angled bust darts, back darts and hip darts. From here it is a simple step to the cutting of curved bodice seaming and other contour seams which incorporate the dart shaping.

Back darts

Swinging the darts does not have to be confined to the bodice front: attractive effects can also be achieved at the back.

1. As the shoulder blades are a much flatter area than the bust, a little more flexibility as to the exact position of the darts is possible So, rather than attempting to work them out on paper and perhaps being disappointed with the final result, decide more or less where you would like the darts and then cut your fabric with plenty of surplus seam allowance.

2. Ask a friend to fit you—on one side only—first placing two or three pins down the center back to hold the fabric in place. Then gently stroke the fullness into the desired position and pin a dart.

3. Take off the back and carefully mark both stitching lines of the dart before unpinning it.

4. Fold the bodice along the center back and mark the dart through to the other side.

5. Consider the position of the darts carefully as some possible shoulder dart positions could be very unflattering to any figure, possibly giving a widening or round shouldered effect.

Hip darts

6. Hip darts, too, can be swung with very attractive results. As a rule the purpose of hip darts is to take the surplus fabric above the hipbone up into the waistline. There is, however, no reason why they should not be swung in any direction you like, apart from the usual practical considerations that apply to all darts— fabric, grain, pattern and, naturally, your own shape.

Make sure that the hip darts coordinate with the darts on the bodice. In addition, to look really good, the angle of both sets of darts usually needs to be the same—this sort of touch is one of the marks of a good design.

Hipbones vary in both shape and prominence and, as with the shoulder blades, this area is flatter than the bust point; so again there is a certain amount of flexibility as to where they may start.

If a really close and exact fit is wanted two darts may give a better result than one, though this will also depend on the figure type and the prominence of the stomach.

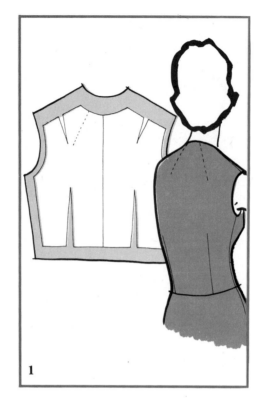

Remember, on a dress which is really closely fitted at the waist, unless you have an exceptionally flat stomach, the skirt waist at the front should always be slightly larger than the corresponding part of the bodice. The extra length is eased in during stitching.

Most women like to look slim-waisted, so you will notice that nearly all the darts in the sketch slant inward toward the waist. Even the exceptions are placed so that they give a slimming effect.

7. Hip darts that slant outward into the waist would flatter no one.

8. The back hip darts can also be varied if you wish, but beware of giving a big-bottomed look.

9 and **10.** Particular care must always be taken to see that any darts that meet at a seam do meet, and very precisely (**9**); nothing looks worse than a near miss (**10**). It helps to keep a tape measure handy when moving darts around.

11. Sometimes, instead of stitching the darts in the normal way, a good idea is to leave them as tucks or folds.

12. Here the darts are stitched a little way down but not right to the points.

13. Alternatively the darts could be topstitched on the right side instead of, or as well as, the usual stitching. This detail usually corresponds to similar stitching detail elsewhere on the garment.

14. Another idea is to stitch the darts in the usual way but to the outside of a garment; here too the rest of the design should be carefully planned to echo this detail in some way.

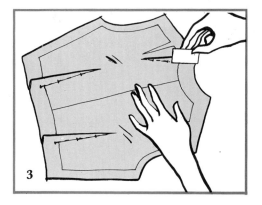

3

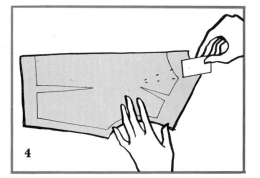

4

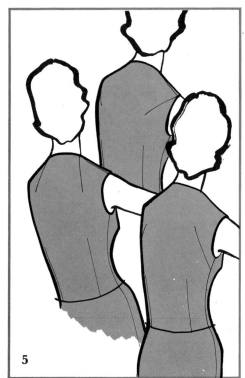

5

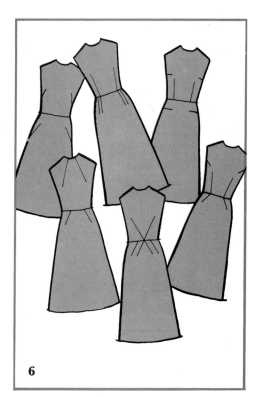

6

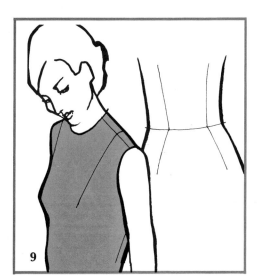

8

9

10

12

13

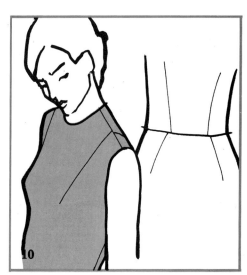

14

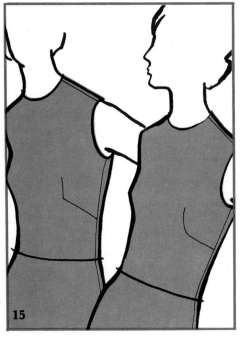

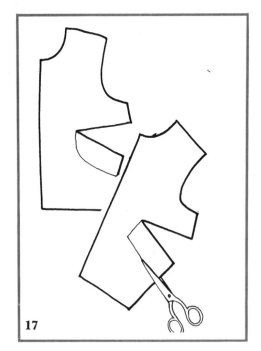

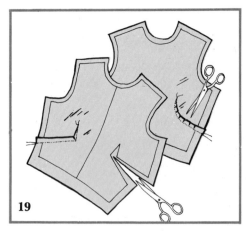

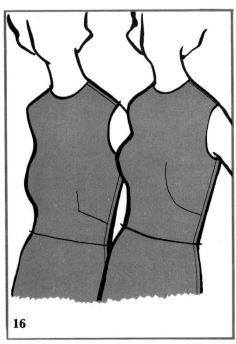

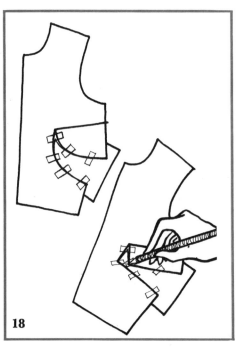

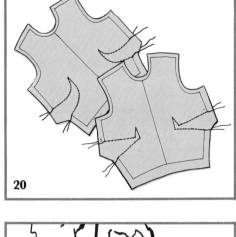

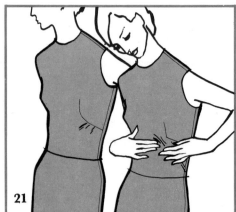

Curved and angled darts

15. As well as ordinary straight-cut darts and the variations already mentioned, it is a simple matter to cut the rather more decorative curved darts, or darts with corners. Both these are particularly flattering to small busts and help to give a nice long, closely-fitted body line under the bust.

16. But they are not very good for a large or low bust, tending to make it look even larger or lower.

17. Use exactly the same method of dart manipulation, having first swung all the fullness into one dart. Draw the new shaped dart position on the paper pattern, right to the bust point, then cut along it.

18. Close the original darts and draw in the new one, remembering that the point must always be a certain distance from your actual bust point.

19. These darts will have to be cut through the center before they are stitched, and obviously the raw edges will need to be clipped in places to make sure that there is no distortion or pulling on the right side of the garment.

20. It is advisable, before cutting them, to reinforce the stitching line with a line of machine stay stitching, particularly if you are using a fabric that frays or stretches easily.

21. It is also advisable to try on the dress with the dart basted so that you can check on the fit and see whether there is any pulling or fullness that needs to be eliminated before stitching. It may be that you will be able to take in the dart to some extent to get a closer fit, possibly smoothing the fabric under the dart outward toward the side seam; or it may just need some slight adjustment on account of the fact that the nearer one side (or part) of a dart comes to the true bias of the fabric the more it stretches.

Curved bodice seams

22. You may have noticed earlier that some of the bodice variations achieved by swinging the darts had one dart, and some had two. Provided that you attempt to

1538

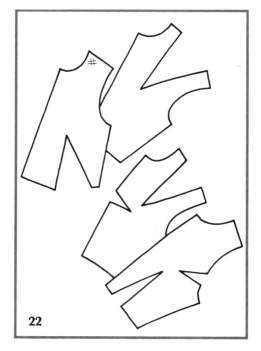

22

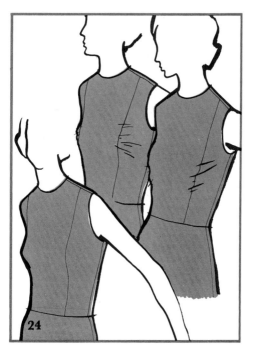

24

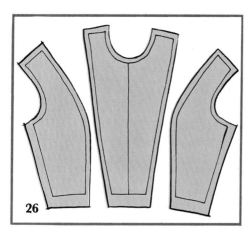

26

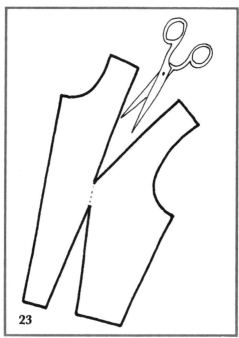

23

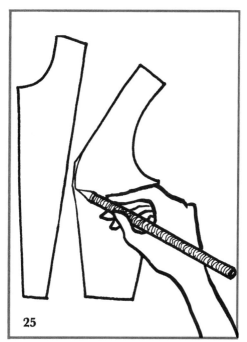

25

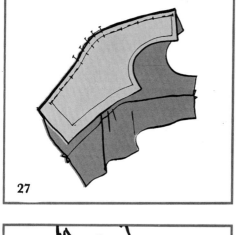

27

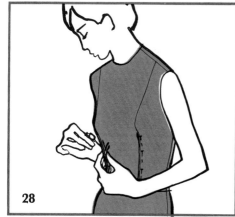

28

take in no more and no less than the amount of surplus fabric exactly right for your figure—and the degree of fit you require—you can have as many darts as you wish.

23. Supposing you had two darts, as in this pattern, it is easy to see how the pattern could be cut in two and seamed up instead of darted.

24. The more closely fitted the garment, however, the more important it is that the seam should pass precisely over the bust point. If it passed to the inside it would drag across the bust. If it passed to the outside it would be too loose, and possibly cave in at the side of the bust. So the first step is to extend the darts to the

bust point.

25. Then the original straight lines must be redrawn to a smooth and continuous curve. Be particularly careful not to add a lot more fullness to one side of the pattern without taking the same amount away from the other while drawing these lines, otherwise you will find yourself with a lot of surplus fabric which will have to be disposed of at a later stage.

The reverse also applies—if you take away from one side you must add to the other.

26. Add seam allowances to both edges when cutting out the dress.

27. Before stitching the seam, pin it from both ends toward the bust point, easing in evenly any slight fullness along the

center of the curve over the bust.

Baste and then try on the bodice. Smooth and adjust it where necessary if there is any unwanted fullness or, perhaps, if any difference in grain has stretched the fabric on one side of the seam more than on the other. Pass fullness up or down, trim off surplus at shoulder- or waistline.

28. It is a simple matter to get exactly the degree of fit, or semi-fit, you want by taking in or letting out very small amounts of these seams. Apart from the fact that the fitting of some figures is made much easier with this type of contour seaming they can also be helpful in disguising some figure faults—in particular, disproportion.

1539

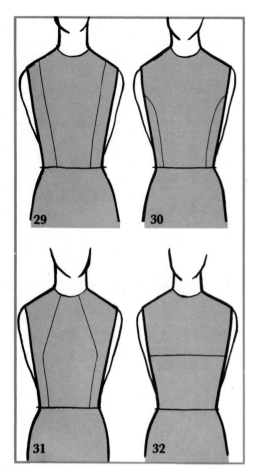

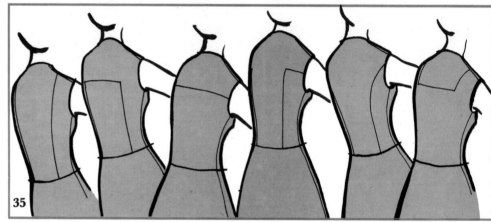

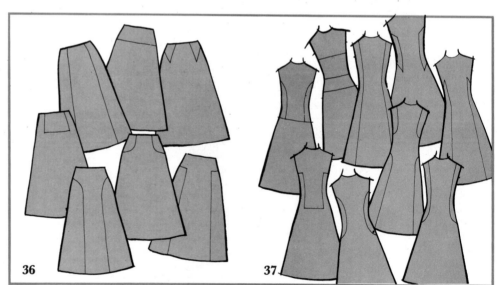

29. For instance, these vertical seamlines can be slimming to the bodice.

30 and **31.** These lines give the effect of a wider shoulderline (**30**) while these appear to narrow the shoulders (**31**).

32. By using the same method a seam line can be made to run across the body, giving a wider look to the bust.

33. As an alternative to cutting the bodice with seams, separate decorative sections can be cut to shape it instead.

34. These sections can, if you like, be made in other colors or fabrics and can be

designed to produce slimming or widening effects.

They can be useful, too, in using up odd pieces of fabric—in which case it is often a good idea to use the same fabric elsewhere on the garment or on a matching coat or jacket. This decorative variation can sometimes be an excellent, easy and well disguised way of letting out a garment.

35. Using the same method, the darts at the back of the bodice can be swung, cut through and redrawn as seams—or cut as sections.

36. So can skirt darts, back and front. Always bear in mind the eventual over-all effect—whether it is slimming or widening, or possibly too unusual or eye-catching, serving only to draw attention toward a figure fault.

37. It is easy to see how bodice and skirt patterns can be joined together to make dresses that are entirely shaped with seams instead of darts; provided that the seams pass exactly over the bust points and hip-bones, all kinds of beautiful variations can be the result.

1540

Crafts/fabric collage

What is fabric collage?

The word collage is derived from the French phrase *papier collé*, or pasted paper, and means, literally, the art of sticking pieces of paper, sticks, wood, and fabric onto a background to make a picture.

In fabric collage, although the picture is mainly composed of material, other things such as beads, lace, shells, feathers or braids can be introduced to give texture, and sometimes a few stitches are added for decoration or to hold down a piece of fabric. The art of making fabric pictures is a long established one, but because present day adhesives have more reliability and are easier to use the art of fabric collage has developed fairly recently.

There are one or two charming examples in museums dating from the late nineteenth century, made chiefly of paper with figures dressed in fabric, and these show that the interest has always been there, if not the technique.

▲▼ Swan queen collage with printed silk background, the swan worked in metallic fabrics and padded

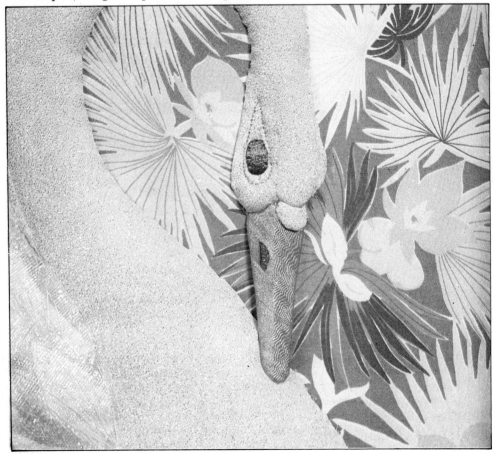

Designs for collage

Almost any pictorial design can be turned into collage, and for a beginner children's books will provide some delightful illustrations for inspiration. Make sketches of scenes which appeal to you and keep a scrapbook of cuttings collected from magazines and newspapers. Poems, music, and television programs can all be sources of inspiration for picture making, and so can the shapes and colors of nature. Look carefully at a bunch of flowers or an old stone wall—they will give you lovely ideas for color schemes which can be incorporated into your work. Look again at a favorite painting, and see how the artist used color to represent fabric. Museums and art galleries will also give you a wealth of ideas for collage pictures, and you can buy postcard reproductions of works of art which can be taken home and studied carefully. Animals, birds, flowers, fruit, fish, the countryside, city streets, children, the kitchen, your garden — inspiration for collage is all around you, for the taking.

Equipment and materials for collage

You will need:

- ☐ Scissors for cutting fabric and paper, large for general cutting, small for fine work (it's better to have more than one pair of each, so that if one gets lost among the fabrics, another is at hand)
- ☐ Scrap paper, for roughing out designs
- ☐ Pencil
- ☐ Pins and needles
- ☐ Adhesives suitable for fabric work (i.e. latex adhesives)
- ☐ Spreader for use with adhesives and some cocktail sticks
- ☐ Sewing thread, wools and silks for the odd stitching required
- ☐ Iron and ironing board
- ☐ Strong, firm fabrics for backing, such as Pellon, paper-backed burlap, felt, cotton, mattress ticking
- ☐ White cardboard for mounting (not brown, it may discolor fabrics)
- ☐ Tweezers to grasp delicate bits of fabric more easily
- ☐ A weight of some sort to hold materials in place while the adhesive sets, such as a felt covered brick
- ☐ Set square and ruler

Fabrics

These are the raw material of collage and from them ideas will grow for pictures. Save scraps from dressmaking and ask your friends to save them for you too. Go to rummage sales and buy old clothes. Don't part readily with old dresses. If you

can persuade a storekeeper to let you have them, pattern books and sample swatches will provide a wide selection of colors and textures. Felt is useful because it doesn't fray, and it is dense enough to prevent adhesive seeping through.

Nets will come in handy for misty, romantic effects. Small bits of fur fabric are invaluable for animal pictures. Gold and silver Lurex fabrics will add a touch of luxury and splendor. Dull-surfaced fabrics will also be needed to offset bright ones, so keep some of those in your scrap bag and some strong firmly textured fabrics for backgrounds. Patterned fabrics which will suggest forms and shapes for pictures are invaluable—corduroy for plowed fields, green chenille for trees, black lace for wrought iron, red and white striped cotton for awnings, and so on. Textures can be as important as colors in fabric collage, so look for tweeds and other

nubby materials, and shiny, sleek and velvety surfaces. Raffia, Lurex yarn, fringes, ribbons, lace, bits of crochet work, string, beads, absorbent cotton, cords, silks, wools, feathers, braids, sequins, buttons— all of these should be saved and kept for collage.

Storing materials

You need to keep your bits and pieces in some sort of order, otherwise you will never be able to find anything when you need it.

Large, transparent plastic bags are one of the best ways of storing materials. Either store them in bags by color, or, if you prefer it, in textures, thin and thick, furry, shiny, and so on. Patterned bits can go together, and small items, such as braids and buttons, need a home of their own. For these, a set of transparent plastic containers is excellent.

Ordinary large glass storage jars can be used, too. It is important to store things so that you can easily see them.

How to start

For your first picture choose a simple design in a few colors on a plain background, such as the circles and squares design in this chapter. It's best not to try to be too realistic, or to aim for three dimensional effects to begin with, but to concentrate on improving your eye for color and pattern.

Also, it's best at first not to have too many pieces overlapping each other, or you might become confused.

Choose the background material, and cut it a bit larger than the intended measurements of the finished picture; you can trim down more easily than you can add. The frame will cover a bit of the background all around the edge, so allow for this when

you plan your design. For your first attempt don't make the picture too big —about 12in by 15in or even smaller is a good size to start with. Iron all the fabrics flat before cutting out (except velvet, which should be steamed). Draw your design on paper. Then, either trace the design onto tracing paper, cut up the shapes and use them as a pattern for cutting out each shape, or cut up the drawing and use that as a pattern for the fabric. When you have more experience, you will

be able to draw the shapes lightly in pencil directly onto the fabric, or even cut out directly from the fabric. Place the background material onto a piece of cardboard, and baste all around the edge one inch in to mark the overlap which will be needed for the mounting later on.

Place all the fabric pieces in position on the background, and move them around a little to make sure that you are satisfied with the color harmony and design.

Pin them down and mark the position of

each piece with a pencil where it won't show, as a guide to sticking them down.
It is best to do figures and complicated pieces of design separately, then stick them down as a whole unit.

Using latex adhesives
Spread the adhesive on the smaller bits of fabric with a cocktail stick, and use a spreader for the larger pieces. The most important points to remember when using latex adhesives are not to use too much,

and always to follow the directions on the container. Generally, the adhesive is spread thinly on one of the surfaces to be joined, then pressure is applied and the work allowed to dry. When fixing light-weight materials, apply latex sparingly to both surfaces and allow them to dry for a minute or two. Then place the two surfaces together. Nets can be stuck down success-fully by spreading the background itself with adhesive, then pressing the net down onto it under a weight. If you do make a mistake while sticking on fabrics, most manufacturers of latex adhesives can supply a solvent which will remove it. Most clear adhesives can be removed with acetone, and most white adhesives can be removed with a damp cloth while they are tacky, or a very damp cloth when dry.

Finishing off for framing

Press the finished work under a damp cloth—except areas with sequins. Cut the mounting cardboard an inch or so smaller than the background fabric, first making sure with a set square that all angles are right angles. Then, following the basted stitches as a guide, turn the edges of the background fabric back over the card-board, mitering the corners neatly, and lace the picture together at the back with strong thread. Easily frayed material can be pressed onto self-adhesive non-woven fabric before gluing, or the edges can be overstitched, or a little glue can be run along the edges.

Knitting design/sleeves

Now that you know how to design a top and a skirt, the next most important stage in designing is the planning of sleeves. Sleeves and their shapes are very important in designing garments and a poorly shaped sleeve can mar an otherwise perfect garment. It is therefore important to fully understand the different kinds of sleeves, their shapes, and how to fit them.

A dress, like the one illustrated, can be made by joining the basic skirt and top at the waist, adding short sleeves and linking the whole with stripe detail.

There are many different types of sleeve, each with its own characteristics, but to begin with it is important to understand the construction of the basic sleeve shape and the terms used to identify the various parts. All sleeves are divided into two groups:

Group 1. Sleeves sewn into an armhole which has been formed by the back and the front of the garment being joined with a shoulder seam.

Group 2. Sleeves which extend over the shoulder to the neck edge such as both the raglan and saddle cap varieties and those

garments with a circular yoke. This style removes the need for a shoulder seam entirely.

The parts of a sleeve
Sleeves consist of two sections:
Section B is the lower part of the sleeve—all the sleeve from the top of the seam at underarm down to the lower edge, irrespective of the length.
Section A is all the sleeve above section B, and is called the cap of the sleeve.
For a sleeve belonging to group 1 (that is, a set-in sleeve fitting into an armhole) sections A and B will resemble figure **1**. The area called the cap of the sleeve, section A, is shaded.
Sleeves from group 2 (where the sleeve extends to the neck edge) will be dealt with later in this chapter.

The set-in sleeve — group 1

The basic rule in planning group 1 sleeves is that the entire length of the sleeve, both sections A and B plus the length of the shoulder seam, must equal the body measurement from the point on the arm where the lowest edge of the sleeve is to be, up the arm and along the top of the shoulder to the neck edge (see illustration).

Planning section B and taking measurements
Planning the lower section of a sleeve follows basic rules for both group 1 and group 2.
Figure **2** shows a simple, slim fitting, long sleeve. Draw a similar chart and add your own measurements.
AB is the measurement required for the lower edge of the sleeve and should be the actual measurement of the arm at this point, plus whatever tolerance is required (AB can be at any point of the arm from above the elbow to the wrist, depending on the length of sleeve desired). A fitting cardigan or pullover sleeve will have very little added for tolerance whereas a coat may have 2 or more inches added. A full sleeve gathered into a cuff will naturally be very much wider.
CD is the measurement required at the widest point of the upper arm, plus the addition of any extra width required.
EF is the length required from the lowest edge of the sleeve to a point underarm, say $\frac{1}{2}$ inch below the actual armpit.

Planning section A
The most usual type of sleeve cap in group 1 looks like figure **2**, whether on a long or a short sleeve. The next measurement to calculate is FG.
Tie a piece of tape around the arm at

underarm level to give the equivalent of line CD. Measure carefully from the center of this line to the point where the sleeve will join the shoulder seam. This measurement is FG (see illustration). It is essential that the piece of tape is level around the arm before measuring. If it is allowed to slope upward the lines of knitting in the finished sleeve will pull downward because the cap of the sleeve is too shallow. If the tape is allowed to sag then the lines of knitting will slope incorrectly and sag unbecomingly. Correctly measured, the finished sleeve will hang perfectly and will also be comfortable to wear.

The line CGD is curved, and varies depending on the shape of the armhole. To fit an armhole shaped like that of the top in the previous chapter, it should be of a shape similar to that in figure 2.

Planning the sleeve cap on graph

Work out the shape of the sleeve cap on 1 inch squared graph paper. First, mark out the number of squares required for the measurement CD.

The points H and I are marked next and are found by binding off at the beginning of the next 2 rows the same number of stitches as are bound off for the beginning of the armhole on front and back of the garment.

The width of the last row at the extreme top of the sleeve cap is the next stage to decide and is determined only by your personal choice. Not less than 3 inches is advisable, however, otherwise the sleeve has a pinched look. Mark this measurement on the chart.

The final shape will depend on how the remaining stitches are decreased to leave the correct number on the last row. It is best not to decrease too rapidly at the beginning. If the cap becomes narrow too quickly, when it is worn it will pull the armhole edges onto the arm during wear, giving the arm insufficient room to move comfortably. It is usual to decrease one stitch at each end of the next 4 or 6 rows and then to decrease more gradually, probably one stitch at each end of every other row until the sleeve is nearly the required length. Surplus stitches can then be bound off at the beginning of the next 4, 6 or even 8 rows until the correct number is obtained for the final row. It is preferable to reduce stitches more rapidly at this point rather than decreasing the total width nearer the lower part of the cap. Map out the shape on graph paper. If you see a better way of arranging the stitches it is a simple matter to redraw before you

start to knit.

If you decide to alter the armhole shape when you are planning the top then the sleeve must also alter as the relationship between sleeve and armhole must be maintained.

Variations of sleeve caps

In many continental sweaters the shoulderline of the garment is below the natural shoulderline, making a longer shoulder seam. The sleeve cap is charted in exactly the same way, but it will look different because the distance between F and G will be less, making it necessary to reduce the number of stitches more quickly because there are fewer rows in which to work. The basic rule still applies because the total measurement of both sleeve sections plus the shoulder seam are equal to the measurement from the lower edge of sleeve to the neck edge. The shape of the dropped shoulderline sleeve is shown in figure 3.

On a casual jacket or housecoat the sleeve may consist of a lower section only. In this case, the shoulder seam measurement must be extended so that with the lower section the correct measurement is obtained.

Group 2 sleeves

The basic rules for planning group 2 sleeves are the same as for group 1 sleeves, but the sleeve may become part of back and front, as in a circular yoke, making it necessary to consider the garment measurements as a whole. The upper section of the sleeve may be separate for a few rows or it may become part of the yoke at the end of section B. The total number of rows above the sleeve on the yoke must still produce the required measurement.

A raglan sleeve will have seams on either side of the sleeve cap, but again, in planning it must be related to front and back of garment as the number of rows must be the same. Figure 4 shows two possible raglan sleeve shapes. Saddle capped sleeves must be related to the armhole shaping, but instead of being bound off at the shoulderline the sleeve cap is continued as a straight panel until the sleeve and panel length equal the length from sleeve edge to neck. When complete the shaped edges are seamed to the armhole and the bound-off shoulder edges are sewn to the sides of the center panel. Figure 5 shows the shape of a saddle cap sleeve.

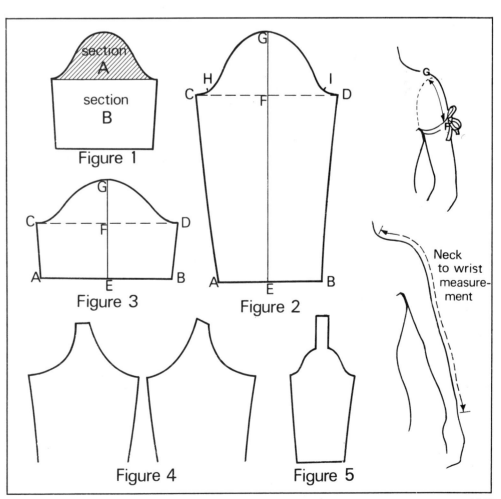

Figure 1

Figure 3

Figure 2

Figure 4

Figure 5

Neck to wrist measurement

Knitting pattern/classic dress

The yarn used for this very attractive dress, worked mostly in stockinette stitch, gives a tweed effect. A garter stitch edge gives a crisp finish and the front opening running into a high neckline adds fashion detail. This dress looks equally good worn unbelted or with the addition of a ready-made belt or silk scarf. Careful choice of accessories will give either a daytime or evening look.

Sizes
Directions are for 34in bust. The figures in brackets [] refer to the 36, 38 and 40in sizes respectively.
Length, 33[34:35:36]in.
Sleeve seam, 3[3:3½:3½]in.

Gauge
6 sts and 8 rows to 1in over st st worked on No.4 needles.

Materials
Unger Derby
16[17:18:19] balls
One pair No.4 needles
One pair No.2 needles
8 buttons
½yd grosgrain ribbon

Back

Using No.2 needles, cast on 126[132:138:144] sts.
K 8 rows.
Change to No.4 needles and continue in st st beg with a K row.
Work until 7[7½:8:8½]in from beg ending with a P row.
K2 tog at both ends of next and every following 10th row until 102[108:114:120] sts rem.
Continue without shaping until work measures 26[26½:27:27½] in from beg ending with a P row.

Shape armholes
Bind off 6 sts at beg of next 2 rows.
K2 tog at both ends of every other row 6[7:8:9] times.
78[82:86:90] sts.
Continue without shaping until armholes measure 7[7½:8:8½]in ending with a P row.
1548

Shape shoulders
Bind off 6[6:7:7] sts at beg of next 6 rows, then 5[6:4:5] sts at beg of next 2 rows.
Slip rem 32[34:36:38] sts on holder.

Front

Work as given for Back until 108[114:120:126] sts rem.
Work 1 row after last dec.

Divide for front opening
Next row K51[54:57:60], cast on 6 sts, turn, slip rem sts on holder.
Next row K2, P to end.
Keeping 2 sts at inside edge in garter st, continue dec at side edge on every 10th row until 54[57:60:63] sts rem.
Continue without shaping until work measures the same as Back to armholes ending with a WS row.

Shape armhole
Bind off 6 sts at beg of next row, then K2 tog at armhole edge on every other row until 42[44:46:48] sts rem.
Continue without shaping until armhole measures the same as on Back ending with a WS row.

Shape shoulder
At arm edge, bind off 6[6:7:7] sts every other row 3 times, then 5[6:4:5] sts once.
Slip rem 19[20:21:22] sts on holder.
Mark position of buttons on front edge as follows: first button 1in from beg of opening, 2nd button level with first row of shoulder shaping, then 3 more buttons spaced evenly between these two.
Attach yarn to sts on holder, K to end.
Next row P to last 2 sts, K2.
Rep these last 2 rows for 1in ending with a WS row.
Next row K3, bind off 2 sts, K to end.
Next row Work to end, casting on 2 sts over those bound off on previous row.
Continue work to correspond to first side, working buttonholes as before level with button markings, reversing shaping.

Sleeves

Using No.2 needles, cast on 68[71:74:77] sts and K 4 rows.
Change to No.4 needles and continue in st st.
Inc one st at both ends of 5th and following 6th row.
Continue without shaping until sleeve seam measures 3[3:3½:3½]in ending with a P row.

Shape cap
Bind off 6 sts at beg of next 2 rows.
K2 tog at both ends of next and every other row until 36[37:38:39] sts rem ending with a P row.
Bind off 2 sts at beg of next 8 rows, then 3 sts at beg of next 4 rows.
Bind off rem 8[9:10:11] sts.

Pocket flaps

Using No.2 needles, cast on 21 sts and continue in garter st for 1¼ in.
Next row K1, K2 tog, K to last 3 sts, K2 tog, K1.
Rep the last row until 9 sts rem. Bind off.

Neckband

Join shoulder seams.
Using No.2 needles and with RS facing, K across all sts on holders.
Keeping 2 sts at each end in garter st, continue in st st for 10 rows more and working buttonhole as before on 6th row.
K 4 rows. Bind off.

Finishing

Press work under a damp cloth and using a warm iron.
Sew in sleeves. Join side and sleeve seams.
Face right Front edge with grosgrain ribbon. Buttonhole-stitch around buttonholes, cutting through ribbon.
Sew down underwrap at beg of Front opening. Press all seams.
Sew on buttons. Sew on pocket flaps with a button on each.

This short sleeved dress has a simple elegance ▶

1549

Stitchery pattern/stool and pillow

This unusual design in wool embroidery makes an equally pleasing decoration for either a stool top or a pillow cover. The original design was worked on a background fabric of fine wool, but even-weave linen would also be suitable. Crewel yarn could be substituted for tapestry yarn.

Footstool and pillow
A delightful embroidered footstool and matching pillow cover, worked in long and short stitch for the leaves and satin stitch for the flowers.

Using Appleton's Tapestry yarn, two skeins each of numbers 1 and 10, one skein each of the remainder.
1. 991 white; **2.** 943 pale, bright rose pink; **3.** 438 leaf green; **4.** 253 grass green; **5.** 353 light gray green; **6.** 355 dark gray green; **7.** 243 light olive green; **8.** 542 early English green; **9.** 403 light sea green; **10.** 406 dark sea green; **11.** 752 pale rose; **12.** 946 deep, bright rose pink; **13.** 501a scarlet; **14.** 755 mid rose pink; **15.** 144 dull rose pink.

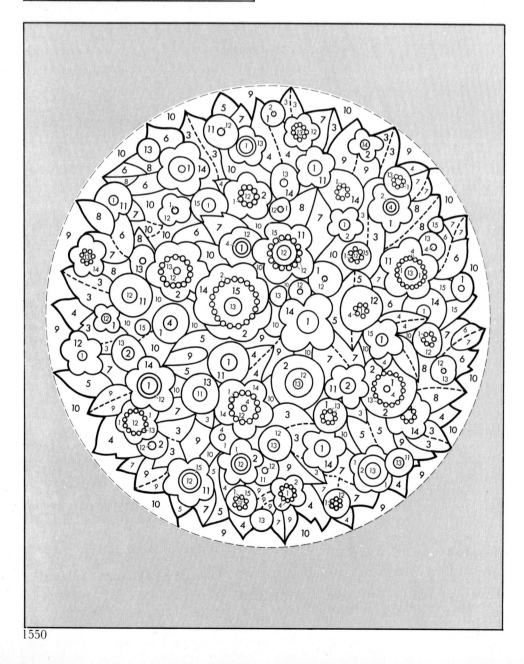

1551

Stitchery design/grouping shapes

Progressing from single shapes, the next stage is to learn how to make a more elaborate design. Still using the original simple pear shape as inspiration, the panel illustrated shows what can be achieved by grouping.

The designer has chosen to create a decorative panel by grouping and overlapping the pear shape, contrasting the texture of heavy slubbed burlap and smooth woolen fabric in the same color and tone for the background. You can try a grouped arrangement like this for yourself by tracing the pear shape given in chapter 1 and cutting out several identical pears from several thicknesses of paper. Lay the shapes on a large sheet of paper and move them around until a satisfying arrangement is obtained. In this design the designer has cut away some sections of the pear's outline to give a more subtle effect, and other lines are then added. These lines contrast with the applied areas and link shapes in a free and flowing way, the shapes between being as important to the design as the actual pear shapes. Notice that all the lines and shapes in this design are curved and belong to the same family. The alternative arrangement illustrated shows a different approach using parts of the pear shapes which break in and out of rectangles. When this stage is reached, it does not mean that the designing process is complete. The comparative textures and weights of fabric and thread may need reducing or increasing as the work develops. The selection of threads and stitches is part of the design process, inseparable from the overall concept. Things tend to alter all the time unless one is an exceptional visualizer, and it is this that makes designing one's own embroidery so much more exciting and satisfying than copying from someone else's design.
The focal point of the panel illustrated is obtained by grouping different kinds of round shapes, French knots, large wooden beads and woven wheels over beads. Thus the focal point, which is essential to a good design, is achieved—not only because of its placing, but also because it forms the most positive area of texture and color.
The stitches used, mainly twisted chain, double knot stitch, couching and outline are a good choice for lines, because they stand up well from the background. The threads—shiny, highly twisted, soft and matte, vary as much in texture and weight as the fabrics themselves.

Relating embroidery design to use
One should always start by relating an embroidery design to it's use, asking oneself whether the object will fit permanently in a room scheme, for instance. Planning the decoration for an embroidered pillow, for example, immediately presents limitations: the general style and color scheme of the room, the shape, fabric and color of the chair or sofa with which the pillow will harmonize or contrast. Is the pillow to form an unobtrusive or a dominant feature? Do the furnishings in this room receive hard wear? What about washing or cleaning? These questions will affect the embroiderer's choice of materials and technique.
The interests and tastes of the maker and the eventual user of any embroidered object also dictates the choice of design and technique to some extent. Love of animals, flowers, geology, pop art, fishing or brass rubbing—any of these can reveal themselves in design.
The embroiderer who can use a camera will find photography a rich source of ideas. An abstract design might originate from a close-up of bare, gray fig tree branches taken on a Portuguese holiday; a vivid and exciting panel might result from a photograph of the heart of a rose.
Ideas will come at odd moments and must be jotted down as soon as possible—on a theater program, on the corner of a magazine on a journey, and ideally, the student of design should carry a small sketch book from which she is never parted.

Summarizing the principles of embroidery design discussed in these chapters, two different designs were worked out by an embroiderer using the pear shape as a basic motif (see diagrams below). She traced off and cut out several pear shapes and then arranged and rearranged them under a sheet of tracing paper until a pleasing design appeared. She then drew the outlines of the paper shapes using a soft pencil, and rubbed out some parts of the outlines and added other lines and solid areas, roughing in those tones which were to become textured and contrasting areas eventually. The piece of embroidery illustrated shows how the embroiderer finally interpreted one of her original inspirations (the diagram on the right), into threads, fabric and beads. Two textured fabrics have been used for the background, a thick, coarsely woven burlap and a smooth even-weave fabric. The pear shapes themselves have been treated in a wide variety of ways; some are cut from fabric—velvet, wool jersey, tweed, silk —and applied to the background, others are incorporated into the design in embroidery threads and stitches or outlined in silk cord. The embroidery stitches chosen by the designer are mainly twisted chain, outline stitch, double knot stitch and couching. Beads were used for the focal part of the embroidery, some grouped in the center and others used in graduated sizes. Tones of purple, chosen for the strongest colors in the design, are repeated in the beads, large wooden ones for the central area, with smaller ones grouped around.

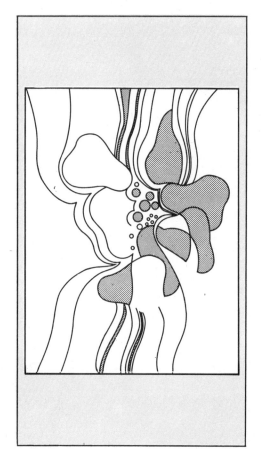

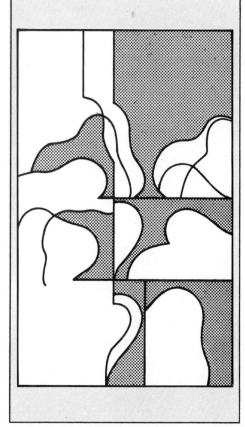

1553

Home crochet/bedspread

Crocheted in separate squares, this heavily textured bed-spread can be made larger or smaller by varying the number of squares used.

Size
About 98in by 112in.

Gauge
Each square measures about 14in.

Materials
Coats and Clark's O.N.T. Speed-Cro-Sheen
About 2¾ balls per square
One No.C crochet hook

Square motif

Ch10 and join with a ss to form a ring.

1st round Ch3, 2dc into ring, (ch3, 3dc into ring) 3 times, ch3, ss into 3rd of first 3ch.

2nd round Ss to ch3 sp, ch3, (2dc, ch3, 3dc) into the sp, *ch1, (3dc, ch3, 3dc) into next sp, rep from * twice more, ch1, ss into 3rd of 3ch.

3rd round Ss to ch3 sp, ch3, (2dc, ch3, 3dc) into sp, *ch2, 1dc into next sp, ch2, (3dc, ch3, 3dc) into sp at corner, rep from * twice more, ch2, 1dc into next sp, ch2, ss into 3rd of 3ch.

4th round Work first corner as 2nd round, *(ch2, 1dc into next sp) twice, ch2, (3dc, ch3, 3dc) into sp at corner, rep from * to end finishing with a ss into 3rd of 3ch.

5th round Begin as 2nd round, *ch3, 1dc into next sp, ch3, 6dc into next sp, take out hook and insert through top of first dc, then through loop which was left and pull loop tight—called knot 1—, ch3, 1dc into next sp, ch3, (3dc, ch3, 3dc) into sp at corner, rep from * to end, finishing as on all previous rounds.

6th round Begin as 2nd, *ch3, 1dc into next sp, ch3, knot 1 in next sp, 3dc into knot, knot 1 in next sp, ch3, 1dc into sp, ch3, (3dc, ch3, 3dc) into corner, rep from *, end as before.

7th round Begin as 2nd, *ch3, 1dc into next sp, 1554

ch3, knot 1 in next sp, 3dc into knot, knot 1 into 2nd of 3dc, 3dc into knot, knot 1 into sp, ch3, 1dc, ch3, (3dc, ch3, 3dc) into corner, rep from * ending as before.

8th round Begin as 2nd, *ch3, 1dc in next sp, ch3, (knot 1, 3dc) 3 times, knot 1, ch3, 1dc, ch3, (3dc, ch3, 3dc) into corner, rep from * ending as before.

9th round As 8th but working 5 knots.

10th round As 8th but working 6 knots.

11th round As 8th but working 7 knots.

12th round Begin as 2nd, *ch3, 1dc into next sp, ch3, knot 1 into next sp, 2dc over knot 1 of previous round, 1dc into each of next 3dc, 2dc over knot 1 of previous round, (knot 1, 3dc) 3 times, knot 1, 2dc over knot 1 of previous round, 1dc into each of next 3dc, 2dc over knot 1 of previous round, knot 1 into next sp, ch3, 1dc into next sp, ch3, (3dc, ch3, 3dc) into corner, rep from * ending as before.

13th round As 12th but working 11dc and 3 knots on each side.

14th round As 12th but working 15dc and 2 knots.

15th round As 12th but working 19dc and 1 knot.

16th round Begin as 2nd, *ch3, 1dc in next sp, ch3, knot 1 in next sp, 2dc over knot 1 of previous round, 19dc,

2dc over knot 1 of previous round, 19dc, 2dc over knot 1 of previous round, knot 1 into next sp, ch3, 1dc into next sp, ch3, (3dc, ch3, 3dc) into corner, rep from * ending as before.

17th round Begin as 2nd, *knot 1 into 2nd of 3dc at corner, 3dc into next sp, knot 1 on next dc, 3dc into next sp, knot 1 into next knot, (skip next dc, 3dc into next dc, skip next dc, knot 1 into next dc) 3 times, 20dc, (knot 1 into next dc, skip next dc, 3dc into next dc, skip next dc) 3 times, knot 1 into next knot, 3dc into next sp, knot 1 into next dc, 3dc into next sp, knot 1 into 2nd of 3dc at corner, (3dc, ch3, 3dc) into corner, rep from *, ending as before.

18th round As 17th but with 24dc between grs of knots.

19th round As 17th but with 28dc between grs of knots.

20th round As 17th but working 32dc between grs of knots.

Fasten off. Make 56 squares.

Finishing

Press each square into shape under a damp cloth and using a warm iron.
Join the squares into 8 strips of 7 squares each, then join the strips. Press again.
Make a knotted fringe all around using about 8 strands for each knot.

Fifty six squares make a spread large enough for a double bed ►
▼ Close-up detail of the central motif of a square

Design in dressmaking/pockets

1

Studying the fashion reports in the press you will notice that in some seasons pockets are very much a fashion feature. Pockets are usually the easiest of all ideas to copy as they are not normally structural and so can be cut out in paper or muslin, pinned on, moved around, altered and then discarded if you don't like the result.

Functional or decorative
1. Here is a variety of pockets designed as important fashion features of the garments they decorate.
If pockets are added to a design simply for looks they don't even have to be made functional or be placed within easy reach. But there is much to be said for basically functional details like pockets—and fastenings too—that really do work.
On the practical side it is easy to see that many garments look better with the addition of pockets which are well designed and thoughtfully placed: we
1556

need them for handkerchiefs; a small ticket pocket in the lining of a jacket or coat saves all that frantic searching for tickets or small change when traveling; winter coats need pockets in which gloves can be safely stowed away.

Planning the pocket
When deciding whether or not to have pockets on a garment the strength, weight and transparency of the fabric must be considered in relation to the size and purpose of the pocket you would like. Then, if the fabric is right, the size and placing of the pocket needs careful thought.
2a. Take a simple basic dress. Although pockets are probably the most easy-to-make variation possible, they can completely transform the entire look of a garment. Cut out shapes in paper—or the dress fabric itself—and experiment by pinning them in different positions.
There are some parts of a woman's anatomy, such as the hips and possibly the

bust, which look very unattractive with added bulk.
2b. Also, pockets are eye-catching, and it is essential that attention is not inadvertently drawn to figure faults such as a big bust or wide hips by pockets being placed where they would only serve to emphasize them. Bad placing can give a pinch-chested or droopy-busted look where none exists, and a pocket too near the hem looks as though it might fall off at any moment. If the pockets are to be functional the size must be right for the hand and the likely contents. The position is also important: not too low for fingers to reach down to the bottom, or so high into the waist that you have to stretch up and lean over in the opposite direction before you can get your hand into it.
For those who are going to sit around most of the time, pockets on skirts will need to be placed much lower than usual for convenient use as the position changes appreciably when one sits down.

2a

2b

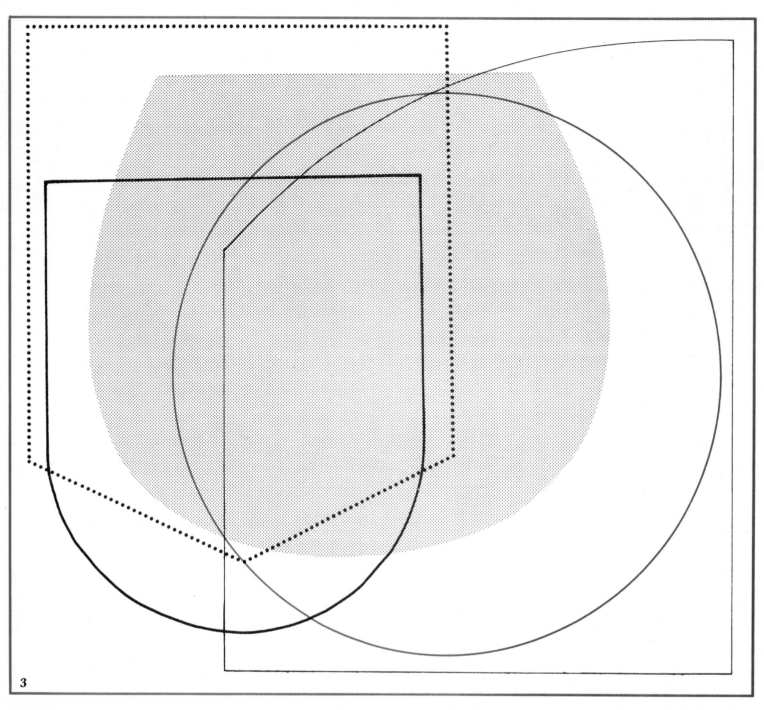

3

Patch pockets

3. Patch pockets can be made any shape you like—here are a few ideas and tracing patterns.

4. Even if a pocket is designed for utilitarian purposes it can be very decorative too—surely the ideal to aim for whatever you are designing. Cut to the desired size and made up as already described in Golden Hands Dressmaking chapter 23, simple patch pockets can be attractively placed wherever they are most useful —the back of a pair of pants, the yoke of a jacket.

5. Patch pockets can look good in contrasting colors or textures. They will be very eye-catching, so be sure to place

1558

them where they will not attract attention to parts of you which are best not noticed.
6 and **7.** Patch pockets can be tucked, have pleats, be turned down and buttoned (**6**) or have cuffs (**7**).
8. Gathered patch pockets are simple to cut and make but usually look best if there are gathers elsewhere in the design.
9. Patch pockets can have holes or openings of any shape which are faced or bound before the pocket is stitched to the garment.
Alternatively, a hole can be cut and bound on the garment and then a pocket stitched on the inside with topstitching to fit in with the rest of the design.
10. Patch pockets can sometimes be used

to conceal, but great care must be taken to see that they really do look like an intentional part of the design. They can be used to hide a cigarette burn, a flaw or join in the material, or an irremovable stain.
11. In very hot weather, a see-through blouse with strategically placed pockets enables one to go without a bra and remain marvelously cool and comfortable —and entirely decent too.
12. For security, or simply for looks, pockets can be closed with zippers—either in seams or superimposed.
13. Pocket flaps can be added. Make them plain and simple, or cut them to any shape or size you like.

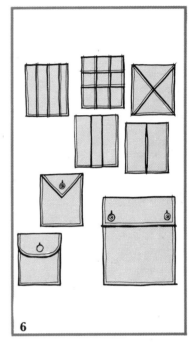

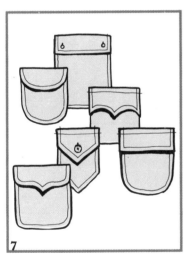

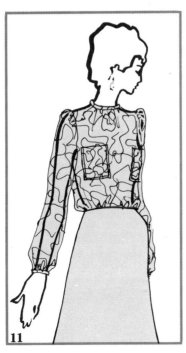

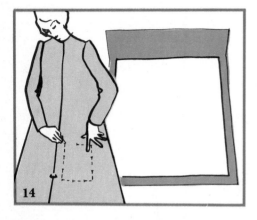

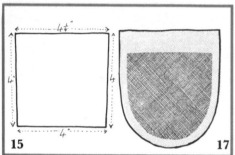

Applying the patch pocket

14. To make your own pocket design simply chalk or pin whatever shape you like on your garment and trace it off. Smooth and correct the outline if necessary and add the usual seam allowances before cutting out in fabric.

15. To allow for really easy access some pattern cutters recommend cutting the top edge of a rectangular pocket a fraction longer than the bottom, with the sides slanting outward toward the top. When the pocket is stitched to the straight grain of the garment there is room for the hand to slip in more easily.

16. To make a gathered patch pocket, chalk or pin the required shape on the

garment, trace off and cut out a pattern. Slash the pattern and spread it until you have the required amount of fullness to be gathered in, then draw around the edge onto another piece of paper. Round off the pattern to a smooth line and add seam allowances.

The gathered edge can be bound, faced, shirred or smocked, or it can be gathered onto a lining cut from the original shape before it was slashed.

17. For a crisp effect a pocket can be stiffened with iron-on interlining. Cut the interlining the exact size of the pocket without the seam allowances.

18. Whenever you want identical pockets, one on each side of a garment, mark one

side only. Then fold the garment exactly down the center and mark through to the other side with pins.

19. The pocket should be pinned in place when the garment is actually on the body, and therefore rounded, rather than when it is laid out flat on a table. If you don't take this precaution the hang of the garment is likely to be distorted.

Bound pockets

20. Bound pockets (see Golden Hands Dressmaking chapter 60) can be placed where you like and made in self or contrasting fabric. They can have zippers or flaps. They can be set straight or at an angle, as you wish.

Crafts/beadweaving

Although the earliest beads used for woven bead jewelry and garments might have been seeds, and the loom most likely a few pieces of stick, the craft of beadweaving is certainly a very ancient one. It is a traditional folk-craft in the north of South America, where the women weave themselves intricately patterned bead aprons, and was well-known to the North American Indians. Two forms of beadweaving are covered in this chapter. One uses a loom and produces a woven ribbon of beads. The other uses a cord-knotting technique to produce larger pieces of beadwork which can be used to make jewelry and accessories.

Materials and equipment

Very little equipment is required for beadweaving. To produce a flat ribbon of closely woven beads a bead loom is essential.

Wood or metal beading looms are inexpensive to buy, or a simple one can be constructed from a wooden box with tacks hammered into it. Even a cardboard box with notches cut in the edges can be used as a loom, but threads must be stretched very tightly before work is begun, and only very small pieces of beadweaving can be worked by this method.

Beads. Small embroidery beads made of plastic, ceramic or glass, colored wooden beads and natural wooden beads of all sizes can be used for weaving.

Needles. Long, thin beading needles, fine enough to go through the beads twice, are best.

Thread. This also must be fine enough to go twice through the beads. Either linen carpet thread or special beading cotton are recommended. If neither of these are available, thin crochet cotton may be used, but nylon thread must not be used as it is too rigid.

Designs for beadweaving

Beginners will find it easier to follow a chart, but after a little practice you will be able to work a simple design without having to follow a pattern. You can make a chart yourself on graph paper, when each small square will represent one bead of your design. Color the squares with the colors of the beads you intend to use—this makes it much easier to follow a pattern. Charts for needlepoint or cross stitch can be used for beadweaving and one bead will replace each stitch marked. If you are inventing your own pattern, start with an uncomplicated design, working up into more ambitious, three or four color patterns. When creating a design for bead work, remember that curved lines have to be built up row by row, just as in needlepoint.

After planning a design, work a few trial rows first, and count how many beads you will need for the completed work.

Setting up the loom

The lengthwise stretched threads are known as the warp, and the beads lie between them, so the distance between the threads should correspond to the size of the beads you are using. There must always be one more warp thread than there are beads in the width of the pattern, and to give added strength to the edge of the weaving the two outside warp threads should be doubled. Therefore, if your pattern is 20 beads wide, you will need to stretch up 23 threads.

For a thin belt you can use as few as 10 beads across the pattern, but for a bag made of small beads you will need more threads and beads to give you the correct width.

Cut the warp threads to the length of beading you desire plus 6 inches. Knot these threads in bunches of 5 around the square stick at the end of the loom, stretch them tightly across the combs, and secure them at the other end of the loom in the slot. You will find it quicker to keep beads of different colors separated in small, shallow containers. Small plastic boxes with lids can be bought and these are ideal. Sprinkle a few beads onto a piece of felt, ready to be picked up.

Beginning to weave

Thread the needle with the working thread, and attach the end of it to the double stretched thread on the left. Don't make the working thread too long, as it tangles easily. 15 inches is long enough. Work four rows without beads in darning stitch to make the top of the weaving firm, finishing on the left. Thread onto the working thread the beads required for the first row of the pattern, counting the pattern from the left.

This string of beads is now placed underneath the warp threads so that one bead is positioned under and between each two warp threads.

Press the string of beads up between the threads with the first finger of your left hand. Pass the needle from right to left back through the hole of each of the beads, thus securing them. Pull the thread fairly tight at the end of the row to make it firm, but be sure to keep the tension even because the edges of the weaving can easily become distorted. Begin the second row of the pattern working from the left again, and continue in this way until you have finished the pattern. Pull the thread back and forth through the previous rows every now and then for added strength.

If you happen to leave a warp thread exposed by mistake don't worry, it will be captured by the next line of beads.

1562

To make long articles, first weave the length of the loom, then, loosening the warp threads from the slot, wind the weaving around the square stick, and then stretch the newly exposed threads.

Tighten the warp and proceed as before.

Finishing off

Work two or three lines of darning without beads with the last working thread, then take the working thread back through the next to last row of the beads. Tie a knot and cut the thread.

Lift the warp threads off the loom, take two warp threads at a time back through the beads, knot again, then cut. Run the knots up to the beads on a pin.

Fancy finishes

To make a five-bead side fringe.

Tie the working thread on the left-hand double warp threads, and thread on a row of beads in the usual way, according to the pattern, but add five extra beads for the side fringe. When turning at the end of the row, ignore the number five bead, but thread the working thread back through the four fringe beads, then work through the pattern beads in the normal way. For a fringe at both sides, as soon as the pattern beads have been worked through thread on five extra beads, turn, ignore the first bead but thread the working thread back through the four extra beads. Thread on the pattern beads and continue.

To make a side U loop (Five beads)

Tie the working thread on the left-hand double warp threads and thread a row of beads in the usual way, according to the pattern. Add on an extra five beads, then, without turning, thread on another row of pattern beads. Press up these two rows of pattern beads and catch them with the working thread, starting from the left-hand warp for the first row, and going back as usual from the right-hand warp for the second row. Ignore the extra five beads at the end and they will form a loop. If you want a side U loop at both sides of the work, at the end of these two rows add an extra five beads, thread on your pattern beads, add five extra beads, thread on the pattern beads, and then catch these two rows of pattern beads, ignoring the extra five at each end, which will form loops.

For a longer loop, thread on more extra beads. For a scalloped edge, add three extra beads only.

Top: two different handmade looms
1. *Passing beads behind warp threads*
2. *Passing needle back through the beads*

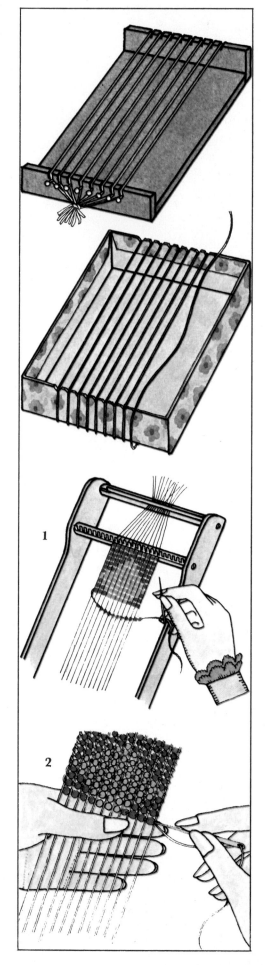

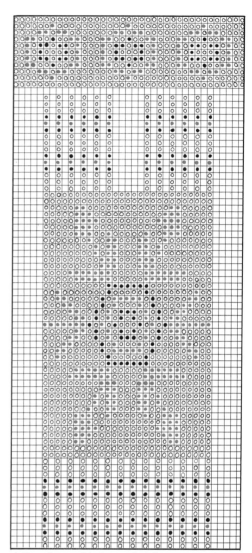

Chart for the three-color necklet—top right   *Chart for the fringed bracelet—bottom right*

▲ *Complete necklet's panel and remove work from loom. Hand-thread beads onto six pairs of threads on left and right, cut central five threads to 2ins and thread back into work. Proceed with side strips to pattern shown above.*

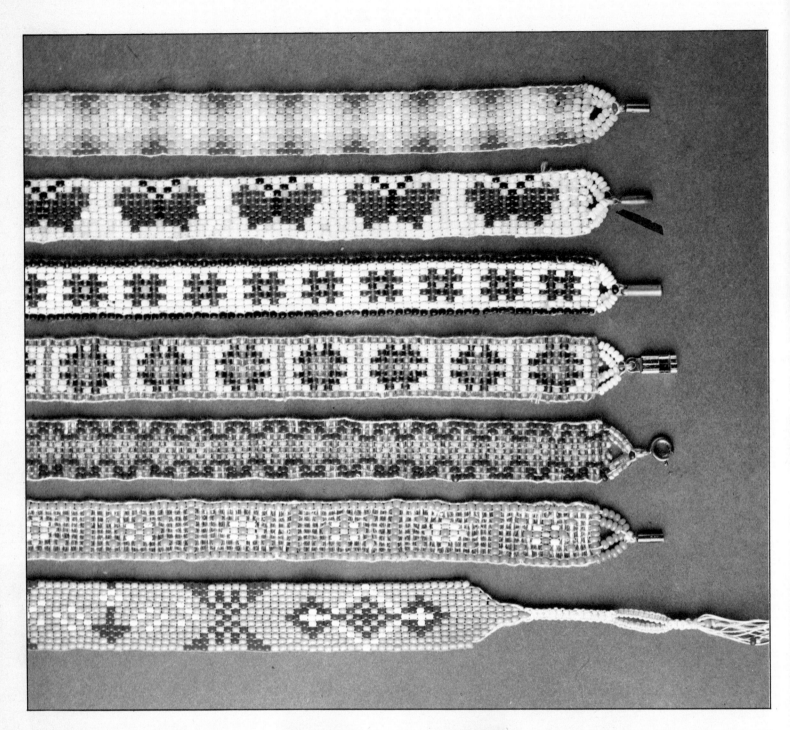

Six of the chokers shown above have been finished off with conventional necklace fastenings, the threads worked back through the last few beads before knotting off. The lower necklet and the belt on the right have been finished with macramé square knots with additional beads interthreaded. To make a macramé square knot on four threads follow the diagram and work as follows: pass the left thread under the center two threads and over the right-hand thread to form a loop. Pick up the end of the right-hand thread and pass it from front to back through the loop and draw it up tightly. This forms a half knot. Now pass the right-hand thread under the center threads and over the left-hand thread and put the end of left-hand thread through loop for a square knot.

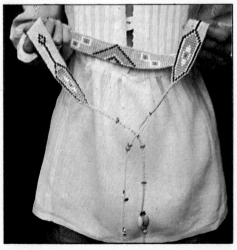

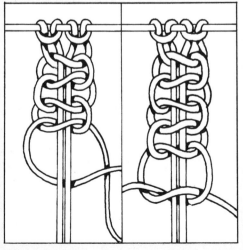

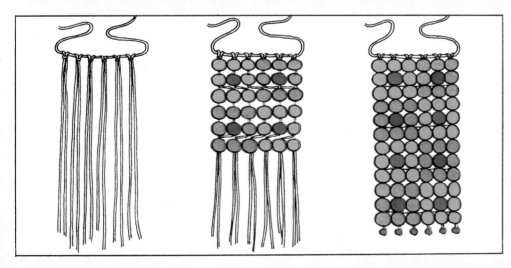

▲ The two belts and the pendant illustrated
are made by various cord-knotting techniques
which can also be used for making large
beadwork items such as vests. The
diagrams show one pattern of cord-knotting.
Knot six thin cords onto a thicker cord,
using a macramé knot. Dip the ends of the
thin cord into melted candle wax to make
bead threading easier. Thread beads onto the
pairs of cords. After two rows of beads have
been threaded, working from the left, string
the first bead onto a single cord, and take its
pair across to the second bead. Take one of
the second beads' cords across to the third bead
and so on to the last bead which has three
cords through it. After two more rows, take
the cords back across again.

Knitting design/variations on a dress

The skirt, top and sleeves already designed can form the starting point for an endless variety of designs based on these shapes.

The simplest variation is to combine the skirt and top to create a dress and add simple, short set-in sleeves.

Bodice

The top of the dress is designed in exactly the same way as the sleeveless top in Knitting Design chapter 2. The main point to remember is that the lower edge of the top is knitted onto the top edge of the skirt and the join is actually on the waistline.
The top and the skirt must therefore have the same number of stitches at the waist.

Skirt

For an all-in-one dress without a seam at the waistline, the amount of shaping between the hipline and the waistline will probably need to be reduced considerably.

Neckline

If you charted the neckline for the top on graph paper and are using the same yarn and stitch for the dress, there is no need to make another chart for a different neckline, provided the number of stitches from the armhole upward remains the same.
A lower, round neckline can easily be planned by working a similar curve to the neckline as the top but starting it one or two inches lower.
A V-neckline is also quite simple to plan but it is always best to work one over an odd number of stitches so that there is one center stitch around which to plan the V. Leave the center stitch to be picked up when working the edge and plan the V on either side of this stitch after deciding where you want the point of the V to commence.
Mark the altered neckline on your graph using a different color so that the two sets of markings are easily distinguished.
Rechart the neckline, however, if the gauge or stitches differ in any way.

Varying designs

One of the simplest methods of varying the basic designs in these chapters is to add stripes of contrasting or toning colors. First decide the dimensions of the stripes and how many rows they are to cover, marking them on your chart.
As in the dress illustrated, a very individual

look can be given to an easy stockinette stitch garment if the stripes are cleverly placed and are repeated on bodice or sleeves. This kind of pattern gives continuity and does not look as if it had been added as an experiment, or as an afterthought.
A dress as simple as this can also be given an exclusive, festive look by the careful addition of beads or sequins on the sleeves or on the cuff and neckline.

Basic shape alterations

Once you begin to feel that you know what you are doing and are finding it easier to chart, you will want to make more complicated alterations to the basic shapes. To plan simple alterations it is easiest to draw a diagram of the original shape and mark out any alterations on it in a different color. This can help when you are beginning to design, because although you are making a change, the overall measurement must still be achieved by the new shape.

Dividing the top for a button fastening
Draw a diagram of the top front. Using a different color, draw a line down the length of the center front. For a ribbed

button strip to be added after the garment is completed, decide on the width and draw a line half this width to one side of the center line. Repeat this to the other side of the center line as shown in figure **1**. Again, you may be able to use your original chart, subtracting the number of stitches equal to the width of the button strip from the total and working each side on the stitches required. Work the button strip after completing the other pieces and sew it to the center front edges.
For buttonholes on the actual garment the diagram will differ.
Draw a diagram of the front and mark the center line. On the center line mark the buttonholes and make a note of how many stitches wide they are to be. To this, add at least 2 edge stitches working toward the right so that the buttonholes will not be too near the edge. Add 1 stitch for the folded edge and then calculate the number of stitches required for the underside. This should consist of the same number of stitches, 2 or more to the buttonhole, the same number of stitches for the under buttonhole and 2 or more stitches to complete the underside (see figure **2**).
The left-hand side of the garment is similar in width but is worked omitting the button-

holes. For a less bulky fastening the underside of the left-hand side can be omitted and grosgrain ribbon used in its place.

Forming a yoke on the basic top
A yoke can easily be planned from your basic diagram. Draw a line on the back top diagram, from side to side, at the required depth below the center back neck. On the section of the back which comes below the yoke line you will need to add extra stitches for fullness (see figure **3**).

This is added to the total and, as it in no way affects the shaping of the armholes, can be worked using the original chart.

If the back is to be seamed onto the yoke it will make the finished work neater if the fullness is decreased across the width while working the last or 2nd last row so that the bound-off edge measures the same as the cast-on edge of the yoke.

The front of the top is altered in the same way for a yoke and can also be divided for a buttonhole opening if desired.

To turn the top into a full dress add additional length as well.

Alterations for raglan sleeves
This is a larger alteration because back, front and sleeve all have to be altered and must fit together row by row when complete. The calculations up to the armholes will be the same but from there on they will differ.

On a sheet of graph paper, mark the number of stitches required across the back just below the armhole level. Work out the number of rows to give the correct center back measurement and also the width across the back neck and mark both on the paper. The shaping of the raglan slope must now be fitted in between armhole and neck edge. It is unlikely that you will have exactly the number of stitches to allow you to decrease one stitch at either end of every other row and you will have to decide where and how the extra stitches are to be reduced. As with a set-in sleeve a few stitches may be bound off at the very beginning of the shaping, but if it is necessary to have a place where the decreasing is more rapid it should be as close to the top as possible.

The front raglan shaping should match the back. From the beginning of the armhole shaping, the sleeve must have the same number of rows as the back and front and it is therefore easiest to chart all three across the width of a large sheet of graph paper. Thus, the start and finish of the raglan shaping can be kept in line from the first calculation (see figure **4**).

Sometimes, because of the gauge being used and size required, fewer stitches may have to be reduced on the sleeve and you will therefore have to space the decreasing. This is perfectly alright so long as the number of rows are constant on all three pieces. The opposite can also occur and the neatest way of disposing of the extra stitches is to work a shoulder dart by decreasing in the center of the sleeve after you are above shoulder level. These decreases, spaced evenly from shoulder edge to neck edge, can be used decoratively to add interest to the design.

Alterations for a circular yoke
A circular yoked sweater can have the yoke beginning as low as the armhole or the back, front, and sleeves may be worked separately for an inch or two before all the stitches are worked together. Whichever is the case, the yoke from then on takes the place of the sleeve cap and of the top of both back and front. First plan how deep the yoke is to be and how many rows it must cover. It must be shaped to reduce the neck edge to the number of stitches required for a good fit. This reduction should be planned in gradual stages decreasing more rapidly toward the neckline.

For a neatly fitting circular yoke, it is advisable to curve the upper edges on both front and back so that at the armhole edge there is an extra length to the point of the yoke to accommodate the shoulder. The extra length to be added can be calculated by deciding on the yoke depth at center back and subtracting this amount from the measurement of the sleeve at the same point from the armhole to the neck edge. The basic rule given in Knitting Design Chapter 3 for neck to sleeve edge length still applies, and the sleeve and yoke together must give the total length required (see figure **5**).

Alterations for a saddle-capped sleeve
This is another alteration which affects all parts of the garment although it is not difficult to achieve.

The ordinary set-in sleeve chart can be used, but instead of binding off at the top of the cap a panel is added and worked to the same length as the front and back edges onto which it will be seamed. The width of this panel can be anything you decide upon, from 1½ inches upward. Divide this width in half and subtract the amount from both front and back shoulder measurements, giving a shallower armhole.

This is the basic principle for saddle shoulders but there are many variations. One of the most popular is to bind off the shoulders at the new level in a straight line. To compensate for this the continuation of the sleeve needs to be increased toward the neck edge, either at each side or in the center.

Whatever kind of alteration you want to make to the basic top plan it in this way. Before you start to knit check the alterations you have made to see that all the measurements are still correct.

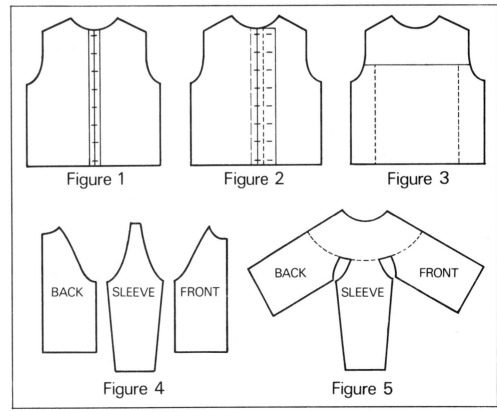

Figure 1   Figure 2   Figure 3

BACK   SLEEVE   FRONT

Figure 4

BACK   SLEEVE   FRONT

Figure 5

Knitting pattern/baby set

Here is a pretty two-piece baby set. The top buttons at the shoulders for quick and easy dressing and undressing, and the elastic-waisted pants are cleverly shaped for freedom of movement.

Size

Top. Directions are for 18in chest.
The figures in brackets [ ] refer to the 20 and 22in sizes respectively.
Length at center back, 10¾ [11:11¼]in.
Sleeve seam, 1½in.
Pants. All around widest part, 22[24:26]in.

Gauge
12½ sts to 2in in width and 22 rows to 2⅛in in depth over patt worked on No.5 needles.

Materials

Reynolds Versailles 3[4:4] balls
One pair No.3 needles
One pair No.5 needles
6 small buttons
3yds shirring elastic

Top back

Using No.5 needles, cast on 80 [86:92] sts.
K 5[5:7] rows garter st.
Commence patt.
1st row (RS) K.
2nd row P.
3rd row K2, ytf, K2 tog, *K1, ytf, K2 tog, rep from * to last st, K1.
4th row As 3rd.
5th row K.
6th row P.
7th row As 3rd.
8th row As 3rd.
9th row K.
10th row P.
11th-15th rows K.
16th row P.
17th row K.
18th row P.
19th row K10[13:16] sts, (K2 tog, K27) twice, K2 tog, K10[13:16] sts. 77[83:89] sts.
20th-22nd rows K.
Rep 1st to 18th rows once more.
41st row K3[6:9] sts, (K2 tog, K12) 5 times, K2 tog, K2[5:8]
1568

sts. 71[77:83] sts.
42nd-44th rows. K.
Rep 1st to 18th rows once more.
63rd row K2[5:8] sts, (K2 tog, K6) 8 times, K2 tog, K3[6:9]. 62[68:74] sts.
K 5[7:9] rows.

Bodice
1st bodice row K.
2nd bodice row P.
3rd bodice row As 3rd patt row.
4th bodice row As 3rd patt row.
Rep 1st and 2nd bodice rows once more.

Shape armholes
1st row Bind off 3 sts, K2, ytf, K2 tog, (K1, ytf, K2 tog) 17[19:21] times, K4.
2nd row Bind off 3 sts, K2, ytf, K2 tog, (K1, ytf, K2 tog) 17[19:21] times, K1. 56[62:68] sts.
Keeping bodice patt correct, dec one st at each end of next and every other row until 52[56:60] sts rem.**
Continue without shaping until 9 complete patts have been worked from beg of bodice.

Shape shoulders
Bind off 8[9:9] sts at beg of next 2 rows and 8[8:9] sts at beg of next 2 rows. 20[22:24] sts.
Bind off.

Front

Work as given for Back to **. 52[56:60] sts.
Continue until 6 complete patts have been worked from beg of bodice. Work first row of next patt.

Shape neck
Next row P21[22:23] sts. Turn.
Complete right shoulder on these 21[22:23] sts.
Dec one st at neck edge on next 5 rows. 16[17:18] sts.
Continue without shaping until Front measures same as Back to shoulder, ending at armhole edge.

Shape shoulder
Bind off 8[9:9] sts at beg of next

row, patt to end.
Work 1 row.
Bind off rem sts.
With WS of work facing, sl next 10[12:14] sts onto holder and leave for center neck.
Attach yarn to rem 21[22:23] sts, P to end.
Work as given for right shoulder, reversing shaping.

Sleeves

Using No.3 needles, cast on 40[42:44] sts.
K 7 rows garter st.
Change to No.5 needles.
Next row K2, *ytf, K2, rep from * to end.
Next row P2, *P1 tbl, P2, rep from * to end. 59[62:65] sts.
Rep 3rd patt row as given for Back twice, then 1st to 4th bodice patt rows and then 1st and 2nd bodice patt rows.

Shape cap
Rep 1st and 2nd rows as given for armhole shaping but read 16[17:18] times instead of 17[19:21] times. 53[56:59] sts.
Dec one st at each end of next and every other row until 49 [50:51] sts rem.
Bind off 6 sts at beg of next 6 rows. 13[14:15] sts. Bind off.

Neck borders

Using No.5 needles and with RS of Front facing, pick up and K12 sts down left side of neck, K10[12:14] sts from center front neck holder, pick up and K12 sts up right side of neck.
K 2 rows.
Change to No.3 needles.
K 2 rows. Bind off.
Using No.5 needles and with RS of Back facing, pick up and K20[22:24] sts along neck edge.
Work as for Front neck border.

Shoulder borders

Press each piece on WS under a dry cloth and using a warm iron. Join shoulder seams leaving 8 sts open at neck edges. Press seams lightly.
Using No.3 needles and with RS facing, beg at back edge of left shoulder and pick up

and K11 sts, pick up and K1 st at shoulder seam and pick up and K11 sts along front shoulder.
1st row (K1, K2 tog, ytf) 3 times, K14.
2nd row K. Bind off.
Work right shoulder to correspond, reversing first row.

Finishing

Sew sleeves into armholes easing in fullness around top. Press seams.
Join side and sleeve seams. Press seams. Sew on buttons to shoulders.

Pants back

Using No.3 needles, cast on 65[71:77] sts.
1st row P1, *K1, P1, rep from * to end.
2nd row K1, *P1, K1, rep from * to end.
Rep these 2 rows 4 times more.
Change to No.5 needles.
K 1 row. P 1 row.

Shape back
Next row K36[39:42]. Turn.
Next 2 rows Sl 1, P6. Turn. Sl 1, K12. Turn.
Next 2 rows Sl 1, P18. Turn. Sl 1, K24. Turn.
Next 2 rows Sl 1, P30. Turn. Sl 1, K36. Turn.
Next 2 rows Sl 1, P42. Turn. Sl 1, K48. Turn.
Next 2 rows Sl 1, P54. Turn. Sl 1, K to end.
Next row P.
K 4 rows.

Side shaping
**K 1 row. P 1 row.
K 1 row inc one st at each end of row. P 1 row. K 4 rows.
Rep last 8 rows 6 times more.
**79[85:91] sts.
K 1 row. P 1 row.

Shape leg edges
Continue in st st, binding off 4 sts at beg of next 4 rows.
Bind off 3 sts at beg of next 16[18:20] rows.
Work 2 rows st st. Bind off.

Front

Using No.3 needles, cast on 65[71:77] sts.

Work 10 rows rib as given for pants Back.

Change to No.5 needles. Beg with a K row, work 4 rows st st.

Work 4 rows garter st.

Rep from ** to ** as given for pants Back. 79[85:91] sts.

K 1 row. P 1 row.

Shape leg edges
Bind off 9 sts at beg of next 6 rows.

Bind off 3 sts at beg of next 2[4:6] rows.

Bind off 2 sts at beg of next 2 rows.

Work 12 rows st st. Bind off.

Leg borders

Press as given for Top. Sew together two bound-off edges. Press seam.

Using No.3 needles and with RS of work facing, pick up and K76[82:88] sts along leg edge.

Next row K1, *K2 tog, K4, rep from * to last 3 sts, K2 tog, K1. 63[68:73] sts.

K 6 rows garter st. Bind off.

Work other leg border in same manner.

Finishing

Join side seams. Press seams lightly. Thread 4 rows of elastic through WS of waist ribbing and secure.

Angelic top and matching pants ▶
Close-up of stitch detail ▼

Stitchery design/church embroidery

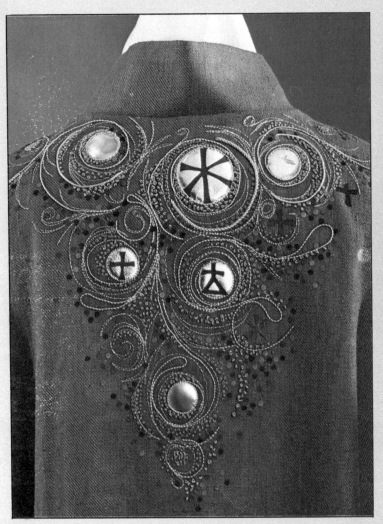

In the thirteenth and fourteenth centuries England was famed throughout Europe for the quality and design of her ecclesiastical embroidery. The name it was known by, "Opus Anglicanum", is still synonymous with the highest craftsmanship. There is a strong resurgence of interest in the embroidering of vestments and furnishings for old and new churches and, as Opus Anglicanum was typical of the thirteenth and fourteenth centuries, so is modern ecclesiastical embroidery typical of the twentieth century. Some examples of the best modern work are illustrated, each showing sensitivity to materials and good workmanship.

In the green chasuble of moiré home furnishing fabric, the design is basically a pattern of circles in gold kid, combined with machine embroidery, emphasized with couched metal cord and twist threads; French knots in thick silk thread and leather spots add depth to the embroidery. The beautiful white altar frontal is part of a set at St. Margarets, Prestwich, in Lancashire, England, and as it is used at Christmas and Easter, Alpha and Omega symbols (the beginning and the end) are

incorporated in the design together with the cross. The most imaginative ecclesiastical embroidery is largely based on applied shapes, some of which are padded; in the white altar frontal a half ping-pong ball has been covered with gold thread, mirror buttons and beads to catch the light in the center of the design. The purple burse and veil from Hey Church, Hey, Cheshire, England, show how the simplest cross motif can be repeated to form an extremely effective overall design; basically patchwork, the crosses have been elaborated with appliquéd ribbons and metal threads of varying thicknesses.

The colorful red stole shows how a geometric design based on symbols of the Trinity can be made interesting and varied by a sensitive use of appliqué, gold thread and multi-colored French knots.

Finally, the miter in blue home furnishing silk illustrates how a modern tracery of lines can retain the richness of traditional work by using a variety of gold threads and kid combined with beads.

The embroideries shown here demonstrate a high standard of proficiency in both design and execution attained by training and experience.

Inspiration for design

There are several possible sources of inspiration in ecclesiastical embroidery; if the church is named after a saint, find out his or her particular symbol. For instance, the lion for St. Mark, the eagle for St. John and so on. Stone or wood carvings or tile decoration can form the basis of a design or the name of the parish or district might also suggest an idea. When designing for a particular item, whether an altar frontal, pulpit fall, kneeler or chasuble, remember that the design must relate to the shape of that one piece alone.

Planning color schemes

Consideration must be given to the size of the church and the lighting. Try the design drawn out on paper to full size and in color, in situ, to insure that it is effective. Vestments, altar frontals, and pulpit falls are usually seen from a distance, so basic shapes must be both bold and simple. In an older church, new embroideries should harmonize with existing colors in the building. Rather than a mixture it is often more effective to let one color predominate, such as red or blue.

A collection of kneelers in a wide range of colors can look chaotic rather than jewel-like.

Materials and techniques

The method of embroidery to be used is dictated by the skill of the available workers. Most people can cope with simple stitches on canvas, and although appliqué needs considerable care in initial preparation, afterward it is a quick and effective technique, using either hand sewing or machine stitching. Metal thread work requires some technical skill and expertise. Nowadays, a variety of materials may be used for church embroidery, from Thai silks to home furnishing fabrics, but generally damasks and brocades should be avoided as the addition of embroidery on these fabrics produces an over-decorative effect. For ordinary stitchery, bold colored embroidery threads, weaving or knitting yarns or cords are frequently used as they show up well from a distance. Even string can be used if it suits the embroidery, but on smaller articles, a burse for example, finer threads such as stranded floss or pure stranded silk, pearl cotton, etc, are more suitable.

Stitchery pattern/magazine rack

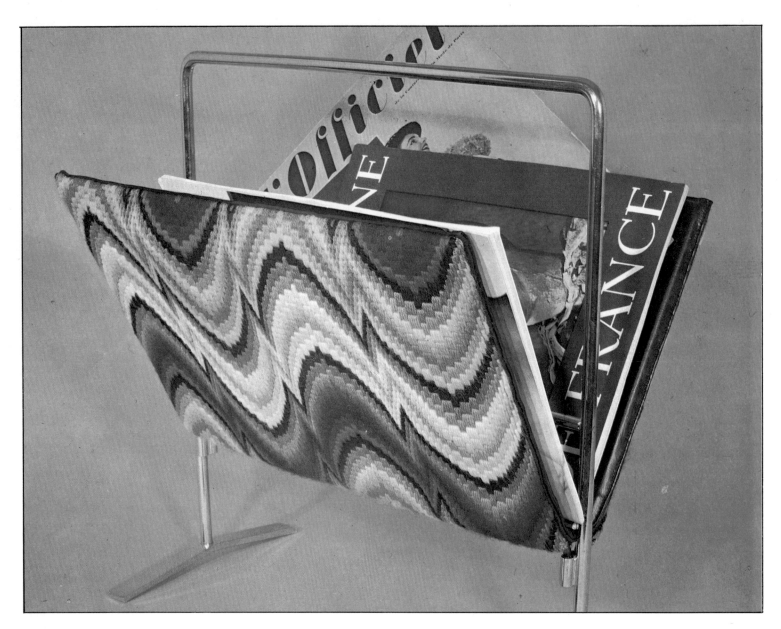

This gay, all-over Florentine design is worked in eleven different colors of tapestry yarn. The design can also be used on a wide variety of items such as chair covers, pillows, casual bags and waste paper baskets.

To make the magazine rack cover measuring 10 inches by 16 inches you will need:
- [ ] Two pieces of canvas measuring 14 inches by 20 inches with 16 single threads to 1 inch
- [ ] D.M.C. Tapestry yarn in the following colors and amounts:
  3 skeins: beige 7501; beige 7503; yellow 7476; red 7108. 4 skeins: yellow 7434; yellow 7473; red 7106; red 7107. 6 skeins: gray 7273; gray 7275 and black
- [ ] Two pieces of Pelomite fusible interlining measuring 10in by 16in
- [ ] Magazine stand of brass tube
- [ ] Tapestry needle No.18

1572

Instructions

Following the grain of the canvas, mark a rectangle measuring 10 inches by 16 inches, 2 inches in from all edges with basting stitches. This marks the area to be embroidered.

The embroidery, executed in tapestry yarn, consists entirely of Florentine stitches. Each line of the grid represents one thread of canvas, and each heavy line represents one stitch passing vertically over six threads on the canvas. The chart shows one motif to be repeated in width as well as height. The arrow marks the center of the work. In order to find the exact center for the undulating line, mark the center of the longer side on the lower edge of the rectangle. Count thirty threads to the left and commence the first row (in red 7108) by the three stitches of the lower group of the design. Follow the working chart, first toward the left side of the design, then come back

toward the first stitch to the right. Continue in horizontal rows from left to right, the second overlapping the first, changing shades as follows: red 7107; 7106, gray 7273; 7275, black, beige 7501; 7503; 7501, gray 7273; 7275, black, yellows 7434; 7473; 7476; 7473; 7434, gray 7273; 7275, black, red 7106; 7107 and 7108.

Repeat from the beginning. Fill in the empty spaces below the first row in the same way. Repeat for second rectangle.

Making the magazine rack

Strengthen the two embroidered parts with the interlining basted onto the wrong side and ironed with a warm iron. Trim the excess canvas to within 1 inch all around. Turn raw canvas to the back of the work and secure in place with herringbone stitch. Take the cover off the rack frame and either stitch or glue the two sides in place. Refit cover onto frame.

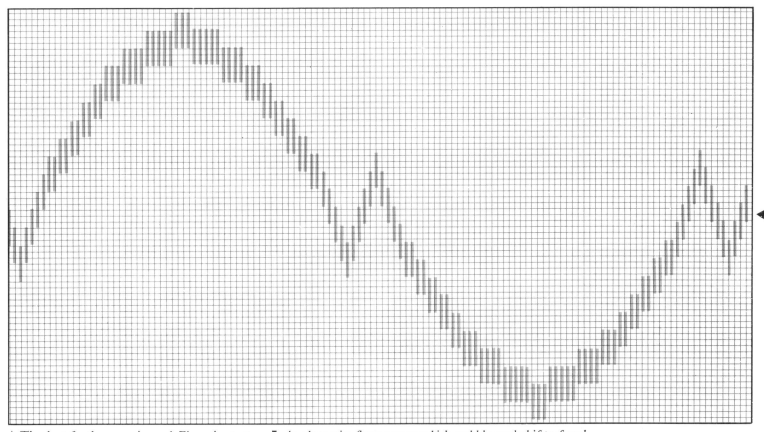

▲ *The chart for the magazine rack Florentine pattern* ▼ *An alternative flame pattern which could be worked if preferred*

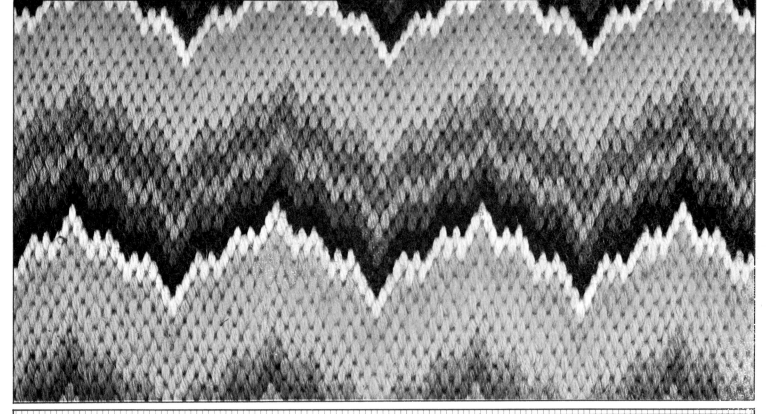

Costume design/Eleanor of Aquitaine

To achieve an authentic look when making period costume use textiles in colors which would have been easily available at the time, and choose accessories to match the outfit as closely as possible to the original. This woman's outfit is typical of the costumes worn in Europe at the beginning of the 12th century.

Fabrics and colors

Fabrics in 1100 A.D. would have been woven from wool and were mostly rather coarse in texture, although ladies sometimes wore woven linen for special occasions. Materials were dyed with vegetable dyes and although red, blue and green colors were possible, the tones were soft and dull compared with the bright chemical dye colors of today. Choose black, brown, dark brown-red, russet, yellow, cream and gray to be more in keeping with the 12th century.

The robe

The robe is full length and closely fitting with an exaggerated flare to the skirt. The sleeves fit tightly on the upper arm, widening from below the elbow, and can be knotted if they are too cumbersome to manage. The dress neckline is round with a slashed front opening.

Darts and zippers should not be used for shaping this garment, but if you feel that a more fitted effect is required, long back parts can be made or a zipper inserted in the back seam, out of sight. Alternatively, when the main pieces are being cut out, one or more "keyhole" shapes cut from the side seams, below the armhole, can be adjusted to fit by extending and tying the ends.

The mantle

This is semicircular in shape and floor length; it can be lined if preferred, although the original garment would not have been. Hold the mantle in place with thongs at the neck or fasten with a large chunky brooch.

The headdress

The headdress consists of a narrow band worn around the head, holding a fine, white circular veil in place. Pleat this around the face and fasten with pins.

Hair, accessories and decoration

Hair was worn long in the 12th century, loose if a lady was very young, braided if she was older. For this costume, hair should be parted in the middle and braided; add false braids to give extra length, sheathed in ribbons, or woven cord. **Shoes** should be flat-heeled with pointed toes and stockings knitted in natural colored wool. If decoration is added to the costume, it should be in the form of woven braid in geometric designs, edging the robe sleeves and mantle.

The headband can be a highly decorative part of the costume. Use braid with a geometric pattern and pick out the design with beads and metal threads to represent jewels. A belt made of braided leather or silk threads, worn around the hips, with long ends hanging down the front, completes the outfit.

Making the 12th century costume

You will need:
☐ **The veil** 1¼yds white voile
☐ **The robe** 2yds 55 to 60 inch wide stretch fabric (cotton knit, wool, nylon jersey)
☐ **The mantle** 3½yds 55 to 60 inch wide non-stretch fabric of heavier weight than the robe
☐ Leather thongs for mantle fastening and belt
☐ Woven braid edging for sleeves and cloak hem and for the headdress

Make a paper pattern from the graph chart and separate the pieces of pattern.

Making the robe
Fold the robe fabric in half lengthwise and place the pieces of robe pattern along the fold. Cut out each piece twice. Cut out the "keyhole" shapes if required and slash the neckline. Stitch the shoulder seams. Stitch the extra flare section into the skirt. Dart the back if desired for fit. Stitch side seams and sleeve seams. Finish neck edge, sleeve edges and hem. Add the braid decoration.

Making the mantle
Lay the fabric out single thickness and pin the mantle pattern to the straight of the material Cut out and hem all around or bind the edges with bias binding. Add braid decoration.

The veil
Cut a complete circle of fabric as large as the material will allow. Cut a hole in the center 7 inches in diameter. Hem the outer and inner edges as finely as possible. The smaller hole fits on the crown of the head, the veil being taken back over the brow and secured with the headband. The main features of this costume are the full-length fitted robe with long sleeves, the floor length mantle and the soft headdress. An under-robe or chemise with long, tight sleeves should be worn under the robe for complete authenticity.

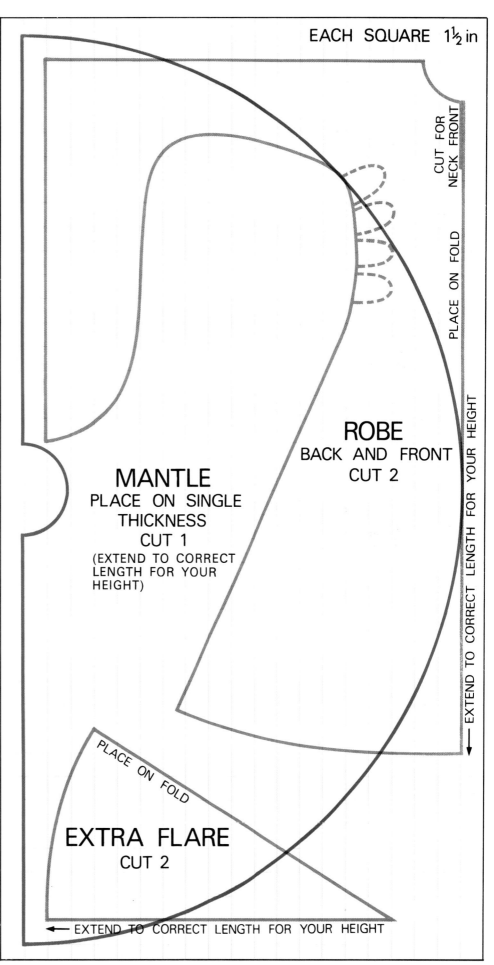

EACH SQUARE 1½ in

CUT FOR NECK FRONT

PLACE ON FOLD

ROBE
BACK AND FRONT
CUT 2

EXTEND TO CORRECT LENGTH FOR YOUR HEIGHT

MANTLE
PLACE ON SINGLE THICKNESS
CUT 1
(EXTEND TO CORRECT LENGTH FOR YOUR HEIGHT)

PLACE ON FOLD

EXTRA FLARE
CUT 2

← EXTEND TO CORRECT LENGTH FOR YOUR HEIGHT

Design in dressmaking/necklines

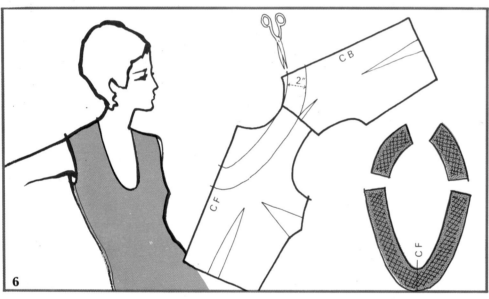

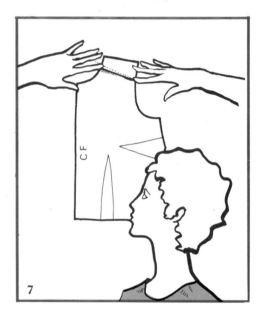

The neckline is one of the most important parts of a dress because it draws attention to the face. A wise choice of neckline can flatter a face and neck in the same way that a good hairstyle does, and at the same time draws the eye away from parts of the body that are best unnoticed.

1. This drawing shows an example of the above—however elegant a perfectly fitted plain dress with a simple high round neck may look, unless there is some focal point well away from the too large hips the eye will be constantly drawn there.

2. There are several absolutely basic points to remember. The first is that the head must be able to get through the neck opening. This would appear at first to be an obvious statement since most dresses today have a center back opening up to the neck edge. But many dresses could perfectly well be designed with an opening elsewhere, such as in the side seam, which many people find easier to manipulate.

3. The neckline must then be big enough

for the head to pass through without a struggle—or it must open elsewhere, either down the center front with a short zipper or buttons, or split at the center back, or the shoulder seams can be made to fasten with zippers or buttons, or hooks and eyes. It is a simple matter to alter the basic shape of a neckline, but be careful; you will probably have realized early in your dressmaking how easy it is to cut away too much fabric, and whereas $\frac{1}{2}$ inch on the double may be just right, $\frac{3}{4}$ inch could spoil the overall proportions of a dress completely.

As a rule, really low necks are only suitable for evening, beach or jumper dresses.

4. A plain, high, round neckline is ideal for a perfect young neck, but it can show up an ageing or imperfect one cruelly. Any detail will soften the look and take away from the uncompromising harshness —stitching, trimming, bows, tabs—all without altering the basic pattern shape

in any way.

5. Try soft folds—swing the bust darts into the neckline and leave as unpressed pleats or gathers. To do this, slash the pattern in several places from the neckline toward the bust and spread it.

6. But when you do want to alter the basic shape simply cut a pattern to the shape you want, shaping the back of the neckline too, if you like. Cut 2 inch wide facings for the new neckline shape and interface for added strength or crispness if you think the design, or the fabric, needs it.

Some neckline problems

If you have trouble in getting your necklines to set well, here's how to deal with them:

7. If necklines never lie closely around the front of your neck, try taking a tiny pleat in the pattern before cutting out a dress, starting at the neck edge and tapering to nothing at the armhole.

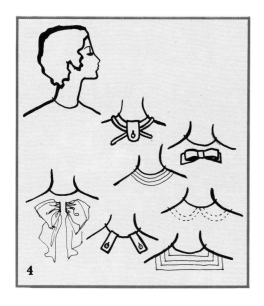

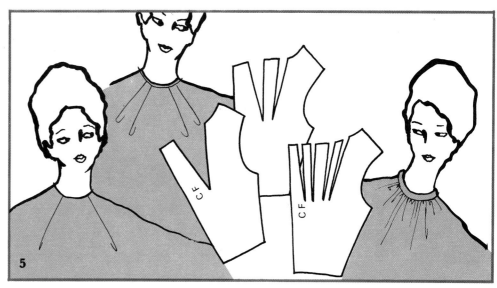

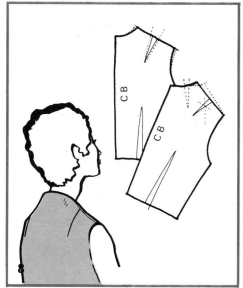

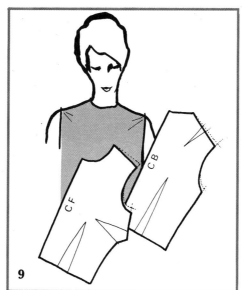

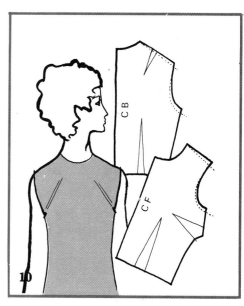

8. If the necklines stand away at the back, increasing the size of the shoulder darts (and lengthening the back shoulder seam a corresponding amount) might help; or you could try swinging the shoulder darts into the neckline (a more easily adjustable position for fitting) and ask a friend to fit you.

9 and 10. If your shoulders are more square than average, take this into account when cutting out (**9**); likewise if they are more sloping (**10**).

11. If your necklines always drag to one side, this means that one shoulder is higher than the other, so cut one shoulder of your dress a fraction higher than the other and extend the neckline slightly at that side.

12. If your design includes the addition of buttonholes, or a tab that buttons down onto the dress, reinforce it where you need the extra strength by increasing the depth of the facing, again interfacing it if necessary.

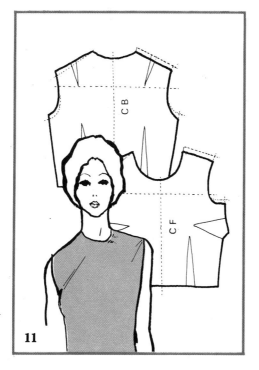

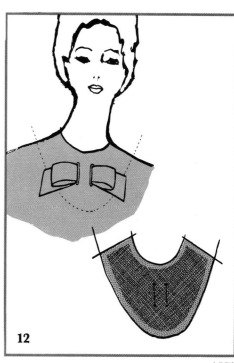

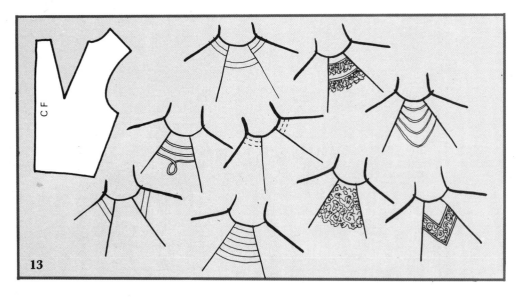

13

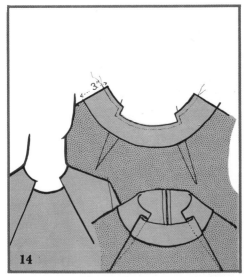

14

finished depth × 4
+ turnings

← neck measurement + 2in + turnings →

17   18

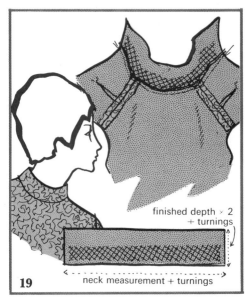

finished depth × 2
+ turnings

← neck measurement + turnings →

19

Variations with neck darts

13. By swinging the darts around into the neckline many variations are possible. The center front section, or the sides, can be trimmed or decorated in a variety of ways while the work is still flat. Then the dress is completed in the usual way.

14. To make this step effect cut away the top 1 inch of the center section. Face with a 3 inch facing before folding the dart into position, stitching it, and catching it down by hand.

Decorative facings

15. Another decorative idea is to have the facing on the outside instead of the inside in same or contrasting fabric.

16. If the finished band is to be 2 inches wide, first stitch the shoulder seams to 2 inches from the neck edge (**a**). Tie the threads securely, clip the turning, press and turn through. Finish stitching the seam on the right side of the work (**b**). Cut the facing to required width plus

1578

seam allowance all around, preferably in one piece. Cut a fusible interfacing without seam allowance, and iron to the facing. Turn in the seam allowance along lower edge and press (**c**). Attach the neck edge of the facing to the wrong side of the dress. Clip the neck edge (**d**). Turn the facing to the right side, and baste in place. Press. Topstitch the outer edge then invisibly slip stitch the fold to the dress by hand.

The same detail can be used for a variety of differently shaped necklines, and a combined neck and armhole facing could also look very attractive. The edge of the facing could be bound or, if you prefer, invisibly stitched.

High necklines

17. Turtlenecks are warm and elegant and easy to make. Measure the neckline of your dress and cut a bias strip that length, plus a couple of inches by four times the finished depth, plus turnings all around. When the collar is basted in place

and tried on you may find that the extra length should be trimmed off.

Fold the collar lengthwise and stitch the sides before attaching to the dress.

18. The collar at the back can fall away or be fastened with hooks and eyes, or the zipper can run on up to the point where the collar folds over.

19. A crew neck is cut and fitted in the same way, but here the bias strip is only twice the finished depth, plus turnings; probably you will need to stretch the bias strip slightly when attaching it to get a good close fit. To give a firmer finish, a fusible interfacing can be ironed to half of the collar before it is basted in position.

20. If you want the collar to stand away from the neck, cut away the side of the neckline a fraction and then on around the front. Try a little at a time—you cannot put fabric back once it's been cut away.

21. This neckline, apart from being warm, softly flattering and yet casual, looks far better at the back than most turtlenecks.

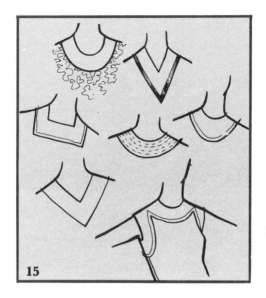

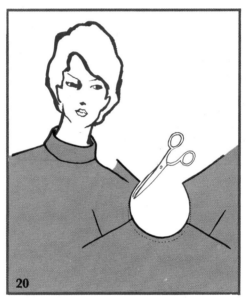

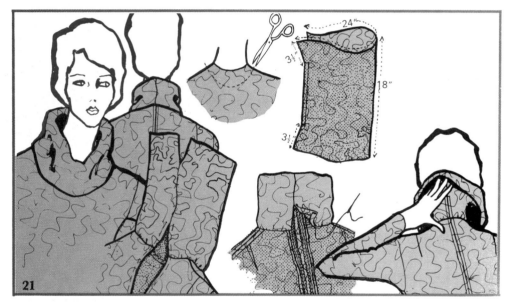

First widen the neck at the sides so that the finished shoulder will measure 4 inches; lower the front to suit yourself. Cut a piece of fabric on the bias about 24 inches by 18 inches; stitch the two shorter sides together, but leaving 3½ inches unstitched at both ends. Baste the collar in place, gathering it very slightly all around the front edge. Notice how the center back zipper runs on up to 3 inches above the back neckline—to be covered when the collar falls over into place.

Try the dress on to see that you have achieved the desired effect; also check that you can get it on and off without a struggle.

Flattering necklines

22. A well chosen neckline can do much to disguise a neck that is too long; crew necks or turtlenecks are good (**a**), rouleau loops or a fat bias binding padded with a strip of foam would be flattering (**b**), so would a tie (**c**) or a funnel neck (**d**).

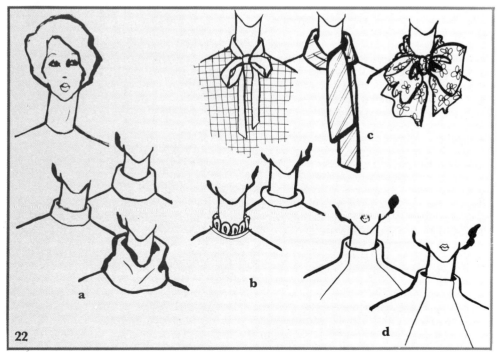

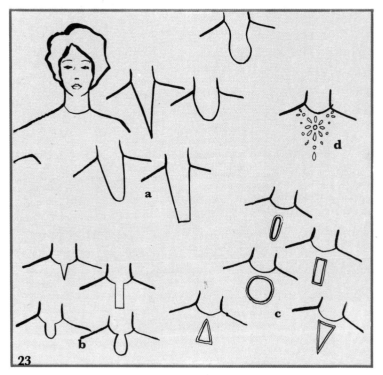

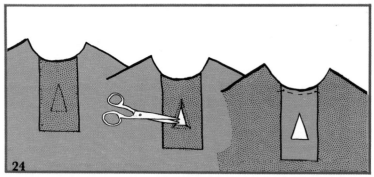

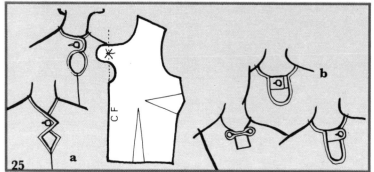

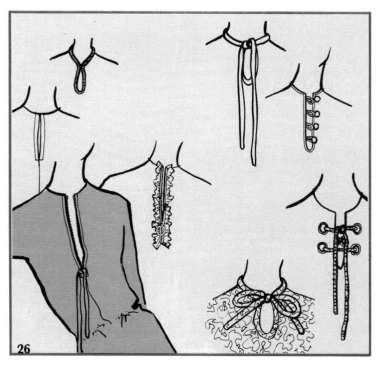

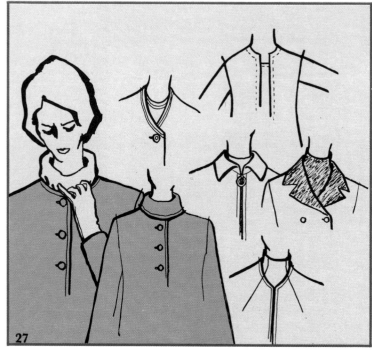

23. Obviously a neck that is too short needs to be given the illusion of increased length. This can be achieved with a deep neckline, but be careful to avoid the illusion of extra width at the shoulders (**a**). Notches are also flattering to a short neck (**b**), so are keyholes of any shape (**c**) as they extend the color of the face and neck in a vertical line.

Cutout machine embroidery will give the same sort of illusion (**d**).

24. Cut the keyhole facing long enough to reach the neckline edge, stitch around the keyhole shape, cut away the center 1580

and clip the turnings. Turn through, press very carefully and then baste the facing to the neckline edge. All this should be done while the work is still flat. Then proceed as usual, binding or facing both edges together as one.

25. A keyhole opening with a buttoned fastening can be cut in one with a center front seam (**a**), or a separate tab or rouleau buttonhole can be stitched across a notch or split seam when the facings are being attached to give a keyhole look (**b**).

26. All splits give an illusion of length; either leave the top three or four inches

of a center front seam unstitched or simply slit down from the neckline. Face or bind the edges and incorporate a fastening of some kind—a hook and eye, buttons and rouleau loops, a tie or lacing.

27. Finally, a point to remember with any neckline—if the dress is to be worn under a coat or jacket, both necklines must be designed to look good and to feel comfortable together. For instance, it would be no good having a dress with a stand-away or bulky neckline if the coat to go over it has a closely fitted one.

Crafts/enameling

The art of enameling has been practiced for at least two thousand years and may have originated in Western Europe: early Greek writers describe the colorful designs of the enamel-decorated weapons and armor used by northern barbarians. In early examples of Greek and Celtic enamel work only opaque enamels were used, and it was not until the 12th century that glowing, translucent colors appeared in the work of the Gothic enamelers. The craft gradually developed, and fine examples were produced by the jewelers of Elizabethan England and in France in the 18th century. By the early 20th century, the enamelers of the Russian firm of Carl Fabergé were producing work of incredible precision and technique. In recent years, the art of enameling has enjoyed a revival, and artists are again using techniques which have not changed, basically, for many hundreds of years.

The word "enamel" is sometimes used to describe a substance such as paint or varnish applied to glaze a surface. Enameling, in the context used here, is a technique whereby a kind of glass ground to a powder, and colored by the addition of metal oxides, is fused by heat to a metal surface. Copper, silver and gold are the metals most commonly used with glass powder enamel, and of these copper has the advantage of being inexpensive, of standing up to fairly rough treatment, and of having a high melting point. Silver gives a greater degree of reflection and is most suitable for the transparent green and blue enamels. Gold is the supreme metal for enameling, and is particularly suitable as a background for transparent red colors, although its price puts it beyond reach of most amateur enamelers.

The techniques of enameling

The five basic enameling techniques in use are still known by their French names, and date from the 11th or 12th centuries. These are Limoges, cloisonné, champlevé, basse-taille, and plique à jour.

Cloisonné is thought to be the oldest technique. The name comes from the word "cloison" (meaning "enclosure"), and in this work narrow wires are soldered onto a base plate in a pattern, with the spaces in between filled with the enamel, which is usually opaque.

In champlevé enameling (the word means "raised field") hollows are carved out of the metal and are then filled with enamel. This is somewhat similar to basse-taille (meaning "low-cut"), a more advanced form of champlevé in which the recesses are also decorated with low relief carving which shows through the transparent enamels used in this process.

Transparent enamels are also used in plique à jour ("light of day") which produces an effect similar to that of a stained glass window.

These processes all involve filling recesses with enamel, but the Limoges technique, named after the town in France where it originated, does not rely on metal carving or cloisons, and is therefore the most suitable for the beginner.

Equipment and materials

It is usually supposed that enameling is a process involving high temperature firing and quantities of expensive equipment, and is therefore unsuitable for the amateur. This is not entirely true. It is possible to produce enameled pieces suitable for jewelry using a small kiln, or even a Bunsen burner or a gas torch. In some circumstances it is even possible to fire pieces on a gas or electric stove.

Enamel powders and copper shapes are obtained from craft shops. The only other equipment necessary for the craft are shaker boxes or sieves made from wire mesh (80 or 60 mesh) used for sprinkling the enamel powders. A mesh bottomed tea or coffee strainer makes a good shaker, and this gives a good idea of the coarseness of the material needed if you decide to make your own. Matchbox trays with the base removed and replaced with a small piece of cotton organdy make effective shakers. Some enamels come in glass jars with a sieve lid, which saves using a shaker.

A spatula or palette knife is useful for placing pieces in and removing pieces from the kiln or flame, but an old kitchen knife will do just as well, if it is flexible.

◄ *The pendant worn with a matching bracelet*

Making a simple pendant

This piece is made by the Limoges method, in which the entire surface area of the metal is covered with enamel. The enamels can be applied by dusting, painting or stenciling, and chunks of enamel or glass beads can be introduced to vary the surface structure. The method for a simple dusting and painting technique is given here.

You will need

A small enameling kiln (or an improvised firing arrangement, such as a Bunsen burner under a piece of wire mesh on a tripod stand).
Copper shapes, either preformed or cut from 18 gauge copper (No.2).
Enamel in powder form (two colors).
Two shaker boxes.
Spatula or palette knife.
Sheets of paper.
Light machine oil (sewing machine oil) or glycerine.
Brushes (No.1 or 2) and steel pen nibs in holders.
Fine steel wool.
Vinegar.
Leather thong.

Stage 1. Prepare the copper shape by filing and smoothing the edges and cleaning the entire surface of the shape with fine steel wool, so that the enamel will fuse with the metal.
Immerse the copper in vinegar and leave for a minute or two, then wash in water and dry. This will remove any grease or dirt. After cleaning, the copper should be handled only by the edges. The point to remember is that the copper has to be clean and grease-free to allow the enamel to fuse properly.

Stage 2. Lay the prepared copper shape on a clean piece of paper, with a coin to prop it up at one corner so that the spatula can be inserted easily underneath. Using the shaker box, dust the enamel powder over the whole surface of the metal until an even coating of enamel powder covers the copper shape.

Stage 3. Lift the sprinkled piece with the spatula or knife, and place it in the kiln. The excess enamel powder which has fallen on the sheet of paper can be replaced in the shaker.

Stage 4. It is now time to turn on the heat. Follow the manufacturer's instructions for heating the kiln. If a Bunsen burner is being used, turn it on fully to get as much heat as possible, and place the flame directly under the piece to be fired. During firing, which takes two or three minutes, the enamel will at first

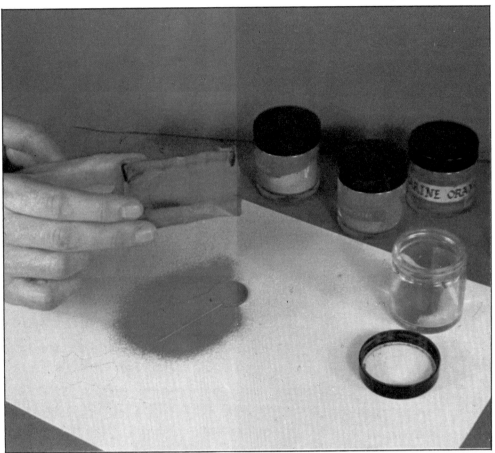

▲ *Stage 2 of the process, where the first color is sifted over the copper shape*
▼ *Once an even coating of powder has been applied, lift the piece with a spatula*

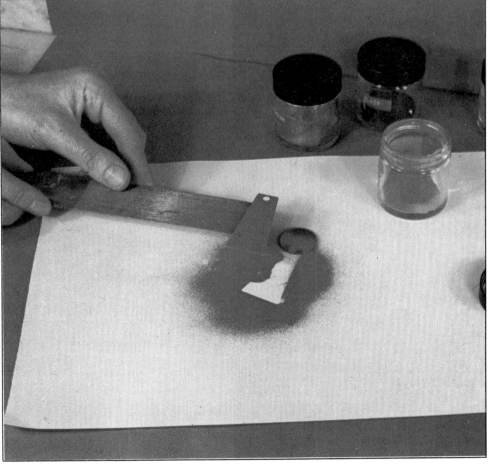

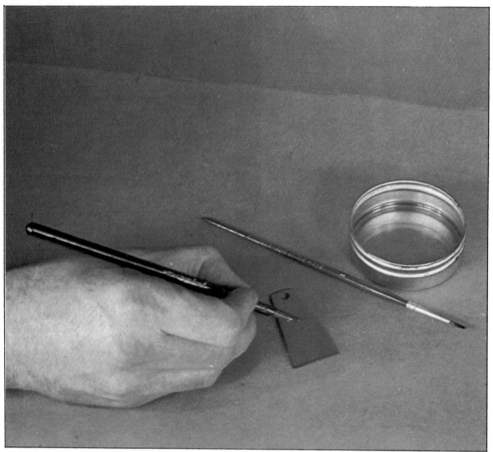

▲ *After the first firing, paint the design on the surface using a brush and oil*
▼ *Stage 5, with the second color powder adhering to the oil-painted design ready for second firing*

appear to discolor, and will then glisten as it begins to melt and fuse with the copper. If a closed kiln is used, and there is no observation hole, it is possible to open the door slightly and check the visual appearance of the work. But this must be done carefully in order not to lose too much heat.

When an even, glassy appearance can be seen, the heat is turned off and the piece allowed to cool.

Stage 5. Having achieved a nice, evenly colored surface on the shape, you can now add a second dusting of color to create a decorative pattern. During the second dusting it is important to make sure that no fire scale from the back of the copper shape becomes mixed with the enamel, as this would spoil it for future use. To avoid this possibility, clean the back of the piece after the first firing with steel wool, or else apply a saline solution to the back beforehand which will facilitate the removal of fire scale. One tablespoonful of salt to a cup of water makes a suitable solution. Apply it with a brush. Follow this procedure between each firing.

Either glycerine or a light oil are used as adhesives for the second and subsequent colors. Having preplanned a design draw it on the clean enamel surface in oil or glycerine using either a pen or fine brush.

A second dusting of enamel powder in a contrasting color is then applied from a shaker and will adhere to the oil drawing. Any excess powder is removed by tapping the piece on its end.

When the second dusting has been completed, return the piece to the kiln for refiring.

The second color will melt and fuse with the first layer which will also remelt, and the process is complete when an even, glassy finish is obtained.

Stage 6. Allow the piece to cool, then clean the edges and back with steel wool and metal polish. When cleaning the edges always rub away from the enamel surface to avoid chipping the actual edge. Complete the pendant by adding a leather thong and perhaps giving the back a coat of metal lacquer.

This pendant uses only two colors, but others can be added by the same method, cleaning off between firings.

Experiment with different finishes and effects by dusting the second color through a paper stencil or by sifting the powder all over the first firing and then scratching a design with the end of a matchstick. Once the technique has been mastered and you are happy with the results, you can progress to larger and more involved pieces of work.

▲ *The buckle is the result of two firings, one black, the second yellow and green* ▼ *The oblong pendant in this picture is an example of the cloisonné technique*

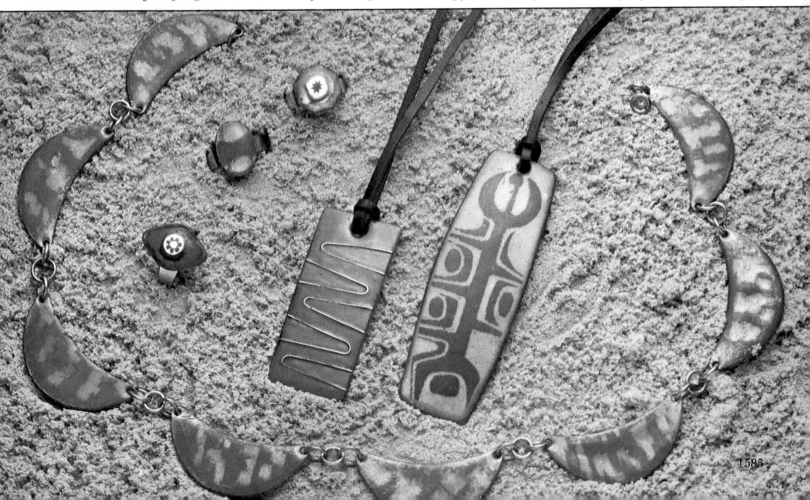

Knitting design/stitches and patterns

Good shaping is essential for a successful garment design, but other factors also play an important part. A perfect shape can be completely ruined if insufficient consideration is given to color, texture and stitch, or to the planning of small details.

A change of color can give a favorite knitted design quite a different look. The stockinette stitch top and skirt in earlier chapters were made in a multicolor yarn. In this chapter, they are made with the top in blue and the skirt in blue and green, using a simple two-color stitch. Yet another look would have resulted from a patterned top over a plain one-color skirt.

When more than one color is to be used in a design the overall effect must be considered in relation to stitch and pattern. Work a sample before buying the amount of yarn needed for the complete garment, to try out unusual combinations of colors.

Stitches in designing

The simple garments in previous chapters have all been worked in stockinette stitch, but with consideration given to stitch characteristics, other stitches can be used to produce more exciting effects.

An experienced knitter will already know the type of stitches she enjoys working and will quickly find ways of using them to their best advantage. Knitters with less experience can quickly learn if different patterns are tried in as many different yarns as possible for practice. A knitter will always design better using a stitch which she enjoys, but she must also choose the stitch because it is suitable for both wearer and type of garment.

Stitch characteristics

Different stitches cause the finished fabric to have different characteristics, and these should be used to their best advantage when designing.

Any stitch based on ribbing, for instance, will tend to be elastic, and the garment will cling to the figure. Therefore this stitch is not likely to be suitable for an entire garment, and should be used for those areas where fit is required, such as cuffs, waist and neckband. The remainder of the garment might be worked in a different, less elastic stitch, or one which is not elastic at all such as stockinette stitch or garter stitch. Extra interest could be added by using the waist ribbing up to a yoke line and then working in blocks of alternating rib like a basket stitch pattern. Or, instead of alternating the rib, the upright lines of the ribs could be knitted or embroidered together to give a "smocked" appearance.

Combined stitches

When one stitch is to be used throughout the entire garment there are fewer problems to consider than when two or more types of stitches are combined. It is unwise to try to combine too many stitches or types of stitches into one design unless the stitches come from the same family. For instance, if the background is stockinette stitch, and a lace panel is desired, the lace used must also be based on stockinette stitch. Similarly, for a garter stitch background, a lace based on garter stitch is needed. If the purl or reverse side of stockinette stitch is being used then the lace must be based on a pattern using the purl side of the lace as the right side. Trying to combine a stockinette stitch background with a large Aran design interspaced with garter stitch based lace will only lead to a confusion of stitches lying in too many different directions to complement each other.

An easy variation on the basic top, skirt and dress designs already given is the addition of lace patterned stripes on a stockinette stitch background, with the stripes either horizontal with stockinette stitch between them, or vertical as they are in the paneled V-necked sweater illustrated.

Combined gauges

The same degree of consideration is required if the stitches combined produce two different gauges. Take as an example a skirt worked in bands of stockinette stitch three inches wide, with a lace pattern four inches wide between the plain areas. It is most likely that when a sample of both stitches is worked and measured, the lace pattern will have fewer stitches to the inch than the stockinette stitch, although the number of rows may be the same. One cannot simply continue on one size of needle, hoping for the best. Alterations must be made, and this can be done in one of two ways.

Method 1. The size of needle on which the lace is worked can be altered to one size smaller, and then the sample measured to see if this change gives the same gauge as the stockinette stitch. If it does, a finer needle can be used each time the lace stitch is worked, remembering to return to the larger needle for stockinette stitch. A check must be made also to see what the effect is on the number of rows, and allowances made for this.

▼ Lace panels on a stockinette stitch pullover knitted in Sportsyarn

Method 2. The knitter can decrease on the last row of the stockinette stitch band or the first row of the lace so that the required number of stitches for the width of the lace is obtained. If this method is chosen, remember that an increase has to be made before returning to stockinette stitch, and that this adjustment must be made each time a change is made from one band to the next.

When working with a lace pattern one must also make sure that there is always the correct number of stitches into which the lace repeat will divide.

When working a design which uses more than one color, such as Fair Isle or Norwegian designs where the colors not in use are stranded or carried across the back of the work, similar changes of needle size can be necessary, particularly if the pattern is worked in bands. Theoretically, Fair Isle patterns are supposed to be worked at the same gauge as the surrounding stockinette stitch, but most knitters find that they need to work the patterned area on one size larger needle to counteract the tendancy to pull the work tighter when carrying the colors across the back. Again this alteration in needle size must be made each time a change is made from one band to the next.

Designing with intricate patterns

Large repeats or complicated patterns can produce problems when it comes to working shapings. On garments where the shaping, other than the side shapings of armholes, is slight, it is possible to overcome this by changing needle size to alter the gauge rather than trying to work out intricate methods of increasing or decreasing a complicated pattern. For example, an evening top can be shaped by changing to one size smaller needle just below the waistline, then changing to yet a smaller size needle after another two inches have been worked. Once past the waistline area the width is increased by using the needle a size larger, and again after two or three inches returning to the original size of needle.

This method is useful in shaping patterned sleeves and skirts.

Never be content with any proposed design unless you have considered all the above factors. Once you are certain that it is going to be perfect for its intended purpose, that the fastenings and trimmings in no way spoil it, that the stitch is entirely suitable, and that you have not tried to combine more ideas than are wise, you will be able to work the design with every chance of success.

Top and skirt in Sportsyarn ►

Knitting pattern/gaucho suit

Knit yourself this distinctive gaucho suit.

Sizes

Directions are for 32in bust. The figures in brackets [ ] refer to the 34 and 36in bust sizes respectively.
Gauchos. Inside leg, 16½[17:17½]in.
Sweater. Length, 23[23½:24]in. Sleeve seam, 17in.

Gauge
Gauchos. 5 sts and 7 rows to 1in over patt on No.8 needles.
Sweater. 5 sts and 6 rows to 1in over patt on No.10 needles after pressing.

Materials

Bernat Germantown
Gauchos. 8[9:10] balls main color A, red
Sweater. 6[7:8] balls main color A, red
6[7:7] balls contrast B, black
One pair No.5 needles
One pair No.6 needles
One pair No.8 needles
One pair No.10 needles
One cable needle
One stitch holder
One No.F crochet hook
8 ⅝in diameter rings
1yd 1in grosgrain ribbon
2 1in buckles
¾yd elastic

Gauchos right leg

Using No.8 needles and A, cast on 109[115:121] sts.
1st row K1, *sl 1, K1, rep from * to end.
2nd row P.
Rep these 2 rows until work measures 12in, ending with a WS row.
Inc one st at each end of next and every following 8th row until there are 115[121:127] sts.
Continue without shaping until work measures 16½[17:17½]in, ending with a WS row.

Shape crotch

Bind off 4[5:6] sts at beg of next row, then 8[9:10] sts at beg of next row.
Dec one st at each end of next and every other row until
1588

89[93:97] sts rem.
Continue without shaping until work measures 6[6½:7]in from beg of crotch shaping and ending with a WS row.
Change to No.6 needles. Continue without shaping for 3in.
Change to No.5 needles and continue without shaping until work measures 11[11¼:11½]in from beg of crotch shaping and ending with a WS row.
Next row K1, *P1, K1, rep from * to end.
Next row P1, *K1, P1, rep from * to end.
Rep last 2 rows for 1in. Bind off in rib.

Left leg

Work to correspond to Right leg, reversing shaping.

Leg bands

Using No.5 needles and A, cast on 9 sts and work in patt as on Legs for 15in or desired length, ending with a WS row.
Dec one st at each end of every row until 3 sts rem. Bind off.

Sweater back

Using No.10 needles and A, cast on 87[93:99] sts.
K 1 row.
Continue in patt as follows:
1st row (WS) Using B, P3, *sl 1, P2, rep from * to end.
2nd row Using B, K2, *sl next st onto cable needle at front of work, K2, sl st from cable needle onto right-hand needle without knitting it—called CR2R—, rep from * to last st, K1.
3rd row Using A, *P2, sl 1, rep from * to last 3 sts, P3.
4th row Using A, K1, *sl next 2 sts onto cable needle at back of work, sl next st onto right-hand needle without knitting it, K2 from cable needle—called CR2L—, rep from * to last 2 sts, K2.
Rep last 4 rows until work measures 16in, ending with a WS row.

Shape armholes

Bind off 5 sts at beg of next

2 rows.
K2 tog at each end of every other row 4[5:6] times.
69[73:77] sts.
Continue without shaping until armhole measures 7[7½:8]in, ending with a WS row.

Shape shoulders

Bind off 5 sts at beg of next 6 rows, then 5[6:7] sts at beg of next 2 rows. Bind off rem 29[31:33] sts.

Front

Work as given for Back to armholes, ending with a WS row.

Shape armholes and divide for neck

Bind off 5 sts at beg of next 2 rows.
Next row K2 tog, patt 36[39:42]. Turn and slip rem sts on holder.
Keeping neck edge straight, dec one st at armhole edge every other row 3[4:5] times.
Continue without shaping until armhole measures 4[4¼:4½]in, ending with a RS row.

Shape neck

Bind off 14[15:16] sts at beg of next row. Continue on rem 20[21:22] sts until armhole measures the same as on Back, ending with a WS row.

Shape shoulder

Bind off 5 sts at arm edge every other row 3 times.
Bind off rem 5[6:7] sts.
With RS facing, attach yarn to sts on holder, K2 tog, patt to last 2 sts, K2 tog.
Complete to correspond to the first side.

Sleeves

Using No.10 needles and A, cast on 45[48:51] sts.
K 1 row.
Continue in patt as on Back, inc one st at each end of 9th and every following 8th row until there are 63[66:69] sts.
Continue without shaping until sleeve seam measures 17in, ending with a WS row.

Shape cap

Bind off 5 sts at beg of next 2 rows.
K2 tog at each end of every other row 15[16:17] times.
Bind off 3 sts at beg of next 4 rows. Bind off.

Finishing

Pin all pieces out to size and press under a damp cloth using a warm iron.
Gauchos. Join back, front and leg seams. Face leg bands with ribbon. Sew buckles on straight ends of leg bands. Sew bands to legs, gathering legs to fit and allowing about 2in of band to thread through buckle. Sew elastic inside waistband with casing-stitch.
Sweater. Join shoulder seams. Sew in sleeves. Join side and sleeve seams.
Using No.F hook and A, with RS facing, work 1 row sc around lower edge. Turn.
Next row (WS) Ch3 to count as first dc, inserting hook into back loop of sc only work 1dc into each sc, ending with a ss into first sc. Fasten off.
Work same around sleeves.
Work around neck edge in the same way, starting at beg of slit and working up right side of slit, around neck and down left side of slit. Turn.
Next row Ch3 to count as first dc, work 1dc into back loop only of each st to top of slit, keeping last loop of each on hook work 1dc into each of next 3 sts, yoh and draw through all 4 loops on hook—called 3dc tog—, 1dc into each st to inside corner, 3dc into next st, continue in dc to inside corner at left side of neck, 3dc into next st, continue to next corner at top of slit, work 3dc tog, continue in dc to end.
Fold all edges to right side (the line between the sc and dc will make the turning line) and slip stitch in place.
Press all seams.
Buttons. Using No.F hook and A, work in sc around each of the 8 rings until covered. Fasten off A and fill in the center of the rings by overcasting with B. Sew on as shown.

Stitchery design/kneelers

Kneelers are popular projects for church embroidery, either worked individually or as a group activity. This chapter suggests some symbols for designs and gives two charts to work from, one based on the Vine and the other symbolizing the Dove of Peace.

Materials and stitches
As embroidered kneelers receive hard wear and must last for many years the stitches used must cover the canvas completely, be well padded on the back, and be well integrated with the canvas—tent stitch and rice stitch for example. For a beginner, the whole kneeler can be worked in a single stitch such as cross-stitch, but in simple bold designs, such as the cross and the IHS design, a variety of stitches can be worked to add textural interest, and for this kind of embroidery single thread canvas is best.

On coarse canvases (10-12 threads per inch) carpet thrums are quickly worked and are particularly hard wearing, but on finer canvases either tapestry yarn or crewel yarn would be more in scale. Carpet thrums have a limited color range, whereas the other yarns present a much wider choice.

Designs in church embroidery
Most design in church embroidery is based on symbolism, and the kneelers illustrated in this chapter represent the Holy Spirit (the dove) and the Redeemer (the vine).
Cross—The Crucifixion.
These designs could also be adapted for use on a pulpit fall, worked on the ends of a Bible marker or repeated to form a long communion rail kneeler or carpet. In some churches, kneelers are left on the floor or on a low shelf and the design is then only seen horizontally. In other churches, kneelers are hung on the back of the pew in front and are thus seen vertically. The kneeler designs in this chapter have been planned so that they can be seen both vertically and horizontally. Other symbols represent:
IHS and PX (the Chi Rho)—monograms of Christ.
Lilies—purity and innocence, associated with the Virgin Mary.
Dove with olive branch—peace.

Canvas quantities
On the charts, each square represents one stitch, and the scale of your canvas, i.e. how many threads per inch, will determine the finished size of the design itself. The following is an approximate guide:
10 threads per inch—finished size of design 9 inches by 12 inches.

14 threads per inch—finished size $6\frac{3}{4}$ inches by $8\frac{1}{2}$ inches.
18 threads per inch—finished size 5 inches by $6\frac{3}{4}$ inches.
As a guide to canvas quantities, the top of the kneeler on the next page measures 9 inches by 12 inches and a 1-$1\frac{1}{2}$ inch border forms the sides, plus a 2 inch turning allowance, making the final canvas size that will be required 16 inches by 19 inches.

Working the kneeler
Find the center of the canvas and of the chart and mark both. Begin at the center of the design and work outward to insure that the motif is correctly placed on the canvas.
Complete the top of the kneeler and leave two (on finer canvas, 3) threads unworked before starting the border; when the embroidery is finished, block and stretch the canvas.

Making the kneeler
Fold the worked canvas along the un-worked threads and embroider these with long-armed cross-stitch. Seam the corners very firmly on the wrong side, either by hand or with two accurate rows of machine stitching, one on top of the other for strength. Trim the seam and overcast raw edges. Turn the kneeler to the right side and work long-armed cross-stitch over the corner seams.

The padding can be either layers of carpet felt, or a piece of foam rubber or plastic foam, but the pad must be $\frac{1}{2}$ inch larger than the kneeler's finished size in all measurements. Place the padding inside the kneeler and push it firmly into the corners. Lace the canvas over the padding on the back using strong, fine string, beginning with the two long sides and finishing with the two short sides. Trim and make the corners neat by overcasting. Cover the base of the kneeler with upholsterer's black lining fabric or some other sturdy lining.

If the kneeler is to be hung, sew a large curtain ring to the edge of the kneeler, stitching through base lining and canvas.

Working chart for a kneeler. This design of grapes symbolizes The Redeemer ▶

▼▲ *Border of the dove kneeler and working chart*

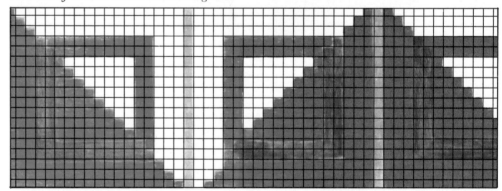

▼ *Border design which can be worked for either the grapes or dove kneeler*

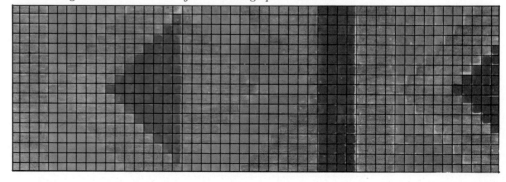

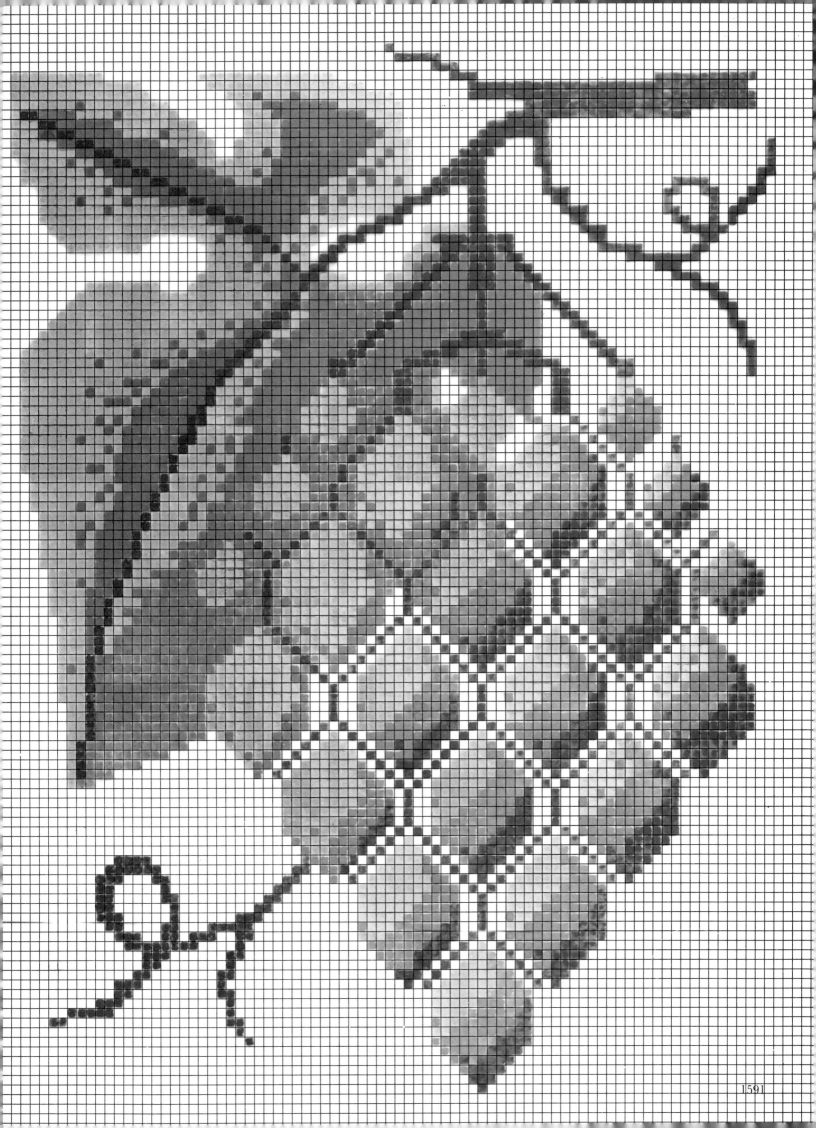

1591

Stitchery pattern/flower handbag

The lively design of this summer hand-bag worked on white, coarse, even-weave linen is emphasized with clear, bright colors. The flowers are worked without shading in 6-strand floss and crewel wool, using a small but varied range of stitches. Choose a lining fabric to match one of the flower colors. The instructions given here suggest working the design on both back and front of the bag, but the back could be left plain equally well.

To make the handbag, which measures 10 inches by 10½ inches, you will need the following:
White even-weave linen, two pieces 12 inches by 12 inches
Lining, two pieces, 12 inches by 12 inches
Non-woven interfacing fabric, two pieces,

12 inches by 12 inches
Sewing thread, white
Handbag frame, 10 inches wide
D.M.C. 6-strand floss, three skeins of **1**, eight skeins of **4**, and one of each of the remainder
1. 350 geranium; **4.** 742 gorse yellow; **7.** 301 chestnut; **8.** 445 canary yellow; **9.** 310 black. Appleton's Crewel Yarn, two skeins of **2** and **6** and one of **3** and **5**. **2.** 804 fuchsia; **3.** 566 sky blue; **5.** 405 sea green; **6.** 545 early English green
Crewel needle No.5
Sharps needle

Working the design
Mark the center of the pieces of linen fabric. Transfer the design to the fabric using the tissue paper method. The shading on the tracing design indicates the type and

direction of the stitches. For the most satisfactory result, work the looped, but-tonhole stitches without a hoop and the flat, satin stitches in a hoop.
With six strands of thread work the small flowers (geranium, color **1**) with straight stitches and finish at the center with a French knot. Six strands of thread are used for the two brick stitch flowers (gorse yellow, color **4**). Use two strands of crewel yarn and three strands of floss for other parts of the design.

Making the handbag
Press the finished embroidery. Interline with the interfacing fabric and join the back and front of the bag, leaving the top open. Make a hem at the top edges to fit the rods. Cut, make and fit the lining. Slip stitch in place.

1595

Design in dressmaking/collars

1. This is the first of two chapters dealing with collars. After a preliminary section on collars and figure types, you will be shown how to draft any of the collar shapes featured here. Then, on the last page, are tracing patterns for various collar shapes for those who still do not feel confident enough to draw their own.

The second chapter will cover the drafting of tailored collars, collars on low necklines, including middy collars, and collars with revers.

For the sake of simplicity the Golden Hands Pattern Pack dress pattern has been chosen as a starting point for the collar drafting, but any pattern with a plain high neckline will do.

Collars, necks and figure shapes

Even more effectively than most necklines, collars can frame and flatter the face and if carefully chosen can do much to disguise necks and proportions that are less than perfect. A collarless style can look and feel somewhat bleak, and certainly reveals every flaw.

2. It is obvious that a woman with a short neck would be unwise to hide what neck she does have behind a big, high collar. The attention must be drawn in a vertical direction by a long narrow collar, or an extended opening, maybe.

3. A woman with too long a neck should always go for big, bulky or wide collars, making sure that she chooses styles which cut across that length horizontally.

4. Women with big busts and small hips tend to look overpowering and top-heavy in large collars (**a**), while women with big hips should balance their proportions with big collars—small ones look rather lost and self-effacing (**b**).

Making a collar

A collar that does not sit well, or one that is not perfectly finished, can truly spoil the look of an outfit. Here are some general basic points:

A collar must be interfaced. Many people find the iron-on variety of interfacing the easiest to use. It can be cut on the bias, where appropriate, and can be stretched or eased in with the fabric as dictated by the style and cut of the collar. It is a good idea to cut and fuse all interfacings at the same time as cutting out a garment so that they are ready to sew without further preparation.

5. The collars of delicate fabrics can be interfaced with a very fine fabric, such as lawn or organdy; for transparent fabrics try a flesh-toned interfacing for the collars, tabs, belts or cuffs.

Stitch it in such a way that the turnings are underneath and out of sight once the collar or detail is turned through. For instance, on a collar interface the top collar so that the seam allowance will be covered by the interfacing when turned.

6. The outside edge and any topstitching must be smooth and perfect. If your dressmaking is not yet up to standard,

practice stitching on odd pieces of fabric until you are sure you can stitch lines exactly as you want them—straight, curved, zigzagged, around corners, $\frac{1}{2}$ inch from the edge, $\frac{5}{8}$ inch from the edge, etc. Careful pressing during the making of a collar is essential for a professional finish.

Ways of attaching a collar

A collar can be attached to a garment in one of four ways. Which method you use will depend upon the weight and bulk of the fabric and the style of the garment.

7. To a facing (**a**).

By means of a bias strip (**b**).

To a lining—or part-lining (**c**).

With all the seam allowances turned in out of sight as in a shirt collar, which is always attached this way (**d**).

Collar patterns

8. If you want to cut a particularly complicated or exotic collar, or if you don't quite trust your own capabilities yet, you can always use a commercial pattern. Provided that you first cut your neckline to match that of the commercial pattern there is no reason why the collar should not fit perfectly. One word of caution—be very sure that design-wise it will look right on your particular garment; there is more to designing dresses than simply making permutations of all possible variations of shape and detail without taking into account scale, fabric and general suitability.

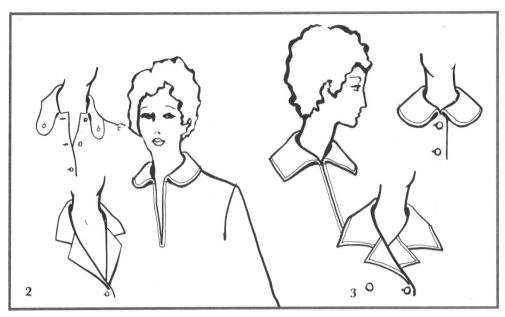

2

3

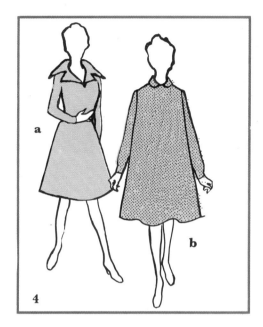

4

a

b

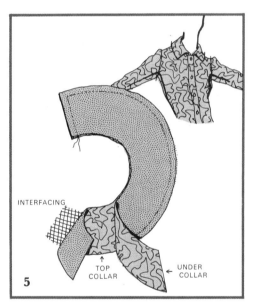

INTERFACING

TOP
COLLAR

UNDER
COLLAR

5

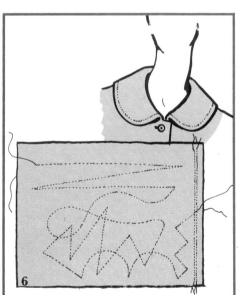

6

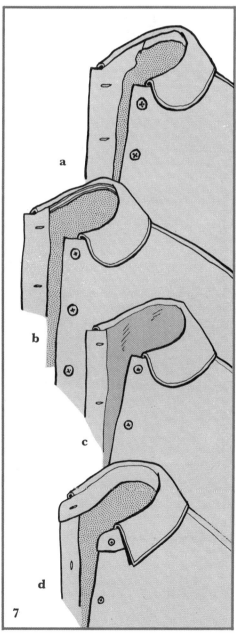

a

b

c

d

7

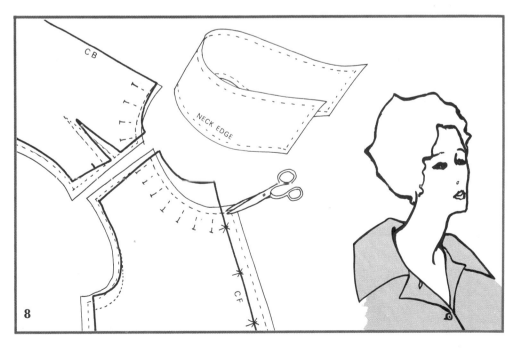

C B

NECK EDGE

C F

8

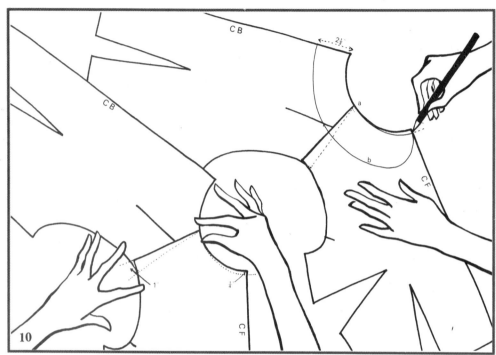

9. However, it is much more fun and altogether more rewarding to draft your own collar patterns.

Let's start with a Peter Pan collar. There is a little more to it than just putting back and front patterns together at the shoulder seams and drawing in the collar shape. This would give an unattractive flat look with a wavy edge, while what you really want is a snug fit around the neck with the collar rolling over smoothly.

10. First close the shoulder dart. Lay back and front bodice patterns together at shoulder seam, overlapping them 1 inch at the outer, shoulder edge only.

Measure down $\frac{1}{4}$ inch from the neck at the center front and draw your collar neck edge in a smooth curve from that point

tapering off to nothing at the shoulder point (**a**). Now simply draw the rest of the collar, say $2\frac{1}{2}$ inches deep all around (**b**). If you find curves difficult to draw freehand any circular objects around the house will serve as a template.

11. Try drawing other collars on this neckline—any shape or depth you like.

12. If you are using the tracing patterns on page 1600, and your dress neckline is larger or smaller than the size given, slash the collar pattern along the line indicated and spread or overlap the edges until the pattern measures the right size.

13. Notice that all these collars meet at the center front and do not extend to the wrap edge on a garment that buttons.

14. Cut out the collar, the under-collar and the interfacing, all with the straight

grain at the center back.

15. Trim off $\frac{1}{16}$ inch all around the outer edge of the under-collar, tapering off to nothing at the center front neck. This insures a smoothly rolled edge with no chance of the seam showing.

16. Trim away your turnings from all around the interfacing. If you are not using a fusible one, catch stitch the interfacing to the top collar. When stitching, the top collar—which is slightly longer—should be underneath so that the teeth of the machine will ease it in as it is stitched.

17. If you want to have a collar on a garment with a center back zipper, cut it with the straight grain to the dotted line. Cut the under-collar and interfacing in the same way.

12

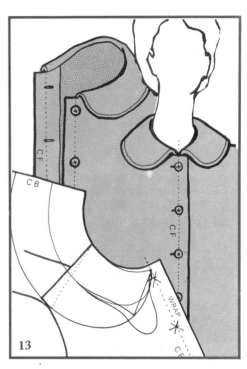

13

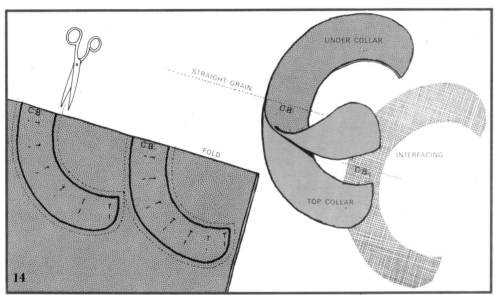

UNDER COLLAR

STRAIGHT GRAIN

C B

FOLD

INTERFACING

C B

TOP COLLAR

14

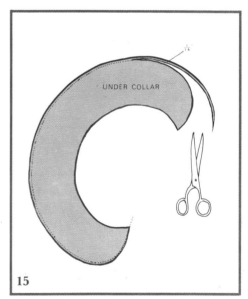

UNDER COLLAR

C B

UNDER COLLAR

15

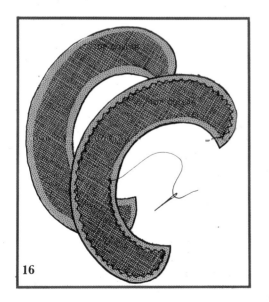

16

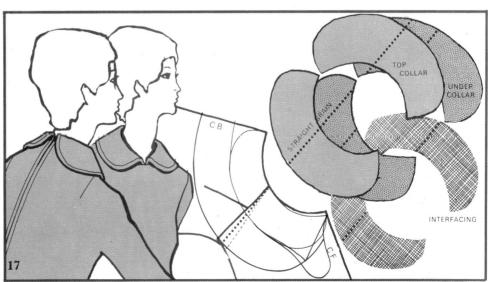

TOP COLLAR

UNDER COLLAR

STRAIGHT GRAIN

C B

INTERFACING

C F

17

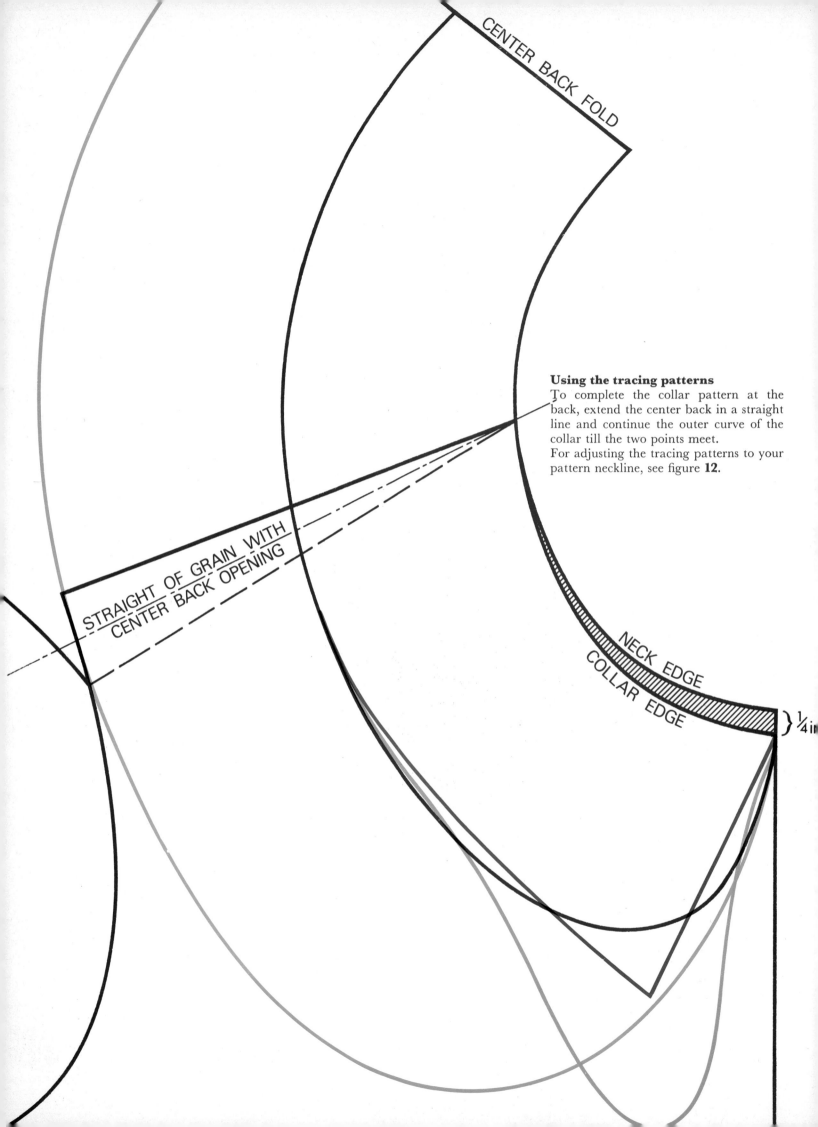

CENTER BACK FOLD

STRAIGHT OF GRAIN WITH
CENTER BACK OPENING

NECK EDGE
COLLAR EDGE

} ¼ in

Using the tracing patterns
To complete the collar pattern at the back, extend the center back in a straight line and continue the outer curve of the collar till the two points meet.
For adjusting the tracing patterns to your pattern neckline, see figure **12**.

Crafts/preserving flowers

It doesn't matter whether you have a big garden or a small one, or even none at all, as long as you can get into the countryside there are masses of flowers, grasses, seedheads and leaves that can be picked and preserved for decorations.

A charming Victorian art revived, it is this easy accessibility of the basic materials which makes the craft so appealing.

Dried flowers have dozens of possibilities for decoration: preserved whole they make formal vase arrangements, table displays, wall plaques, and Christmas and party decorations. Pressed flat, they make charming collage pictures, table mats, bookcovers, bookmarks, and greeting cards, to name but a few.

The choice of flowers

Gather flowers for preserving in the spring and summer, and for best results as soon as they have opened. If blossoms are too full blown, they are likely to either disintegrate or lose their color. Flowers which will dry easily fall into two categories, the everlasting flowers such as Rodanthe and Acroclinium and others called "soft flowers", some of which can be dried successfully if the process is quick. Here is a short list of flowers which can be preserved for whole flower decorations:

- ☐ Rodanthe: a small, deep red everlasting flower.
- ☐ Acroclinium: a rosy colored annual everlasting flower.
- ☐ Statice sinuata: long stems of pink, mauve, violet, white and yellow.
- ☐ Statice limonium (sea lavender).
- ☐ Honesty: sometimes called "silver pennies".
- ☐ Chinese lanterns: orange, lantern-like bracts.
- ☐ Cornflower: pink and blue.
- ☐ Love-in-the-mist: excellent for seed pods.
- ☐ Hydrangea: mature flower heads can be preserved.
- ☐ Delphiniums: blues, mauve and purple; small spikes preserve best, picked young.
- ☐ Golden rod: yellow gold spikes.
- ☐ Godetia: pink and red.
- ☐ Star of the Veldt: mixed colors.
- ☐ Marigolds: yellow and orange.
- ☐ Larkspur: pinks, mauve and purple.
- ☐ Sunflowers: double varieties of perennial types can be dried successfully.

Choosing for pressing

Almost any kind of flower can be gathered for pressing but it should be remembered that in pressing, bright colors will fade. Blues can fade to pale brown and bright red is likely to turn into chocolate brown,

▲ *A standing arrangement of dried flowers, grasses, ferns and poppy seed heads*

that some of the stems should be pressed in a curve for variety. Here is a list of grasses suitable for preserving:

☐ Briza maxima: nodding heads—ideal for Christmas decoration when glittered.
☐ Lagurus ovatus: (hare's tail grass)—like a squirrel's furry tail.
☐ Stipa pennata: (feather grass).
☐ Timothy grass

Leaves

Many wooded stemmed leaves such as beech, pittosporum, lime and laurel can be preserved on the branch by using a glycerine solution. Beech leaves are popular for this kind of preserving because the range of colors which can be achieved is so beautiful. The earlier branches of beech are cut, the deeper the color will be after preserving. Branches gathered later will turn a light tan color. Elaeagnus, camellia, box and many evergreens are also well worth preserving using the glycerine treatment.

For pressing purposes, tree leaves should not be picked when they are green because they fade. The colors of autumn foliage are beautiful and will keep their colors without fading, and fallen leaves can be collected, even if they are damp. Include the leaves of plants such as clematis and those with gray and silver colors, such as cineraria, diamond, artemisia, and absinthium in your collection. Raspberry leaves are gray on the underside and so is the gazania leaf, and the addition of these leaves to a collection is recommended.

Seedheads and berries

Some seedheads, collected while they are still green and unripe, can be successfully preserved by the glycerine method. Experiment with different kinds of flowers and plants to find out the colors and effects. Many are prettier left until they are ripe, and are preserved by drying—poppies, spiraea, delphiniums, columbines, for instance, and, of course, honesty. Chinese lanterns are gathered when the lower lanterns are just beginning to color.

Some vegetables produce attractive seedheads for flower arrangements—parsley, fennel, onions and leeks, for example, as do many wild flowers and shrubs. Look for plants such as knapweed, types of cow parsley, dock, ripple-wort and teasels. Berries can be preserved, but for only a few weeks, by brushing them with a thin glue soon after they are picked.

Methods of preserving

Drying flowers

Wherever possible, cut flowers with long

so make allowances for these changes when a pressed flower collection is being built up. Experiment with different kinds of petals and flowers and note the color changes as they dry. Beautiful collage pictures can be made in tones of beige, pale browns, gray and silver white. Yellow flowers are good for pressing—buttercups, for instance, retain their colors for about a year—but even if flower petals are inclined to turn to tones of brown, their colors, combined with silvery leaves and autumn leaves, will give a wonderful color range with which to work. Ideally, flowers should be picked

in the middle of the day when they are dry—try to avoid picking when damp.

Grasses

Grasses should be picked before they are fully mature to prevent their shedding seeds. A collection of grasses can therefore be started quite early in the summer and a good variety should be gathered, including some of the less decorative kinds. In whole flower arrangement, grass stems can be used for mounting flower heads and leaves, their flexible stems falling into pleasing curves quite naturally. Grasses can be pressed too, remembering

▲ *Hanging ornament using sycamore, barley ears and wild grass*

▲ *Hanging ornament using larch cones, ash and brome grass*

▲ *Thank-you card using flowers, ferns and seed heads*
▼ *Bookmark using flowers and birch leaves*

▲ *Matchbox top using buttercups, grasses, rush and vetch*
▼ *Table mat with a bird motif using leaves and honesty pod*

▲ *Door finger plates using spring and summer flowers and mounted under glass*

such as a shed or outbuilding. The darker the better because light will turn the grasses into hay.

Preserving leaves

Split branch stems upward for about two inches and immerse them immediately in warm water. Leave the branches for a few hours and discard any on which the leaves curl. Make a solution of one part glycerine to two parts hot water and insert the stems. As the stems only require two or three inches of solution, use a narrow vessel—a tin can for instance— for the preserving fluid, and stand the tin in a bucket so that the branches are supported. The leaves will "turn" in about three weeks.

Stems

As the stems of some dried flowers turn brittle, the stem can be strengthened by inserting a piece of fine wire through the center of the flower, giving it a twist under the calyx. Alternatively, paint the stem just under the flower head with latex adhesive. This will dry stiff and clear and looks quite natural.

Natural looking false stems for flower heads and odd leaves are made with preserved grass stems—Timothy grass is particularly useful for supporting flower heads. Pierce the center of the flower with a match stick and thread the grass through, stem first, until the grass head touches the flower center. Trim the grass head off and pull it through a little more until it is almost invisible. Separate leaves can be attached to grass stems with a touch of latex adhesive.

Pressing flowers

Method 1. Pick the whole flower and place it as soon as possible between two sheets of blotting paper and then immediately between the pages of an old book which has absorbent paper pages. Several flowers can be arranged together on the sheets as long as they do not touch. When one sheet is complete, turn six or seven pages on in the book and proceed through until the book is full. Then place a heavy weight on the book—bricks or a flat iron will do, and leave it undisturbed for about four weeks. Do not look at the flowers at all while they are pressing. Leaving them undisturbed with the heavy weight on top is the secret of successful pressing.

Method 2. For flowers with a hard center or a hard formation, use a flower press.

Presses are often inclined to spoil delicate flowers and the book and brick method is better for these types of flowers.

stems. Tie into small bunches and hang heads downward in a cool shady place with air circulation. It is important that the place be dry because damp conditions will make the flowers go moldy, and if there is too much light the colors will fade. Some flowers, such as helichrysums, lose their heads when the stems are dried out. These can be mounted on false stems. An alternative method of drying whole flowers involves the use of powdered borax or Silica gel. Flowers dried in borax dry in about three weeks—only three days are required for flowers buried in Silica gel.

Method. Cover the bottom of a box or

cookie tin with the powder and then either lay flowers face down or stand them on their faces, depending on their structure. Pour more powder all over and around them, lifting the petals now and then, so that the flower is surrounded by powder but still retains its shape. Leave the flowers for the required time until they are brittle and dry. Be very careful when removing the flowers from the powder.

Drying grasses

Tie grasses into tight bundles (they shrink during drying) and hang them heads downward in a cool, dark place,

Pressing separate petals

In many cases, a far prettier effect in collage is achieved if petals are pulled off flowers for pressing and then reassembled when dried and pressed.

Decorations with whole flowers

Table arrangements using whole dried flowers can be made on a base of styrofoam or plasticine, but some of the easiest decorations to make with dried flowers and grasses are hanging ornaments. These are best made with a styrofoam center which is lightweight. Use a ball of styrofoam and tie it in halves and then quarters with colored string or ribbon, leaving the ends for hanging. Fix a ribbon bow at the base with a long pin and then fill in the four quarters of the ball with dried flowers and seedheads. Should some of the flowers prove difficult to insert by their stems, pin them in place through the head of the flower into the foam.

Slightly more delicate in appearance are stars with cone centers, in which grasses or flower stalks are glued to the scales of a pine or larch-cone. Alternatively, a small cardboard disk can be used as a center, and with combinations of sycamore seeds, oat grains and dried flowers and grasses glued to both surfaces. Gilded or colored, they make pretty Christmas decorations. Thistles can also be used as a base for hanging ornaments and so can hogweed, acorn-cups and yarrow-stalks.

Ideas using pressed flowers

Besides collage pictures, lovely accessories for the home and gifts can be made using pressed flowers. The finger plates illustrated in this chapter are a charming example.

To make finger plates, cut white cardboard to the size of a plastic finger plate and position the flowers and stalks. Stick the flowers down in the way described and cover with the plastic plate.

Matchboxes with a flower decorated top make acceptable gifts. Arrange small flowers and leaves on the lid of a large box previously covered with white paper and stick them down. Place a piece of adhesive plastic sheeting over the flowers, smoothing it down carefully. Once in position the adhesive plastic cannot be removed, and one should make sure that the flowers are firmly in position before applying it.

Larger surfaces can be treated in the same way (notebooks, calendars and greeting cards, for example).

Another idea particularly suitable for the use of pressed flowers is a set of table

▲ *"Iceberg" flower collage. White rose petals were used for the two central flowers*

mats. Make them in sets, and to any dimensions, with a backing of colorful felt or tweed. The top surface of the mat is glass, cut to size by a glazier, in a 24oz or 32oz thickness which will resist the heat of all but the very hottest dinner plates. The edges of the mat are finally sealed with tape chosen in a color that seems most suitable.

Collages with pressed flowers

Pressed flower collage is a most absorbing and creative craft, the petals, flower heads, stems, grasses and seeds forming an

integral part of the composition itself. The theme of the collage may be more than a design of pressed flowers; it can become a picture, the shapes of leaves and flowers themselves providing the inspiration.

A latex based adhesive is best for sticking down flowers and petals. Choose one which is easily removed when it is rubbed off with a finger and leaves no stain on the paper. A soft paint brush is ideal for lifting petals and for arranging them in position. Tweezers are not recommended because they can damage the flowers. Always use adhesive sparingly in dried flower collage.

Knitting design/darts and shaping

Darts worked for front shaping

Darts worked from waist and shoulder to reduce fullness, method 1

As well as being able to work out their own simple knitwear designs, many knitters enjoy adapting commercial patterns to their personal needs.

This chapter is about enlarging patterns and working darts for waistlines, shoulders and bust shaping.

Obviously to adapt a 38 inch bust pattern to fit a 40 inch bust size two inches must be added across the chest, one inch to the front piece and one to the back, but without experience it is difficult to know what other alterations need to be made to cope with the additional stitches. Although bust, waist and hip measurements can increase by as much as two inches per size, the shoulder width measurement remains almost the same, increasing by only $\frac{1}{4}$ inch per size. For this reason, stitches added to increase a bust measurement, for instance, have to be reduced between the beginning of the armhole and the shoulderline. It is inadvisable to increase the width of the shoulderline to cope with any of these extra stitches, except by perhaps one or two stitches, which can be added to the width of the neck on both back and front without spoiling the garment fit.

To give some examples: if six stitches are to be added to the front of a sweater, one extra stitch can be added to each shoulder, leaving four stitches to be worked into the armhole, two each side. For a set-in sleeve, it is advisable to bind

off one stitch extra at the beginning of the armhole and decrease one stitch extra at the end of the curved armhole shaping. If eight stitches are to be added, two of the stitches can be added to the width of the neck on both back and front, either as stitches to be bound-off or left on the holder. The remaining six are reduced as before.

The side seam length of the back and front of a garment usually remains the same in a size increase although the armhole itself increases by $\frac{1}{4}$ inch on both back and front pieces. Because the armhole has altered, the sleeve cap itself also has to be altered slightly, but it is inadvisable to add more than two or three stitches to the cap shaping or a baggy sleeve will result; the measurement of the upper arm varies only very slightly in size and, as knitted fabric is pliable, it is better to stretch the sleeve cap slightly when sewing it into the armhole.

Although the upper sleeve may require the addition of stitches, it is unlikely that many extra stitches will be required at the wrist, and this fact will alter the number of increases to be worked on the length between cuff and underarm. This means that the number of rows between increases must be recalculated and altered if necessary. Whether on the body of the garment or on the sleeve, carefully measuring and recalculating is the only sure method of producing a well fitting garment. When altering pattern sizes, think

alterations out carefully and consider the effects of the change on other sections—facings, collars, etc.

Front shaping on knitted garments

Knitted fabrics are so pliable and elastic that fronts of knitted garments are usually made without any different shaping from the back. Because of the characteristics of the fabric this is possible, although it is not the best way of obtaining a perfect garment. Knitting directions in printed form, whether in a leaflet or a magazine, are written to take up as little space as possible, and for this reason the words 'Front—work as for Back', are given rather than detailed directions for placing and working waist, bust or shoulder darts. When planning ones own designs, written directions are not a consideration and front shaping can therefore be included in the form of darts, to give a better fitting garment.

Shaping with darts

Bust darts are usually worked about two inches below the armhole and extending toward the center. When the point where the dart is to begin is reached, graduated rows are worked, each row being a few stitches shorter than the row before, until enough have been worked to give the additional length required. Figure **1** shows a possible chart for a bust dart worked over fourteen rows, each being five stitches shorter than the row before.

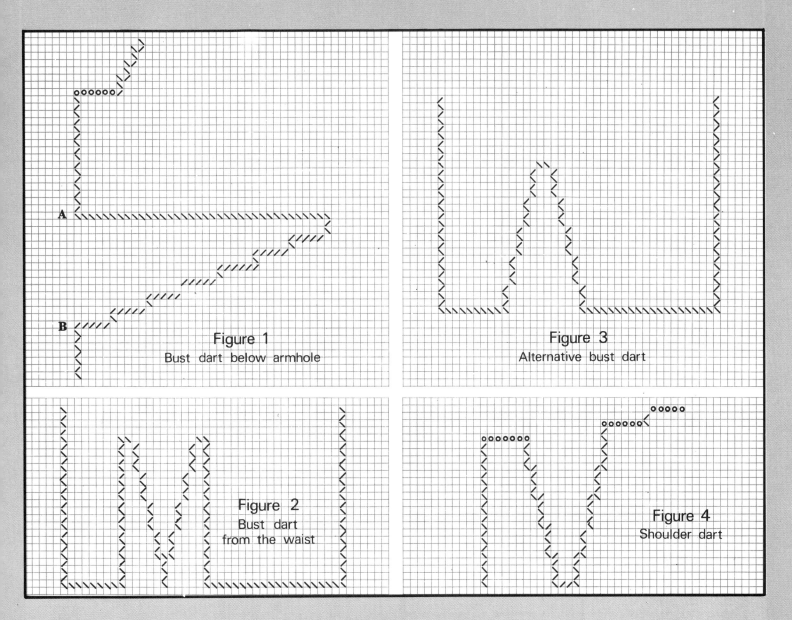

Figure 1
Bust dart below armhole

Figure 3
Alternative bust dart

Figure 2
Bust dart
from the waist

Figure 4
Shoulder dart

Reducing fullness with darts

Where the bust measurement is greater than usual it may be difficult to keep the garment waistline from being too bulky or to reduce a sufficient number of stitches at the armhole. This can be overcome in two ways:

Method 1. Two darts are worked on each side of the front, one running from the waist up to the bust and the other running from above the bust, tapering up to the shoulderline (see illustration).

Method 2. Instead of increasing only at the side edges from the waistline upward, additional stitches are increased at intervals, usually in a straight line below the center of the bust area, until the required number of stitches have been worked to give the total width.

Between the armhole shaping and the shoulderline the additional fullness must be decreased and it may be greater than can adequately be dealt with by the armhole shaping alone. By tapering in a

straight line, this time upward, to the shoulderline, stitches are decreased while the correct number for the shoulder are produced.

Both of these methods and working bust darts require a different method of charting because the alterations and shaping take place in the center of the work and not at the side edge.

Charting darts

When working a dart from the waist upward toward the bust, decide first on the position of the dart and mark this number of stitches along from the center front, leave a gap over the number of spaces required for the stitches which are eventually going to be increased, then mark the remaining number of stitches for the waistline on the chart. As work proceeds upward for the length of dart required, mark the increases on the chart until the gap has been closed. Figure 2 shows a chart for a bust dart from the waistline

where 10 stitches have been increased evenly on either side of a center stitch, increasing two stitches on every 4th row. Figure 3 shows a different method of charting the same dart.

Although this dart now looks like an opening, the chart is read across the gap, as though ignoring it. Remember that a chart is a map, and not a paper pattern. The shoulder dart required to decrease the fullness will look very similar but will be in reverse as it is decreasing the number of stitches instead of increasing (figure 4).

On the bust dart chart in Figure 1 the total side length is the length up to point A plus the length from B to armhole, the rows between A and B do not exist as far as the side seam measurement is concerned.

The lines of increase and decrease may be incorporated into the design, being accentuated by openwork, twisted stitch or even cable panels.

Knitting pattern/mini-dress

This slimming mini-dress has an unusual wide rib which gives a smooth fit, and a patterned yoke and sleeves.

Sizes

Directions are for 32in bust. The figures in brackets [ ] refer to the 35 and 38in sizes respectively.
Length, 26[27:28]in.
Sleeve seam, 3in.

Gauge

6 sts and 8 rows to 1in worked over st st on No.5 needles.

Materials

Bernat Nylo Sports
5[6:6] balls
One pair No.3 needles
One pair No.5 needles
One set of 4 No.3 double-pointed needles
2 stitch holders

Back

Using No.3 needles, cast on 101[110:119] sts.
1st row K4, *P3, K6, rep from * to last 7 sts, P3, K4.

A close-up detail of the plain ribbing and yoke patterning ▼

2nd row P4, *K3, P6, rep from * to last 7 sts, K3, P4.
Rep these 2 rows until work measures 2in.
Change to No.5 needles and continue in rib until work measures 20[20½:21]in, ending with a WS row.
Next row (patt row) K4, P3, *yon, sl 1, K2 tog, psso, (K1, P1) into the thread between the last st and the next st, K2 tog tbl, move this st back onto left-hand needle and slip the next st over it, move st back to right-hand needle, yon, P3, rep from * to last 4 sts, K4.
Next row P4, K3, *P6, K3 rep from * to last 4 sts, P4.

Shape armholes

Next row Bind off 6 sts, rib to end.
Rep this row once more.
Next row K2 tog, rib to last 2 sts, K2 tog.
Next row Rib.
Next row K2 tog, K4, P3, work as patt row to last 6 sts, K4, K2 tog.
Working patt row on every 6th row, continue dec at each end of every other row until 75[82:89] sts rem.
Continue without shaping until armhole measures 6½[7:7½]in, ending with a WS row.

Shape shoulders

Bind off 5[6:6] sts at beg of next 6 rows, then 4[4:7] sts at beg of next 2 rows. Slip rem 37[38:39] sts on holder.

Front

Work as given for Back until armhole measures 4½[5:5½]in, ending with a WS row.

Shape neck

Next row Patt 27[30:33], turn and slip rem sts on st holder.
At neck edge, bind off 2 sts every other row twice, then dec one st at neck edge every other row until 19[22:25] sts rem.
Continue without shaping until armhole measures the same as on Back, ending with a WS row.

Shape shoulder

At arm edge, bind off 5[6:6] sts every other row 3 times. Work 1 row. Bind off rem 4[4:7] sts.
Return to the sts on holder, slip 21[22:23] sts on holder for neck and patt to end.
Next row Patt.
Next row Bind off 2 sts, patt to end.
Complete to correspond to first side.

Sleeves

Using No.3 needles, cast on 73[73:82] sts.
1st row P2, *K6, P3, rep from * to last 8 sts, K6, P2.
Continue in rib, working patt row every 6th row and inc one st at each end of every 6th[4th:6th] row until there are 79[83:88] sts.
Continue without shaping until sleeve seam measures 3in, ending with a WS row.

Shape cap

Bind off 6 sts at beg of next 2 rows.
K2 tog at each end of every other row until 47[47:48] sts rem.
Bind off 2 sts at beg of next 12 rows, then 3 sts at beg of next 4 rows.
Bind off rem 11[11:12] sts.

Neckband

Join shoulder seams.
Using set of 4 No.3 dp needles and with RS facing, work in K6, P3 rib across Back neck sts matching the rib, pick up and K25[24:23] sts down side of Front neck, rib Front neck sts matching the rib, pick up and K25[24:23] sts up other side of Front neck. 108 sts for all sizes.
Next round *K6, P1, P2 tog, rep from * all around. 96 sts.
Continue in rounds of K6, P2 rib for 1in. Bind off in rib.

Finishing

Press lightly under damp cloth, using a warm iron. Sew in sleeves. Join side and sleeve seams.

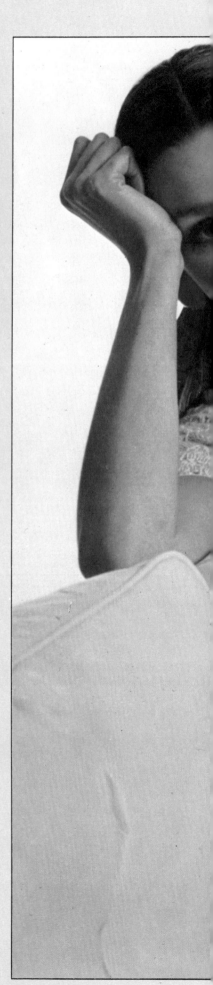

Stitchery pattern/butterfly wall panel

Excluding the frame, the panel measures 21 stiches by 10½ inches. To work it you will need:
- [ ] White linen 24 inches wide by 13½ inches deep
- [ ] White cardboard 21 inches wide by 10½ inches deep
- [ ] Fabric adhesive

- [ ] D.M.C. six-strand floss, three skeins of each color and four of No.5: **1.** 798 cobalt blue; **2.** 806 peacock blue; **3.** 797 azure; **4.** 906 parrot green; **5.** 500 grass green
- [ ] Blue and green beads
- [ ] Small blue and large green glass "jewels"

- [ ] Beading needle
- [ ] Crewel needle No.6
- [ ] Embroidery frame

Working the design
Mark the center of the fabric in each direction. Transfer the design to the fabric using the tissue paper method and frame

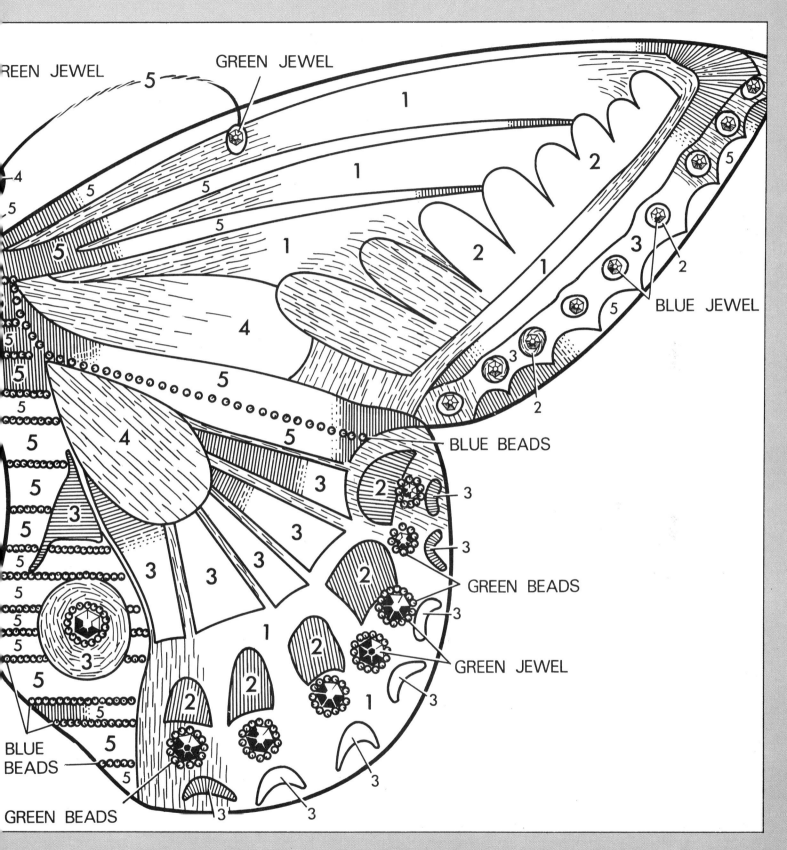

GREEN JEWEL

GREEN JEWEL

BLUE JEWEL

BLUE BEADS

GREEN BEADS

GREEN JEWEL

BLUE BEADS

GREEN BEADS

the work. Use four strands of floss in the needle, and following the directions indicated in the outline drawing, work in a free, rather than an exact manner. For the background areas of the patterned wings work split stitch in open rows. Work the satin stitch blocks so that they slightly overlap the split stitch areas.

Stitch the jewels in position and surround with beads. Fasten the beads upright with a stitch at each side.

Preparing for framing
To avoid breaking the beads, use an extra thick ironing pad. Place the embroidery face downward and press lightly.

Mount on the cardboard, either by lacing across in each direction with a strong thread, or with fabric adhesive and keeping the horizontal and vertical threads of fabric in line with the edges of cardboard. Half of the butterfly and half of the stitch chart is shown, reproduced slightly less than the size of completed panel.

Stitchery design/flat stitch rugs

This chapter deals with materials and techniques for flat stitch rugs. The next chapter will give the stitches used for pile rugs.

Materials

Canvas. Double mesh rug canvas. The canvas is made from either cotton with 4 or 5 holes to 1 inch or linen with 7, 8 or 10 holes to 1 inch. Canvas with 5 holes to 1 inch is the best size mesh to start on. Single mesh canvas is also used and the type most commonly worked on is made of closely woven jute with 8 threads to 1 inch. Each stitch is worked over two threads of the canvas. This gives 4 stitches to the inch.

The number of stitches to the inch influences the design. A more flowing and intricate design can be planned on a fine mesh canvas, whereas the same design would have an angular, stepped appearance on coarse canvas.

Wools. It is essential that all wool used is of the best quality and not of a wool/cotton or wool/synthetic mixture.

2-ply Axminster thrums or hanks are used for the coarse canvas, whereas for finer canvas Brussels or worsted thrums or hanks, and crewel wool are used. For flat stitched rugs allow 6 to 7 ounces of thrums to each square foot of canvas.

Needles. Carpet needles with blunt points and large eyes are used for coarse canvas and tapestry needles for finer canvas.

Scissors. A 6 inch pair of surgical scissors with one blunt and one sharp point is ideal. This point must be very sharp.

Designs for needle-made rugs

It is far more satisfying to make a rug to your own design, and the best method is to plan the design on graph paper using each square to represent one stitch.

Before planning a design there are some points to be considered.

A rectangle is the natural shape for a rug. Square rugs do not fit well into most areas. Unusual shapes such as half moons are not suitable for needle-made rugs because they waste a considerable amount of canvas; they can only be used in one position and the problems of working a curved edge are practically insurmountable. As a rug is to be used on the floor the design should show up clearly from varying heights and different angles.

The border of a rug should measure at least ⅙th of the area. For example, a rug measuring 27 inches across should have a border at each side measuring a least 4½ inches. A border is often divided into sections, with one more important border edged on either side with smaller supporting borders. Some motif or part of the main

design should, if possible, be included in the border as a unifying link.

When designing a rug which is not being made to fit into a particular area, the normal proportions are for the length to measure 1¾ times the width. Always remember when buying canvas to allow for the turn over at each end of the rug and at least ¼ yard extra for any alterations which occur when planning the design onto the canvas.

Making a working chart

It is only necessary to make a chart of half the rug design if the pattern has a natural repeat.

Halve the rectangle and mark the depth of the border lightly with a pencil in case this has to be adjusted later. Plan the motifs on a separate sheet of graph paper and select parts of these to be included in the border. With a free flowing border it is often desirable to have a connecting motif at the corners.

A corner is visually most important and so should be planned first.

Outlining

Outlining the motifs in a design greatly enhances the general effect. This can be done with one line of stitches or, for a stronger effect, a double outline can be worked. Never outline in black as this is too harsh; navy blue or dark brown are more effective.

Stitches

The stitches used for flat rugs are the same as those used for needlepoint—cross-stitch, long-legged or Portuguese stitch, deep long-legged cross-stitch (worked over 2 bars instead of 1), rice stitch, tent stitch (worked diagonally), Soumak stitch, interlocking Gobelin stitch and backstitch, which is used mainly to fill the gaps between other stitches.

Preparation of canvas and edge stitching

Whatever type of canvas is used, the cut edges must be dealt with immediately or they will fray. Fold the cut edges of the canvas over to the wrong side for flat stitched rugs and to the right side for tufted rugs. The turning should be of 2 to 2½ inches for small rugs and a little more for larger ones.

When using double mesh canvas, a double bar should lie along the folded edge to insure that the large holes of the turned over canvas correspond exactly with those below. Herringbone stitch the top cut edge firmly to the canvas using a complete cross-stitch. The other end of the canvas

should be oversewn roughly along the cut edge to prevent initial fraying. This lower edge is dealt with as the rug nears completion. If the sides of the canvas are cut then these must be turned over to the same depth and the corners mitered. Do not cut any canvas away, work through all thicknesses for strength.

The next important step is the edge stitching which should completely cover the canvas. The strongest method is plait stitch for all types of canvas, but when working on single mesh jute there are three alternative methods, i.e. single crochet, blanket stitch and twisted cable stitch. They should be worked between every thread of canvas and about 3 or 4 threads deep.

Before plait stitch is commenced, work a row of oversewing with one thread in the needle along the edge, taking a stitch into every hole of the canvas.

Corners

The corner points are difficult to cover neatly and it helps to paint the canvas in the same color as the wool being used for the plait. When the paint is dry, work a single cross-stitch over the point as an extra covering.

As the plait approaches the corner it should be shortened: when an "on 3" stitch finishes in the corner hole it should be followed by back 2 on 2, back 1, on 1, so that the last stitch as well as the first along the edge is a simple cross-stitch. Oversew the corner point, neatly covering the cross-stitch already worked and commence the plait down the selvage as before with a cross-stitch, the first half of which should be sloping in the direction in which the plait is to be worked. For pile rugs the edging stitch is always worked first, but for flat stitched rugs it is a matter of personal choice. If, for instance, the rug has to be stretched, it is often preferable to work the plait after stretching.

Fringes

These are not really practical as they wear badly and can be a nuisance when vacuum cleaning; however, if desired, a fringe may be worked as an alternative to the plait stitch as an edging on needle-made rugs.

Finishing

Most flat stitched rugs are improved by stretching, though it is rarely necessary to stretch a pile rug. Stretch the rug face down as for needlepoint and dampen thoroughly. The rug should be left stretched for one week to allow it to dry completely. Brass nails should be used to keep the rug free of rust stains.

Flat stitches

Soumak stitch

This is a particularly interesting stitch to work and somewhat unusual in appearance, resembling the weave texture of the Soumak rugs of the East which are woven on a loom. The stitch is worked, as shown in the diagrams, in vertical rows from top to bottom, in horizontal rows from right to left, or diagonally. The working position of the canvas is different from that used for any other type of needle-made rug. The rug must be held with the unworked length of canvas lying to the left, and the V which each stitch forms is pointed toward the worker.

Vertical method

Using a single thread in the needle, each stitch is commenced at hole 1 between two threads of canvas (i.e. splitting the bar).

Insert the needle upward over two warp bars into hole 2, take it under a weft double bar from right to left into hole 3, and return it to the original starting point at hole 1. Drop it down between the threads of the next double bar to hole 4. The stitch is completed as before to form vertical rows.

Horizontal method

Working from right to left, insert the needle between the double bar to the left of the completed stitch instead of dropping down.

Diagonal method

For a diagonal line descending from right to left, the needle drops down one bar diagonally each time.

For a diagonal line upward from right to left, the needle moves up one bar diagonally.

In all four methods it must be remembered that each single stitch must be worked and completed according to the basic method instructions.

When using Soumak stitch it is necessary to work a row of backstitch between the first and last row of stitches and the edge stitches to avoid leaving small gaps in the canvas.

When planning a design for this stitch there should be one more hole in the canvas than the total number of squares on the chart.

Interlocking Gobelin stitch

This stitch is quick and easy to do and is worked backward and forward in horizontal rows. It is ideal for striped rugs and can be worked across the rug or in lengthwise stripes.

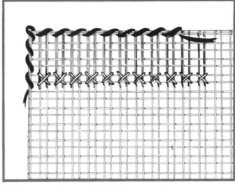

▲ *Corner point and double oversewing*

Soumak stitch—stages of vertical method ▼

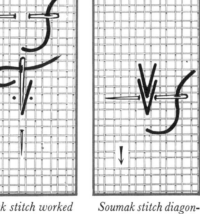

Soumak stitch vertical method completed ▼

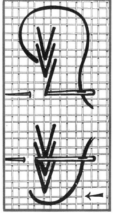

Soumak stitch worked horizontally ▼

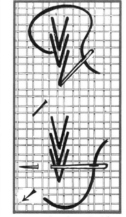

Soumak stitch diagonally right to left ▼

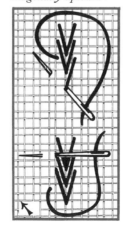

Soumak stitch diagonally upward ▼

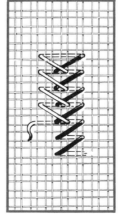

Working interlocking Gobelin stitch ▼

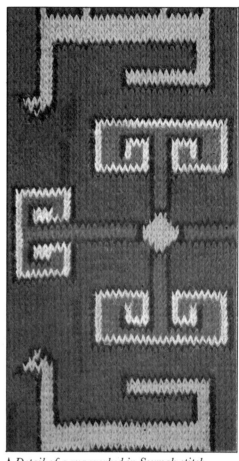

▲ *Detail of a rug worked in Soumak stitch*
▼ *Example of interlocking Gobelin stitch*

Home crochet/window pelmet

This pretty idea from Scandinavia gives an attractive decoration for the top of a window while allowing the maximum of light to filter through. As crochet can be seen from either side the valance looks well from outside, too.

Size
Top. Each band measures about 3in (thus 5 bands as illustrated will give a depth of 15in).
Frill. Each scallop measures about 13in wide.

Gauge
6½dc to 1in over top.

Materials
Coats & Clark's O.N.T. Speed-Cro-Sheen
About 1 ball for each scallop and 1 ball for the equivalent width of top as required
One No.C crochet hook

Frill

Ch20 and join with a ss to form a ring.
1st row Ch2, 17dc into half of ring. Turn and work in rows.
2nd row Ch2, 1dc between each dc to end. 18 sts.
3rd row Ch7, *(2tr, ch3, 2tr) between 3rd and 4th dc, skip 3dc, rep from * to end finishing with ch4, 1tr into last dc. 5 points.
4th row Ch7, *(3dc, ch3, 3dc) into ch3 sp, ch4, rep from * to end finishing with 1dc into 4th ch at edge.
5th row Ch7, *1sc into both ch4 loops of previous rows, ch4, (3dc, ch3, 3dc) into ch3 sp, ch4, rep from * ending with 1sc into last 2 ch4 loops, ch4, 1dc into 4th ch at edge.
6th row Ch14, *1sc into ch3 sp, ch10, rep from * ending with 1tr into 4th ch at edge.
7th row Ch3, 12dc into first ch loop, work 13dc into all other ch loops and positioning the 13th dc on the last loop into the 4th of the 14ch of previous row.
8th row Ch5, 1dc between 2nd and 3rd dc of previous

1614

row, *ch1, skip one sp, 1dc into next sp, rep from * to end finishing with 1dc into top of 3ch. 40dc.
9th row Ch5, *1dc into ch1 sp, ch1, rep from * ending with 1dc into 3rd of 5ch.
10th row Ch7, skip first ch sp, *(2tr, ch3, 2tr) into next sp, ch4, skip 2 sps, rep from * ending with 1tr into 3rd of 5ch. 13 points.
11th row Ch7, *(3dc, ch3, 3dc) into ch3 sp, ch4, rep from * ending with 1dc into 4th of 7ch.
12th row As 11th.
13th row Ch7, 1sc into all 3 ch4 loops of previous rows, ch4, (3dc, ch3, 3dc) into ch3 sp, *ch4, 1sc into all 3 ch loops, ch4, 3dc into ch3 sp, ch41, turn, beg at 3rd ch from hook work 1dc into each of rem 38ch, 3dc into same ch3 sp, rep from * 3 times more, **ch4, 1sc into all 3 ch loops, ch4, (3dc, ch3, 3dc) into ch3 sp, rep from ** twice more, then rep from * to ** once, ch4, 1sc into all 3 ch loops, ch4, (3dc, ch3, 3dc) into ch3 sp, ch4, 1sc into all 3 ch loops, ch4, 1dc into 4th of 7ch. Fasten off.
Work second scallop in the same way until 12th row has been completed.
13th row Ch3, 1sc into edge loop on previous scallop, ch4, 1sc into all 3 ch loops of previous rows, ch4, 3dc into ch3 sp, ch1, 1sc into corresponding point on previous scallop, ch1, 3dc into same ch3 sp, rep from * to ** on previous scallop. Turn. Ch9, weave first dc strip on previous scallop over and under the 4 strips just worked, then work 1sc into top of strip, (ch9, weave next strip in the same way but alternately to first, then work 1sc into top of strip) 3 times but working last sc into top of 2 strips together, continuing along other side of point made by these strips (ch9, 1sc into top of next strip) 3 times, ch9, 1sc into loop of point on first scallop (the same point as 4th strip was worked from). Turn. *Ch4, (2tr, ch3, 2tr) into

ch9 loop, rep from * 8 times more working into each ch9 loop and into the sc at point where sc was worked into 2 strips together and ending with ch4, 1sc into 3rd dc on 13th row of scallop. Turn. *Ch4, (3dc, ch3, 3dc) into ch3 sp, rep from * 8 times more ending with ch4, 1sc into same loop as previous row. Turn. Ch5, 3dc into first ch3 sp, ch1, 1sc into loop of first free point on previous scallop, ch1, 3dc into same ch sp as before, *ch4, 1sc into two ch4 loops, ch4, (3dc, ch3, 3dc) into ch3 sp, rep from * ending with ch5, 1sc into same loop as at previous turn. Continue with 13th row on first scallop, ch4, 1sc into 3 ch loops, ch4, 3dc into ch3 sp, ch1, 1sc into point loop of braided part, ch1, 3dc into same ch3 sp as before, complete as for 13th row of first scallop.
Make as many scallops as are required for the width of the valance, joining each as already given. On the end scallops work one set of strips only, leaving the outer edges plain. When all scallops are completed, along the top edge work 1dc, *ch2, skip 2 sts, 1dc, rep from * to end. Fasten off.

Top section

Make a number of ch divisible by 19, plus 4. Example shown here, 99.
1st row (3dc, ch3, 3dc) into 4th ch from hook, *skip 2ch, 1dc into each of next 14ch, skip 2ch, (3dc, ch3, 3dc) into next ch, rep from * to end, 1sc into 3rd of turning ch on frill top edge.
2nd row Ch4, 1sc into next dc on frill top, (3dc, ch3, 3dc) into ch3 sp, *ch14, (3dc, ch3, 3dc) into ch3 sp, rep from * to end.
3rd row Ch4, (3dc, ch3, 3dc) into ch3 sp, *1dc into each of 14ch, (3dc, ch3, 3dc) into ch3 sp, rep from * to end, 1dc into turning ch, 1sc into next dc on frill.
Rep 2nd and 3rd rows for width required.

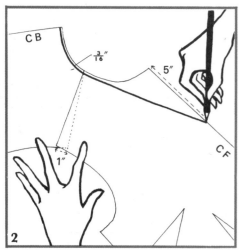

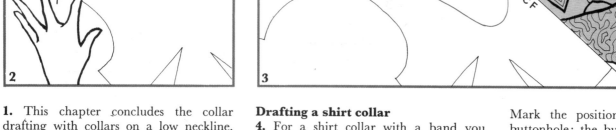

1. This chapter concludes the collar drafting with collars on a low neckline, tailored collars and rever collars, including a middy collar.

Some tracing patterns for these are given on pages 1618 and 1619.

Drafting a collar on a low neckline

2. For a collar on a low neckline, overlap the shoulder seams at the outer edge 1 inch as before. From the center back as far as the shoulder seam draw in a new neckline for both garment and collar $\frac{3}{16}$ inch in from the original. Then carry on the line to as low at the center front as you wish—the illustration shows a neckline starting 5 inches down from the neck edge.

Make sure that you will be able to get your head through the neck if you have no other opening.

3. Draw the collar any shape you like and cut out with the center back fold on the straight grain of the fabric.

Drafting a shirt collar

4. For a shirt collar with a band you will need a ruler.

5. A few construction lines first: draw a line half the length of your neck measurement with a line at right angles to it at each end and one through the middle. Mark one end center back and the other center front.

6. Follow the diagrams step by step; written directions would sound unnecessarily confusing (**6a, b, c** and **d**).

7. Now draw the "fall" of the collar as in the diagram (the points can be any shape you like).

8. For a one-piece collar draw the "stand" parallel to the curve of the collar by using the higher construction lines of the two sets. Extend the lines at the center front to form the tab of the collar (**a**). How far you extend them depends on the size of your wrap, or, as the trade calls it, "button stand". The top edge of the tab is usually rounded (**b**).

Mark the position of the button and buttonhole; the buttonhole starts $\frac{1}{8}$ inch on the outside of the center front.

9. For a two-piece shirt collar, use the lower construction lines of the two sets to draw the band. Extend and mark the tab as before. Extend the neck edge of the band at the center back and draw in the center back fold line at right angles to this extension. This collar has a 1 inch stand and a 2 inch fall; you could have a $\frac{3}{4}$ inch stand and a $1\frac{1}{2}$ inch fall.

10. To increase or decrease the size of the collar if you are using the tracing pattern simply add or take away from the length at the center back.

11. The band alone can finish the neck line most attractively.

12. You will not need the usual center front facings with any of these collars, or the neck band finish. Instead, cut a 2 inch turning on the front edges which can be interfaced, stitched and pressed in place before the collar is stitched on.

4

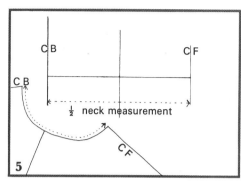

5 C B   C F

C B

½ neck measurement

C F

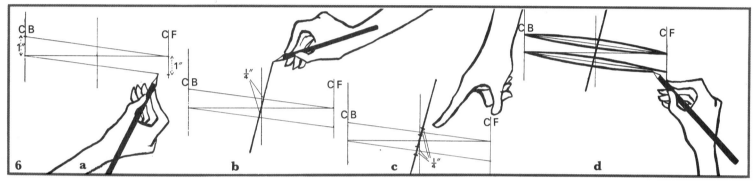

6   **a**   **b**   **c**   ¼"   **d**

C B   C F
1"   1"

¼"

C B   C F

C B   C F

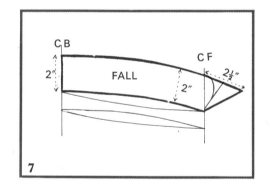

7

C B
2"

FALL

C F
2½"
2"

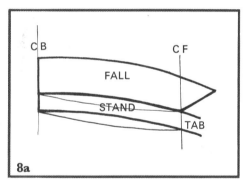

8a

C B   C F

FALL

STAND

TAB

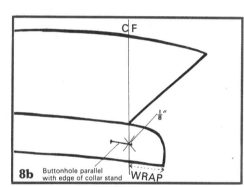

8b

C F

⅛"

Buttonhole parallel
with edge of collar stand   **WRAP**

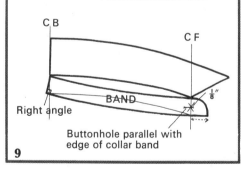

9

C B   C F

BAND   ⅛"

Right angle

Buttonhole parallel with
edge of collar band

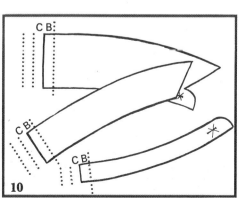

10

C B
C B
C B
C B

11

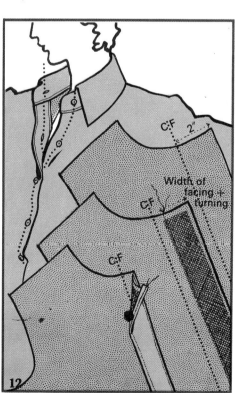

12

C F   2"

Width of
facing +
turning

C F

C F

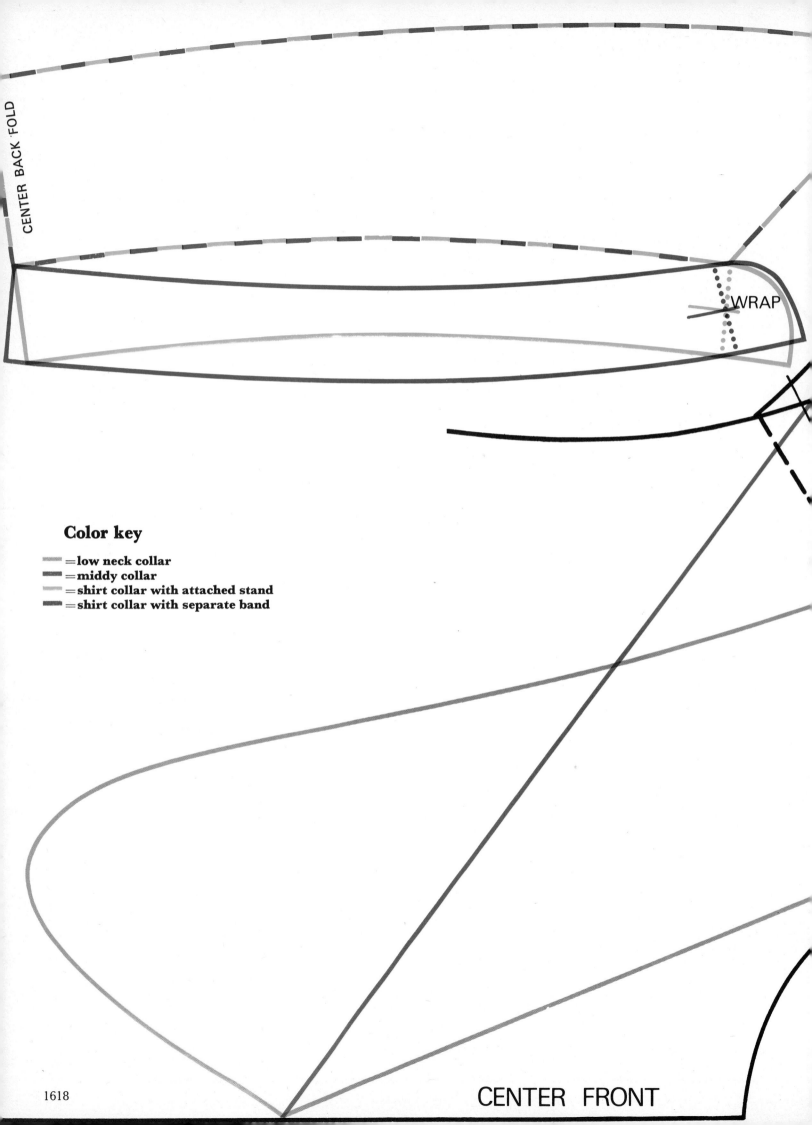

CENTER BACK FOLD

WRAP

Color key

━━━ =low neck collar
━━━ =middy collar
━━━ =shirt collar with attached stand
━━━ =shirt collar with separate band

CENTER FRONT

1618

To alter the size of the shirt collar see figure 10.

The middy and low neck collars are altered as for the tracing patterns in the previous chapter, figure 12.

CENTER BACK FOLD

GRAIN LINE
WITH CENTER BACK OPENING

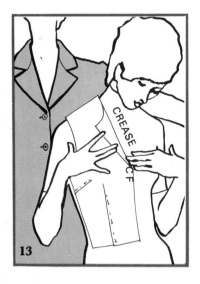

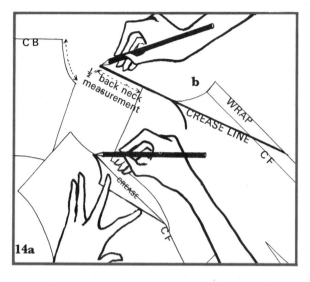

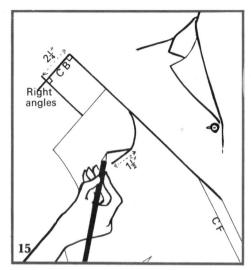

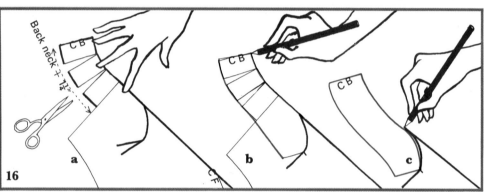

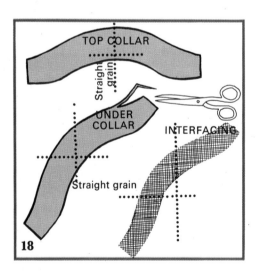

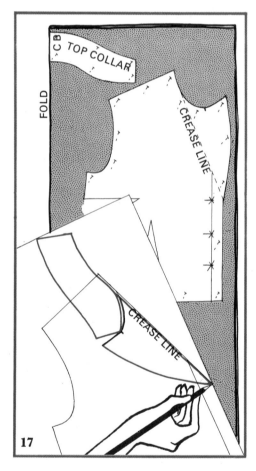

Collar with revers

13. To draft a simple collar and rever use only the front of your pattern. Hold it against yourself and crease it where you want the rever.

14. Draw around the curve before opening the pattern out flat (**a**). Place the pattern on a sheet of paper and draw in the crease line. Extend the crease line at the front to the edge of the wrap. Extend the other end up through the shoulder point and continue for a length of half the back neck measurement (**b**).

15. Draw in the $2\frac{1}{4}$ inch center back line

of the collar at right angles to the extended crease line, using a set square or book, and draw another line back to the shoulder as shown. To make the notch, extend the rever about $1\frac{1}{2}$ inches, then draw the "notch" of the collar any shape or size you like.

16. Slash the top section twice, from the outer edge, and spread so that the slashed edge measures $1\frac{1}{4}$ inches longer than before (**a**). Then draw in the top collar (**b**). Finally, for a good line on the collar, draw from notch to collar point, making the curve slightly less than the same edge

on the rever (**c**).

17. Complete the drawing of the rever, very slightly curving the line—it looks better that way. Using the new lines make new front and collar patterns.

18. The under-collar and interlining are cut on the bias, and trimmed away as described in the last chapter, so that the seam will remain hidden. Cut top collar with center back on the straight grain.

19. Use the front pattern to cut a rever facing pattern. Extend it for $\frac{1}{16}$ inch as shown. This will give a good roll to the edge, with no seam showing.

Crafts/paper sculpture and paper craft

Many people have tried their hand at papercraft at some time or another, either as children, or later when they've attempted to make a paper flower, or perhaps tried to fold a paper napkin attractively for a party table. This chapter is about the art of folding and bending paper to produce three-dimensional effects.

The limitations imposed by using paper as a raw material are in a way an advantage, especially to the beginner. It is impossible to reproduce realistically in paper, so one is compelled to use imagination and originality and interpret what is seen in stylized form.

Once a few simple rules and techniques have been mastered, there is no limit to the wonderful objects and designs that can be made—table decorations, lampshades, masks, standing figures, animals, pictures in frames, fancy dresses, wall plaques, hanging mobiles—even stage scenery. Paper is surprisingly robust when treated correctly, and creations made from it last as long as they are needed.

Materials and tools

Paper. There are dozens of different types of paper, and it's important to choose one that is right for the work in hand. For a large relief, thin mounting cardboard is used, and for a small, light piece of work a good quality thick cartridge

▲ A sturdy London policeman, made in paper for a magazine promotion

▲ Penguin in paper sculpture designed for a paper company promotion

paper is best. Anything thinner than this is unsuitable because the paper will not stand up under its own weight, nor will it bend or fold properly. Above all, paper must be of good quality, strong enough to stand well, and sufficiently pliable to bend easily.

Foil-covered and surfaced papers, colored papers and those colored on one side only can be very effective for paper craft, although scoring is likely to expose the white backing on the latter. If only white paper is obtainable, and a colored effect is required, spray-paint the paper before starting or paint the sculpture when it is completed. Never mix white papers in one piece of work unless a contrast is required. There are several different shades of white and one will clearly show against another.

Scissors. These should be sharp. It is best to have two pairs, a large pair for cutting big areas, and a small, pointed pair for delicate, detailed work.

Knife. For a cleaner cut, many people

use a blade in preference to scissors, but it is a matter of personal choice. If a blade is used, it must be sharp, and because pressure will be exerted on it, a guard of some kind is essential. A stencil knife is ideal. A scalpel blade is also recommended—obtainable with a special holder, or a proper cutting tool with changeable blades. These are all available at craft shops. Razor blades are not recommended because they break under pressure.

Scoring tool. Scoring is an important part of paper sculpture and tools are obtainable from art and craft shops. A suitable scoring tool can be made by fixing a blunt darning needle into a pen holder, or even by tying one to a pencil.

Adhesives. A clear cellulose acetate glue is best for sticking paper. Rubber cement can be used and is easily removed by rubbing off when dry.

Paper can also be stuck together with double-sided tape, which is less messy than glue, and can also be used to reinforce

delicate areas.

Ruler. A metal ruler or one with a metal edge on one side is necessary to cut against. Wooden or plastic rulers without a metal edge should not be used for cutting, because there is a danger with these that the knife will skid onto the ruler and cut the fingers.

Set square. For true right angles.

Compasses. For drawing circles.

Pencils. An HB pencil is probably the best to use. Anything softer will smudge and wear down quickly, and anything harder will make a line that is too faint to see. Keep pencils well sharpened.

Cutting board. Either use a piece of hardboard or an old pastry board but do not use boards with a noticeable grain. Cover the cutting board with thick paper and cut out on this, replacing the paper when necessary.

Handling paper and glue

Cutting. When cutting paper into a shape, first mark the line to be cut in pencil. Then cut against the metal edge of the ruler, cutting evenly and gently three or four times along the marked line until unwanted paper falls away, rather than trying to exert heavy pressure on the knife, and doing it all at one time.

Scoring. Scoring is an important part of paper work, enabling thick pieces of cardboard and paper to be folded without breaking or wrinkling. Scoring is simply cutting halfway through the paper. Mark the line to be cut in pencil, place the ruler against it as for cutting, then cut without exerting very much pressure. With scoring and folding, sharp, clear-cut effects of light and shade can be obtained.

Curling. Sometimes a design may call for a piece of paper to bend gracefully and this means curling the paper. If you are right-handed, hold the paper to be curled in the left hand, and a ruler or a scissor blade in the right hand. Place the implement under the edge of the piece of paper, securing it by placing the thumb of the right hand on top of it. Still holding the paper firmly on the ruler with your thumb, draw the ruler away and toward the edge of the paper. It will curl away from the thumb and down over the ruler or blade (see illustration). Curling gives soft, gentle effects of light and shade.

Applying adhesives

Keep paper, hands and tools scrupulously clean while working and try not to get adhesives on the fingers. Keep adhesives capped when not actually in use and use a spreader wherever possible. A narrow strip of cardboard, cut into four inch lengths, makes effective spreaders for small areas, and a toothpick is also useful for applying dots of adhesives.

An important rule to remember—don't swamp the work with glue; it doesn't necessarily result in a better bond. Two sparingly gummed surfaces left to partially dry will fix quite firmly.

Simple projects

Try the following folds and cuts and observe the shapes and effects which result. Make some basic forms, boxes, hexagons and cones and vary the surfaces with fan pleats. Concave pleats are made by scoring the paper on the surface and convex pleats by scoring on the underside. For rounded shapes, give the paper a cylindrical bias by drawing the paper under a ruler before starting to fold and score.

Try each fold and cut and see what effects are achieved. The diagram extreme right bottom illustrates the method for curling paper.

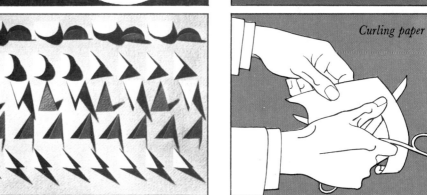

Curling paper

Shadow folds

Score diagonal lines on one side of the paper, reversing it to press in sharp creases. Scoring and creasing are indicated by a solid line for the right side of the paper and a dotted line for the back of the paper. Curvy or wavy folds are made by scoring a reversed curved line followed by a parallel curved line, scoring on alternate sides of the paper.

Different patterns can be made by varying the depth or shape of the folds (figure **1**).

Cut surface designs

Cutting into paper at regular intervals gives a design of light and shadow, useful for indicating fish scales, feathers, leaves, etc.

Another useful effect can be created by raising the cuts and placing darker or colored paper underneath the design. Patterns can be drawn geometrically, but for texture designs such as feather effects they are best cut freely (figure **5**).

Cone formation

To make a cone, draw a circle and cut out. Remove a segment and join the edges together. The circle in the diagram has three inner circles, two drawn on one side

(solid line) and one on the reverse side (dotted line). Score these circles and cut out a quarter segment. Bend the scoring on both sides, mold into a cone and secure (figure **3**).

Curves

For curves, first draw an "S" formation and cut out. Score with a knife down the center, following the shape, and mold

by bending the scoring to the "S" shape. This multi-scoring and molding strengthens the paper, and these curved pieces can be made into many beautiful and different forms (figure **4**).

Stylized flower

Draw a flower shape from the diagram, cut out and draw a circle on one side of the paper (shown as a solid line). Turn

the shape over and draw a circle slightly larger than the first (shown as a dotted line). Score both circles, one on each side of the paper, and cut between two petals from the outside edge to the center of flower. Pull A over B, covering one whole petal and glue. Crease the center scoring to make a deep cone. Small flowers are made with only one circle scored in the center (figure **2**).

Knitting design/working up, down and across

The previous Knitting Design chapters have shown you how to chart your own measurements and plan your own designs for pullovers, skirts and dresses. The U-necked pullover shown is worked on the basic pattern for a sleeveless top, and is knitted in a three color Fair Isle stitch. A chart is given to help you plan the pattern. Work out other patterns of your own.

So far, all the garments in these chapters have been designed to be worked upward, from a hem or lower edge. Although this is the most usual approach to knitting, there are good reasons for considering other approaches when designing garments.

Knitting from the top downward
Knitting downward has certain advantages. Skirts worked in this way are more easily lengthened or shortened because the bound-off edge is on the hem and it is an easy matter to unravel the bound-off edge to knit on an extra piece, or unravel back to a shorter length. In flared skirts particularly this method of lengthening works well. It is more satisfactory to add from the hem, continuing to increase until the new length is achieved, than to add to the waist with the risk of altering the measurements.

Sweaters, particularly childrens' pullovers, benefit from being knitted from the top downward. On a child's garment, the wear occurs first through stretching and breaking of the waist and cuff edges and, of course, the sleeves and body length become too short as the child grows.

In both cases, if the garment has been knitted downward, the worn edges can be replaced easily with new knitting and the length increased as required.

There is an advantage too when working raglan sleeved garments. The shaping of the raglan is formed by increasing instead of decreasing and it can be made to look almost invisible by working downward from the top. It is a simple matter also to make open work increases, which sometimes look very attractive in a design.

Knitting from side to side
A completely different look can result from side to side knitting worked in simple stitches, and it is often easier to work in colors. For instance, a few rows of a second color alternative with the main color is all that is required to produce vertical stripes, difficult to obtain working either upward or downward. Skirts, flared or straight, can be most successful knitted from side to side. A skirt can be flared by adding extra rows, turning before the row is complete, repeating with

1626

fewer stitches in each row to the required skirt length, and then working back again until the row consists of all the stitches, much as you would do in working a bust dart. The edge with the extra rows is the flared hem edge. This technique is charted in the same way as for darts in the last chapter. Dresses are too awkward to knit sideways in one piece, but it is possible to make skirt and bodice separately, seaming the pieces on completion. When knitting side-to-side pullovers or cardigans, it is far more satisfactory to work the fabric for the body first, omitting the edges. When the sections are complete the stitches are picked up along the edges and the edgings worked downward for the required depth.

Designing seamless knitting
Seamless knitting is a little more difficult to design but it can present the designer with great pattern possibilities. For jackets and coats with center front openings the number of seams can be reduced by working the main section from one front edge, around across the back to the other front edge, with shoulders seamed afterward and sleeves set into armholes. A jacket can be worked without seams, other than shoulder seams, in two ways. It can be charted from the bottom upward, working across the entire width of front and back and dividing for the armholes. Alternatively, it can be worked across the width of the garment beginning at one center front edge and working across back and front, working all the necessary shaping for back and armholes at one side of the work. The other edge is kept straight for the lower edge of the garment. When working in this way it must be remembered that in calculating, the number of stitches gives the length instead of the width, and the number of rows to one inch gives the width and not the length.

Alternatively, a garment may be entirely seamless with sleeves worked circularly and joined at underarm with a circular yoke or raglan shaping. Because of the opening, the sleeves are circular with the entire main section of the jacket worked in rows, although the finished result would be seamless.

Without openings of any sort the garment becomes completely circular in working although each part, whether sleeve, skirt or bodice, retains all the necessary shaping. Circular knitting does not mean that the finished garment will be tubular and shapeless.

Designing diagonally
There are two methods of working diagonally.

Method 1. Where rows are planned diagonally across the work, charting can be complicated because of the amount of shaping which is necessary. This is one instance where it is easier to make a paper shape exactly as you require the finished section to be. After calculating gauge and the number of stitches required at various points, knit the garment shaping as required, measuring constantly against the paper shape.

Method 2. A bias or slope can be given to a panel by increasing at one side and decreasing at the other, thus drawing it across to one side of the work. Again this creates an effect which can be achieved in no other way. It gives a sideways slope to a cable, Fair Isle or patterned panel. This is not easy to chart and again is more successfully worked using a diagram.

Charting patterns
Before attempting to chart in different directions for patterns, experiment with charting where the stitches themselves make the pattern, such as in cable or Aran patterns and in Fair Isle or Norwegian designs where more than one color is being used to build up a pattern.

The pullover illustrated has a simple Fair Isle pattern worked across the entire width of the garment in stripes. A knitter may want to chart only one pattern repeat or she may prefer to chart the position of the entire pattern to arrive at the best placing of pattern across neck and armholes.

Planning color patterns
Decide first how many colors are to be used in a pattern and decide upon a symbol to represent each color. For the pullover illustrated, you might decide to leave a square blank for the background color, X might represent yellow, and O represent brown. If a lot of colors are being used decide upon symbols as different from each other as possible and mark them clearly on the chart. Different colored pencils can be used if preferred.

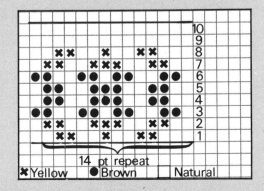

Knitting pattern/sleeveless dress and jacket

This outfit has the simple elegance of uncluttered lines in a smooth stockinette stitch.

Sizes

Directions are for 34in bust. The figures in brackets [] refer to the 36 and 38in sizes respectively.
Dress. Length, 35[36:37]in.
Jacket. Length, 25½[26:26½]in. Sleeve seam, 16in.

Gauge

7 sts and 9 rows to 1in over st st worked on No.4 needles.

Materials

Unger English Crepe
Dress. 15[16:17] balls
Jacket. 13[14:15] balls
One pair No.2 needles
One pair No.4 needles
5in zipper

Jacket back

Using No.2 needles, cast on 125[133:141] sts and work in st st for 1½in, ending with a P row.
Next row K1, *ytf, K2 tog, rep from * to end.
Next row P.
Change to No.4 needles and continue in st st until work measures 18in from hemline (eyelet row) and ending with a P row.

Shape armholes

Bind off 7 sts at beg of next 2 rows, then 2 sts at beg of next 2 rows.
K2 tog at each end of every other row 5[6:7] times. 97[103:109] sts.
Continue without shaping until armholes measure 7½[8: 8½]in, ending with a P row.

Shape shoulders

Bind of 6 sts at beg of next 8 rows, then 5[6:7] sts at beg of next row.
Next row Bind off 5[6:7] sts, K to end.
Change to No.2 needles.
Beg with a K row, continue in st st for 1¼in. Bind off.
1628

Jacket left front

Using No.2 needles, cast on 63[67:71] sts and work in st st for 1½in, ending with a P row.
Next row K1, *ytf, K2 tog, rep from * to end, turn, cast on 8 sts.
Next row P.
Change to No.4 needles.
Next row K to last 9 sts, sl 1, K8.
Next row P.
Rep last 2 rows until work measures 16in from hemline, ending with a P row.

Shape front edge

Next row K to last 19 sts, K2 tog, K8, sl 1, K8.
Continue dec in this way on every 4th row until work measures same as Back to armholes, ending with a P row.

Shape armhole

Continue dec on front edge on every 4th row as before *at the same time* bind off 7 sts at beg of next row, then 2 sts at beg of following row at arm edge. K2 tog at armhole edge every other row 6[7:8] times, then continue to dec at front edge only on every 4th row until 37[38:39] sts rem.
Continue without shaping until armhole measures the same as on Back, ending with a P row.

Shape shoulder

Bind off 6 sts at armhole edge every other row 4 times.
P 1 row. Bind of rem 13[14:15] sts.

Jacket right front

Work as for left Front, reversing all shaping.

Sleeves

Using No.2 needles, cast on 51[55:59] sts and work in st st for 1½in, ending with a P row.
Next row K1, *ytf, K2 tog, rep from * to end.
Next row P.
Change to No.4 needles and continue in st st.
Inc one st at each end of 17th and every following 8th row until there are 81[85:89] sts. Continue without shaping until sleeve seam measures 16in from hemline, ending with a P row.

Shape cap

Bind off 7 sts at beg of next 2 rows.
K2 tog at both ends of every other row until 39[41:43] sts rem, ending with a P row.
Bind off 2 sts at beg of next 8[10:10] rows, then 3 sts at beg of next 4 rows. Bind off rem 11[9:11] sts.

Pockets

Using No.4 needles, cast on 33 sts.
Work 4 rows in st st beg with a K row.
Work in patt as follows:
1st row K15, K2 tog, ytf, K16.
2nd and every other row P.
3rd row K14, K2 tog, ytf, K1, ytf, sl 1, K1, psso, K14.
5th row K13, K2 tog, ytf, K3, ytf, sl 1, K1, psso, K13.
7th row K12, K2 tog, ytf, K5, ytf, sl 1, K1, psso, K12.
9th row K11, K2 tog, ytf, K2, K2 tog, ytf, K1, ytf, sl 1, K1, psso, K2, ytf, sl 1, K1, psso, K10.
11th row K10, K2 tog, ytf, K2, K2 tog, ytf, K1, ytf, sl 1, K1, psso, K2, ytf, sl 1, K1, psso, K9.
13th row K9, K2 tog, ytf, K2, K2 tog, ytf, K3, ytf, sl 1, K1, psso, K2, ytf, sl 1, K1, psso, K9.
15th row K8, K2 tog, ytf, K2, K2 tog, ytf, K5, ytf, sl 1, K1, psso, K2, ytf, sl 1, K1, psso, K8.
17th row K7, (K2 tog, ytf, K2) twice, K2 tog, ytf, K3, ytf, sl 1, K1, psso, K2, ytf, sl 1, K1, psso, K7.
19th row K6, (K2 tog, ytf, K2) twice, K2 tog, ytf, K1, (ytf, sl 1, K1, psso, K2) twice, ytf, sl 1, K1, psso, K6.
21st row K5 (K2 tog, ytf, K2) twice, K2 tog, ytf, K3, (ytf, sl 1, K1, psso, K2) 3 times, K3.
23rd row K4, (K2 tog, ytf, K2) twice, K2 tog, ytf, K5, (ytf, sl 1, K1, psso, K2) 3 times, K2.

25th row K6, (ytf, sl 1, K1, psso, K2) twice, ytf, sl 1, K1, psso, K1, (K2 tog, ytf, K2) 3 times, K4.
27th row K7, (ytf, sl 1, K1, psso, K2) twice, ytf, sl 1, K2 tog, psso, ytf, K2, K2 tog, ytf, K2, K2 tog, ytf, K7.
29th row K8, (ytf, sl 1, K1, psso, K2) twice, ytf, sl 1, K1, psso, K1, (K2 tog, ytf, K2) twice, K6.
31st row K9, ytf, sl 1, K1, psso, K2, ytf, sl 1, K1, psso, K3, (K2 tog, ytf, K2) twice, K7.
33rd row K10, ytf, sl 1, K1, psso, K2, ytf, sl 1, K1, psso, K1, (K2 tog, ytf, K2) twice, K8.
35th row K11, ytf, sl 1, K1, psso, K2, ytf, sl 1, K2 tog, psso, ytf, K2, K2 tog, ytf, K11.
37th row K12, ytf, sl 1, K1, psso, K2, ytf, sl 1, K1, psso, K1, K2 tog, ytf, K12.
39th row K13, ytf, sl 1, K1, psso, K3, K2 tog, ytf, K13.
41st row K14, ytf, sl 1, K1, psso, K1, K2 tog, ytf, K14.
43rd row K15, ytf, sl 1, K2 tog, psso, ytf, K15.
45th row K16, ytf, sl 1, K1, psso, K15.
46th row P.
Work 4 more rows st st.
Next row K1, *ytf, K2 tog, rep from * to end.
Change to No.2 needles and beg with a P row, continue in st st for ¾in.
Bind off.

Dress back

Using No.2 needles, cast on 151[159:167] sts.
Work in st st for 1½in, ending with a P row.
Next row K1, *ytf, K2 tog, rep from * to end.
Next row P.
Change to No.4 needles.
Continue in st st for 6½[7:7½]in, ending with a P row.
Next row K12[13:14], sl 1, K1, psso, K28[30:32], sl 1, K1, psso, K63[65:67], K2 tog, K28[30:32], K2 tog, K12[13:14].
Work 15 rows.

Next row K12[13:14], sl 1, K1, psso, K27[29:31], sl 1, K1, psso, K61[63:65], K2 tog, K27[29:31], K2 tog, K12 [13:14].
Continue dec in this way on every 16th row until 127[135: 143] sts rem, then on every 8th row until 119[127:135] sts rem.
Continue without shaping until work measures 28[28½: 29]in from hemline, ending with a P row.

Shape armholes

Bind off 7 sts at beg of next 2 rows, then 2 sts at beg of next 4 rows.
K2 tog at both ends of every other row 8[9:10] times. 81[87:93] sts.
Continue without shaping until armhole measures 3[3½:4] in, ending with a K row.
Next row P38[41:44], K2, K2 tog, K1, P to end.
Next row K40[43:46]. Turn. Slip rem sts on holder.
Next row K2, P to end.
Keeping 2 sts at inside edge in garter st, continue without shaping until armhole measures 7[7½:8]in, ending with a WS row.

Shape shoulder

Bind off 6 sts at arm edge every other row 3 times.
Bind off 6[7:8] sts at beg of following row at arm edge.
Slip rem 16[18:20] sts on holder.
With RS facing, attach yarn to first set of sts put on holder and K to end.
Next row P to last 2 sts, K2.
Continue to correspond to first side.

Dress front

Work as given for Back until work measures 26[26½:27]in from hemline, ending with a P row.
Next row K58[62:66], K2 tog, ytf, K59[63:67].
Next row P.
Next row K57[61:65], K2 tog, ytf, K1, ytf, sl 1, K1, psso, K57[61:65].
Continue to work center sts in patt as on Pocket until work measures the same as Back to

armholes, ending with a P row.

Shape armholes

Keeping center sts in patt correct, shape armholes as on Back.
Continue without shaping until the 46 rows of diamond patt have been completed.
Continue without shaping until armholes measure 5[5½:6]in. End with a P row.

Shape neck

Next row K29[31:33]. Turn. Slip rem sts on holder.
Bind off 2 sts at beg of next row.
Dec one st at neck edge on every other row until 24[25:26] sts rem.
Continue without shaping until armhole measures the same as on Back, ending with a P row.

Shape shoulder

Bind off 6 sts at arm edge every other row 3 times.
P 1 row. Bind off rem 6[7:8] sts.
With RS facing, slip first 23[25:27] sts on holder for neck, attach yarn and K to end.
Complete to correspond to first side.

Neckband

Join shoulder seams.
Using No.2 needles, K sts of left back neck, pick up and K20 [21:22] sts down side of front neck, K front neck sts, pick up and K20[21:22] sts up other side of front neck, K sts of right back neck.
Keeping 2 sts at each end garter st, continue in st st for ¾in, ending with a WS row.
Next row K3, *ytf, K2 tog, rep from * to last 2 sts, K2.
Continue in st st for ¾in more. Bind off.

Armhole borders

Using No.2 needles and with RS facing, pick up and K107 [115:123] sts around armhole.
Continue in st st for ¾in, ending with a P row.
Work row of eyelets, as before, then continue in st st for ¾in more. Bind off.

▲ *A pretty dress and jacket for day wear* ▼ *Detail of the motif*

Finishing

Press work under a damp cloth and using a warm iron.
Jacket. Join shoulder seams. Join side and sleeve seams and sew in sleeves. Turn up hems and slip stitch in place.

Turn in front facing and back neck facing and slip stitch in place. Turn in hems at top of pockets and slip stitch in place. Sew on pockets. Press all seams.
Dress. Join side seams. Turn in hems and slip stitch in place. Sew in zipper. Press all seams.

Stitchery design/pile stitches

The technique of carpet knotting originated in the East.

Canvas and yarn

Work stitches on double mesh canvas with 4 holes to 1 inch. Use 2-ply carpet thrums, 4 strands in needle for pile and 3 strands for rows of flat stitching.

Method of working

Separate each row of Surrey stitch with rows of deep long-legged cross-stitch.
Work three rows of deep long-legged cross-stitch for a 2 inch pile and four rows for a 2½ inch pile. To avoid pulling the canvas out of shape work the rows of deep long-legged cross-stitch in opposite directions. Work long-legged cross-stitch over 4 holes of the canvas at each end of every pile row to prevent the pile of the rug from hanging over the edge. When the first pile row is worked, the cut pile should just reach the edge of the rug. Work one row of long-legged cross-stitch after the final pile row is completed.

Surrey stitch

Work this stitch in rows from left to right and pull each stitch tightly to form a knot. To change color, cut end of yarn to same length as previous stitch and work next stitch in the new color. When each row is completed, cut the loops, making sure that the ends are of equal length.

Turkey or Ghiordes knot stitch

This stitch is worked in rows from left to right and forms a pile similar to that of Surrey stitch.

Method of working a pile rug

Work plait stitch edging on a pile rug before working the main part. A single row of long-legged cross-stitch is usually worked between the pile and the edge stitch.
A pile rug is commenced at the bottom left-hand corner and stitched in rows across the canvas from selvage to selvage, working away from the worker. As the stitched area of the rug grows, roll it up out of the way.

Yarn quantities for pile rugs

Use 2-ply carpet thrums double on 5 holes to the inch canvas; use Rya yarn double on 7 holes to the inch canvas and use Rya yarn wool single on 10 holes to the inch canvas.
Rya type rugs require 10-12 ounces per square foot.
The pile rugs use the same quantities as given for flat stitch rugs in the previous chapter.

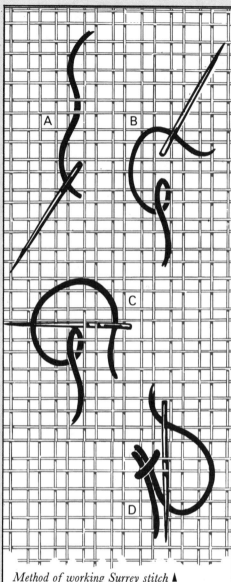

Method of working Surrey stitch ▲
Method of working Turkey knot stitch ▼

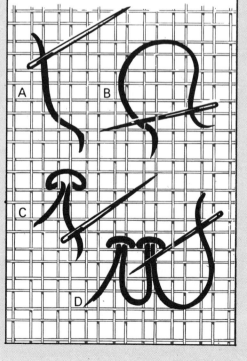

Detail of a needle-made Rya rug ▲
Long-legged stitch separating pile stitches ▼

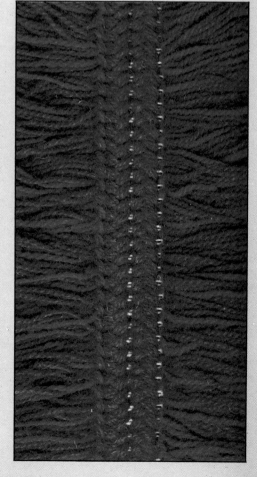

◀ *Modern interpretation of a Persian rug*   *Detail of the rug* ▼   ▼ *The back view of the rug*

Stitchery pattern/flowered bedspread

To make the bedspread measuring about 80 inches by 100 inches you will need:

☐ 4½ yards 54 inch wide heavy woolen fabric, or a ready-made bedspread
☐ Pieces of light weight woolen fabric in the following colors and amounts: ½ yard dark pink, ⅝ yard pink, 1½ yards green, 2 yards dark green
☐ Sewing thread
☐ Crewel needle No.8

To make the bedspread

Cut the 4½ yard length of fabric in half, making two 2¼ yard lengths. Cut one of these lengths in half along the crease line of the fabric. With a flat-fell seam join a narrow panel to either side of the wide panel.
Press well.

To decorate

Spread the bedspread out flat. Make a template and cut out flowers and leaves from the colored fabrics. Arrange them on the bedspread and pin them down. Baste in place and link the flowers and leaves with curving stems cut from scraps of fabric. Alternatively, stems could be embroidered if desired.
Using a zigzag stitch on the machine, stitch around the shapes. If preferred, the shapes can be cut with narrow turnings, the raw edges turned and basted to the wrong side. Then apply to the background with a slip stitch or fine hemming stitches. Finish the edges with a 1 inch deep bias-cut border in the dark green fabric.

Alternative techniques

The simple flower and leaf shapes could also be worked in machine embroidery for a different effect.
Crewel wool embroidery would be effective too, using long and short stitches and French knots. For a combination of appliqué and surface embroidery techniques, work the flowers in chain stitch, working large stitches around and around to the center of the petals. The stems could be made of flat braid applied to the surface.

Same size template shapes for the flower and leaves

Crochet pattern/five bright pillows

These five crochet pillow covers are bright and gay enough to bring sparkle to any room. They are made with a simple background and four of them have modern appliquéd flower motifs.

Sizes
Round pillow. 19in diameter.
Rectangular pillow. 19in by 24in.

Gauge
4dc to 1in on No.G hook.

Materials
Columbia-Minerva
Nantuk Sports Yarn
Round pillow with tassel.
2 skeins orange, A
Round pillow with flower.
1 skein orange, A
2 skeins white, B

1634

1 skein brown, C
White rectangular pillow.
5 skeins white, B
1 skein terracotta, D
Terracotta rectangular pillow.
1 skein orange, A
1 skein white, B
5 skeins terracotta, D
Orange rectangular pillow. 4 skeins orange, A
1 skein white, B
1 skein brown, C
For all pillows. One No.G crochet hook (except Round pillow with tassel) One No.D crochet hook Pillow forms to measurements (lined)

Round pillow with tassel

Using No.D hook and A, ch8. Join with a ss into ring.

1st round Ch2 to count as first dc, 21dc into ring, ss into 2nd ch.
2nd round Ch4 to count as first tr, 1tr into same st, 2tr into each st to end, ss into 4th ch.
3rd round Ch4 to count as first tr, 1tr into each st, ending with ss into 4th ch.
4th round Ch5 to count as first tr and 1ch, *1tr into next st, ch1, rep from * to end, ss into 4th of 5ch.
5th round Ch6, *1tr into next st, ch2, rep from * to end, ss into 4th of 6ch.
6th round Ch7, *1tr into next st, ch3, rep from * to end, ss into 4th of 7ch.
7th round As 6th.
8th round Ch8, *1tr into next st, ch4, rep from * to end, ss into 4th of 8ch.
Continue in this way, working one more ch between darts on

every other round until work measures 19in in diameter. Fasten off.
Make a second piece in the same manner.
Press work under a damp cloth, using a warm iron.
Join the two pieces leaving an opening for pillow form.
Make 2 tassels and sew one to center of each side.

Round Pillow with flower

Using No.D hook and B, make 2 pieces as for Round pillow with tassel.
Press work and join the pieces.

Flower center
Using No.G hook and C, ch4 and join with a ss into ring.
1st round Ch1, 5sc into ring, ss into first ch.

hook, 1dc into each ch to end. 84 sts.

2nd row Ch2 to count as first dc, 1dc into each st to end. Rep the 2nd row until work measures 38in. Fasten off. Press work under a damp cloth, using a warm iron. Fold in half and join sides leaving an opening for form.

Flower center
Using No.G hook and B, ch4 and join with a ss into ring.
1st-3rd rounds As 1st and 2nd rounds on Flower center of Round pillow with flower, break off B, attach D and work 3rd round. Fasten off.

Petals
Using No.G hook and B, ch5.
1st round 1sc into 2nd ch from hook, 1sc into next ch, 3sc into last ch, turn and work along other side working 3sc, then 2sc into last st.
2nd round Ch1, 2sc into next st, 3sc, 3sc into next st, 3sc, 2sc into next st, 1sc. Break off B, attach D.
Continue in this way, working 2sc into first st and second-last st and 3sc into center st at other end for 2 rounds. Fasten off.
Make 6 petals in all. Sew the petals to the Flower center. Make 7 more flowers in the same way, then sew to front of pillow placing 3 along top, 3 along bottom and 2 in center as illustrated.

Terracotta rectangular pillow

Using No.G hook and D, make pillow as for White rectangular pillow.

Flower center
Using No.G hook and D, ch4 and join with a ss into ring.
Work as for Flower center on Round pillow with flower working 2 rounds D, 2 rounds A, one round B. Fasten off.

Petals
Using No.G hook and D, ch9.

Work as for Petals of Round pillow with flower, working 2 rounds D, 2 rounds A, 2 rounds B.
Fasten off.
Sew the 6 petals around the center. Make 3 more flowers and sew to pillow as illustrated.

Orange rectangular pillow

Using No.G hook and A, ch85.
1st row 1dc into 3rd ch from hook, 1dc into each ch to end. 83 sts.
2nd row Ch2 to count as first dc, 1dc into each of next 2 sts, *ch1, skip 1dc, 1dc into next dc, rep from * to last 2 sts, 1dc into next dc, 1dc into turning ch.
Rep the 2nd row until work measures 38in.
Next row Ch2 to count as first dc, 1dc into each of next 2 dc, *1dc into ch sp, 1dc into next dc, rep from * to last 2 sts, 1dc into next dc, 1dc into turning ch. Fasten off.
Press work under a damp cloth, using a warm iron. Fold in half and join sides, leaving an opening for form.

Larger flower center
Work as for Flower center on Terracotta rectangular pillow working 2 rounds A, 2 rounds C, 1 round B.

Larger flower petals
Work as for Petals on Terracotta rectangular pillow, working 2 rounds A, 2 rounds C, 2 rounds B.

Smaller flower center
Work as for Flowers on White rectangular pillow, working 2 rounds C, 1 round B.

Smaller flower petals
Work as for Petals on White rectangular pillow, working 3 petals with 2 rounds C, 2 rounds B, and 3 petals with 2 rounds A, 2 rounds B.
Make 4 flowers in all, sewing Petals to Centers and then positioning on pillow as illustrated.
Press.

2nd round Ch1, 1sc into first st, 2sc into every st to end sc, ss into 1ch.
3rd round Ch1, 2sc into next st, *1sc into next st, 2sc into next st, rep from * to end, ss into 1ch. Break off C, attach B.
4th round Ch1, 1sc into next st, 2sc into next st, *1sc into each of next 2 sts, 2sc into next st, rep from * to end, ss into 1ch.
5th round Ch1, 1sc into each of next 2 sts, 2sc into next st, * 1sc into each of next 3 sts, 2sc into next st, rep from * to end, ss into first ch.
Continue in this way, working 8 more sc in every round and working one more round B, 4 rounds A. Fasten off.

Petals
Using No.G hook and C, ch9.
1st round 1sc into 2nd ch

from hook, 1sc into each of next 5ch, 3sc into next st, continue along other side of ch working 1sc into each of 6 sts, then 2sc into last st.
2nd round Ch1, 2sc into first st, 1sc into each of 7sc, 3sc into next st, 7sc, 2sc into next st, 1sc.
3rd round Ch1, 2sc into next st, 9sc, 3sc into next st, 9sc, 2sc into next st, 1sc.
Continue in this way, working 3 rounds B, 4 rounds A.
Fasten off.
Make 6 petals in all.
Sew the petals around the flower center. Attach flower to pillow. Press.

White rectangular pillow

Using No.G hook and B, ch86.
1st row 1dc into 3rd ch from

Tailoring one/introduction

Tailoring is not difficult but you must work patiently—with a little care the rewards are great. You might find it easier to make a successful and professional looking coat than a dress, and will be surprised at how few people guess you have made it yourself. In addition you can save a great deal of money and you will have a garment uniquely yours.

A tailored garment should have a fresh look, appearing as though little work and even less handling has been done. This is achieved by means of accuracy, attention to detail, basting, pressing, molding and fine hand stitching.

How to use the tailoring chapters

At the end of these chapters you will be able to attempt any coat pattern you wish. Each chapter takes you a step further in the construction of a coat, dealing with various alternatives rather than a separate complete coat in each chapter. For instance, in this chapter the coat is cut out, in the next it is fitted, and when it comes to making the collar stage the different types are covered in turn. So, choose your coat pattern and follow the relevant instructions in each chapter. The beginning of each chapter outlines the contents and the main sections are marked as A, B, C . . . etc. An asterisk * in the text refers to the "Terms and stitches" used, at the end of each chapter. Numbers in bold refer you to the appropriate diagram.

In this chapter

A. What you need for tailoring: coat fabrics; fabric designs; linings; interlinings; interfacings; padding; pattern and notions; general equipment.

B. Pressing equipment

C. Cutting out: preparing the fabric; cutting out; marking fabric; interlining.

D. Interfacing: cutting out; darts and seams.

*Terms and stitches

A. What you need for tailoring

Coat fabrics

The fabric you choose for making a coat should be as good a quality as possible and not too heavy in weight. The weave should be close and firm, as the looser weaves tend to fray, causing difficulties during construction.

☐ An ideal fabric is a 100% wool cloth made from short wool fibers which are processed to lie over each other in all directions. This produces a soft dense

cloth with a slightly rough look as found in tweeds and flannels.

☐ Equally good is a 100% wool worsted cloth made from long wool fibers which are processed to lie parallel to each other, producing a smooth fabric, usually with a well defined weave as found in suitings, serge and gabardine.

☐ These two are often combined to make some very attractive fabrics.

☐ It is best to avoid those fabrics with a large proportion of man-made fibers as they do not always respond well to the techniques of pressing.

Fabric designs

There are many designs to choose from—herringbone, small checks, self-colored, tweeds etc. It is wise to avoid large patterns and checks as these cause matching problems and some wastage of fabric.

Linings

The lining you choose should complement the coat fabric in weight. So it is safer to buy both at once.

☐ Satin: a smooth, soft and shiny lining. Avoid a cheap one as it doesn't wear well. Good for all weights of cloth.

☐ Japanese silk: a thin and soft lining, good for lightweight cloth, but expensive.

☐ Satin backed crêpe: a satin with a crepe finish. A suitable heavy-weight lining for tweeds.

☐ Milium: a satin weave backed with aluminum for warmth. Useful in winter coats.

Interlinings

An interlining is used to give body to a light fabric or a loose weave, and to prevent creasing. It is basted to the back of the main fabric, and interlining and fabric are then made as one.

☐ Mull: a light, woven cotton.

☐ Organdy: an extremely light cotton with a very close weave. Avoid nylon organdy.

☐ Silesia: a heavier weight organdy.

Interfacings

An interfacing gives body to, and helps retain the shape of, a garment. It is placed between the fabric and the lining. There are two groups of fabric used for interfacing.

☐ Mixed fiber hair canvases: used for all fabrics and containing the following mixtures.

Wool and hair: very springy and non-crease, the best of all canvases for keeping shapes molded into it.

Cotton and hair: slightly springy, but can crease.

☐ Single fiber interfacings.

Pure wool: very springy and soft, useful for

the lightweight tweeds.

Linen canvas (or shrunk duck): a soft canvas that will maintain a crease. Used with very light cloths and as a backing for pockets.

French (or collar) canvas: made with warp and weft * threads of equal weight to give firm control to the under-collar.

Padding

☐ Tailor's wadding: used for making shoulder pads and padding sleeve caps.

☐ Felt or loosely woven, lightweight filler: these are used for light padding at chest or back to give shaping without weight.

Patterns and notions

Paper patterns: When choosing a style, look for one which has clean, uncluttered lines. The pattern should be fashionable but not so extreme as to be unwearable in six month's time.

As it is not too easy to mold the end of a wide bust dart, choose a pattern with a seam over the bust or one with side front seams and a small bust dart.

Buy your usual size pattern as any extra ease needed will have been allowed for by the designer already.

Stay tape: $\frac{1}{2}$ inch wide linen tape for holding the front seams of coats.

Threads: a variety are used in tailoring.

☐ Silk: used for all hand stitching.

☐ Mercerized cotton: for all machine stitching. Use a 50 for light to medium weight fabrics and 40 for heavy weight fabric.

☐ White and colored basting threads: for tailor's tacks and basting.

☐ Silk buttonhole twist: for handworked buttonholes.

☐ Gimp: for buttonholes (if unavailable, two thicknesses of buttonhole twist can be substituted).

Buttons: The choice is very wide, but be sure to choose ones which will suit the coat style: plain for a country tweed, self fabric for a town coat, leather for a car coat, silver or gilt for a blazer.

Good notions stores will make buttons from your fabric, and if you wish, will incorporate leather, silver or gilt for an

Here, and on page 1638, are a few styles from the wide range of coat patterns available. They have been chosen to represent different style details. Right: A Vogue pattern, made in blue and white tweed, shows a simple coat with step collar. Far right. Top (and cover): From Butterick, a red gabardine coat with a belt across the back and an inverted back pleat. Middle: Vogue 2573 in tweed. Bottom: Butterick coat in checked angora; jacket, Butterick 6528. Page 1638. From left to right: Vogue 2671, Vogue 2222, Butterick 6462, Butterick 6462.

1637

individual touch.

General equipment

☐ Sewing machine: keep oiled and clean,
Fit a new needle and adjust tension to
give 10 to 12 stitches per inch on the
material to be stitched. Always test
tension on a double scrap of the fabric
before stitching.

☐ Shears: very sharp to give a good line
when cutting out.

☐ Small pointed scissors: for snipping
and buttonholes, pockets etc.

☐ Stiletto: for shaping hand buttonholes
(**1**).

☐ Sewing needles: 7 to 8 Sharps for felling,
basting, catch stitching and hemming.
5 to 6 Betweens for pad stitching, side
stitching, basting, tailor's tacks.

☐ Pins: long steel dressmaker type.

☐ Tailor's chalk: for marking alterations.

1638

B. Pressing equipment

☐ Iron: a dry domestic iron, the heavier
the better.

☐ Ironing board.

☐ Cotton pressing cloth: used dry with
iron or wet where extra steam is needed.

☐ Wool cloth: a fine wool cloth is used to
prevent shine when top pressing.

☐ Tailor's ham: for pressing curved seams.
This can be simply made:

2a. Cut two ovals of muslin or close weave
cotton as shown. With right sides facing,
sew together leaving a 4 inch gap.

2b. Turn to the right side and stuff very
firmly with sawdust.

2c. Hem opening to close.

☐ Pressing roll: used for pressing seams
open without the turning being impressed
into the garment. Made as follows:

3a. Either cover a wooden rod with

blanket, sewing the edge with herringbone
stitch*.

3b. Or make a tight roll of blanket, again
sewing the edge with herringbone stitch*.

☐ Wooden clapper: for pressing away
steam and for making turnings wafer-thin
after steaming (**4**).

If you find a clapper hard to find an
old iron or back of a large flat wooden
clothes brush will do just as well.

C. Cutting out

Preparing the fabric

To prevent press marks which may occur
on woolen fabrics it is advisable to steam-
press the length before cutting out.

Unfold the fabric and lay it right side
down on a clean blanket, preferably on
the floor to avoid creasing.

Steam press all over, lifting the iron each

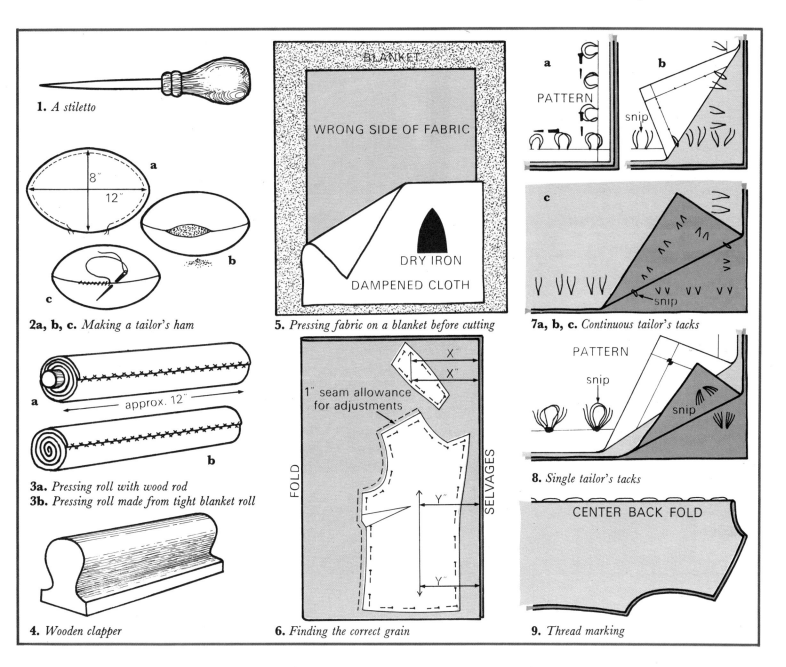

1. *A stiletto*

2a, b, c. *Making a tailor's ham*

3a. *Pressing roll with wood rod*
3b. *Pressing roll made from tight blanket roll*

4. *Wooden clapper*

BLANKET
WRONG SIDE OF FABRIC
DRY IRON
DAMPENED CLOTH

5. *Pressing fabric on a blanket before cutting*

1" seam allowance for adjustments
FOLD
SELVAGES

6. *Finding the correct grain*

PATTERN
snip

7a, b, c. *Continuous tailor's tacks*

PATTERN
snip
snip

8. *Single tailor's tacks*

CENTER BACK FOLD

9. *Thread marking*

time. Do not push the iron as this tends to distort the grain.
5. Cover the fabric with a thoroughly dampened cloth and press with an iron hot enough to hiss as it touches the cloth. Hang the cloth to dry.

Cutting out

Trim the paper pattern to the cutting line.
6. Following the instruction sheet layout place the pattern pieces on the fabric. To make sure the grain lines * are correct, measure out equal distances from the selvage to each end of the arrow on the pattern as shown. Smooth the paper and pin every 2 inches along the stitching line. Cut out carefully. It is wise to make seam allowances of 1 inch at shoulders, armholes and side seams to allow for alterations.

Marking the fabric

Transfer pattern markings to the fabric using tailor's tacks and thread markings. Chalk and tracing paper lines are not permanent enough for tailoring, as accuracy in following pattern lines is essential for a perfect fit.
Always work with pieces laid flat.
Use the following markings:
☐ Tailor's tacking—continuous: used for marking stitching lines.
7a. After cutting out and before removing the paper pattern, mark all stitching lines with continuous tailor's tacks. To do so, thread a needle with double thread and, on the stitching line, make stitches through both layers of fabric and the pattern, a loop being made at each stitch.
7b. To remove the pattern snip through the center of each loop, unpin the pattern and gently ease the paper away.

7c. Gently pull the fabric edges apart and cut the stitches, leaving tufts on both sides. Mark the wrong side of each piece with a chalk cross.
☐ Tailor's tacks—single: used for marking balance marks and style details.
8. Using a double thread, take a stitch through the dot or hole in the pattern and both layers of fabric.
Repeat, leaving a loop.
Snip the loop before removing the pattern.
☐ Thread marking: used for marking center back, center front and alteration and style lines.
9. Thread marking is a continuous line through one layer of fabric as shown.
Color code: if a color code routine is adopted in this marking it saves confusion later—so tailor's tack seamlines in white and use colors for matching balance points.

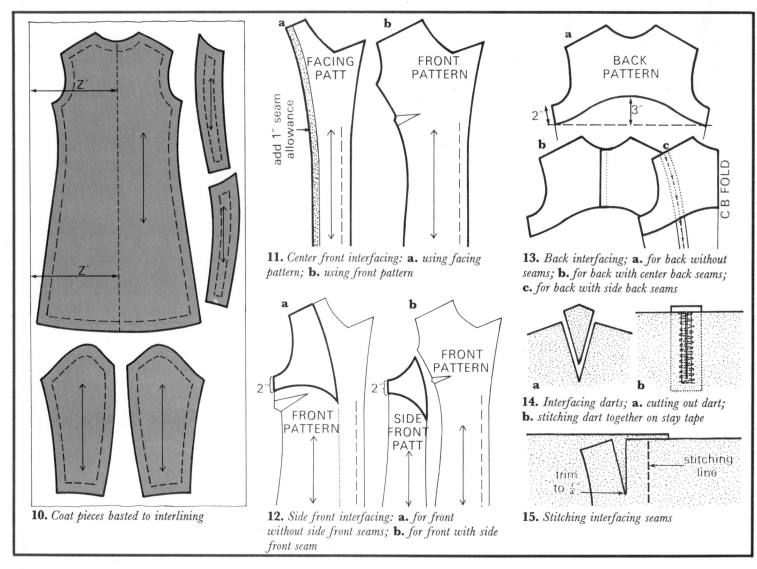

10. *Coat pieces basted to interlining*

11. *Center front interfacing:* **a.** *using facing pattern;* **b.** *using front pattern*

12. *Side front interfacing:* **a.** *for front without side front seams;* **b.** *for front with side front seam*

13. *Back interfacing;* **a.** *for back without seams;* **b.** *for back with center back seams;* **c.** *for back with side back seams*

14. *Interfacing darts;* **a.** *cutting out dart;* **b.** *stitching dart together on stay tape*

15. *Stitching interfacing seams*

Inter- or underlining

If it is necessary to interline the fabric, works as follows:

10. After the coat fabric has been cut out, marked up and separated, place each back, front and sleeve piece onto the single interlining fabric. Place the wrong side to the interlining, matching the grain. Baste together all around 1 inch in from the stitching line.

Cut out and work interlining and coat fabric as one.

D. Interfacing

This relates to all tailored coats.

Cutting out

Interfacing should be steam pressed before cutting out to prevent shrinkage during shaping.

Coat and interfacing grains should coincide to avoid the possibility of distortion.

11a and b. For each front, cut one piece of canvas as for the facing, adding an extra 1 inch seam allowance at the inner edge (**a**). If your pattern has a side front seam use the front pattern complete instead of the facing pattern (**b**).

12a and b. Cut a second piece of interfacing for each front to include the armhole as shown, using the front, or side front, pattern as a guide.

13a, b and c. For the back, cut canvas to include the neck and armhole, using the back pattern as a guide and curving the lower edge as shown (**a**). If there is a center back seam cut two pieces of canvas and join them at the center back (**b**). Where you have side back seams, overlap the pattern pieces on the stitching line and cut as shown (**c**).

Darts and seams

There are two ways to give shaping to the canvas interfacings, but you must fit the basted canvas and coat before shaping.

14. Darts. Cut the dart shape out along the stitching line. Place the cut edges together over stay tape. Machine stitch.

15. Seams. Overlay on the stitching line, machine stitch and then trim the seam allowances to $\frac{1}{4}$ inch.

Press the canvas over a tailor's ham to retain its shape.

*Terms and stitches

Grain lines (16): lengthwise grain, or warp threads, run parallel to the selvage. Crosswise grain, or weft threads, run across the fabric from selvage to selvage.

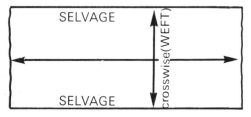

Herringbone stitch (17)

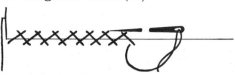

Warp and weft: see grain lines.

Crafts/tie-dye

The process and method

Tie-dye is the term given to a process where patterns are dyed into cloth, and it's so simple even a child can do it—and many children do produce beautiful examples.

The craft consists of taking a piece of fabric, then tying, folding, binding, knotting or sewing it so that when the fabric is dipped in a dyebath the color penetrates the untied areas and a pattern appears on the areas which have been protected from the dye. More complex patterns can be created by using more than one color, and retying first one area, then another. Tie-dye can be worked on lengths of fabric for home furnishings, on household linens or on garments. Dresses, blouses, skirts, pants, ties, pillowcases and curtains, can all be decorated with the tie-dye process.

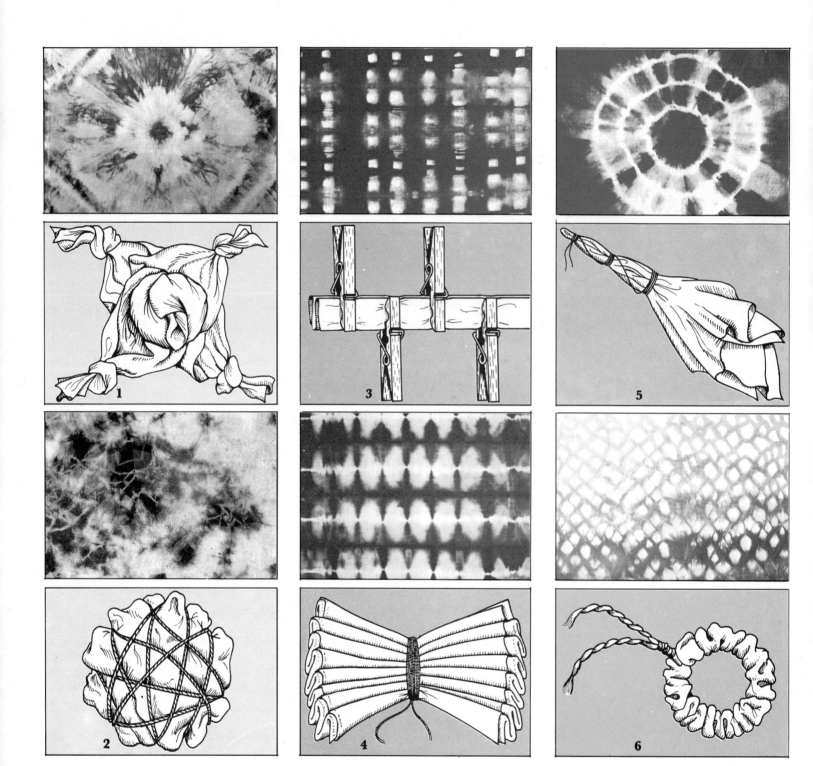

How to make patterns

There are countless ways of tying up a bundle of fabric to produce a design. A picture guide is given in this chapter showing just a few of them and the patterns that will result.

1. Knotted squares. Pick up a point of fabric in the center of the square, knotting the point and each corner.

2. Marbling. Crumple up the fabric in the hand. Bind into a hard ball. Crumple in different places for each color used. For a large garment, bunch along the length, section by section, making a long firm roll.

3. Pleat a piece of fabric and secure with clothes pins.

4. Stripes. Fold a piece of fabric in four, pleat it and then bind with string.

5. Small circle. Pick up a piece of fabric to form a "furled umbrella" shape and bind with thread.

6. Ruching around cord. Roll a piece of cloth around a length of cord and ruch.

7. Clump-tying. **A.** Bind a cork into a piece of fabric.

8. Clump-tying. **B.** Tie a number of different sized stones into a piece of fabric.

9. Small circle. Pick up a piece of fabric to form a "flared umbrella" shape and cross bind with thread.

10. Fold a piece of fabric in half and pleat it. Bind at various intervals with string, raffia and thread.

11. Twisting and coiling. Fold the cloth in half, pleat, then twist until it coils back on itself like a skein of yarn. Bind at ends and at intervals.

12. Simple double knots.

Experiment and discover which pattern is the most suitable for the fabric or garment being dyed. Marbling makes a pretty, all-over pattern for most things and stripes are particularly effective on towels and curtains.

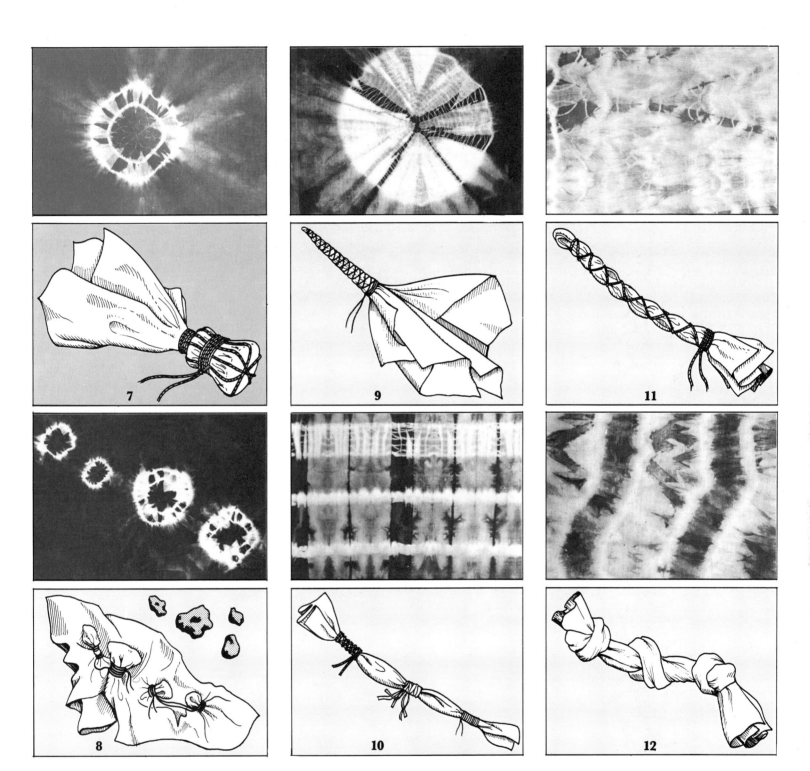

Fabrics and equipment

Cold water dyes will dye natural fibers such as silk, cotton and linen in bright colors. They are easy to use and the results are wash- and light-fast. Cold water dyes come in a large range of shades, and one tin of dye is required for each ½lb (250 grams) of dry fabric—i.e. two to three square yards of medium weight fabric. For example, a dress weighing one pound to be dyed blue and red will require two tins of each color. Some dyes are very concentrated and will dye larger quantities.

When fast color, cold water dyes are not available a hot water dye can be used, but the dyed garment should always be laundered separately. Hot dyes are also available in a wide range of colors, and will dye natural and some synthetic fabrics. Simmering will give the intensity of color intended, but the manufacturer's instructions for hot water dyeing should be followed exactly.

Fabrics

It is not advisable to tie-dye woolen sweaters as the tying may make them go out of shape. Woolen fabrics can be dyed, but manufacturer's special instructions for dyeing wool should always be followed. Generally, cold dyes are a better choice for woolen fabrics than hot ones.

Fabrics unsuitable for dyeing are polyester/wool mixtures, acrylics (Orlon, Acrilan), and acetate rayon. Fabrics with special finishes resist dyeing and should not be chosen for tie-dyeing. Polyesters like Dacron, when dyed with triple strength hot dye in dark shades, will come out as pretty pastel shades.

Shirts, linens, towels and anything which is going to need constant washing should be dyed with a cold water dye, which is color fast.

Other materials needed

- ☐ Salt
- ☐ Soda (for cold dyeing, not needed for hot dyeing)
- ☐ Wooden spoon to stir with
- ☐ Rubber gloves to protect hands
- ☐ Container, big enough to submerge the tied fabric; plastic or glass for cold water dye, a heat resistant container for hot dye
- ☐ Pitcher to hold one pint
- ☐ Thread, elastic bands, cork, pebbles, string, raffia, cord, cotton, or anything else needed to make the patterns.

Hints and tips

• New fabric may have dressing in it which will resist dye, so boil the garment or fabric first, ironing it smooth again when it is dry.

• When making tie-dyed dresses, always tie-dye the material first, and then make the dress. The finished garment will have a much more professional look.

• Tie up a sample piece before immersing the whole piece of fabric in the dye bath. Dye, rinse, wash, and untie it, to see whether the resulting pattern and color is as required. Don't forget that the color will look darker when the fabric is wet.

• If an old, colored garment is to be tie-dyed to freshen it, remove the original color with color remover, but test a sample first to find out if the dye is fast.

• When two or more colors are used they will blend with one another, so choose color combinations carefully, remembering that red and blue make purple; red and yellow make orange; yellow and blue make green; and that a lot of colors mixed together will usually make mud!

How to start

Bind the fabric in any of the ways shown in this chapter. Leave two inches of thread when starting binding, and when binding is completed return to the starting point and tie the two ends together. This will help to insure that the whole thing does not unravel in the dyebath.

If several bindings are being used on one garment, just use a slip knot and carry the thread onto the next binding.

For a sharp pattern, thoroughly wet the item before putting it in the dye bath. For a softer outline, put the item in the dye bath dry.

Prepare the dye. Always work the lightest color first.

For cold water dyes, dissolve the dye in one pint of warm water, stir well, and pour into the dye container. For each tin of dye used, dissolve 4 tablespoonsful of salt and one tablespoonful of common

▲ *An unusual way of using tie and dyed fabrics.* ▼ *Four neckties to make*

soda in one pint of hot water. Stir well, and when everything is ready to dye, add the salt and soda to the mixture. Once the soda is added to the dye, it is only effective for about two hours, so don't add until everything is ready. Otherwise, follow directions for your dye.

Neckties from sheeting
The four ties illustrated were made from tie-dyed cotton sheeting.

Tortoiseshell banded tie. Dye colors: coral red and café au lait.
Method: Fold a length of cloth 52 inches long by 7 inches wide in half along the length. Tie as many knots along the length as possible. Dye in coral red, rinse, untie, rinse again. Retie and dye in café au lait.

Red ovals tie. Dye colors: nasturtium and camellia.
Method: Fold length of cloth 52 inches by 7 inches lengthwise. Pick up small tufts of cloth along the fold and bind them narrowly, leaving a ¼ inch gap between each tie. Widen the tufts toward the end. Dye in nasturtium. After rinsing and while still tied, bind each tuft again below the original tie. Dye in camellia.

Purple chevron tie. Dye colors: French navy and camellia.
Method: Cut two pieces of cloth on the bias, each 28 inches by 8 inches. Fold each piece in half lengthwise. Roll the doubled cloth diagonally into a tube, beginning at the corners and working toward the folded edge. Make narrow bindings at 1 inch intervals along this tube. Dye each roll in French navy. Rinse, and while still wet, add further bindings between the original ties. Let the rolls dry and then dye again in weakly-made camellia colored dye (¼ teaspoonful of dye made up to 1 pint with 2 teaspoonsful of salt and ¼ teaspoon of soda added).
Rinse well, hot wash and rinse again. Make a necktie by joining two pieces together and pointing the ends.

Wide red tie. Dye color: Camellia.
Method: Cut two lengths of cloth 52 inches by 6 inches. Fold in half lengthwise. Follow this procedure for both pieces. Pick up a piece of fabric, on the fold, about 4 inches from the end. Pull it into a tent shape and bind diagonally right up to the point, then back to the beginning and tie the thread ends. The tent shape by now should be a finger shape. Leave little gaps in the binding so that as the dye partially penetrates a criss-cross texture is achieved. Each of these bindings will make a circle. Make as many circles as required, decreasing in size toward the center. Tie from the other end in the same way. Wet the cloth and dye.

Knitting design/pants and continental patterns

Once the intricacies of charting shapings have been mastered, designing and charting a pair of knitted pants is comparatively simple. Combined with the garments already given in the previous design chapters, smart two-piece outfits can be designed. This chapter also explains how to work from continental patterns.

Drafting

The main measurements required for a pair of pants are:

1. The total side length from waistline down the outer side of the leg to the ankle or the desired length.
2. The total measurements around the upper hip.
3. The hipline at the widest point.
4. The required width around upper leg, taken 3 inches below the crotch
5. The required width around the leg just above the knee.
6. The required width of the lower edge.
7. Length from the lower edge to the top of the knee.
8. Inside leg length from lower edge to crotch.

Pants diagram

Begin by marking the center line AB. This is the total side length from waistline to the desired length (measurement 1). Using the line AB as the center line mark on it O, which is the distance between lower edge and top of knee (measurement 7). Mark P on the line, measuring from just above knee to the point where the upper leg measurement was taken. Q is the length from lower edge to the crotch—the inside leg measurement. R is the point at which the upper hipline measurement was taken.

Using AB with the marked points as a center line mark the following:

CD—half the total waist measurement plus required tolerance ($1\frac{1}{4}$ inches is recommended for this design).

EF—half the upper hips measurement plus tolerance ($1\frac{1}{4}$ inches for this design).

GH—half the measurement around the hips plus tolerance (for this design $4\frac{1}{2}$ inches total tolerance is recommended).

IJ—the actual circumference of the upper leg plus tolerance.

KL—the actual circumference of the leg just above the knee plus tolerance.

MN—the width required at lower edge.

The shape of the pants leg is a matter of design choice. It can be sloped from GH to MN for a flared look or, if the pants are to have fitted legs, the lines will slope inward.

Mark a point S on the chart 1-$1\frac{1}{2}$ inches above point D. This is to give extra

length to the back seam to allow for ease in sitting down. Draw a slightly curved line from A to S. In the same way the center front point C can be dropped slightly to shorten the front seam, but on knitted fabric, which is very elastic, it is not essential.

The curve from G to C is sharp where it starts at G and curves to E, then it is less shaped to C, much the same way as on an armhole curve.

The back curve from H to F can be more gradual.

Draw the diagram to look like figure 1, and this is your working diagram for the left pants leg. Prepare a gauge and pattern swatch and mark in numbers of rows and stitches to one inch.

The leg shaping is usually fairly easy to arrange but from the line GH it is easier to work out the shaping on graph paper. Remember that this diagram is for the left leg. For the right leg it is necessary to reverse the shaping above GH to the waistline.

Because of the degree of elasticity in knitted fabric it is quite easy to obtain a well fitting pair of pants that have no side opening and are fitted with elastic at the waist. A more tailored pair of pants would be similar from the hipline upward to a skirt pattern, and could have the fullness reduced by darts as well as by shaping over the hipline.

Pants in circular knitting

Pants also lend themselves to being worked without seams using circular needles. Each leg is worked circularly and then joined just above the crotch where a small seam is necessary, so that the body is also worked without seams.

Continental-type charts

Continental designs, seen in magazines and leaflets, often suggest an idea which appeals to the knitter, but they are impossible to understand if one lacks the knowledge of technical terms in another language. Often, however, foreign directions do away with the need to understand every word by the clever use of diagrams.

Figure 2 is typical of these diagrams and shows half the back of a stockinette stitch sweater, slightly shaped toward the waist with a narrow edge of ribbing, and with the waistline defined by a ribbed panel. The number of stitches to be cast on is indicated under the diagram and in some diagrams this may be for half the pattern or it may indicate that although only half the back is shown, the total number of stitches to be cast on has been stated. A quick check as to the gauge

one obtains with the chosen yarn will determine the number of stitches that are to be cast on.

The ribbing at the lower edge is usually indicated by tiny upright lines and may have the depth indicated beside it, i.e. 2cms (2 centimetres).

The distance between the ribbing and the waist ribbing will have a measurement against it, and decreasings marked by a small dot. Figure 2 indicates one decrease four times in all at each side. To determine the number of rows between, calculate how many rows will be needed to reach the required measurement and then divide this into even sections.

The waist ribbing is again indicated by small vertical lines and above there is an area with dots to indicate the number of times increases are to be worked—four in figure 2.

At the armhole, the 3 and 2 indicate that 3 stitches are bound off first. On the next row 3 stitches would be bound off on the

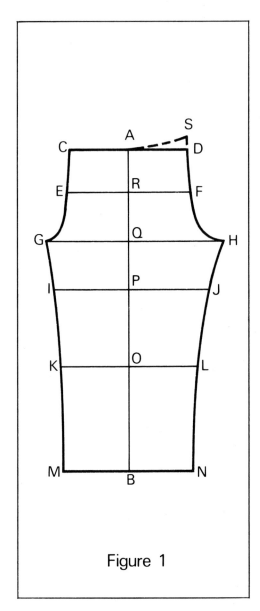

Figure 1

other side of the work and then 2 stitches at the beginning of the next 2 rows. The dots above this indicate again where stitches are decreased and how often they are worked. Close together on an armhole curve they would be worked every other row. In the same way the remaining numbers refer to the stitches to be bound off for neck shaping and the number of times you bind off for the shoulder.

Because the diagram takes up a great deal less print space than row by row instructions many continental designs give more varied methods of shaping than American designs. Apart from sweaters many designs have backs which are narrower than the front. This gives an exceedingly good line when the garment is finished because the side seam tends to be toward the back instead of centrally below the armhole. When measuring this type of design do not simply double the front or back measurement to see if it is the size you require, but add both back and front together.

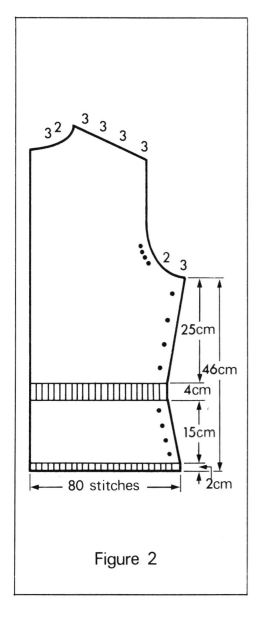

Figure 2

Knitting pattern/striped for two

These knitted outfits are as sturdy as they are attractive. If you are knitting for a little girl there's double value—the top can team with skirt or pants. The patterns couldn't be simpler. All in stockinette stitch, the pullover has four row stripes, the skirt and pants are edged with ribbing.

Sizes

Directions are for 21in chest. The figures in brackets [ ] refer to the 22 and 23in chest sizes respectively.
Pullover. Length, 13½[14½:15] in. Sleeve seam, 9[10:11]in.
Skirt. Length, 9[9½:10]in, adjustable.
Pants. Inside leg, 13[14:15] in, adjustable.

Gauge
5 sts and 7 rows to 1in over st st worked on No.6 needles.

Materials
Columbia-Minerva
Nantuk Sports Yarn
Pullover. 2[2:2] skeins main color A, red
2[2:2] skeins contrast B, white
Skirt. 2[2:3] skeins A, red
Pants. [2:2] skeins A, red
One pair No.4 needles
One pair No.6 needles
One set of 4 No.4 double-pointed needles
Waist length elastic for pants
2 buttons for skirt
Stitch holder

Pullover back

Using No.4 needles and A, cast on 53[55:57] sts.
1st row K1, *P1, K1, rep from * to end.
2nd row P1, *K1, P1, rep from * to end.
Rep these 2 rows once more, inc 5[5:6] sts evenly across the 2nd row. 58[60:63] sts.
Change to No.6 needles and attach B.
Continue in st st working 4 rows B, 4 rows A throughout until work measures 8½[9:9½]in
1648

from beg. End with a WS row.

Shape armholes
Bind off 2 sts at beg of next 2 rows.
Next row K1, sl 1, K1, psso, K to last 3 sts, K2 tog, K1.
Continue dec in this way on every 4th row 2[2:3] times more, then on every other row until 24[24:27]sts rem. End with a P row.
Slip sts on holder.

Front

Work as given for Back until 34[34:37] sts rem. End with a P row.

Shape neck
Next row K1, sl 1, K1, psso, K6. Turn and slip rem sts on st holder.
Next row P to end.
Next row K1, sl 1, K1, psso, K to last 2 sts, K2 tog.
Rep the last 2 rows twice more, then the first of these 2 rows once more.
Next row K1, sl 1, K2 tog, psso.
Next row P2 sts.
Next row K2 tog. Fasten off.
Return to sts on holder. Slip first 16[16:19] sts on holder for neck, K to last 3 sts, K2 tog, K1.
Complete to correspond to first side.

Sleeves

Using No.4 needles and A, cast on 25[27:29] sts and work in rib as given for Back for 2in, ending with a WS row and inc 8 sts evenly across last row. 33[35:37] sts.
Change to No.6 needles and attach B.
Continue in st st working in stripes of 4 rows B, 4 rows A throughout, inc one st at each end of every 8th row until there are 41[43:45] sts.
Continue without shaping until sleeve seam measures about 9[10:11]in from beg, ending with the same row as Back at armholes.

Shape cap
Bind off 2 sts at beg of next 2 rows.
Next row K1, sl 1, K1, psso,

K to last 3 sts, K2 tog, K1.
Continue dec in this way on every 4th row 2[2:3] times more, then every other row until 5 sts rem, ending with a P row. Slip sts on holder.

Neckband

Join raglan seams.
Using set of 4 No.4 dp needles and A, K left Back neck sts and left Sleeve sts, pick up and K9 sts down side of neck, K Front neck sts, pick up and K9 sts up other side of neck and K right Sleeve sts. Join. 68[68:74]sts.
Continue in rounds of K1, P1 rib for 1½in. Bind off loosely in rib.

Finishing

Press work lightly under a damp cloth, using a cool iron. Joins side and sleeve seams. Sew in sleeves. Fold neckband in half to inside and slip stitch in place. Press all seams.

Skirt back

Using No.6 needles and A, cast on 73[77:83] sts.
Work in rib as given for Back of Pullover for 4 rows, inc one st at end of last row. 74[78:84] sts.
Beg with a K row, continue in st st until work measures 8[8½:9]in from beg, or length desired, ending with a P row.
Dec one st at end of last row.

Waistband
Change to No. 4 needles.
Continue in rib as at beg for 10 rows. Bind off in rib.

Front

Work as for Back as far as waistband.

Waistband
Change to No.4 needles.
Continue in rib for 4 rows.
Next row Rib 13[14:14], bind off 2 sts, rib to last 15[16:16] sts, bind off 2 sts, rib to end.
Next row Rib to end, casting on 2 sts over each 2 sts bound off.
Work 4 rows more in rib. Bind off in rib.

Straps

Using No.4 needles and A, cast on 11 sts.
Work in rib for 15½[16:17]in or length desired.
Dec one st at each end of every row until 3 sts rem.
Break off yarn, thread through sts, draw up and fasten off.
Make a second strap in the same manner.

Finishing

Press work lightly under a damp cloth, using a cool iron. Join seams. Sew straight ends of straps to back waistband and sew button to other end of each strap. Press all seams.

Pants right leg

Using No.6 needles and A, cast on 71[73:75] sts and work in rib as on back of Pullover for 4 rows, inc one st at end of last row. 72[74:76] sts.
Beg with a K row, continue in st st until work measures 13[14:15]in or length desired, ending with a P row.

Shape crotch
Next row Bind off 4 sts, K to end.
Next row Bind off 6 sts, P to end.
Dec one st at each end of every other row 4 times.
54[56:58] sts.
Work even until work measures 8[8½:9]in from beg of crotch shaping, or length desired, ending with a P row.
Dec one st at end of last row.
Change to No.4 needles.
Continue in rib for 1in.
Bind off in rib.

Left leg

Work to correspond to right Leg, reversing all shaping.

Finishing

Press work lightly under a damp cloth, using a cool iron.
Join back and front seams.
Join leg seams.
Sew elastic to inside of waistband with casing-stitch.
Press all seams.

1649

Stitchery design/beading and embroidery stitches

Bead embroidery, more than any other form of the craft, lends itself to experimentation with unusual materials. All kinds of objects can be used as an embroidery decoration for clothes and furnishings. In this chapter you will find some clever ideas for working with unusual things and combining them with beads and stitches.

Unusual materials

Besides beads and sequins, all kinds of things can be used to decorate fabrics, and many modern embroidery designers have produced quite striking pieces of work utilizing unlikely materials. Faucet washers, curtain rings and pants buttons, for instance, provide interesting round shapes, and there are dozens more to be found on hardware and notions counters. Hooks and eyes, snap fasteners, pants fastenings, used in groups and rows, look exciting and original. Bits of clock mechanism provide some unusually shaped pieces too, and lengths of plastic-covered wire have been used with effective results. There are no fixed rules about what can or cannot be used in this kind of embroidery —anything goes, so it's up to the embroiderer and her imagination.

Treatment of metal shapes

It may be necessary to varnish some metal objects before using them to prevent them from rusting. Clear varnish is best for a protective covering but there is no reason why colored nail polish shouldn't be used for effect. Finish off with a coat of clear polish to harden the nail polish off.

Beads combined with shapes

Many objects, such as faucet washers, curtain rings and paper clips can be used individually to build up a design, but combined with beads they can look even more interesting. The pants fastenings design illustrated in this chapter has been used in conjunction with beads, the beads used to secure the pants fastening to the background fabric.

Sequin material

Sequin material can be cut with a pair of scissors into almost any shape and size to form giant sequin shapes. This is very useful because the large shapes provide a bold contrast to the smaller beads and sequins.

Sequin waste

This is the material from which the sequins have been cut, and it is full of sequin size holes. This sequin waste can be cut into lengths or an endless variety of shapes that

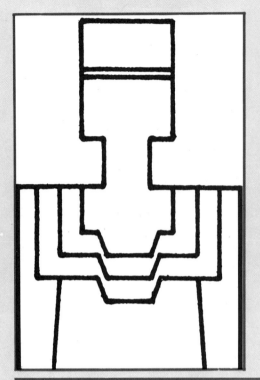

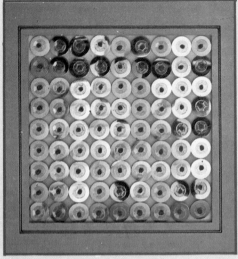

Left: stylized figure for bead embroidery
Above: formal arrangement of sequins
Below: pants fastenings and beads arranged in rows to make a striking border design
Top right: contoured beads and sequins
Bottom right: beads and sequins in a hexagon
Far right: ways of using beads and stitches

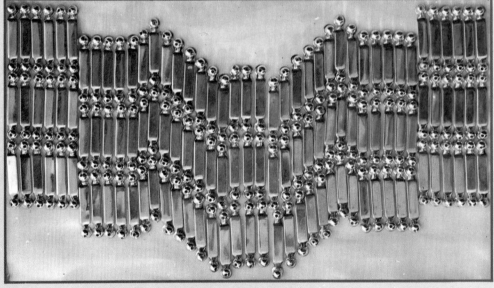

can be caught to the background fabric with embroidery stitches making use of the holes.

Rich borders can be formed with sequin waste by working rows of herringbone stitch or chain stitch in crewel yarn. Lazy daisy stitch worked into six holes and either left as it is or finished off with a tiny bead in the center looks interesting and is simple to do. Spider's web, also worked into six holes, gives a lovely contrast of texture.

Paillettes and mirrors

Paillettes have an attractive dull glow and combine well with bead embroidery. Mirrors have a brighter glitter and are cut by holding the mirror under water in a bowl, cutting it with a pair of old kitchen scissors. One-sided handbag mirrors are ideal for this.

Beads combined with embroidery stitches

This is a most interesting technique with endless possibilities. Stitches such as herringbone, wheatear, outline, fly, feather and buttonhole look completely different when beads are actually worked into the stitches. Herringbone stitch, for example, looks interesting worked with large, oval, wooden beads or glass bugles, which in turn can be caught down at top and bottom with two or three small beads worked in a double backstitch. Lines of the design can be worked in beading broken up with intermittent areas of beading.

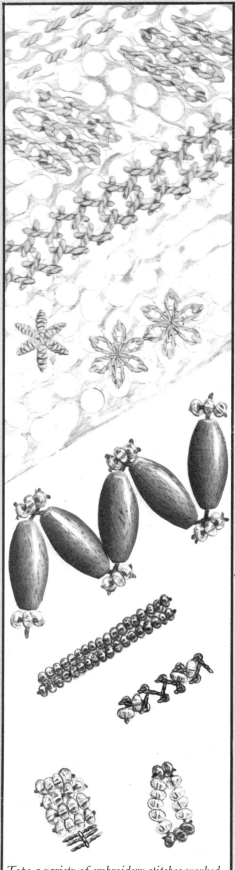

Top: a variety of embroidery stitches worked on sequin waste
Bottom: beads combined with embroidery stitches such as herringbone, Rumanian and coral knot

Stitchery pattern/rose-patterned slippers

A charming yellow rose design in needlepoint for a pair of slippers. Work the pattern exactly the same for left and right foot; the instep shaping is part of the finishing. The slippers can be made to fit any size foot by extending the tapered ends, but cut out the shape in paper before starting to check the fit of the upper.

For working a pair of slippers you will need:
- [ ] Double canvas, 10 holes to the inch, 26 inches by 13 inches
- [ ] Corduroy for lining half yard 36 inches wide
- [ ] Piece of leather "split" or a piece of chamois for the soles
- [ ] One pair of cork soles to foot size
- [ ] Piece of stiff cardboard 12 inches by 12 inches
- [ ] Appleton's Crewel Yarn. Three skeins 761 for the background, one skein each of the following: dull china blue range: 927, 925, 922; brown olive range: 315, 313; early English green range: 542, 546, 544; bright yellow: 552, 554; golden brown: 905; grey green: 352.
- [ ] Tapestry needle No.20
- [ ] Crewel needle No.7
- [ ] Embroidery frame

Working the design
Mark out the two slipper upper shapes on the canvas leaving space between them for making up. Mount the canvas in the frame. Mark the center of each shape and work the design from the center outward.

Making the slippers
Block the embroidery and cut out the uppers, leaving an inch of canvas all around. Using the cork insoles as a pattern cut out two more soles from the cardboard. Still using the cork insoles as a pattern, cut out the shape for each foot in the chamois and then in the corduroy, leaving an extra inch all around. Cover the cardboard sole shapes with the chamois, lacing on the reverse side (see illustration). Cover the cork insoles with corduroy and lace in the same way.

Use the embroidered upper as a guide and cut out the corduroy linings and line the embroidered upper. Run a gathering thread $\frac{1}{8}$ inch from the embroidery edging and drawing it up, then try the uppers on, easing the gathers to fit the foot. Place the foot on the sole covered with corduroy and try the uppers again, turning the 1 inch of canvas to the underside of the insole. Pin and then stitch the uppers to the insole firmly. Glue the insole to the sole, wrong sides facing, using a fabric glue.

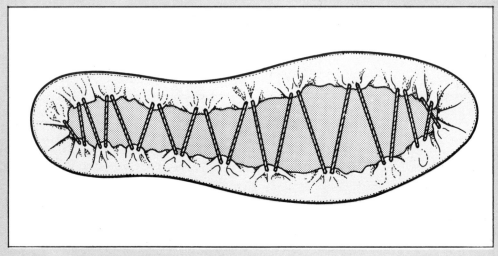

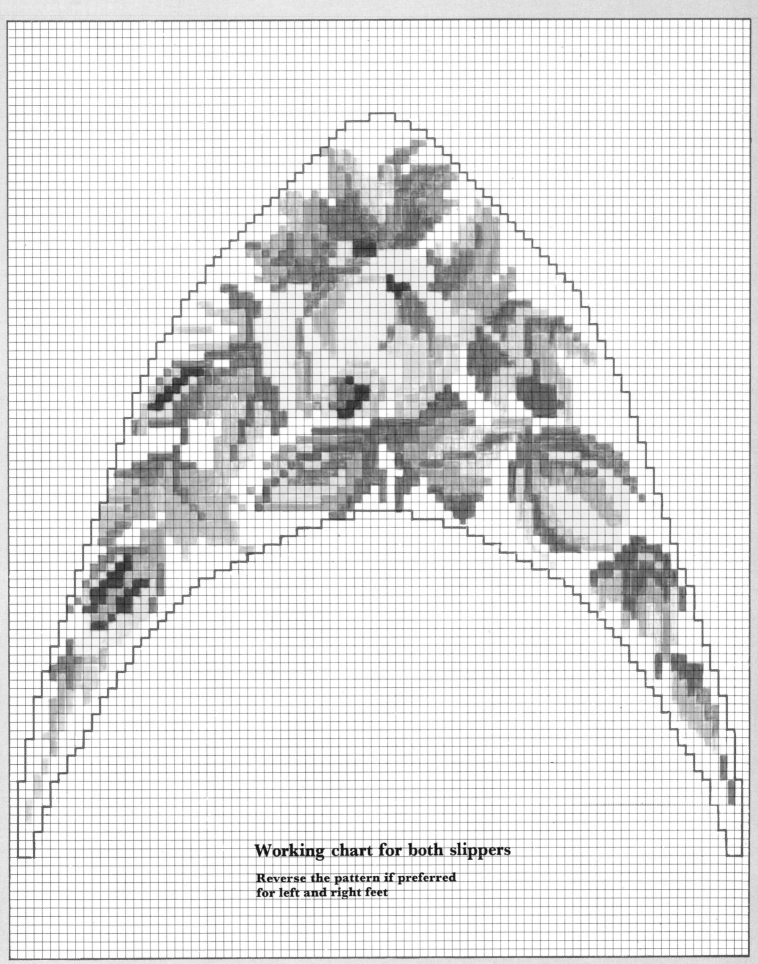

Working chart for both slippers

**Reverse the pattern if preferred
for left and right feet**

Home crochet/fireside rugs

The oval rug is worked from the center, and the round rug is worked in a long strip and then sewn together.

Fiery embers rug

Size
About 27in by 38in.

Gauge
5sc to 3in and 2 rows to 1in using double yarn worked with No.K hook.

Materials
Unger Scheepjeswool 1654

1 skein medium red, A
4 skeins scarlet, B
5 skeins raspberry, C
6 skeins dark red, D
5 skeins black, E
One No.K crochet hook.

Rug

Using No.K hook and one strand each of A and B, ch18.
1st round 1sc into 2nd ch from hook, 1sc into each of next 15ch, 3sc into end ch, continue along other side of ch working 1sc into each of next 16ch, 2sc into turning ch, ss into first st. Turn.

2nd round Ch1, 1sc into same st, 2sc into each of next 2 sts, 1sc into each of next 16 sts, 2sc into each of next 3 sts, 1sc into each of next 16 sts, ss into ch1. Turn.

3rd round Ch1, 1sc into same st, 1sc into each of next 17 sts, (2sc into next st, 1sc into next st) 3 times, 1sc into each of next 16sc, (2sc into next st, 1sc into next st) twice, ss into ch1. Turn.

4th round Ch1, 1sc into same st, 1sc into each of next 2 sts, (2sc into next st, 1sc into each of next 2 sts) twice, 1sc into each of next 16 sts, (2sc into next st, 1sc into each of next

2 sts) 3 times, 1sc into each of next 16 sts, ss into ch1. Break off A.

Continue in this way into 3 sts at the curve on each round by placing one more st between inc on each round and keeping straight sides correct.

5th—7th rounds Work with 2 strands B.

8th—11th rounds Work with one strand each of B and C.

12th—14th rounds Work with 2 strands C.

15th—17th rounds Work with one strand each of C and D.

18th—20th rounds Work with 2 strands D.

21st—23rd rounds Work with one strand each of D and E.

24th—26th rounds Work with 2 strands E. Fasten off.

Spiral rug

Size
About 26in diameter plus fringe.

Materials
Columbia-Minerva Rug Wool
3 skeins main color, A
1 skein contrast, B
1 skein contrast, C
1 skein contrast, D
1 skein contrast, E
1 skein contrast, F
One No.K crochet hook

Main Section

Using No.K hook and one strand each of A and B, ch3.

1st row 1sc into 2nd ch from hook, 1sc into next ch. 3 sts.

2nd row Ch1 to count as first sc, 1sc into next sc, 1sc into turning ch.

Rep these 2 rows until work measures 10in.

Break off B and attach C, thus continuing with one strand each of A and C for 10in more.

Continue in 10in sections, using yarn as follows:
A and E, A and F, A and D, A and B, A and C, A and E, A and F, A and D, A and B, A and D, A and C, A and E, A and F, A and C, A and E, A and B, (A and F, A and C, A and B, A and D) twice, A and E, A and C, A and F, A and D, A and B, A and E,

A and C, A and F, A and D, A and B, 36 sections. Fasten off.

Finishing

Working on a flat surface, shape strip into a circle, overcasting on the wrong side with A and positioning colors as illustrated.

Fringe

Cut about 150 8in strands A and 75 8in strands B. Using 2 strands A and one strand B together throughout, knot into the edge of the rug at 1in intervals. Trim fringe evenly.

1655

Tailoring two

In this chapter
A. About basting: seams and details; seams with ease; back shoulder dart; overbasting.
B. The first fitting: preparing for the fitting; fitting points; correcting the faults; pinning alterations; marking alterations; preparing to stitch.
C. About stitching: seams; shoulder seams; topstitching.
D. Pressing: using a tailor's clapper; pressing seams; pressing eased seams; pressing darts; top pressing.
E. Pleats: inverted pleat; knife pleat; slit opening.
*Terms and stitches

A. About basting

Always work on a flat surface when basting* seams, details and canvases. This insures that the grain is kept correctly aligned and not pulled out of shape.

Seams and details
1. Lay the pieces flat, right sides together, notches and balance marks matching exactly. Pin at right angles to the stitching line.
Using double thread, baste together, starting with a tailor's knot* and finishing with a backstitch.

Seams with ease*
2a. Lay the pieces together, right sides facing, with the one to be eased on top. Pin the notches and divide ease equally along the length.
2b. Push ease down with fingers and baste, taking a small section at a time.

Back shoulder dart
In most cases it is better to ease in the back shoulder dart for a smoother line rather than stitch the dart. Exceptions are with linen, or fabric with a high man-made fiber content, because it is not easy to shrink these fibers.

Overbasting
3. Overbasting is used when basting for a fitting to give a smooth line and a better indication of fit.

B. The first fitting

Preparing for the first fitting
Before any sewing is done the coat must be basted together, tried on to see that it fits, and the initial alterations made.
4a. On the back, baste the style seams and baste the canvas to the wrong side along the neck and armholes.
4b. On the front, baste the style seams and the canvas darts or seams, then baste the
1656

canvas to the wrong side.
Baste the sleeve seams.
4c. Baste the center back seam of the under-collar then baste the collar canvas to the wrong side of the under-collar.
4d. Overbaste the side and shoulder seams and the under-collar to the neck.
Baste the sleeves to the coat taking great care to spread the ease evenly at the sleeve head.

Fitting points
A well fitted coat feels comfortable, adjusts naturally to the activities of the wearer, is becoming in line and amount of ease, and is consistent with the current fashion.
Five interrelated factors are to be looked for when fitting a coat.
☐ Ease: there should be ease for movement without the coat being too large.
☐ Line: all vertical seams should be at right angles to the ground unless they are fashion features designed to be otherwise. All horizontal lines—the bust, waist, hips—should be at right angles to the vertical lines.
☐ Grain: as for line.
☐ Set or fit: a garment which sets well sits on the figure without wrinkles or strain.
☐ Balance: pockets, belts, buttons, hems to be proportioned correctly for the individual figure.

Correcting the faults
Put on the coat, right side out, over the appropriate clothing. Pin the center front lines together and then check the following points. It is better if you can get a friend to help you here.
☐ Is the coat sitting on the figure correctly (**5**)? Are the lower edges level, the center back and center front lines vertical?
☐ Are the style lines right for the figure—sometimes a line over the bust can be moved for better balance (**6**).
☐ Look for strain points shown by wrinkles (**7a**). Unbaste and let seams out till wrinkles have gone. Repin.
☐ If the coat is too big it will hang in folds (**7b**). Unbaste and repin.
☐ Turn up the hem and check buttonhole and pocket positions. Unless they are fashion features, pockets should be placed so that they are easy to use—the usual position is about 2 inches below the waist and between the center front and side seam. If your hip or stomach is rather large a pocket could be inserted in a seam to give a smoother line (see Golden Hands chapter 39).
☐ Check that the fold of the lapel lies smoothly and continues on the under-collar (**8a, b**). An adjustment to the top button

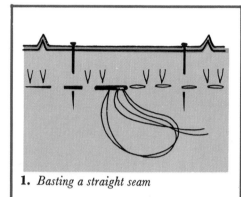
1. Basting a straight seam

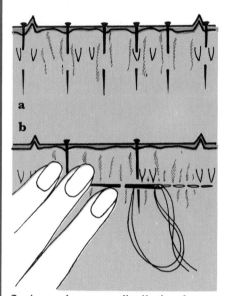
2. An eased seam: **a.** *distributing the ease;* **b.** *pushing in the ease and basting*

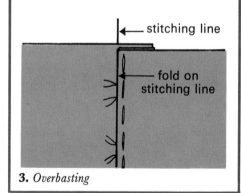
3. Overbasting

position can correct a loose or tight neckline (**8c**). An adjustment at the back neck seam may be necessary for a shawl collar to sit well.
Pin along the folds and thread mark when unbasted (**8a, b**).
☐ See that the sleeve hangs smoothly, that it is not too large or tight, and that the armhole line is well balanced. However, no alterations to the sleeve are made at this stage; the sleeves are put in to check the appearance and balance of the coat.

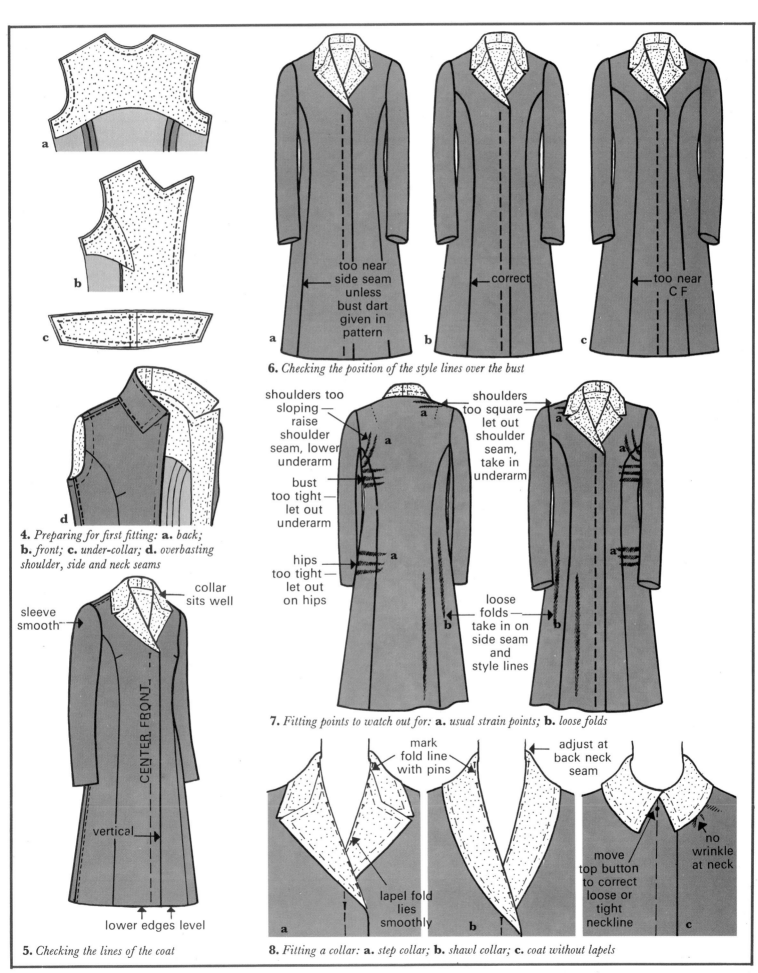

4. *Preparing for first fitting:* **a.** *back;* **b.** *front;* **c.** *under-collar;* **d.** *overbasting shoulder, side and neck seams*

collar sits well

sleeve smooth

CENTER FRONT

vertical

lower edges level

5. *Checking the lines of the coat*

too near side seam unless bust dart given in pattern

correct

too near C F

6. *Checking the position of the style lines over the bust*

shoulders too sloping — raise shoulder seam, lower underarm

bust too tight — let out underarm

hips too tight — let out on hips

shoulders too square let out shoulder seam, take in underarm

loose folds — take in on side seam and style lines

7. *Fitting points to watch out for:* **a.** *usual strain points;* **b.** *loose folds*

mark fold line with pins

lapel fold lies smoothly

adjust at back neck seam

move top button to correct loose or tight neckline

no wrinkle at neck

8. *Fitting a collar:* **a.** *step collar;* **b.** *shawl collar;* **c.** *coat without lapels*

Pinning alterations

9a, b. To let out or take in a seam, first unbaste. Find the correct position for the seam then fold one side on the new stitching line and pin fold to new stitching line on under piece.

Marking alterations

10. On shoulders and side seams thread mark any alterations in a new colored thread.

Mark through the fold and along the under piece.

Remove old markings.

11. On style seams slip baste* any alterations through fold and under piece. Remove old markings.

Preparing to stitch

Unbaste sleeve, under collar, shoulder and side seams, but leave the style seams basted.

C. About stitching

Seams

12. To avoid damage to the fabric remove the tailor's tacks before stitching, and then stitch just outside the line of basting without catching it.

Seams with ease should be stitched with the ease side up as they are easier to control this way.

Shoulder seams

13. Shoulder seams, however, are best hand sewn. For a firm result use a double silk thread and a backstitch. By doing this the ease is controlled, resulting in a straight line.

14. Before a seam is pressed the basting is removed and the edges made neat by overcasting in matching silk thread.

Topstitching

Topstitching gives a professional finish when done carefully, so practice on a piece of fabric folded to the appropriate thickness.

Work the topstitching as the garment is being made, not when it is finished.

For topstitching work as follows:

☐ Set the machine to a large stitch.

☐ Use a number 16 (or 100) needle.

☐ If possible use buttonhole twist in both bottom and top of the machine. If you find this does not work try threading the top only with buttonhole twist.

☐ Check bobbin and refill if low.

☐ Baste just inside the topstitching line (**15**). Then stitch slowly and carefully, using basting, seam and machine foot as guide lines. When turning corners leave the needle in the work and pivot cloth on needle.

1658

D. Pressing

To insure a smoothly finished garment each stage of the work should be pressed as it is finished. This needs care and plenty of patience.

Remember that pressing is not ironing and that the iron should be lifted and pressed upon the part required—not smoothed back and forth.

16. The positioning of the garment or part to be pressed is important and you should work in the direction of the grain.

Always test for the correct iron temperature on a spare piece of fabric. If there are any artificial fibers in the cloth, regulate the heat to these to avoid destroying them.

Using a tailor's clapper

Pressing cloths must be damp rather than wet to avoid spoiling the appearance of the fabric and leaving a rough-dry look.

17. As the iron is lifted after each pressing, quickly remove the damp cloth and hold the tailor's clapper firmly over the pressed section for some seconds. This action helps to set the seam or edge professionally, insuring a crisper fold or flatter surface.

Press and clap the folds of pleats, hems, seams, darts, pockets and edges as the construction of the garment proceeds.

Pressing seams

18. Remove all basting and press the seam flat to blend the stitches.

19. Lay the seam over a pressing roll, making sure that the rest of the garment is well supported. Press open with the point of the iron as shown.

20. Look at the right side to make sure the seamline is flat before pressing with a damp cloth and clapping heavily on the wrong side.

Pressing eased seams

Where a seam has been eased or fabric is to be molded the technique of shrinking* is used.

21. Lay the garment flat on an ironing board, right side down. Shrink away the ease with the point of the iron and a damp pressing cloth.

22. Open the seam, lay over a pressing roll and shrink the eased seam edge. While damp, stretch * the uneased edge.

Finally press and clap the seam.

Pressing darts

23a. After stitching, cut along the fold of the dart, cutting as near to the point as possible.

23b. Lay the dart right side down over a ham and press and clap the dart open, checking for a smooth line.

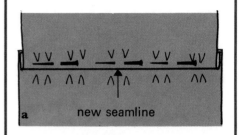
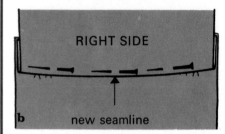
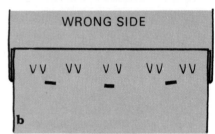

9a, b. *Letting out and taking in a seam*

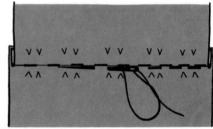

10. *Remarking shoulder and side seams*

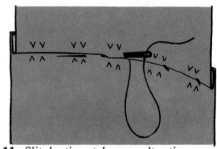

11. *Slip basting style seam alterations*

Top pressing

Top pressing is used for lapels, collars and the final press.

Lay the garment on an ironing board right side up, smoothed into the correct position with the grain undistorted.

Cover with a piece of lightweight wool cloth. Over this, place the pressing cloth and press lightly. This prevents shine and removes any pin, basting or seam marks which might have been accidentally pressed in.

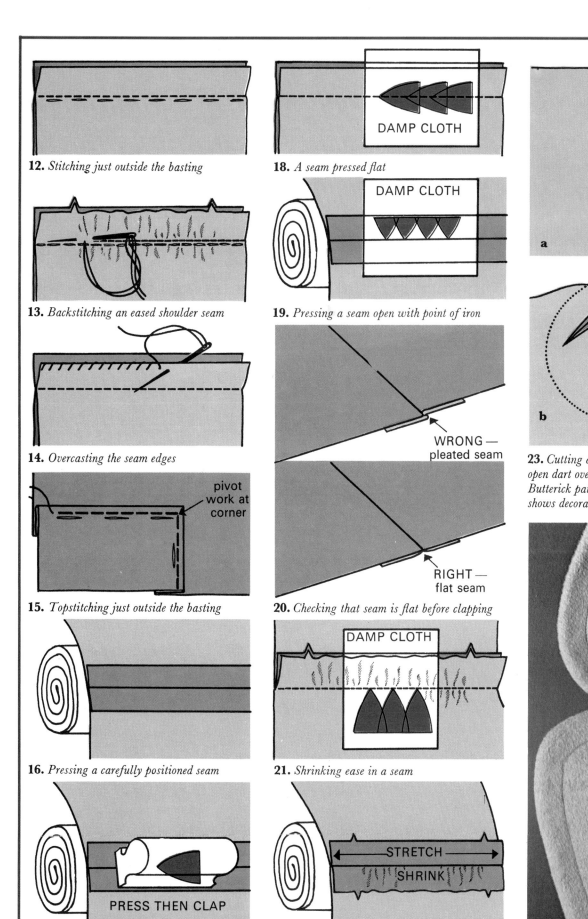

12. *Stitching just outside the basting*

13. *Backstitching an eased shoulder seam*

14. *Overcasting the seam edges*

pivot work at corner

15. *Topstitching just outside the basting*

16. *Pressing a carefully positioned seam*

PRESS THEN CLAP

17. *Using a tailor's clapper*

DAMP CLOTH

18. *A seam pressed flat*

DAMP CLOTH

19. *Pressing a seam open with point of iron*

WRONG — pleated seam

RIGHT — flat seam

20. *Checking that seam is flat before clapping*

DAMP CLOTH

21. *Shrinking ease in a seam*

STRETCH

SHRINK

22. *Pressing the eased seam open*

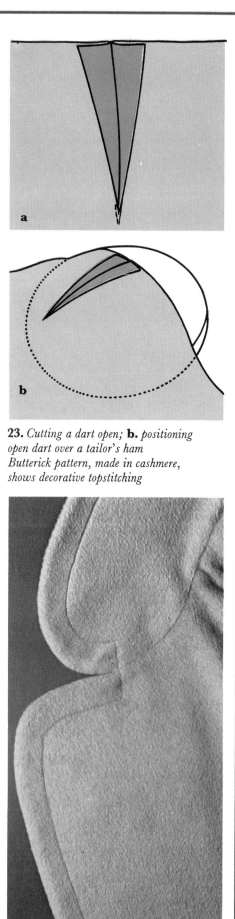

a

b

23. *Cutting a dart open;* **b.** *positioning open dart over a tailor's ham*
Butterick pattern, made in cashmere, shows decorative topstitching

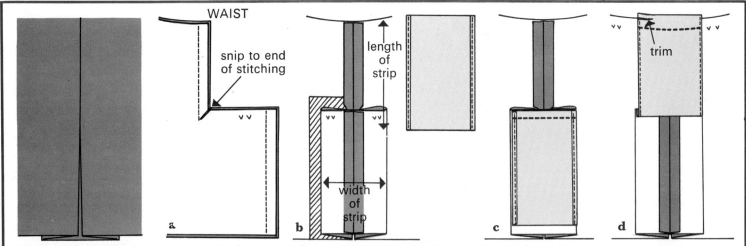

24. *Inverted pleat:* **a.** *stitch, overcast and snip the seam;* **b.** *press pleat and prepare lining strip;* **c.** *lining stitched to top of pleat;* **d.** *trimming top edge of lining strip*

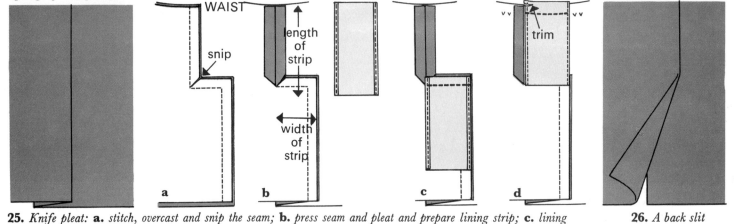

25. *Knife pleat:* **a.** *stitch, overcast and snip the seam;* **b.** *press seam and pleat and prepare lining strip;* **c.** *lining stitched to top of pleat;* **d.** *trimming top edge of lining*

26. *A back slit*

E. Pleats

Because of the heavier fabrics used in tailoring all pleats need to be supported to prevent them from dragging and up-setting the balance of the garment.

Inverted pleat

24a. Baste, fit, stitch, snip and make the seams neat. Press open.

24b. Put seams in line and press pleat, placing brown paper or cardboard under the fold to prevent marking the fabric.
Cut a strip of lining to the pleat width plus ½ inch, and to the length from the top stitching line of the pleat to the neck or waist.
Turn under each long edge for ¼ inch and stitch.

24c. Stitch this strip to each fold of the pleat.

24d. Fold up and stitch it to the coat just above the neck or waist seam. Trim to the curve.

Knife pleat

25a. Baste, fit, stitch, snip and make the seams neat.

25b. Press the coat seam open and the pleat seam flat. Cut a strip of lining fabric to the pleat width plus ½ inch, and to the length from top stitching line of slit to the neck or waist. Turn under the long edges for ¼ inch and stitch.

25c. Stitch this strip to the top of the pleat.

25d. Fold up and stitch it to the coat just above the neck or waist seam. Trim to the curve.

Slit opening (26)

Stitch as given for the slit opening in the pattern, then support as for knife pleat.

*Terms and stitches

Basting: firm basting with ¼ inch stitches.

Easing: instead of a dart, shaping is obtained by easing one seam to another.

Shrinking: to shrink away the extra full-ness which gives ease and to create shaping.

Slip basting (27): used to baste a seam from the right side after altering a seam (also used to match patterns, plaids, stripes etc). Fold top piece under on sewing line. Place fold over sewing line of lower piece. Sew taking a ½ inch stitch through fold then a ½ inch stitch through under piece along the sewing line.

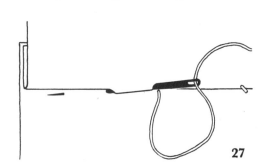

27

Stretching: to stretch fabric to make it lie flat as in curved seams, and to create shaping.

Tailor's knot (28):

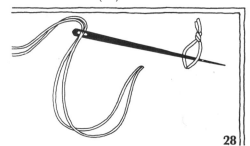

28

Crafts/Making bead jewelry

Beads in fashion

Decorative beads have played an important part in sophisticated fashion for centuries. Archeological finds in Egypt have uncovered ancient glass beads, beautifully shaped, and medieval women wore elaborate bead ornaments in their hair. Among the American Indians bead work was a major art, and their bold designs have influenced many contemporary fashions. In the nineteenth century, Victorian ladies made small beaded accessories as a home craft. Bead jewelry, or some

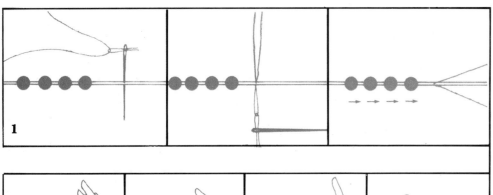

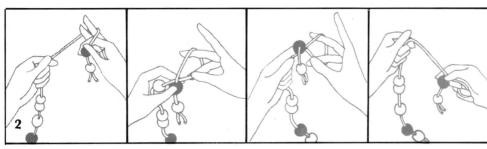

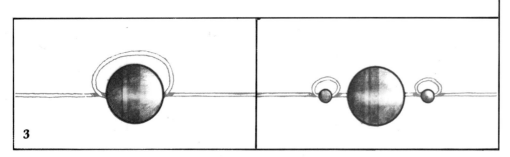

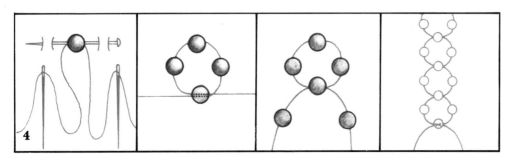

Sometimes, small beads are sold strung on thread. If you break the thread the tiny beads spring apart. A useful tip is illustrated in diagram 1. Thread a needle with cotton thread and pass the necklace thread through the loop of the cotton. Pierce the thread supporting the beads with the needle and pull the thread through. Hold the new bead thread parallel with the old and slide bead across.

Bead knotting

When beads are to be spaced from each other either for appearance or for safety of precious stones, the simple knotting technique here is used. If thread seems too visible, a small bead is strung both sides of a large bead, the thread being strung through the small bead twice. On nylon, if small beads are threaded about 2 inches apart using this method, a pretty effect is achieved. Diagrams 2, 3◄▼

Jeweler's findings

For some necklaces a metal clasp is needed for finishing and fastening. After a necklace or bracelet is finished, the thread ends are taken under the tongue and the back of the clasp and then taken up through the last two beads. Many different kinds of findings are available, some of them with perforated surfaces so that smaller beads can be stitched on. (Not illustrated.)

Two-thread technique

This is the basic technique of beadwork and can be used with endless variations. Take a long thread and run it through a single bead. Push a pin through the bead and fix that to a cushion pad. Now working with both ends of the thread, thread a bead on the left-hand thread and another on the right-hand thread. Cross the threads through the fourth bead and proceed as before. Diagram 4 ◄

form of decoration made from beads, has never been out of fashion for long, whether the feeling has been for the recent simple string of pearls or, by contrast, the heavy Victorian jet collars. Today, with current trends toward soft, informal clothes, beads are a natural accessory. In this chapter some, but by no means all, of the techniques of bead stringing are illustrated. The effects created can be as varied as the imagination and taste of the individual designer —from massive, sparkling necklaces to a single understated medallion on a leather thong.

Materials for beadwork can often be found just lying around, waiting for a sharp-eyed collector, although speciality shops can be an equally good source for discovering beautiful, expensive beads.

Materials and equipment

Beads

Almost anything through which a hole can be bored is usable as a bead: shells, seeds, fruit seeds, sweet smelling spices such as cloves and cardomom, nut shells, kernels, dried berries, animal and fish teeth, pieces of bone, scraps of leather, pieces of wood—all these have been successfully used for decorative jewelry.

More formal and familiar beads are usually either round, oval, square, raindrop or baton shaped and are made of precious and semiprecious stones, mineral substances, coral and jet, glass and crystal, porcelain, pottery, plastics and resins. Beads are obtainable in large or small quantities from craft shops, needlework shops and specialist suppliers.

Start a collection of beads for jewelry making—it can be like searching for treasure. Chain store jewelry counters provide a variety of inexpensive bead necklaces which can be broken up and reassembled. Junk shops and secondhand clothing shops are worth searching for beautiful old beads which are now becoming scarce, and elderly lady friends can be counted on to have a broken bracelet or brooch tucked away. A single beautiful bead can be used as the centerpiece of a brooch and is well worth looking for.

Threads and strings

A variety of different threads and strings can be used for making bead jewelry, depending on the design and the size of bead being used.

Bead silk, strong twist thread, any polyester thread, various weights of nylon thread, thin cords and wire are among

Bead mosaic

The diagrams here show how close, dense surfaces are built up. A row of beads is strung fairly loosely and then the thread is taken back through the last bead but one. A new bead is taken up each time, the thread going back through the second bead of the row before. This principle can be used with cord, nylon thread or wire. Pretty medallions, earrings and pendants can be made. Diagram 5 ►

Working with wire

Working with wire, three-dimensional effects are possible. A pair of pliers is needed for this kind of bead work. The illustrations show how wire is bent into links for beads and how beads are secured by wire. For a dropping bead, for a pendant or an earring, a jeweller's pin is used. To hold a large bead securely at the end of a drop, the wire is threaded through a smaller bead. Diagrams 6, 7 ► ▼

Alternative finishing

If a different kind of finishing is desired, the simplest is a bar and ring made of beads. Knot the threads through a bar bead and finish the ends through six beads making a circle. Glue the ends of the threads before passing them through the last bead. The glue will adhere to the inside of the bead and hold it securely out of sight. Use this method for finishing off thread ends (Not illustrated.)

Pendant earrings

Here are some ideas for pendant earrings. A small, flat-backed bead is used to hide the metal finish of the earclip. Alternatively, glue a piece of fabric or leather to the clip and either cover it with beads or leave it plain. Wooden beads can be split to make half beads by tapping a tack into the hole. Paint them with shiny enamel paint or nail polish ►

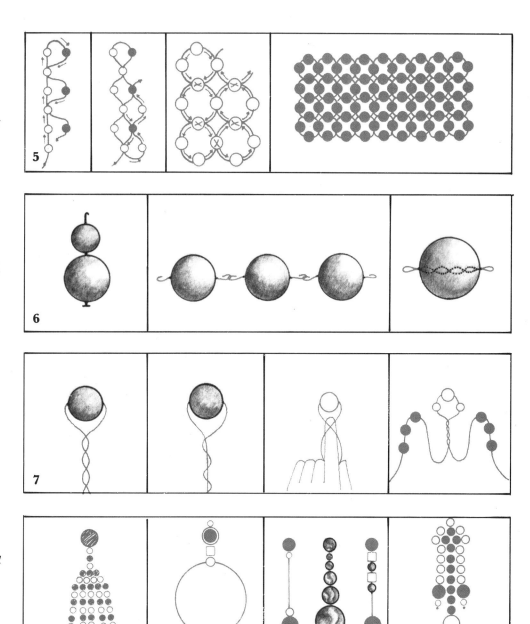

those most commonly used, but leather thongs, thick cords and macramé twine are also used for some types of jewelry. Dental floss, obtainable from most drug stores is also recommended.

Wire for jewelry making is available in soft copper, brass or silver. Copper plated steel wire is also used and is easy to work. Wire is available in a range of gauges. Florist's wire can be used for some techniques in jewelry making.

Needles

Long thin beading needles are useful for threading beads with small holes, and needles of different gauges can be used as long as the eye will pass through the bead. Some threads are stiff enough to be passed through a bead without a needle, and other threads can be dipped in glue or twisted with soap to stiffen the ends.

For working with wire a pair of pointed, half-round pliers, a pair of side cutters for cutting wire, and a fine file are needed.

Clasps and fastenings

Clasps and fastenings for jewelry are called "findings" and are obtainable from specialist suppliers and crafts shops in a wide and varied range of styles.

Pins and working pad

For more intricate beadwork, such as mosaic beading, a working pad similar to that used in lacemaking is advised, a felt-covered brick or a piece of cork mat covered in felt will do. Long, glass headed pins are used for holding bead patterns in position during working.

A felt or velvet lined tray is ideal for making most other kinds of jewelry. The design can be laid out in the tray without

the beads rolling around, and if the fabric is of a dark color the color contrasts show up more clearly. A few small plastic pots near the work tray will conveniently hold beads while they are being worked.

Techniques

Apart from the simple thread and knotting techniques used in single strand necklaces, there are other techniques in bead jewelry making which are more complex and require practice to perfect.

Mosaic beading, for instance, is rather similar to lacemaking and there are several variations on the basic patterns for achieving different effects. These are some of the techniques illustrated in this chapter and after awhile, you will be able to identify which have been used to produce this beautiful jewelry.

for macramé necklace

☐ 4oz cone fine white macramé twine
☐ 24 long beads
☐ 20 round beads

To make the necklace

Lay four lengths of twine together to form holding cords. Set on twenty-four doubled threads across the center of these holding cords.

Thread on beads as shown, working a square knot above the eight center beads and below all twelve beads. Thread on beads in the sequence illustrated, separating them with square knots and ending each column with an overhand knot.

Complete the neckband of the necklace by working square knots on either side of the beads to give the required length to fit around the neck.

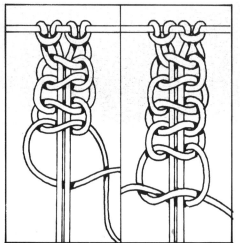

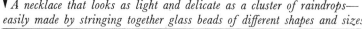

▼ *A necklace that looks as light and delicate as a cluster of raindrops— easily made by stringing together glass beads of different shapes and sizes*

▲ *A white macramé necklace with amber, red and white flat wooden beads*
▼ *Large and small beads strung closely together to make a solid necklace*

▲ *Different effects can be achieved using small colored beads or shells*
▼ *Eye-catching huge wooden beads look good strung on leather thongs*

▲ *Cord of different colors can be used as a contrast to the beads*
▼ *The variety of designs using toning and blending colors is endless*

Knitting pattern/chunky jacket

The fastest thing on two pins is just the way to describe this long line cardigan. Worked on very large needles and using three strands of yarn simultaneously, it's fun to work and quick to complete. The result is a warm, richly textured cover-up to go with casual outfits when the temperature drops.

Sizes

Directions are for 34in bust. The figures in brackets [ ] refer to the 36, 38 and 40in bust sizes respectively.
Length, 31[31:32½:32½]in.
Sleeve seam, 15½[16:16½:17]in.

Gauge

6 sts and 9 rows to 4in over st st worked on Jumbo needles ¾in using 3 strands yarn tog.

Materials

Botany Jiffy
15[18:18:18] skeins
One pair Jumbo needles ¾in
4 buttons

Back

Using 3 strands yarn tog throughout, with Jumbo needles cast on 31[31:33:33] sts.
1st row K1, *P1, K1, rep from * to end.
2nd row P1, *K1, P1, rep from * to end.
Beg with a K row, continue in st st until work measures 8[8:9:9]in, ending with a P row.
K2 tog at each end of the next and following 6th row.
Continue without shaping until work measures 23[23:24:24]in from beg, ending with a P row.

Shape armholes

K2 tog at each end of next and every other row until 9 sts rem, ending with a P row. Bind off.

Left front

Cast on 15[17:17:19] sts.
Work 2 rows in rib as given for Back, inc one st at end of last row. 16[18:18:20] sts.
1666

Next row K5[6:6:7], K into second st on left-hand needle then K first st on left-hand needle and slip both sts off tog—called TW2R —, placing needle behind first st on left-hand needle K into back of second st then K first st and slip both sts off tog—called TW2L —, K to end.
Next row K2, P to end.
Rep last 2 rows until work measures 11½[12:12:12½]in, ending with a WS row.
Next row K3[4:4:5], (P1, K1) twice, M1P, (K1, P1) twice, K to end.
Next row K2, P3[4:4:5], K1, (P1, K1) 4 times, P to end.
Next row K3[4:4:5], bind off 9 sts in rib, K to end.
With a separate length of yarn and a spare needle, cast on 8 sts. Work 3 rows st st, ending with a K row. Break off yarn.
Return to where main piece of work was left.
Next row K2, P3[4:4:5], P the 8 sts on spare needle, P to end.
Keeping the center 4 sts in patt as before, continue without shaping until work measures the same as Back to armholes, ending with a WS row.

Shape armhole and front edge

Next row K2 tog, patt to last 4 sts, K2 tog, K2.
Continue dec in this way at front edge on every other row 4[6:5:7] times more, *at the same time* dec at armhole edge on every other row until 2 sts rem.
Continue on these 2 sts in garter st for 5in. Bind off.

Right front

Work to correspond to left Front, reversing all shaping.

Sleeves

Cast on 13[13:15:15] sts.
Work 2 rows in rib as on Back, inc one st in center of last row. 14[14:16:16] sts.
Next row K5[5:6:6], TW2R, TW2L, K to end.
Next row P to end.

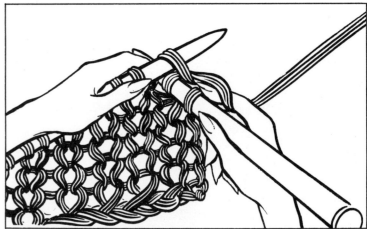

▲ *Showing the size of the Jumbo needles*
▼ *Close-up detail of TW2R which forms the cable-like panel*

Keeping patt correct in center, inc one st at each end of every 5th row until there are 22[22:26:26] sts.
Continue without shaping until sleeve seam measures 15½[16:16½:17]in, ending with a P row.

Shape cap

K2 tog at each end of next and every other row until 4[4:6:6] sts rem, ending with a P row.

Bind off.

Finishing

Press work lightly under a damp cloth using a warm iron. Join raglan seams. Join side and sleeve seams. Join ends of Front bands and sew to Back neck. Make pocket linings from fabric and stitch in place. Sew on buttons using holes in knitting for buttonholes. Press seams.

1667

Stitchery design/candlewicking

Candlewick originated in America in early Colonial days when, with a severe shortage of sewing materials of all kinds, women settlers used the thick cotton wick intended for candlemaking as an embroidery thread, working it into knotted and tufted designs on bedspreads. For many years the use of candlewick was restricted to bedspreads, but it looks effective in many other forms and can be used for pillows, rugs and bathmats as well as for warm garments such as bathrobes.

The tracing design given in this chapter is adaptable for almost any use and builds up well, placing the motifs as linking squares. It can be used for both tufted and smooth candlewicking and parts of the design could be adapted for a matching border motif.

Materials for candlewick

There are two kinds of candlewicking, tufted and smooth, but for both types it is essential that the material on which the embroidery is worked should shrink on the first washing to secure the candlewick in the fabric.

Usually, bleached muslin is used for candlewick, but linen can also be used. It is important to choose a weave which will take two thicknesses of the candlewick cotton.

Yarn. Lily Mills Sugar'n Cream cotton can be used for candlewick and is sold in skeins or balls, available in a variety of colors. Skeins can be cut into 48 inch lengths or, if preferred, wound into a ball and used as required.

Needles. A special candlewick needle is used; this is large in size with a flattened, curved point and a big eye.

Scissors. It is essential to have scissors which are extremely sharp for cutting the loops. A blunt pair will drag and pull the tufts out of the fabric.

Designs

Designs for candlewick are most effective when based on geometric shapes, but flowing designs can also be used if they are large sized. Small, intricate patterns are difficult to work and the shapes become distorted with the tufting. The candlewick can follow the outlines of the design, can fill in some areas, or cover the background completely as an all-over design, giving a solid area of pile texture.

Tufted candlewick

In some early examples of candlewick, French knots and backstitch were used, but in modern embroidery the stitch mainly used is running stitch worked $\frac{1}{4}$ inch—$\frac{1}{2}$ inch apart along the line of the

1668

▲ *A tracing design for working in either tufted or smooth candlewicking*

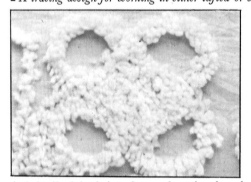 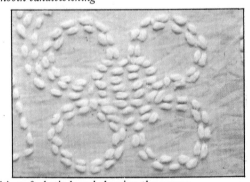

▲ *A detail of the design above, enlarged and worked in tufted stitch and showing the reverse*

design, leaving a small loop between each stitch. To keep the loops of even length place a pencil under the cotton as each loop is made. The candlewick yarn is used double. Cut a length twice as long as is required and thread it through the needle until the ends are even. It is not necessary to finish off the ends when starting or finishing—begin on the right side of the fabric, leaving an end equal to the size of the completed tuft and end in the same way.

When all the design is completely worked cut the loops evenly with a very sharp pair of scissors.

Smooth candlewick

This type of candlewick is worked simply in running stitch. One doubled length of cotton is used in the needle as for tufted candlewick and the stitches are worked about $\frac{1}{4}$ inch long and $\frac{1}{4}$ inch apart. This results in a bead-like stitch giving a beautifully raised, sculptured effect. This type of candlewick is at its best worked in geometric designs built up into solid shapes and covering the entire area of the fabric.

Finishing candlewick

The completed work should be washed so

▲ *Smooth candlewicking in a modern bedspread*

that the fabric shrinks to fix the tufts more securely and to fluff them up. If a washing machine is used, wash for at least 20 minutes in warm soapy water. If washing by hand let the work soak for three to four hours. Do not wring or squeeze, just shake out.

Dry the work out of doors in a strong breeze and shake it frequently while drying to eliminate creasing and to make the tufts fluffier. Brush the tufts lightly with a soft brush before they are quite dry to fluff them up.

It is best to avoid ironing candlewick as this will flatten the tufts.

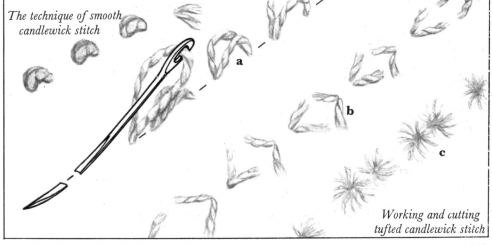

The technique of smooth candlewick stitch

a

b

c

Working and cutting tufted candlewick stitch

Stitchery pattern/flower pillows, two charts

▲ *Floral designs worked on linen are fresh and colorful as a group of pillows or used individually*

The appeal of these pillows depends largely on the use of strong, clear colors to work the bold floral designs. Instructions and a tracing pattern are given here for each of the two pillows shown above right; the next chapter will include those for the two pillows on the left. These are just a few of a wide range of floral possibilities to be worked in the individual's choice of color and stitch.

To make each pillow measuring 15 inches square, you will need:
- ☐ ½yd 36 inch wide even-weave linen
- ☐ Sewing thread to match linen
- ☐ 10 inch zipper

- ☐ Pillow form 16 inches square
- ☐ D.M.C. 6-strand floss

Peony pillow

You will need two skeins of D.M.C. 6-strand floss in each of the following colors:
1. Light blue 813; **2.** Medium blue 826; **3.** Light blue/lilac 334; **4.** Dark blue/lilac 336; **5.** Light lilac 209; **6.** Dark blue 939; **7.** Bright green 911; **8.** Dark green 890; **9.** Olive green 469.

Method

This design is worked entirely in long and short stitch using two strands of thread in the needle. Commence working the

design from the center of the flower with the stitches lying in the direction indicated on the tracing pattern.

Gypsophila pillow

You will need D.M.C. 6-strand floss in the following colors:
1. Light violet 334; **2.** Dark violet 312; **3.** Blue 826; **4.** Turquoise 519; **5.** Light green 955; **6.** Yellow/green 472; **7.** Dark green 905.
Two skeins each of colors 4, 6 and 7.
Three skeins each of colors 1, 2, 3 and 5.

Method

Using two strands of thread in the needle,

▲ *A combination of stitches from the gypsophila*   ▼ *Detail of peony reveals direction of stitches*

the flowers and leaves are worked in long and short stitch. Stitch the petals of the flowers first; then fill in the centers with satin stitch and French knots. Allow the satin stitches of the centers to radiate a little into the petals. With three strands of thread in the needle work all stems in outline stitch.

Finishing

When all the embroidery is completed, press the work carefully on the wrong side. Make into a pillow measuring 15 inches square inserting a zipper centrally along one seam on the pillow. Press and insert pillow form.

Tracing pattern for gypsophila

1672

Tracing pattern for peony

1673

Costume design/19th century ladies

The main features of this costume from the 1880's are the high Empire waistline and the tubular dress skirt with its elaborate hem decoration. This was a graceful and feminine look and exceptionally flattering.

The Dress

The dress has a high waistline with a narrow waistband joining the skirt to the bodice. The skirt is gathered very slightly at the front and more fully at the back, standing away at the hem and finishing above the ankles.

Necklines of this period were either high and worn with puffed sleeves ending well below the wrist, or low with the puffed sleeves ending above the elbow. A frilled muslin neckerchief was worn to fill the low neckline. A Spencer was usually worn over the thin dress for warmth.

Fabrics and colors

Muslin, fine linen and cotton, embroidered or printed with dots, sprigs of flowers, and delicate border prints on white were most popular for day dresses, although soft pastel shades came in later in the period. For evening wear, gauze over colored silk or satin was fashionable. Outer garments were made from woolen or silk cloth; the Spencer was usually either blue or black.

Accessories

Bags of silk (bead embroidered or tubular knitted silk) were carried by ladies, and parasols, short gloves and small fans were necessary to complete an evening outfit.

Shoes were very pointed with tiny curved heels or no heels at all, worn with flesh or white colored stockings.

Hats and hair

Hats were richly trimmed; turbans, berets and tall crowned bonnets were adorned with frills, rosettes, ostrich feathers and ribbons etc. Mob caps which covered the hair and framed the face were worn indoors. Hair was centrally parted and arranged in curls on the temples with short ringlets and curls at the front and sides.

19th century costume

You will need:

The dress. 4 yards 36 inch wide material; cotton lawn, voile, muslin or any soft, light fabric, white, pastel or sprigged on white. Ribbons, flowers etc for decorating the hem.

The Spencer. 2 yards 36 inch wide coat-weight woolen cloth, blue or black.

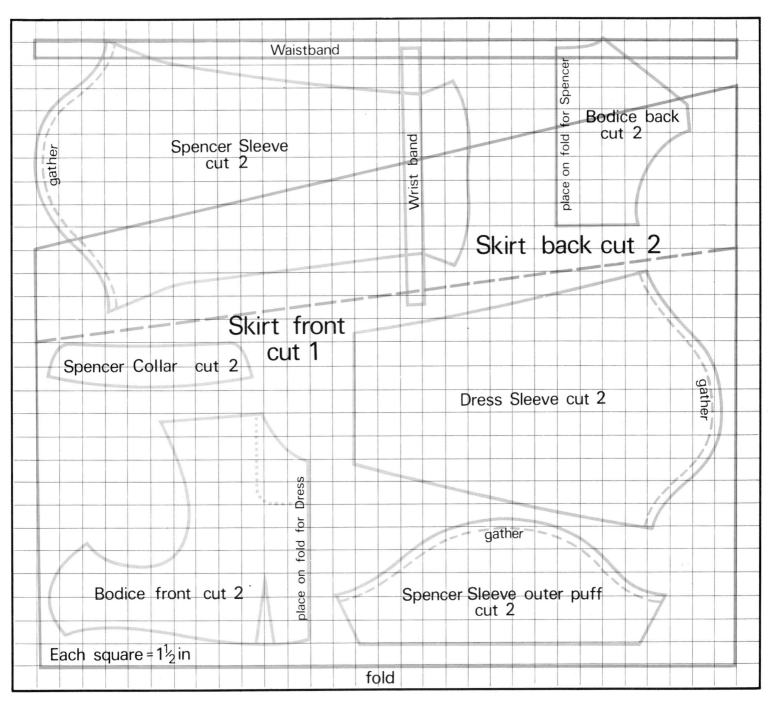

Waistband

Spencer Sleeve
cut 2

gather

Wrist band

place on fold for Spencer

Bodice back
cut 2

Skirt back cut 2

Skirt front
cut 1

Spencer Collar   cut 2

Dress Sleeve cut 2

gather

place on fold for Dress

Bodice front cut 2

gather

Spencer Sleeve outer puff
cut 2

Each square = 1½ in

fold

Matching braid.

(The graph pattern will fit 34 inch bust).

To make the dress

Make a paper pattern from the graph and separate the pieces of pattern.

Place the Skirt Front on the fabric folded lengthwise and cut out. Cut two Skirt Backs, without cutting on the fold, and join front to backs. Seam the center back leaving an opening 8 inches long at the waist.

Place Bodice Front on fold and cut out. Cut two Bodice Backs. Make the waist-bust darts on the bodice front. Join side seams and shoulder seams.

Leave center back open. Cut the Waistband on the straight of the fabric, to diaphragm measurement plus turnings. Sew to the bodice leaving the waist back open. Gather the waist edge of the skirt, gently at the front and more fully at the back. Join the skirt to the waistband, still

leaving the back of the bodice and skirt waist open.

Gather the top of the Sleeve pieces with running stitches. Sew the underarm seam, and pin the sleeves into position, the gathers at the top of the sleeve. Sew the sleeves in.

Face the neck, hem and cuffs. Sew concealed hooks and eyes down the back opening. Adjust the hem length and sew.

To make the Spencer

Cut out one Bodice Back, placing it on the fold of the fabric as indicated on the chart. Cut out two Bodice Fronts. Join the pieces on side and shoulder seams, leaving the front open. Face the front edges with self fabric.

Cut a strip 3 inches wide and long enough to fit the diaphragm measurement on the bias. Fold this to 1½ inches wide and bind the waist edge of the Spencer.

Cut two collar sections in fabric and two

in interfacing. Make up the collar and attach to the neckline adjusting to fit comfortably. Sew hooks and eyes to close the Spencer front edge to edge.

To make the Spencer sleeves, cut out the outer puff section twice and the whole sleeve twice. Gather the top edge of the outer puff section with two rows of stitches and adjust to fit the armhole. Fasten off the thread. Sew the underarm seam. Sew a narrow hem along the puff edge cuff.

Stitch a strip of braid across the sleeve wrists of the main Spencer sleeves where indicated on the chart. Gather the top of the sleeve and adjust to fit the armhole. Sew the underarm seams. Finish off the cuff edge. Slip the puff over the main sleeve, pin both into the armhole and sew. To complete the look of the period, a roll is made by gathering a 10 inch long by 3 inch deep length of taffeta and stitching it to the inside back waist to lift the skirt.

Tailoring three

In this chapter
A. Canvassing the front and back:
padding the front canvas; basting canvas
to the front; basting canvas to the back;
adding a bridle; front stay tape; finishing
the canvassing.
B. Piped buttonholes: marking the
buttonholes; making the buttonholes.
C. Pockets with lining: interfacing a
pocket; straight piped pocket; shaped
piped pocket; piped flap pocket; flap
pocket; false flap pocket; welt pocket.
D. Lining a pocket
* **Terms and stitches**

A. Canvassing the front and back

The canvas is sewn in place after any
style seams, darts and back seams have
been stitched but before the shoulder
seams and side seams are stitched.

Padding the front canvas
After stitching the darts or seams on
the canvas (see Tailoring 1, D) trim off
the seam allowance plus $\frac{1}{16}$ inch on
the underarm, armhole and shoulder to
reduce bulk in seams.
1a, b, c. For a perfect result add a chest
pad of felt or loosely woven filler, stitched
to the canvas by staggered rows of pad
stitching*. This does not add bulk but
gives a rounded line to the chest.
The padding is stitched to the side of the
canvas which faces the lining.

Basting canvas to the front
Lay the canvas flat on a table, padded
side down. Over it lay the corresponding
coat front with the wrong side of the coat
fabric facing the canvas.
Match and pin the center and crease lines
together.
2a, b. Baste the following:
(i) Working from the bustline upward
baste the front edges of the coat to the
canvas, smoothing it up while working to
prevent wrinkles.
(ii) Repeat from the bustline downward.
(iii) Baste the opposite edge of the canvas
in a line from the hem through the bust up
to shoulder.
(iv) Baste around the armhole and along
the shoulder.
(v) Finally, baste along the crease line
of the lapel.

*A wrap-around coat and jacket in luxury
fabrics. The jacket, Butterick pattern number
6528, is made up in cashmere and features
raglan sleeves and a top-stitched step collar.
The coat, Butterick pattern number 6518, is
made up in 100% angora with a Prince of
Wales plaid.*

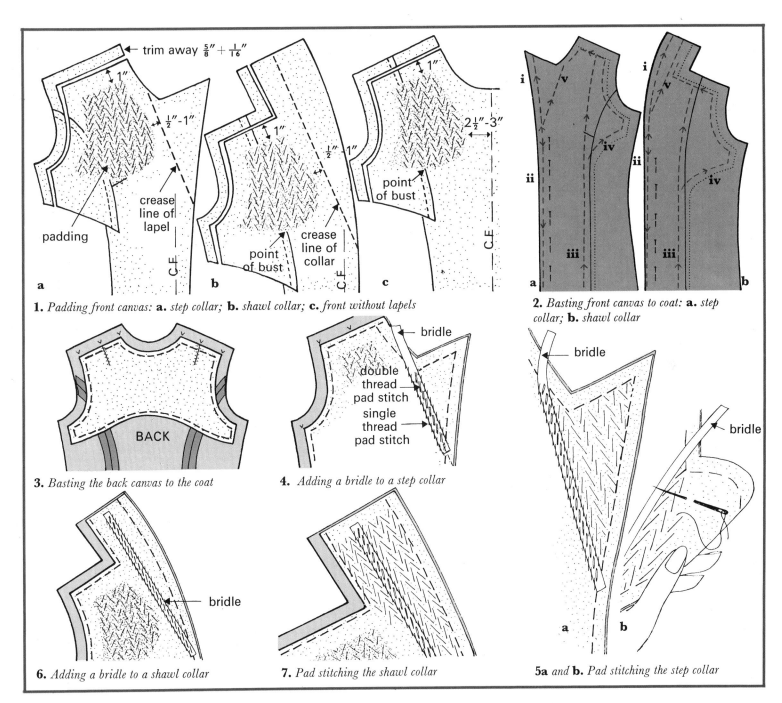

1. *Padding front canvas:* **a.** *step collar;* **b.** *shawl collar;* **c.** *front without lapels*

2. *Basting front canvas to coat:* **a.** *step collar;* **b.** *shawl collar*

3. *Basting the back canvas to the coat*

4. *Adding a bridle to a step collar*

6. *Adding a bridle to a shawl collar*

7. *Pad stitching the shawl collar*

5a *and* **b.** *Pad stitching the step collar*

Basting canvas to the back

Trim off the seam allowance plus $\frac{1}{16}$ inch around underarm, armhole, shoulder and neck edges.

Stitch any darts or seams. Even if you have decided to dispense with the back shoulder dart and ease in the shoulder seam instead, you should make the dart on the canvas.

3. Baste canvas to the wrong side of the coat back as shown, easing the coat fabric to the canvas along the back shoulder seam if necessary.

Adding a bridle

A bridle is a piece of $\frac{1}{2}$ inch wide linen tape sewn to the canvas along the roll line of a lapel, continuing into the step collar for 2 inches or to the center back for a shawl collar.

The linen tape should be shrunk by damp pressing or washing before application to prevent more shrinkage later.

Step collar. Cut a piece of tape to the length of the crease line plus 2 inches to extend into the collar.

4. Pin tape centrally along the crease line with 2 inches extending at the neck edge. Keep the tape taut.

Using a double, matching silk thread, pad stitch the tape in place along the center. This gives a strong central line. Then, with single silk thread, pad stitch along each edge.

5a, b. Starting from the bridle work rows of staggered pad stitching toward the edge. Keep the rows in line with the

bridle and don't sew beyond the seamline. Hold the lapel in a curled position with the left hand.

Shawl collar. Cut a piece of tape to the length of the crease line.

6. Pin tape centrally along the crease line keeping it taut. Using a double matching silk thread, pad stitch the tape in place along the center. Then, with single thread, pad stitch along each edge.

7. Starting from the bridle, work rows of pad stitching toward the edge. Shape the rows slightly at outer edge to allow the collar to set correctly, and don't sew beyond the seamline.

While working, roll the collar in a curled position with the left hand as for the step collar (**5b**).

Front stay tape

8a, b, c. Stay tape is sewn to the front edges. On a coat with a step collar the tape extends from the hem to the top of the crease line (**a**) and on a coat with a shawl collar from hem to center back (**b**). On any other style the tape is taken up the front to the neck edge (**c**).

9. Before adding the stay tape, work as follows:

Trim the front edge of the canvas just within the sewing line to reduce bulk.

Cut linen tape to the required length.

Position the tape and baste the strip taut at the outer edge.

Catch stitch* the inner edge to the canvas.

Finishing the canvassing

Finally, catch stitch the canvas to the coat at the underarm, shoulder and arm-hole on both back and front. Take care not to pull the stitches tight.

Working on the wrong side press well up to the crease line. Fold back along the crease line and allow the collar to roll, but do not press.

B. Piped buttonholes

There are several ways of making fabric buttonholes. For the heavier weight fabrics used in tailoring the following method is very successful.

Marking the buttonholes

The buttonhole length is the diameter of the button plus $\frac{1}{8}$ inch. If you buy the size of button suggested in the pattern then the buttonhole markings will be correct, otherwise, mark again, moving the inside tailor's tacks.

10. To insure that the buttonholes are in line and parallel to each other, prepare tram-lines on the markings, basting through both fabric and canvas. Remove the tailor's tacks.

Making the buttonholes

For each buttonhole cut two pipes in the coat fabric. The pipes should be 1 inch wide and the length of the buttonhole plus $1\frac{1}{2}$ inches, cut in the straight grain of the fabric.

11. Position the pipes on the right side of the garment, with the edges meeting along the buttonhole line and right sides facing. Baste.

Chalk mark the ends of the buttonhole.

12. Working on the right side, stitch along the buttonhole length to each side of the buttonhole marking. The lines should be $\frac{1}{4}$ inch apart for buttonholes (and $\frac{1}{2}$ inch apart for pockets). At each end of the stitching over stitch for about $\frac{1}{2}$ inch to secure ends.

1678

Remove the tram-lines.

13. Working on the wrong side, cut along the buttonhole line making deep mitered v's at the corners at least $\frac{3}{8}$ inch deep. Take care not to cut the pipes.

14. Pull the pipes through the opening to the wrong side. Press the seams open, and the miters away from the buttonhole.

15. Working on the right side adjust the pipes into even folds and oversew to close. Stab stitch * along the seamline as shown.

16. At the back work an oversewing stitch at each end of the buttonhole to hold the facing in position.

17. Fold the garment back and backstitch through pipes and miter as near to the fold as possible.

C. Pockets with lining

Pockets can be functional or decorative. The right place for them varies for each figure type, so make sure at the first fitting that they are in the right position for you.

Interfacing a pocket

All pocket openings are interfaced with a strip of silesia, or duck, basted on the wrong side of the opening to support them.

18. Cut the interfacing with the grain falling along the line of the pocket where possible, and take it into a seam where practicable. Position and baste to the wrong side of the pocket opening, then make the pocket as follows.

19. Straight piped pocket

This type of pocket is attractive if made with contrast pipes. The average pocket length for a coat is $5\frac{1}{2}$ inches to 6 inches. For each pocket cut two pipes 2 inches wide and to the pocket length plus $1\frac{1}{2}$ inches, in the straight grain of the fabric. Make the pocket opening as for bound buttonholes (B); but with the stitching lines $\frac{1}{2}$ inch apart.

To finish, add the pocket backing and lining as shown in D.

20. Shaped piped pocket

Mark pocket position carefully with basting. Then interface the back.

21. To pipe the pocket cut a piece of fabric suitable for the pocket shape as shown, using coat or contrasting fabric. Position the piece of material, right sides facing, over the marked pocket opening, matching any design or check if appropriate.

Baste in place long pocket line.

22. Stitch carefully at equal distances from the basting. The width depends on how you would like the pocket to look.

23. Cut through patch only, as shown, to make pipes.

24. Cut through garment along pocket

8. *Stay tape stitched to front of coat with :* **a.** *step collar;* **b.** *shawl collar;* **c.** *coat without lapels*

opening, mitering corners.

Finish as for a straight piped pocket, snipping any curved seams.

Finally, add the pocket lining and backing as shown in **D**.

25. Piped flap pocket

Make a piped pocket without lining.

26. From the coat fabric cut a pocket flap to the length of the finished pocket and to the desired shape of flap, plus 1 inch on all edges for seam allowance.

Cut a lining for the flap to match.

27. Place pieces together, right sides facing, and stitch as shown. Snip across the corners.

28. Turn to the right side and press, then draw a chalk line 1 inch from the raw edge as shown.

29. Slip flap under top pipe and baste in place through all layers along the stitching line of the top pipe.

30. Turn to the wrong side and stitch in place over the original seam at the back of the top pipe.

To finish, add the pocket backing and lining, as shown in **D**.

31. Flap pocket

Make the flap as for a piped flap pocket (figures **26**, **27** and **28**) and cut one pipe as for a straight piped pocket.

Interface the wrong side of the pocket opening.

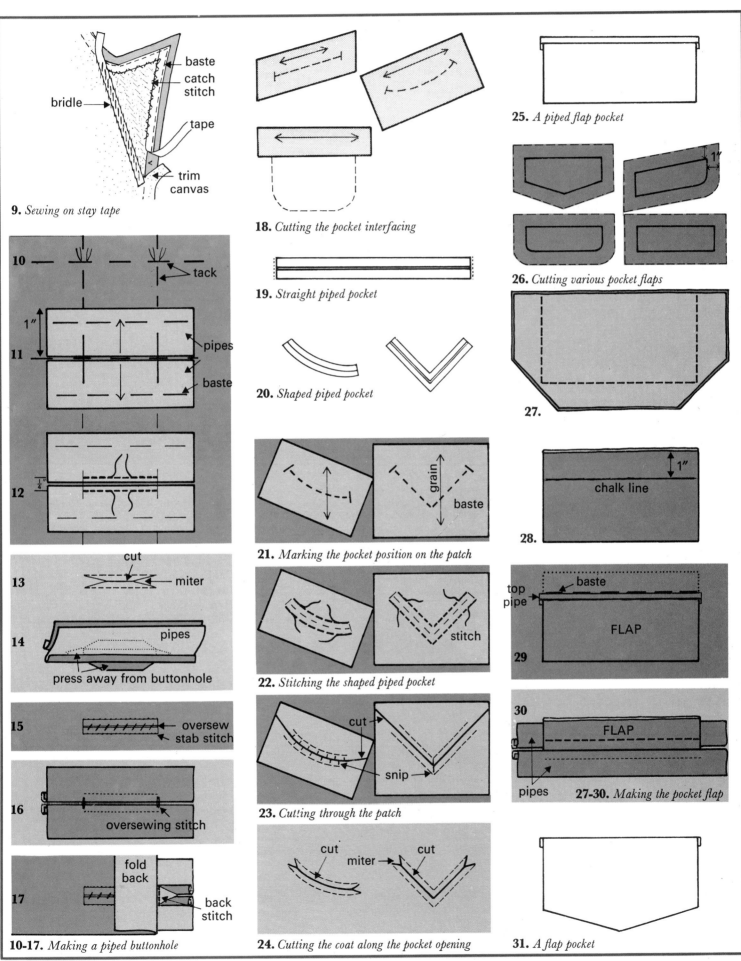

9. *Sewing on stay tape*

baste
catch stitch
bridle
tape
trim canvas

18. *Cutting the pocket interfacing*

19. *Straight piped pocket*

20. *Shaped piped pocket*

21. *Marking the pocket position on the patch*

grain
baste

22. *Stitching the shaped piped pocket*

stitch

23. *Cutting through the patch*

cut
snip

24. *Cutting the coat along the pocket opening*

cut
miter
cut

25. *A piped flap pocket*

26. *Cutting various pocket flaps*

1″

27.

28.

chalk line
1″

29.

top pipe
baste
FLAP

30

FLAP
pipes

27-30. *Making the pocket flap*

31. *A flap pocket*

10.
tack

11.
1″
pipes
baste

12.
¼″

13.
cut
miter

14.
pipes
press away from buttonhole

15.
oversew
stab stitch

16.
oversewing stitch

17.
fold back
back stitch

10-17. *Making a piped buttonhole*

1679

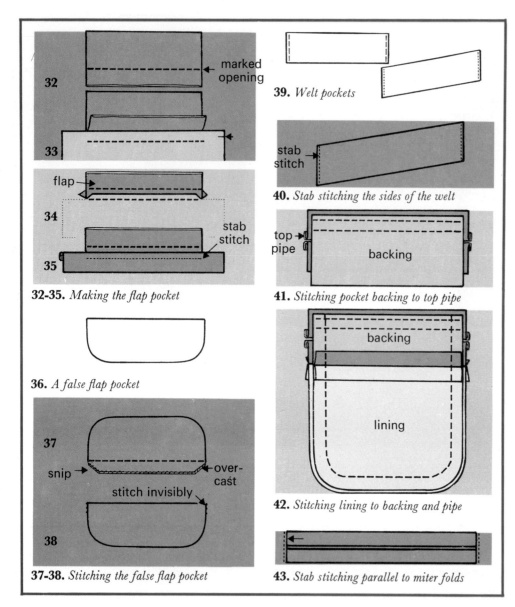

32.
marked opening

33.

34. *flap*
stab stitch

35.

32-35. *Making the flap pocket*

36. *A false flap pocket*

37. *snip* *over-cast*
stitch invisibly

38.

37-38. *Stitching the false flap pocket*

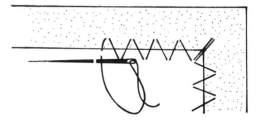

39. *Welt pockets*

stab stitch

40. *Stab stitching the sides of the welt*

top pipe *backing*

41. *Stitching pocket backing to top pipe*

backing

lining

42. *Stitching lining to backing and pipe*

43. *Stab stitching parallel to miter folds*

32. Stitch the flap in place along the marked pocket opening, with right side facing.

33. Fold the flap seam up, out of the way, and stitch the bottom pipe in place as for a piped buttonhole.
Cut through the back of the opening as for a piped buttonhole.

34. Turn the flap seam allowance through the opening to the wrong side, leaving the flap on the right side. Press the flap seam allowance up and the miters away from the opening.

35. Pipe the lower seam opening as for a piped buttonhole.
To finish, add the pocket backing and lining as shown in step **D**.

36. False flap pocket
Make a flap as for a piped flap pocket. (figures **26**, **27** and **28**).

37. Position over opening and stitch. Cut away corners and overcast raw edge.

38. Press the flap down and fasten the sides carefully.

39. Welt pocket
Make the welt as for the flap in figures **26**, **27** and **28**. Then make as for a flap pocket but placing the welt to the lower edge and piping to the top edge.

40. Finish the backing and lining as in **D**. Press the welt up and stab stitch* in place. If the coat is finished with top stitching you can topstitch the sides instead of stab stitching them.

D. Lining a pocket

41. Cut a backing for the pocket in coat fabric, 3 inches deep and to the length of the pipe. Stitch to the top pipe or flap seam allowance as near as possible to the original stitching line. For added strength stitch again $\frac{1}{2}$ inch above first row.

42. For each pocket cut two pieces of lining fabric 4 inches deep and to the length of the pipe. Stitch one piece of lining to the lower edge of the backing and the other piece to the bottom pipe or welt seam allowance.
Round off the lower edges of the lining as shown then stitch around to make the pocket.

43. Working on the right side stab stitch parallel to the miter folds for added strength.

*Terms and stitches

Catch stitch (**44**). Used to catch one fabric to another where bulk is to be avoided. Lift one thread of fabric with each stitch so it will be invisible on right side. Do not pull stitches tight.

Pad stitching (**45**). Worked as shown, the needle to be at right angles to the stitching line. Work with an imaginary grid, coming down one line and going up the next, without turning the work. Stagger the stitches to prevent pleats being formed.
Use small stitches (about $\frac{1}{4}$-$\frac{1}{2}$ inch long) for stitching canvas to lapel and collar to create a roll.
Use medium stitches (about 1 inch long) for lashing padding to canvas.
Use large stitches (about 2 inches long) for quick basting.

Stab stitch (**46**). Used where almost invisible stitches are needed to hold fabric layers together firmly.

a. Working from the right side, push needle down vertically, pull needle through from wrong side.

b. Then push needle up vertically and pull through from right side.
The stitches should be very small.

Crafts/weaving

An introduction to weaving

Weaving is one of the oldest handcrafts known to man, yet the basic techniques have hardly changed since earliest times. It's a craft that almost anyone can master without difficulty, whatever his age—the rag weaving examples shown on this page were worked by children.

Weaving is basically a very simple craft requiring a frame to hold the threads taut so that other threads can be interlaced at right angles.

There are several different kinds of looms and weaving frames available in craft shops. Each of them is designed in a different way to enable the weaver to interlace the yarns in the easiest manner according to the type of fabric to be woven.

The simplest weaving structure is a frame cardboard, a piece of cardboard notched at opposite ends with the warp threads strung between them. This produces small pieces of fabric. At the other end of the scale, a beginner can learn to weave on a four-shaft loom with equal

▲ *Study this picture of the finished frame loom before starting to make it. You will get a clearer idea of the use of various parts*

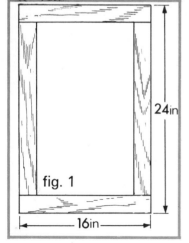

fig. 1

24in

16in

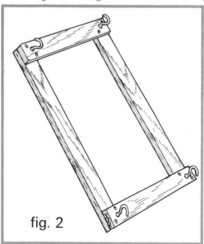

fig. 2

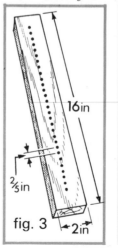

16in

fig. 3

$\frac{2}{5}$in

2in

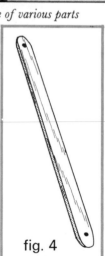

fig. 4

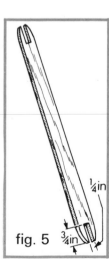

fig. 5

$\frac{1}{4}$in

$\frac{3}{4}$in

chances of success, and produce all kinds of woven fabrics for wall hangings, rugs, mats, table runners, clothes and accessories. As an introduction to this fascinating and absorbing craft, this chapter gives instructions for making a simple frame loom and setting it up for weaving, and suggests some ideas for using the woven fabric.

Glossary of weaving terms

Warp. Threads stretched lengthwise on a loom.
Weft. The cross threads woven into the warp.
Shed. The wedge-shaped opening, created when alternate warp threads are raised or lowered; the space where the weft yarn travels across the warp.
Raddle. (Sometimes called the "reed"). A comb-like implement for separating the warp threads and "beating up" the weft.
Leashes. Strings tied to groups of warp threads, to pull them up to make a shed.
Draft. The way in which the loom is threaded up.
Shed stick. An implement which, when turned on its side, makes a shed for the weft threads to pass through.
Weaving Stick (shuttle). The implement upon which the weft yarn is wound, used to pass the weft threads through the sheds.

A simple frame loom

To make the loom you will need:
☐ Planed lumber 10ft x 2in x 1in
☐ Planed lumber 4ft 6in x 1in x ¼in
☐ 3ft of ½in dowel rod
☐ 4 brass 1¼in hooks
☐ 8 1¼in No. 6 screws
☐ ½lb 2½in round head nails

Constructing the frame
Cut the lumber into required sizes:
☐ 3 lengths 16 inches long and 2 lengths 24 inches long from the 2in x 1in lumber.
☐ 3 lengths 18 inches long from the 1in x ¼in lumber.
Stage 1. Place two 16 inch lengths across two 24 inch lengths to make a frame. Make sure the corners are absolutely square and screw the four pieces together,

using two screws on each corner (figure **1**).
Stage 2. Bore a hole in each corner of the frame between the screw heads, using a bradawl. Screw in the hooks so that the open end of the hook faces outward (figure **2**).
Stage 3. Cut the length of dowel rod in half. This is used to make the rods on which the warp threads are tied. The hooks hold the rods in position (see illustration of completed frame loom).
The Raddle. Draw a line down the center of the remaining 16 inch length of wood. Leaving approximately 1 inch at either end, mark points along the center line at ⅖ inch intervals. Drill ⅛ inch holes approximately ¼ inch deep at each point. Insert a nail in each hole and tap them home until they are firmly embedded. Do not hammer or the wood may split (figure **3**).
Shed stick. Take two of the 18 inch lengths of wood and drill an ⅛ inch hole at both ends of each piece, one inch in from the end. Round off and smooth the ends of both pieces (figure **4**).
Weaving stick or wooden shuttle. Using the remaining 18 inch length of wood, cut slots into each end 1 inch deep by ¼ inch wide as shown in figure **5**.

Setting up the loom

Putting on the warp
Cut warp threads twice the length of the weaving frame (48 inches) plus 10 inches and tie them onto one of the warp rods in the way shown in diagram A, making sure that the ends are of equal length. Space them evenly along the rod.
With a narrow end of the frame toward you, hook the rod into place at the far end of the frame and then tie the warp ends onto the front rod as follows: working from the center take a pair of warp threads and pull them taut over and under the front rod and tie in a single knot as shown in diagram B. This first knot will hold the warp rod in place at the front of the frame while you continue knotting all the warp threads. Make sure that the tension is even. When all the pairs of warp threads are tied, complete the knot as shown in diagram C.
The warp threads are now complete.
Making the first shed. Put the shed stick in position at the top of the frame by sliding it over the first right hand warp thread and under the first left warp thread and working thus across the loom (diagram D). Tie the shed stick with a piece of string through the end holes to prevent it falling out of the loom. When this stick is turned on its side it makes a shed for the weft threads to pass through.

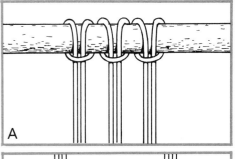

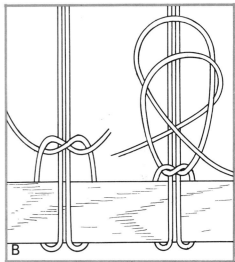

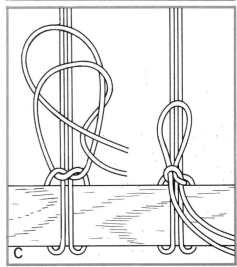

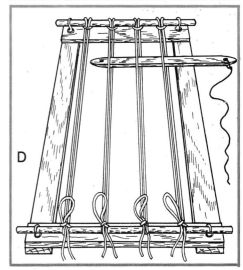

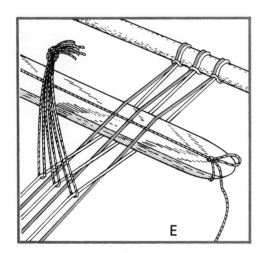

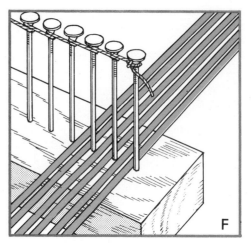

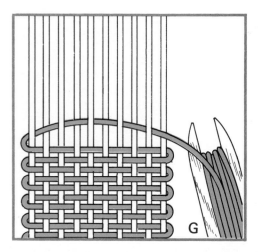

Making the second shed. The second shed is made using leashes and for these use a ball of soft firm string—rough string would damage the warp threads. Cut the required number of strings 18 inches long. Loop a piece of string under one of the right hand warp threads just in front of the shed stick. Knot the ends of the leash together evenly. Knot two more right hand warp threads and then knot the leashes together in groups of three about 4 inches above the warp threads (see diagram E). Tie the remaining leashes across the loom in the same way. The second shed is made by holding the grouped leashes firmly and lifting them so that the weft threads can pass through the space.

Plain weave

To produce a plain weave, first one series of warp threads is lifted by turning the shed stick onto its side and then alternate threads are lifted on the groups of leashes. This means that (by counting from the right) the shed stick lifts even numbered warp threads and the leashes lift odd numbered warp threads.

The raddle

The raddle spaces the warp threads evenly and is also used to beat the weft threads into position. Place the raddle on the loom in front of the leashes so that the warp threads go through the spaces between the nails in pairs. Then loop a piece of soft string around each nail to keep the warp ends from jumping out of position (see diagram F). The frame loom is now ready for the weaving to begin.

Yarns

Because the frame loom has a fairly coarse construction, it is better to use a fairly thick yarn for the warp. Thick rug yarn or thick soft string would be suitable for the first attempt at weaving. Finer

yarns or mixed textures can be used when a little experience has been gained. It is important when choosing the warp yarn not to use anything that breaks or fluffs too easily.

Suitable weft yarns are cotton, wool, linen and string. For fun and more exciting effects try weaving with strips of paper, grass, rushes, cane, dried plants, lengths of beads, lace, ribbon, pieces of thin wood, or strips of colored fabric. Remember when using different yarns and colors to exaggerate the contrast to achieve the most interesting results.

Starting to weave

Wind the weft yarn onto the weaving stick, making sure that it does not get too fat because it is then awkward to use. Turn the shed stick onto its side so that it makes a shed and slide the second shed stick through the space in front of the raddle. Holding the raddle parallel with the front of the frame, pull it firmly toward you until it can go no further. By putting the stick in at the beginning of the weaving you make sure that the warp ends lie evenly spaced for making an even textured cloth (see diagram G). You are now ready to begin using the weft yarn, which is passed through so that it lies in an arc on the warp threads and is then beaten evenly into position again at the front shed stick with the raddle. Lift the leashes and pass the weft through the shed. Begin and end weft threads in exactly the same way, by hooking the thread around the outside warp thread.

It is essential to keep the weaving the same width all the time and this is done by making sure that the weft threads are not pulled too tight. This is why the weft threads are left in an arc before being beaten into place and not pulled in a straight line across the cloth.

When the weaving is complete remove the leashes, the shed sticks and the raddle,

untie the half knots at one end and slide the rod from the other end.

Finishing warp thread ends

For mats the ends of the cloth can either be hemmed and fringed or knotted and fringed.

Weaves

On this draft plain weaves are woven but by free weaving (i.e. lifting the warp threads individually by hand and not using the shed stick and leashes) a greater variety of woven effects can be achieved. Free weaving is used when substances other than yarns are used for the weft.

Things to make

Shoulder bag

Weave brightly colored stripes of plain weave. Remove the work from the loom and sew up the sides. Fringe the warp ends to make an interesting border at the top of the bag. Add a cord for the handle and line the bag with a firm material. For a different effect, weave an inlay pattern on a plain background. Knot the warp ends together to form a side seam and sew up one side for the base of the bag. Add a handle and line with fabric.

Mats

Make a set of mats in plain weave stripes, varying the combination of colors or textures for each mat. Fringe the edges. Rushes, canes, raffia, or string can be used for interesting textures but remember that the mats must be washable.

Wall hangings

One can experiment and use different kinds of yarns and all kinds of objects to make wall hangings because they don't have to withstand wear and tear. If a great deal of color is required, keep the texture and weave simple. If rich texture is the aim, use very simple colors.

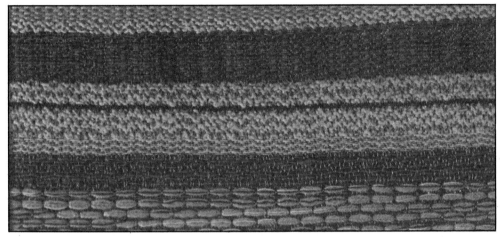

▲ *Fine jute warp, weft of mixed wool and worsted*   ▼ *Plain weave, 4 thin warp threads woven as one*

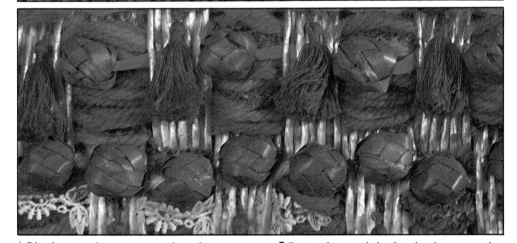

▲ *Plastic warp; lace, rayon tassels weft*   ▼ *Pattern here made by free darning on weaving*

Some of the things which can be made with the fabric woven on the frame loom

Crochet pattern/belted pants suit

This crochet suit is a useful addition to any wardrobe. The jacket has a heavily textured stitch which is repeated in a band around the pants hem. The remainder of the pants is worked in simple double crochet.

Sizes

Directions are for 32in bust. The figures in brackets [ ] refer to the 35in bust size.
Jacket. Length, 27[27½]in. Sleeve seam, 15in.
Pants. Inside leg, 30in adjustable.

> **Gauge**
> 10dc to 3in worked on No.G hook.
> 15 bean sts to 8in and 3 bean st rows to 2in.

Materials

Bernat Berella 4 (Knitting Worsted) 8[9] skeins
One No.G crochet hook
8 buttons
¾yd elastic

Pants left leg

Begin at waistline and using No.G hook, ch52[56].
1st row 1dc into 4th ch from hook, 1dc into each ch to end. 50[54] sts.
2nd row Ch3 to count as first dc, 1dc into each dc to end. Continue in dc, inc one st at each end of 5th and every following 5th row until there are 56[60] sts.
Continue without shaping until work measures 10in.

Shape crotch

Next row Ch8, turn, 1dc into 4th ch from hook, 1dc into each of next 4ch, 1dc into each st to end, attach a separate length of yarn to the end of the row, ch5 and break off, then with original yarn work 1dc into each of 5ch. 67[71] sts.
Work 2 rows.
Next row Patt to within last st. Turn.
Rep the last row twice more. 64[68] sts.
1686

Continue without shaping until leg measures 27½in from beg of crotch shaping, or 2½in less than desired length.
Next row Ch3 to count as first hdc, 1hdc into next st, *(yoh, insert hook into next st and draw through loop, yoh and draw through 2 loops) 3 times into the same st, yoh and draw through all loops on hook—called bean st—, skip one st, rep from * to last 2 sts, 1hdc into each st. 30[32] bean sts with 2hdc at each end.
Next row Ch3 to count as first hdc, 1hdc into next st, 1 bean st into each bean st, 1hdc into each of last 2 sts.
Rep last row once more.
Next row Ch3 to count as first hdc, 1hdc into next st, 2hdc into each bean st, 1hdc into each of last 2 sts. Fasten off.

Right leg

Work to correspond to left Leg, reversing shaping.

Jacket back

Ch67[71].
1st row 1hdc into 3rd ch from hook, *skip 1ch, 1 bean st into next ch, rep from * to last 2 sts, 1hdc into each of last 2 sts. 31[33] bean sts with 2hdc at each end.
2nd row Ch3 to count as first hdc, 1hdc into next st, 1 bean st into each bean st, 1hdc into each of last 2 sts.
Rep the 2nd row until work measures 20in from beg or length desired to armhole.

Shape armholes

Next row Ss over first 2hdc and first bean st, ch3, 1hdc into next bean st, patt to within last 2 bean sts, 2hdc into next bean st. Turn.
Next row Ch3 to count as first hdc, 1hdc into hdc, 1hdc into bean st, patt to within last bean st, 1hdc into bean st, 1hdc into each of last 2 sts.
Next row Ch3 to count as first hdc, yoh, insert hook into next st and draw through loop, insert hook into next st and draw through all 4 loops—

called dec 1—, patt to within last 3 sts, dec 1, 1hdc into last st. 25[27] bean sts with 2hdc at each end.
Continue without shaping until armholes measure 7[7½]in.

Shape shoulders

Next row Ss over 2hdc and 3[4] bean sts, ch3, 1hdc into next bean st, 1 bean st into each of next 4 bean sts. Fasten off. Skip 9 bean sts in center, attach yarn, ch3, 1 bean st into each of next 4 bean sts, 2hdc into next bean st. Fasten off.

Left front

Ch39[43] and work in patt as given for Back until work measures the same as Back to armholes. 17[19] bean sts.

Shape armhole

Next row Ss over 2hdc and 1 bean st, ch3, 1hdc into next bean st, patt to end.
Next row Patt to within last bean st, 1hdc into bean st, 1hdc into each of last 2 sts.
Next row Ch3 to count as first hdc, dec 1, patt to end. 14[16] bean sts.
Continue without shaping until armhole measures 5in, ending at front edge.

Shape neck

Next row Ss over 2hdc and 4[5] bean sts, ch3, 1hdc into next bean st, patt to end.
Next row Patt to within last bean st, 1hdc into bean st, 1hdc into each of last 2 sts.
Next row Ch3 to count as first hdc, dec 1, patt to end. 8[9] bean sts.
Continue without shaping until armhole measures the same as on Back, ending at armhole edge.

Shape shoulder

Next row Ss over hdc and 3[4] bean sts, ch3, 1hdc into next bean st, patt to end.

Right front

Work to correspond to left Front, reversing shaping.

Sleeves

Ch41[45] and work in patt as given for Back for 10 rows. 18[20] bean sts.
Next row Ch3 to count as first hdc, 2hdc into the next st, patt to within last 2 sts, 2hdc into next st, 1hdc into last st.
Rep last row once more.
Next row Ch3 to count as first hdc, 1hdc into next st, 1 bean st into next st, patt to end, ending with 2hdc. 20[22] bean sts.
Work 3 rows without shaping.
Rep the inc rows once more. 22[24] bean sts.
Continue without shaping until work measures 15in from beg.

Shape cap

Next row Ss over 2hdc and 1 bean st, ch3, 1hdc into next st, patt to within last 2 bean sts, 2hdc into next bean st. Turn.
Next row Ch3 to count as first hdc, 1hdc into next st, 1hdc into bean st, patt to within last bean st, 1hdc into bean st, 1hdc into each of last 2 sts.
Next row Ch3 to count as first hdc, dec 1, patt to within last 3 sts, dec 1, 1hdc into last st. Rep last 2 rows 2[3] times more. Fasten off.

Collar

Join shoulder seams.
With WS facing, work 42[46] hdc around neck edge.
Next row Ch2 to count as first hdc, 1hdc into each st to end.
Next row Ch2 to count as first hdc, 1hdc into each of next 3[5]hdc, *2hdc into next st, 1hdc into each of next 2hdc, rep from * 11 times more, 1hdc into each of next 2[4]hdc. 54[58] sts.
Continue in hdc until collar measures 3in. Fasten off.

Belt

Ch8.
Next row 1hdc into 3rd ch from hook, 1hdc into each ch to end.

Continue in hdc until work measures 30[32]in or desired length.

Dec one st at each end of every row until 3 sts rem. Fasten off.

Finishing

Press pieces under a dry cloth using a cool iron.

Pants. Join Back and Front seams. Join leg seams.

Fold over first row at waist and slip stitch in place. Thread elastic through.

Jacket. Sew in sleeves. Join side and sleeve seams.

With RS facing, attach yarn at lower corner of right Front and work 1 row of hdc along front edge, around collar working 2hdc into each corner, then down left front edge, turn.

Mark position of 8 buttonholes on right front edge placing bottom one 2in from lower edge, top one just below neck edge, then 6 more evenly spaced between.

Next row Work in hdc to position of first buttonhole, (ch2, skip 2 sts, 1hdc to next buttonhole) 7 times, ch2, skip 2 sts, 1hdc in each st to end.

Next row Work in hdc with 2hdc into each ch2 sp.

Work 1 more row in hdc. Fasten off.

Work 1 row hdc around lower edge of jacket and sleeves.

Press all seams lightly. Sew on buttons. Sew buckle to straight end of belt.

A stylish suit in simple crochet ►
▼ *Detail of bean stitch and double*

1688

Stitchery design/fairy tale in embroidery

This delightful embroidery hanging illustrates the old fairy tale "The princess and the pea"—and there she is, uncomfortably feeling the pea through seven mattresses. It's simple to do and a young embroiderer might be encouraged to work it for her own bedroom wall.

The mattress pieces are stitched to the background on three sides, leaving the top open. Insert a small amount of teased-out absorbent cotton to pad the mattress and close the top with running stitches. Metal foil has been used for the bed frame, the chamber pot and the princess's crown. Cut out the shapes and then prick the stitching holes with a needle.

The foil shapes must be stitched very loosely to the background or the foil will be damaged by the stitches. The pea is a small white bead, stitched finally under the bottom mattress.

After hemming all four sides of the hanging, stitch two curtain rings to the upper corners.

The hanging illustrated was worked to a measurement of 13 inches deep by 8½ inches wide.

▼ *Two more fairy stories which would make companion wall panels,* Thumbelina and the Little Mermaid

Stitchery pattern/floral pillow

This charming floral design pillow would look attractive in either a traditional or a modern decor.

To make this pillow measuring 15 inches square you will need:

☐ Pieces of single-weave canvas with 14 threads to 1 inch measuring 21 inches square
☐ Piece of fabric measuring 16 inches square for backing
☐ Zipper 10 inches long
☐ Tapestry needle No.18
☐ Pillow form measuring 16 inches square
☐ Appletons Crewel Yarn in the amounts indicated in the following column.

The entire design is worked using diagonal tent stitch, worked over two threads of canvas, with three strands of crewel yarn in the needle.

To make the pillow

When the stitchery is complete, block and trim the canvas leaving ½ inch seam allowances. Make into a pillow using a fabric backing. Leave a 10 inch opening on one side of the pillow and insert the zipper. Insert pillow form.

	Color	No.	Skeins
1	Rose pink	759	1
2	Scarlet	505	1
3	Rose pink	755	1
4	Dull rose pink	144	1
5	Dull rose pink	142	3
6	Mauve	607	3
⊙	Mauve	604	1
⊠	Mauve	602	1
⊡	Putty	981	2
⊟	Putty	983	2
⊘	Putty	985	1
◇	Bright yellow	553	1
⊡	Lemon	996	1
⊿	Chocolate	187	1
▲	Red brown	208	1
✕	Honeysuckle yellow	697	1
●	Drab green	338	1
▼	Drab green	335	2
△	Drab green	332	2
⊙	Drab green	331	1
■	Bright peacock green	835	1
◩	Bright peacock green	832	1
✕	Bright peacock green	831	1
⊘	Peacock blue	641	1
☐	Background—off white	992	12

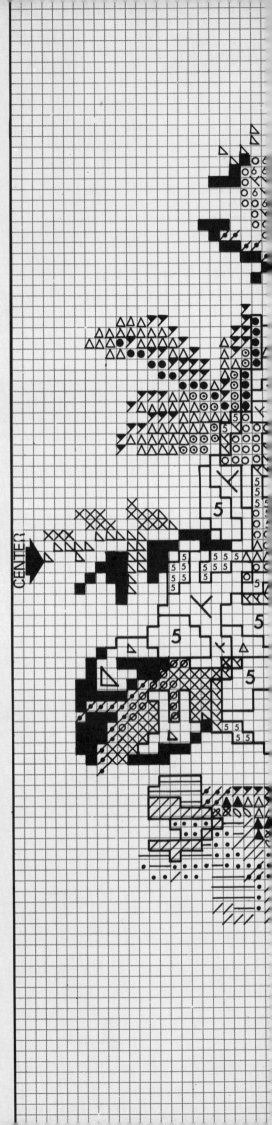

Stitchery design/mola work

San Blas appliqué

Bold, brilliant colors are used in this unique method of appliqué, worked by the Indian women of the San Blas Islands off the coast of Panama. The appliqué designs are now worked in two pieces measuring about 14 inches by 20 inches and are made into blouses called molas.

When the Indians first moved to the islands in about 1850, the molas were simple affairs, made only of dark blue material with a single band of red cloth around the bottom. The designs developed to decorate the lower half of the mola and then developed further to form a major part of the blouse. Later, when traders brought fabrics of brighter colors to the islands, the designs became more elaborate, involving up to five or six layers of fabric in as many colors. Reds, oranges, greens and blues vibrated together in one design. The designs themselves are primitive and gay, representing forms and figures from everyday life on the islands. Gods, goddesses, shapes from nature such as animals and plants and important people are all featured in bold, primitive stylized shapes. Often the designs are copied from pictures in magazines, comic books, calendars and even labels on canned foods. The designs often include English words or letters which are not understood by the Spanish speaking Indians and used with complete disregard of their meaning, but which look decorative and important. The stylized designs of the molas reflect the style of the wooden figures called "nuchus", carved by the Sans Blas men. The layers of fabric are first basted together and then cut away, and the result very much resembles the enamel work of some Mexicans, where layers of color are applied (painted) then incised to reveal color on color.

The molas are an important status symbol amongst the Indians and in some places it is considered improper for a San Blas Indian girl to be married without possessing at least twelve or more unworn molas as part of her dowry.

Fabrics

For the traditional style San Blas appliqué, plain dyed fabrics such as poplin or

▲ San Blas appliqué worked on the hem of a simple wrapover evening skirt

sail cloth are ideal. However, pure silks or shantung would lend themselves beautifully to the technique. For the more ambitious, experiments with textured fabrics such as corduroy or tweed could prove interesting. Felt, suede or leather could also be used but no turnings would be needed.

Uses

This appliqué technique is ideal for fashion where rich, bold effects are required. It would look good worked as a border on a skirt, on an evening cape, on inset panels or on a yoke on a dress or a blouse.

Mola work on curtains would look dramatic and pillow covers, bedspreads, pictures and wall hangings are all suitable subjects.

Method

This appliqué technique is more a method of cutting away than applying pieces of fabric. Parts of the top layers of fabric are cut away to reveal a section of the color below. One, two or three layers of fabric may have to be cut through at the same time to get to the desired color for a particular part of the design. However, if the colors are arranged well, it should not be necessary to have to cut through more than one layer of fabric at a time. Pieces of different colors can be placed under only certain parts of the design.

Experiment with two or three layers of fabric to start with, introducing extra color by applying small areas of fabric to highlight the design.

Place the fabrics in the desired arrangement of colors then baste the layers of fabric together all around the edge and also diagonally across each way to hold them securely.

To reveal the first color under the top layer, use a pair of sharp embroidery scissors and cut away a portion of the top fabric in the desired shape. Clip the edges of the fabric to be turned under on all curves and into all corners and turn in $\frac{1}{8}$ inch. Using a matching color sewing thread, slip stitch the edge to the layer of fabric below. Small appliqués of another color can be added in one, two or more layers using the same technique of cutting out to reveal the color below.

1693

Home crochet/lacy lampshade

This extremely simple pattern for a lampshade cover can either be used to fit in with a room decor or to give new life to an old lampshade. Use the basic stitch pattern of straight and looped chain to make something else for your room to match up with the lampshade, such as a table mat, chair back cover or even curtains.

Size

To fit drum lampshade 11in deep by 10in top diameter by 10½in bottom diameter.

Gauge
5 patts to 2¾ in worked on No.D hook.

Materials

Coats & Clark's O.N.T. Speed-Cro-Sheen
5 balls
One No.C crochet hook
One No.D crochet hook
One purchased drum lampshade 11in deep, 10in top diameter, 10½in bottom diameter

Main section

Using No.D hook, ch192 loosely. Join with a ss into first ch.
1st round Ch7, 1sc into same ch as ss, ch2, skip 2ch, 1sc into next ch, *ch7, 1sc into same ch, ch2, skip 2ch, 1sc into next ch, rep from * to end, working last sc into a ss at beg of round. 64 patts.
2nd round Ss into center of first ch7 loop, *ch2, 1sc into next ch7 loop, rep from * to end, working last sc into center of first ch loop.
3rd round *Ch7, 1sc into same sc, ch2, 1sc into next sc, rep from * to end, working last sc into last sc of previous round.
The 2nd and 3rd rounds form patt and are rep throughout.
Continue in patt until work measures about 5½in.
Change to No.C hook and continue in patt until work measures 11in, ending with a 2nd round (1st patt round).

Top picot edging
Next round *Ch4, 1sc into same sc into next sp, 1sc into next sc, rep from * to end. Fasten off.

Lower picot edging

Using No.C hook, attach yarn to a ch into which sc have been worked.
Work 1sc, ch4 and 1sc into same ch, *1sc into each of the 2 skipped ch between groups of sc of first round, 1sc into next ch, ch4, 1sc into same ch, rep from * until 2ch remain, 1sc into each of next 2sc. Fasten off.

Finishing

Press under a damp cloth, using a warm iron.
Place on lampshade and catch stitch in place around edges.

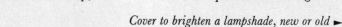
Several ideas for around the home to make from the basic stitch pattern
Cover to brighten a lampshade, new or old ▶

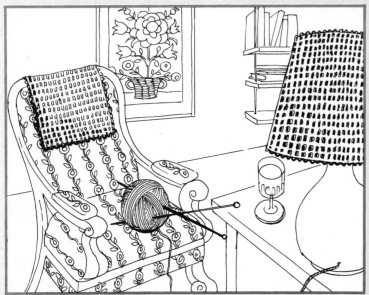

Tailoring four

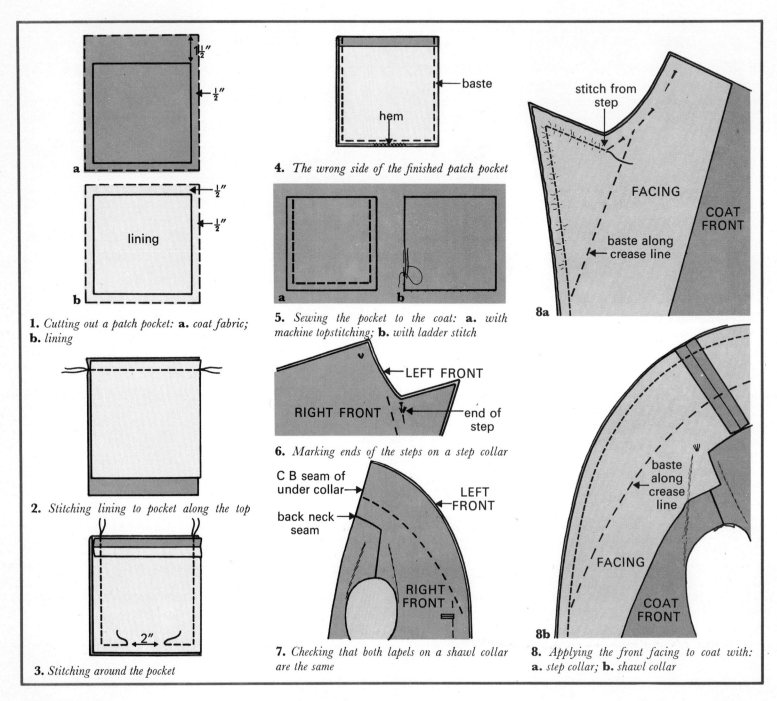

1. *Cutting out a patch pocket:* **a.** *coat fabric;* **b.** *lining*

2. *Stitching lining to pocket along the top*

3. *Stitching around the pocket*

4. *The wrong side of the finished patch pocket*

5. *Sewing the pocket to the coat:* **a.** *with machine topstitching;* **b.** *with ladder stitch*

6. *Marking ends of the steps on a step collar*

7. *Checking that both lapels on a shawl collar are the same*

8. *Applying the front facing to coat with:* **a.** *step collar;* **b.** *shawl collar*

In this chapter
A. Patch pockets
B. Facing the coat front: coat with lapels; coat without lapels.
C. Belts: belt across back; ¼ belt at side seams; ½ belt at back; tie belt; belt with buckle.
D. The second fitting: preparing for the fitting; the fitting stages; set in sleeve; raglan sleeve.
***Terms and stitches**

A. Patch pockets

1a, b. Cut out pocket shape with ½ inch seam allowance all around plus an extra 1 inch along top edge (**a**). Then cut out lining 1 inch shorter than the pocket (**b**).
1696

2. Stitch lining to pocket along the top, taking ½ inch seam. Press seam open.
3. Fold lining to pocket as shown, right sides facing. Stitch, leaving a 2 inch opening at the lower edge. Snip curved seams if any or snip across corners.
4. Turn through the opening, baste flat around edges and hem opening to close. Press and clap.
5. Apply to coat by topstitching (**a**) or ladder stitch* (**b**).

B. Facing the coat front

Coat with lapels
6. If working on a step collar mark the steps on the top edges of the lapels so they are both the same.

7. If working on a shawl collar, stitch and press the center back seam of the under collar, then stitch the shoulder and back neck seams. Press open and clap. Fold the coat in half and check that both sides have the same curve.
8a, b. Lay the facing and coat right sides together. Baste with small stitches to control the slight fullness there may be on the facing of the lapels.
Baste along crease line.
Stitch carefully as given on the instruction sheet, being careful to keep both lapels the same. Note that the step collar is only stitched as far as the end of the step.

This coat from Vogue Patterns has welt pockets and a tie belt ▶

9a, b. Remove basting. Snip across corners, snip into the end of the stitching line if applicable, and layer the seam allowances.

Press the seam open over a pressing roll.

10a, b. Turn facing to the inside. Working on the underside of the lapel, baste the seam edge of the lapel so that it lies away from the top edge and baste along the crease line. Baste the remainder of the facing seam to lie away from the top of the coat.

To press the lapel lay it flat, right side down, on an ironing board. Cover with a damp cloth and press as far as the crease line. Clap.

Press and clap the rest of the front edge. Lay the coat right side up with lapel folded in position and lightly press over a ham, using a woolen cloth under the pressing cloth.

Press the wrong side of the lower coat on a flat board.

11. Side stitch* under the lapel and down the inside front to keep the seam in position.

Coat without lapels

Apply the facing as given on your pattern instruction sheet and follow the steps given above for coats with lapels, ignoring those points referring specifically to the lapels.

12. The whole of the front seam edge should be basted to lie toward the inside of the coat and then side stitched* as shown.

C. Belts

You can add your own belt to a plain coat to give back interest.

13a—e. The belt can be set into the side seams and go right across the back (**a**). It can be set into the side seams and sewn or buttoned at the side back (**b**). It can be set across the center back (**c**). You can have a tie belt (**d**) or a buckled belt (**e**).

14. For all belts you will need two pieces of the coat fabric each to the required width plus $\frac{1}{2}$ inch seam allowance all around and one piece of interfacing cut to the same measurements.

15. If you are making buttonholes, baste the interfacing to the wrong side of one belt piece and make the buttonhole, as shown.

16. Place the belt pieces together, right sides facing, and lay the interfacing on the top. Baste together.

Belt across back

17. Stitch the long edges, layer the seam allowances, turn, baste and press.

18. Topstitch to match coat if required.

9. *Snipping and layering the seams of:* **a.** *step collar;* **b.** *shawl collar*

10. *Edge basting the facing seam on coat with:* **a.** *step collar;* **b.** *shawl collar*

11. *Facing seam side stitched under lapels and down front:* **a.** *step collar;* **b.** *shawl collar*

19a, b. When fitting make sure the belt is correctly balanced for the figure, usually above the waist for a short figure (**a**) and below the waist for a tall figure (**b**).

Quarter belt at side seams

20. Make buttonholes and shape the end.

21. Stitch long edges and across shaped end.

Snip and layer the seam allowances, turn, baste and press.

Topstitch if required.

22a, b. When fitting make sure that both belts are balanced and the same length. The belt should be just above the waist for a short figure (**a**) and just below the waist for a tall figure (**b**).

Half belt at back

23. Make buttonholes and shape ends.

24. Stitch the belt all around leaving a 2 to 4 inch opening along one side.

Snip and layer the seam allowances, turn, baste and press. Hem opening to close.

Topstitch if required.

When fitting check for balance as for the belt across the back (figure **19**).

Tie belt

25. Make as for $\frac{1}{2}$ belt at back.

Belt with buckle

Make up as for $\frac{1}{4}$ belt.

26. Fold unstitched end through buckle. Turn under raw ends and herringbone.

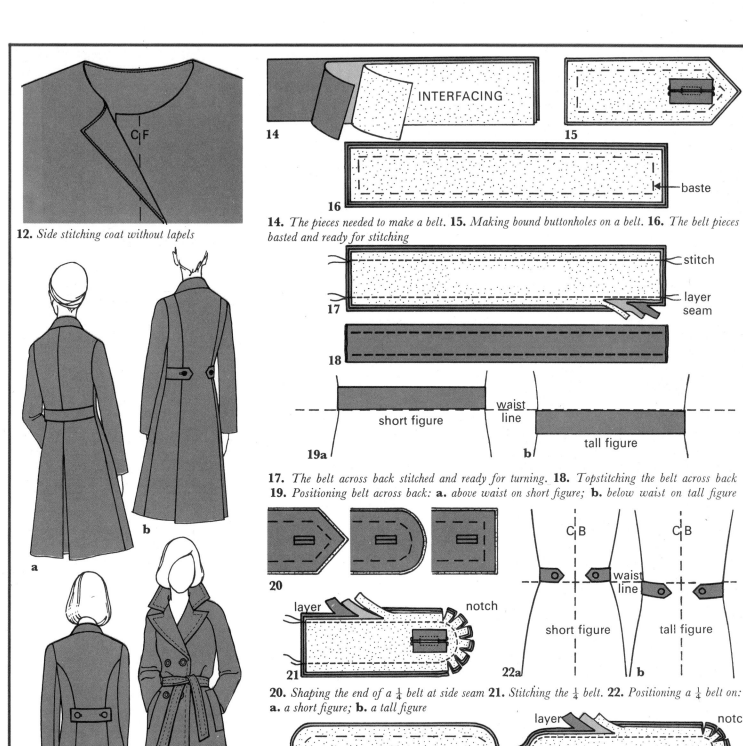

12. *Side stitching coat without lapels*

14. *The pieces needed to make a belt.* **15.** *Making bound buttonholes on a belt.* **16.** *The belt pieces basted and ready for stitching*

INTERFACING

baste

stitch

layer seam

waist line

short figure

tall figure

17. *The belt across back stitched and ready for turning.* **18.** *Topstitching the belt across back*
19. *Positioning belt across back:* **a.** *above waist on short figure;* **b.** *below waist on tall figure*

layer

notch

C B

C B

waist line

short figure

tall figure

20. *Shaping the end of a ¼ belt at side seam* **21.** *Stitching the ¼ belt.* **22.** *Positioning a ¼ belt on:*
a. *a short figure;* **b.** *a tall figure*

layer

notch

2"–4"

23. *The shaped ends and buttonholes on a ½ belt at the back.* **24.** *The stitched ½ belt*

13. *Belts:* **a.** *right across back;* **b.** *¼ belt buttoned at side back;* **c.** *½ belt at center back;* **d.** *tie belt;* **e.** *buckle belt*

25. *A tie belt*

herringbone stitch

26. *Stitching on a buckle*

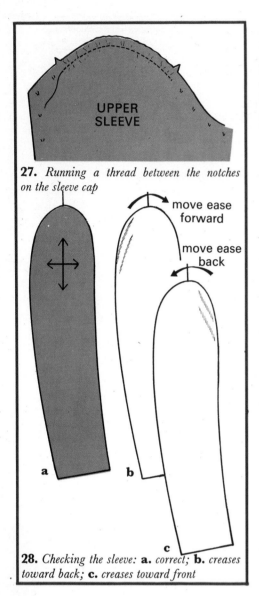

27. *Running a thread between the notches on the sleeve cap*

move ease forward

move ease back

a b

c

28. *Checking the sleeve:* **a.** *correct;* **b.** *creases toward back;* **c.** *creases toward front*

▲ *Close-up of a raglan sleeve set in position. From Butterick pattern 6528*

D. The second fitting

Having made the coat fronts, belt (if required) and stitched the back seams, it is now time for the second fitting.

Preparing for the fitting

Working on the new fitting lines, baste the side seams. Baste the shoulder seams if not already sewn. Over baste the under collar (Tailoring 2, A).

27. Sew a running thread between the notches on the sleeve caps to help distribute the ease and baste the sleeves into the armholes.

Add shoulder pads if required.

The fitting stages

☐ Check all the points made in Tailoring 2.

☐ Turn up the hem. If the coat has a tie or buckled belt, put on the belt before adjusting the hem as the length will be affected.

☐ Other belts are positioned after the

hem has been turned up. The coat must not be cut in half by a belt, it should give a balanced, pleasing look.

☐ Check the length again with the belt in position.

☐ Check that the sleeve is not too tight or too loose.

☐ Turn up the sleeve hem.

Set in sleeve

28a. Take a good look at each sleeve cap. The grain should be square and there should be no creases.

28b. If there are creases toward the back, unbaste and move the ease slightly toward the front. If this is not enough then unbaste the complete sleeve and move it forward.

28c. If there are creases toward the front then reverse the process moving the ease to the back.

Raglan sleeve

Check that the sleeves are not too full at the shoulders. Any fullness should be

pinned into the dart or seam which runs down the shoulder into the arm.

*Terms and stitches

Ladder stitch (29): used for invisibly stitching a pocket to a garment.

Side stitch (30): used for flattening edges of lapels and collars. Make a tiny stitch at right angles to the line of stitching. The stitches should not appear on the right side of the garment.

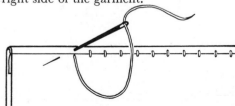

Crafts/making lampshades

Choosing shapes
Lighting plays an important part in home decoration, and a well-placed lamp with a tastefully designed shade can contribute a great deal to the restful atmosphere and charm of almost any room. When considering a shade, choose a style, size and color that will not be out of harmony with the lamp base.

Colors and lamp bases
Some colors are generally thought to be more suitable for lampshades than others. Good colors include gold, pink, red and green, although any color is acceptable if it fits into the color scheme of the room and enhances the overall effect of the furnishings. Generally, blue and dead white shades tend to give a rather harder light than gold and red.

Bases for lamps require a lot of thought and it is advisable to take the base to the store when choosing the shade frame, to see that the size and shape balance the base. A wide variety of ready-made bases are available but it is often possible to pick up a lovely old vase in your local junk shop and convert it. Old brass and silver candlesticks also make elegant bases and it is often worth spending a few dollars to have them properly converted. Wine decanters and bottles rarely make good bases for lampshades.

Cover material and lining
When selecting cover material for a soft lampshade, choose a fabric with plenty of "give", e.g. crepe back satin, rayon dupioni, wild silk and Thai silk. Heavy home furnishing fabrics, cottons, nylons, and materials that do not stretch are not suitable for fitted lampshades.

Crepe back satin is the best choice for lining as it has plenty of give, is reasonably priced, has a shiny surface to reflect light, and is very easy to work. Japanese silk is suitable for small shades only and it is

▲ *Instructions are given for making this empire lampshade*

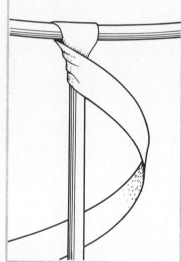

Above left and right: first two stages in taping, figure **1**

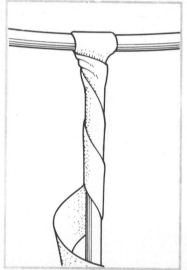
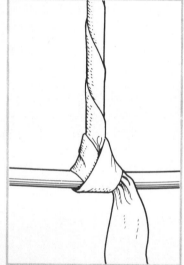

Above left and right: winding and finishing off

not as easy to use as crepe back satin.
The lining of a lampshade has two purposes; to hide the struts, particularly with pendant shades, and to give warmth to an otherwise cold light. A peach or pink lining, for instance, would give a warm glow to a white cover. Different effects can be achieved by using colored linings. A white lining reflects the light and is a good choice when the cover material is dark.

Trimmings

Trimmings can make or mar a lampshade. Before deciding which trimming to use, first consider the type of lampshade being made and the room in which it is to be used. Tailored shades often look most effective with a plain trimming and are easily spoiled by a fussy one.
There are many attractive commercially-made trimmings from which to choose, in various widths and textures, but for a tailored effect try making the trimming
1702

from a piece of bias strip cut from the cover material. A well made and well applied bias strip can look very elegant. It should be made with care and needs "practice to make perfect", but is well worth the extra effort involved. Metallic braids and laces look well used in conjunction with a bias strip trim.

Frames and fitting

The frame and fitting is the first consideration and is the basis of a successfully made lampshade.
Choose a frame made from a good firm wire (copper if possible) and one free from rough edges. If necessary file down any rough edges or they may poke through the binding tape. Check also that the frame is not bent because this is difficult to remedy.
It is advisable to paint the frame with a good gloss paint (allowing a day or two to dry thoroughly) as this reduces the risk of the frame rusting when it is washed.

Making an empire lampshade

To make a 10 inch bowed empire lampshade with a balloon lining you will need the following:
☐ Sharp pair of scissors
☐ Needles—sharps 9 for making silk shades
☐ Steel dressmaking pins or glass headed pins
☐ Good adhesive—UHU
☐ $\frac{3}{8}$in rayon seam tape
☐ Soft pencil
☐ Thimble
☐ Matching silk
☐ $\frac{1}{2}$yd 36 inch fabric for the cover
☐ $\frac{1}{2}$yd 36 inch fabric for the lining

Binding the frame

This is a vital process in the making of a lampshade; if it is not done well, the cover and lining will be loose and baggy instead of taut and firm. For each strut allow twice its length in seam tape. For top

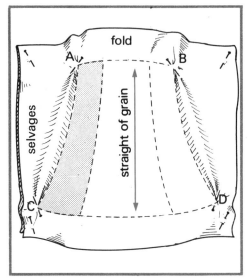

▲ **2.** *Placing the first four pins, figure 2*

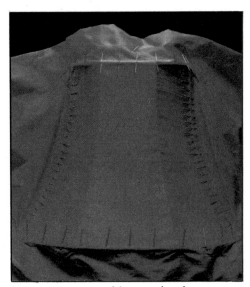

▲ *Side struts, top and bottom pinned*

▲ *Showing the inside at this stage*

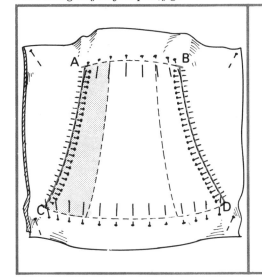

▲ **3.** *Marking struts with a pencil line*

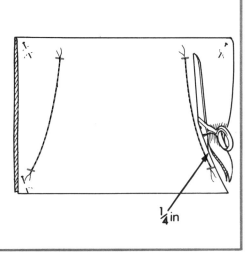

▲ **4.** *Cutting along machining line*

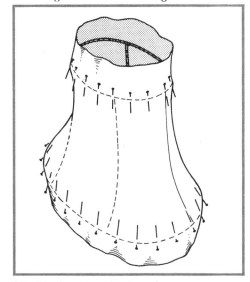

▲ **5.** *Pinning top and bottom rings*

and bottom rings allow twice their circumference. If too much tape is used the struts become bulky and uneven.

Great care must be taken when taping the frame to make sure that the binding is both tight and smooth on the struts and rings. Tape each strut separately and then tape top and bottom rings. Always start and finish taping at the join of a strut and ring, otherwise the tape may work loose. Knot the tape exactly as illustrated. No sewing is necessary, except when braiding rings for hard lampshades where there are no struts (figure **1**).

Fitting fabric onto frame

Fold the cover fabric in half and, with right sides together, place one pin in each corner to hold the pieces together. Place material onto one side only of the frame with the fold at the top and the grain running from the top of the frame to the bottom.

Place a pin at A, B, C, and D to hold

the fabric to the frame (figure **2**).

Start pinning fabric to the side struts (AC and BD), placing pins every ½ inch. Do not pin on top and bottom rings yet, although some wrinkles will appear on the material. Check with the photograph illustrating this stage.

Make sure pins are placed on the side struts with the heads facing the center of the lampshade—this lessens the risk of damaging clothes and body. Now pin the top and bottom. Tighten the fabric as you go, just enough to remove the wrinkles, pinning every 1½ inches and facing pins inward. Complete pinning down the side struts by inserting pins every ¼ inch.

Mark down the struts over the pins with a soft pencil extending pencil line ½ inch beyond the last pin on AB and CD and making a pencil mark ½ inch around the top and bottom ring (figure **3**).

Take out the pins from the frame but keep the holding corner pins in position.

Stitch down the pencil line from top to bottom, using a medium-sized stitch; stretch fabric very slightly while doing this so that when it is pulled onto the frame the stitches do not break (figure **4**).

Trim the fabric away ¼ inch from the stitching line at each side. Cut along the fold at the top edge but do not cut anything at the bottom.

Prepare the lampshade lining in exactly the same way.

Putting the cover on

Press the cover flat (do not press seams open) and slip it over frame with right side outside, making sure that the seams are placed on the side struts. Match horizontal pencil line to top and bottom rings. Pin top and bottom of side seams and then tighten fabric and pin every 1 inch around top and bottom rings (figure **5**). Once again make sure .that the pins are correctly placed to avoid unnecessary damage to clothes.

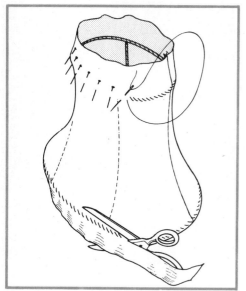

▲ **6.** *Oversewing to frame and trimming*
▼ **7.** *Pinning lining to the frame*

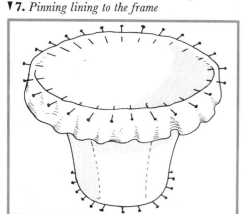

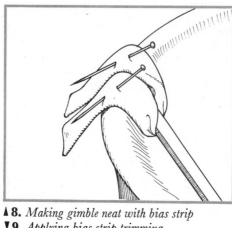

▲ **8.** *Making gimble neat with bias strip*
▼ **9.** *Applying bias strip trimming*

¼ in

▼ *Three more lampshades which can be made following the technique given for the empire shape*

Oversew the cover to the frame using a No.9 sharps needle and a short length of double matching silk thread. If too long a piece of thread is used it will catch around the pins; it is better to use several short lengths. The stitching should be on the outside edge of the top and bottom rings and the oversewing should be done from right to left. Trim away surplus material from top and bottom of lampshade, cutting right up to the stitches (figure **6**).

Inserting balloon lining

Drop the prepared lining into the shade, matching seams and match horizontal pencil marks to top and bottom rings. Pin around top and bottom rings keeping pins on outside edge of lampshade (figure **7**). Tighten the lining by adjusting the pins at top and bottom rings until there is no fullness left. Stitch lining in the same way as the cover, making sure that the stitches come on the outside edge of the lampshade. These will then be completely covered by the trimming.

Note: when fitting the fabric around the top ring, rip the seam down to the horizontal pencil mark and splay out the material to enable the lining to fit neatly around the gimble. Do not try to join up material.

Making gimble neat

Cut a piece of bias strip 1 inch wide and 4 inches long. Turn in ¼ inch at each side to make ½ inch wide strip. Press. Slip under gimble (figure **8**). Pin in position and oversew in the same way as for the balloon lining, being careful to keep the stitches on the outside edge of the top ring.

Bias trimming

Measure around top and bottom of lampshade and prepare enough bias to fit around top and bottom of shade plus 2 inches for turnings. Prepare this in the same way as for the gimble finishing (figure **12a**). Make sure the material is cut on the direct bias and that any joins necessary are made on the bias.

Starting at the side seam apply end of bias strip to outside edge of lampshade, beginning ¼ inch beyond seam.

Apply adhesive carefully and evenly to bias strip, spreading with a small knife. Great care is needed in applying the adhesive, because it will mark the fabric if it is used carelessly.

Stretch the bias strip slightly when applying it to the lampshade, pressing it gently with fingers to make it firm. The bias should just cover the oversewing stitches and should not extend to the inside of the shade. When the strip has been

Two modern lampshades complement William Morris wallpapers, printed from the original pearwood blocks

applied to the top of the lampshade cut off the excess, turn under $\frac{1}{4}$ inch at one end and glue it over the other end (figure **9**). Apply the trim to the bottom edge of the lampshade in the same way, making sure both joins are on the same side of the shade.

Hard lampshades

Hard lampshades are quick and easy to make, and attractive shades can be achieved with a minimum of effort. There are many attractive ready-made materials available from good handicraft shops, but it is also possible to make your own. Use an adhesive parchment to which the material of your choice can be ironed, pressing the material onto the adhesive side with a hot iron. If this method is used, it is advisable to use materials that will withstand a hot iron. The most suitable needles for making hard shades are betweens 5/6. A number of wooden clothes pins are also required. The two lampshades illustrated on this page are hard lampshades. The one on the left requires a pattern; the other is the simplest of all shapes to make.

To make a drum lampshade

Two rings are used for a straight-sided drum lampshade. They must be the same size, but one should be plain and the other should have a fitting, pendant or gimble. Prepare the rings and tape as for the soft lampshade, finishing off the tape on the rings with a few oversewing stitches to keep it firm. Measure around the taped rings for the circumference and decide on the height required for the lampshade.

Cut a pattern from stiff paper or cardboard to test on the rings. Allow $\frac{1}{4}$ inch at the end for the overlap at the seam.

Fit the paper pattern onto the rings with wooden clothes pins and test the height of the shade and the fit of the pattern. Adjust if necessary. Cut fabric using the paper pattern and attach to the rings with clothes pins. Sewing from left to right and using a blanket stitch sew around top and bottom rings. Sew through the lampshade material and onto the tape. This gives a firm finish and the stitches will be covered by the trimming.

When top and bottom rings have been sewn the seam should be glued down. Press down firmly with fingers and hold until stuck.

With a good adhesive apply trimmings to top and bottom of shade, turning in ends $\frac{1}{4}$ inch and butting together. The joins of the trimming should be on the seam of the lampshade.

Making a pattern

This is the quickest and easiest way to obtain a pattern for a lampshade which is smaller at the top than at the bottom: i.e. a cone shape or near drum with side struts. Take a large sheet of cardboard or stiff paper. Placing lampshade frame on paper, draw with a pencil down the side strut and mark top and bottom.

Rotate frame very slowly, marking along the top and bottom rings until the first mark is reached. Allow $\frac{1}{2}$ inch for seam allowance at the end; this can be trimmed down to $\frac{1}{4}$ inch later. Cut out and try pattern onto frame, adjusting if necessary. Note: always try the pattern before cutting into the lampshade fabric.

Cut out fabric from pattern and proceed in the same way as for the straight-sided drum.

This method can be used for making small wall light lampshades.

Crochet pattern/lacy patterned jacket

Crochet this pretty jacket in a lacy pattern.

Sizes
Directions are for 34/36in bust.
The figures in brackets [ ] refer to the 37/39in bust size.
Length, 21[22½]in.
Sleeve seam, 17[17½]in.

Gauge
One rep of patt (one gr and one "V") and 4 rows to 2in on No.E hook.

Materials
Unger Roxanne
8[9] 50 gm balls
One No.E crochet hook
4 buttons

Back

Using No.E hook, ch80[88].
1st row 1sc into second ch from hook, *1sc into next ch, rep from * to end. 79[87]sc.
2nd row Ch1 to count as first sc, *1sc into next sc, rep from * to end.
Rep 2nd row twice more.
5th row Ch3, skip next 2sc, *5dc into next sc—called 1gr —, skip 3sc, 1dc, ch2, and 1dc into next sc—called 1 "V"—, skip 3sc, rep from * to last 4sc, 1gr into next sc, skip 2sc, 1dc into last sc. 9½[10½] patts.
6th row Ch3, *1 "V" in center dc of gr, 1gr in 2ch sp of "V", rep from * to last gr, 1 "V" in center dc of gr, 1dc into 3rd of 3ch.
7th row Ch3, *1gr in 2ch sp of "V", 1 "V" in center dc of gr, rep from * to last "V", 1gr in 2ch sp of "V", 1dc in 3rd of 3ch.
Rep 6th and 7th rows until work measures 13½[14½]in from beg, ending with a 7th row.

Shape armholes
Next row Ss over gr, ch3, 1gr into 2ch sp of next "V", patt to last "V", 1gr into 2ch sp of "V", 1dc into first dc of gr. Turn.
Rep the last row twice more. 6½[7½] patts.
Continue without shaping until armholes measure 7½[8] in, ending with a 7th patt row.
1706

Shape shoulders
Next row Ss over first gr and "V", patt to last "V". Turn.
Next row Ss over first "V" and gr, patt to last gr. Turn. Fasten off.

Left front

Using No.E hook, ch40[48].
Work as given for Back until work measures the same as Back to armholes, ending with a 7th patt row. 4½[5½] patts.

Shape armhole and front edge
Next row Ss over first gr, ch3, patt to end.
Continue dec at armhole edge on next 2 rows as for Back, *at the same time* dec one st at front edge of next 4[8] rows, then every other row until 1[1½] patts have been dec at front edge. 2[2½] patts.
Continue without shaping until armhole measures the same as on Back, ending at armhole edge.

Shape shoulder
Next row Ss over first gr and "V", patt to end. Fasten off.

Right front

Work to correspond to left Front, reversing all shapings.

Sleeves

Using No.E hook, ch40.
Work first 7 rows as given for Back. 4½ patts.
Continue in patt, inc one st at each end of next and every following 3rd row until one whole patt has been inc at each side. 6½ patts.
Continue without shaping until sleeve seam measures 17[18½] in, ending with a 7th patt row.
NB. On the second size the last inch is set into armhole shaping and is not included in sleeve seam measurement.

Shape cap
First size only. Next row Ss over first gr, ch3, patt to last gr, 1dc into first dc of gr. Turn.
Both sizes. Dec 2 sts at each

end of every row until 1½ patts rem. Fasten off.

Bands

Left front
Using No.E hook, ch10.
1st row 1sc into 2nd ch from hook, *1sc into next ch, rep from * to end. 9sc.
Continue in sc until band, when slightly stretched, is the same length as Front edge to beg of shaping, ending with a WS row.
Inc one st at beg of next row, then at this same edge on every 5th row until 17 dec have been made.
Continue without shaping until band is same length as front edge to shoulder measured with band slightly stretched, ending with a WS row.
Fasten off.
Baste band in place and mark position of buttons with pins as follows. Place first pin about 2in from beg, 2nd pin about ¾in below beg of front shaping, then two more pins at equal distances between these two.

Right front
Work to correspond to left front, reversing shaping and working buttonholes to correspond with pin positions.
Buttonhole row (RS) Ch1, 2sc, ch4, skip 4sc, 2sc.
Next row Ch1, 1sc, 4sc in ch4 loop, 3sc.

Collar

Join shoulder seams.
With RS facing, work in sc across 17sc of right front Band, across Back neck, then across 17 sts of left front Band.
Continue in sc for 2in.
Fasten off.

Finishing

Press lightly.
Sew in sleeves. On 2nd size sew the last inch of sleeve seams to first bound-off group at armholes.
Join side sleeve seams. Sew on front bands. Sew on buttons.

Crocheted jacket for cooler days ▶

Knitting pattern/jacket and skirt

This simple knitted suit has a slightly flared skirt which can be made to the length desired, and a jacket with frog fastenings and an interesting detail of slits at the sleeve edges.

Sizes

Directions are for 34in bust. The figures in brackets [] refer to the 36, 38 and 40in sizes respectively.
Jacket. Length, 23½[24:24½:25]in.
Sleeve seam, 16[16½:17:17½]in.
Skirt. Length 20[21:22:23]in, adjustable.

> **Gauge**
> 6 sts and 8 rows to 1in over st st worked on No.5 needles.

Materials

Reynolds Classique
Jacket. 7[7:8:9] balls
Skirt. 4[5:6:6] balls
One pair No.5 needles
One No.E crochet hook
6 buttons
One 7in zipper
Waist length elastic

Jacket back

Cast on 108[114:120:126] sts.
K 15 rows.
Next row K12[12:11:11], *K up 1, K12[13:14:15], rep from * 6 times more, K up 1, K12[11:11:10]. 116[122:128:134] sts.
Beg with a K row, continue in st st for 3in, ending with a P row.
K2 tog at each end of next and every following 12th row until 108[114:120:126] sts rem.
Continue without shaping until work measures 16in from beg, ending with a P row.

Shape armholes

Bind off 5[6:7:8] sts at beg of next 2 rows.
Bind off 2 sts at beg of next 2 rows.
K2 tog at each end of every other row 4 times.
86[90:94:98] sts.
Continue without shaping until armhole measures
1708

7½[8:8½:9]in, ending with a P row.

Shape shoulders

Bind off 7[8:9:10] sts at beg of next 2 rows, then 9 sts at beg of following 4 rows.
Slip rem 36[38:40:42] sts on holder.

Left front

Cast on 56[59:62:65] sts.
K 15 rows.
Next row K12, *K up 1, K12[13:14:15], rep from * twice more, K up 1, K8. 60[63:66:69] sts.
Next row K.
Next row K9, P to end.
Rep these 2 rows for 3in, ending with a WS row.
K2 tog at beg of next and every following 12th row until 56[59:62:65] sts rem, then continue without shaping until work measures the same as Back to armholes, ending with a WS row.

Shape armhole

At arm edge, bind off 5[6:7:8] sts, then 2 sts once.
K2 tog at beg of every other row 4 times, at arm edge.
Continue without shaping on rem 45[47:49:51] sts until armhole measures 5¼[5½:5¾:6]in.
End with a WS row.

Shape neck

Next row K34[35:36:37], turn and slip rem 11[12:13:14] sts on holder.
At neck edge, bind off 2 sts every other row twice.
Dec one st at neck edge on every other row until 25[26:27:28] sts rem.
Continue without shaping until armhole measures the same as on Back, ending with a P row.

Shape shoulder

At arm edge, bind off 7[8:9:10] sts, then 9 sts once.
P 1 row.
Bind off rem 9 sts.

Right front

Work to correspond to left Front, reversing all shaping.

Sleeves

Cast on 26[28:30:32] sts.
K 15 rows.
Next row K5[6:7:8], (K up 1, K8) twice, K up 1, K5[6:7:8]. 29[31:33:35] sts*.
Next row K to end.
Next row P to last 5 sts, K5.
Rep last 2 rows until work measures 2½in, ending with a WS row. Break off yarn and place this piece on a spare needle.
Work a second piece in the same manner as far as *.
Next row K.
Next row K5, P to end.
Rep last 2 rows until work measures 2½in, ending with a WS row.
Next row K to end, then K across the sts of first piece on spare needle. 58[62:66:70] sts.
Next row P24[26:28:30], K10, P to end.
Next row K to end.
Next row P25[27:29:31], K8, P to end.
Next row K.
Next row P26[28:30:32], K6, P to end.
Continue to work 2 sts less in garter st in center of every other row until all sts are in st st.
Continue in st st, inc one st at each end of every 14th row until there are 72[76:80:84] sts.
Continue without shaping until sleeve seam measures 16[16½:17:17½]in. End with P row.

Shape cap

Bind off 5 sts at beg of next 2 rows.
K2 tog at each end of every other row 13[14:15:16] times.
Bind off 2 sts at beg of next 10[10:12:12] rows, then 3 sts at beg of next 2 rows.
Bind off rem 10[12:10:12] sts.

Neckband

Join shoulder seams.
With RS facing, K sts of right Front neck, pick up and K16 sts up side of neck, K Back neck sts, pick up and K16 sts down other side of neck, then K sts of left Front neck.
90[94:98:102] sts.

K 10 rows. Bind off.

Frog fastenings

Using No.E hook, ch25.
Join into ring with a ss.
Into the ring work 14sc, ss into first sc (this makes buttonhole part) then continue around ring working 3sc, ch4, 1sc into the first of these 4ch, 12sc, ch4, 1sc into first of these 4ch, 3sc, ending with a ss into first sc.
Fasten off.
Make 5 more pieces in the same manner. Join into 3 pairs by stitching the ends of the longer loops together at the center of the 12sc.

Skirt Back and Front alike

Cast on 88[92:96:100] sts.
K 16 rows.
Beg with a K row, work 4 rows st st.
Next row K22[23:24:25], K up 1, K2, K up 1, K40[42:44:46], K up 1, K2, K up 1, K to end.
Work 7 rows.
Next row K23[24:25:26], K up 1, K2, K up 1, K42[44:46:48], K up 1, K2, K up 1, K to end.
Continue inc in this manner on every 8th row 3[4:5:6] times more, then on every 16th row until there are 128[132:136:140] sts.
Continue without shaping until work measures 18[19:20:21]in, ending with a P row or to length desired.
Next row K8[10:7:9], *K2 tog, K8[8:9:9] rep from * 10 times more, K2 tog, K8[10:6:8]. 116[120:124:128] sts.
K 14 rows.
Bind off.

Finishing

Press work lightly under damp cloth, using a cool iron.
Jacket. Sew in sleeves. Join side and sleeve seams. Press seams. Sew on buttons.
Skirt. Join seams leaving one side open at top for zipper. Sew in zipper. Sew elastic to waistband with casing-stitch. Press all seams.

1709

Stitchery design / lattice smocking

Lattice smocking is worked without a foundation of gathering and produces an effective form of pleating on the right side of the fabric.

Fabrics

Fabrics with a pile, such as velvet and corduroy, are the best to use, but any heavy quality fabric which does not crease easily, such as satin, will do. Allow approximately double the quantity of fabric to the required finished measurement.

Threads

Use strong sewing threads such as buttonhole twist, button cotton or nylon sewing thread in the needle.

Method

Commercial transfers are made for stamping the dots used in the smocking, but it is possible to mark your own if you prefer. The dots are spaced in rows 1¼ inches apart.

All the smocking is worked on the wrong side of the fabric. The stitches will not show on the right side after the smocking pleats are formed. After the dots are marked on the wrong side of the fabric, start the smocking at the upper left-hand corner. Knot the end of the thread. Pick up the dots by inserting the needle into the fabric to right of dot and out

through the left side of the same dot. The thread is carried from dot to dot on the working side of the fabric. Pick up dot 1 with the needle and make a second holding stitch as shown in figure **1**. Then pick up dot 2, go back to dot 1 and pick up again as shown in figure **2**. Pull dots 1 and 2 together and knot securely as shown figure **3**. Pick up dot 3 then, with the thread above the needle, slip the needle under the thread between dots 1 and 2 as shown in figure **4**, pulling the thread tightly at dot 3 to form a knot. Be sure to keep the fabric flat between dots 1 and 3. Pick up dot 4, then go back and pick up dot 3 again as shown in figure **5**. Pull the dots together and knot them securely. Pick up dot 5 as shown in figure **6**, slip the needle under the thread between dots 3 and 5 and knot as in figure **4**. Continue to work down the row of dots in the same manner, starting with figure **2** and picking up dot 6 next. Secure all the ends firmly.

A different pattern may be obtained by leaving a 1 inch space between each worked row of smocking stitches, resulting in a chevron effect.

Uses

This type of smocking is suitable as a decoration for pillows, hats, handbags, curtains, or items of dress.

Far right: lattice smocking worked in velvet for the sleeves of this delightful dress►
▼ Tracing guide to repeat as necessary　　　　*Step-by-step working instructions►*

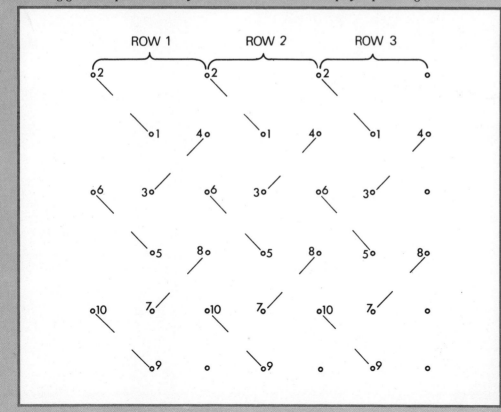

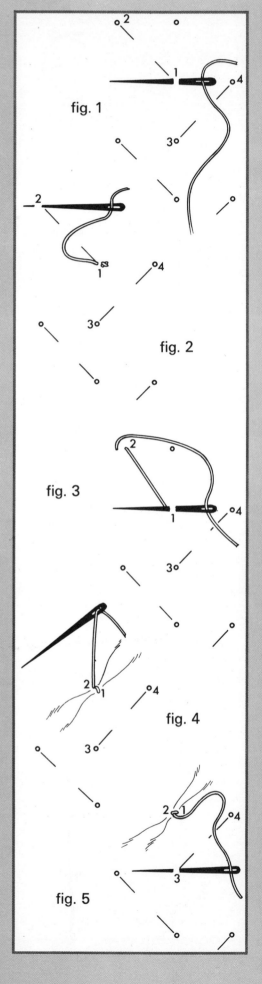

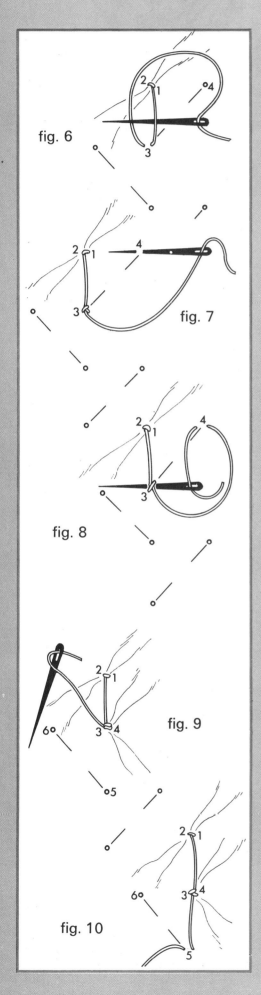

fig. 6

fig. 7

fig. 8

fig. 9

fig. 10

1712

Stitchery pattern/blue town

This blue town picture is worked in a range of blue green shades with highlights of pink and white.

To make the picture, you will need:
- [ ] A piece of dark green linen measuring 23 inches by 16 inches
- [ ] A piece of hardboard measuring 18 inches by 11½ inches
- [ ] Crewel needle No.8
- [ ] D.M.C. 6-strand floss in the following colors and amounts:

  1. pale blue—7301; **2.** light blue—7800; **3.** medium blue—7306; **4.** dark medium blue—7307; **5.** blue—7302; **6.** light navy—7318; **7.** turquoise—7996; **8.** pale yellow—7361; **9.** lime—7773; **10.** light yellow—7431; **11.** gold—7487; **12.** dark green—7387; **13.** very dark green—7389; **14.** dark blue green—7309; **15.** medium gray green—7386; **16.** Pale gray green—7384; **17.** yellow green—7351; **18.** mauve—7226; **19.** deep mauve—7228; **20.** dark slate blue—7241; **21.** pale pink—7132; **22.** deep pink—7133; **23.** white; **24.** brown—7533

One skein each of colors:
6, 8, 9, 11, 12, 13, 16, 17, 18, 20, 21, 22, 23, 24
Two skeins each of colors:
1, 2, 3, 4, 5, 7, 10, 14, 15, 19

Stitches

The stitches used to embroider this picture are running stitch, French knots and couching in a variety of simple methods. The flowers and leaves are worked in freely worked satin stitch.

Use four strands in the needle for the French knots and laid threads, and two strands for the couching and all other stitches. If preferred, small beads could be substituted for the French knots.

Working

It is essential to work this picture in a square embroidery frame to keep the stitching flat and even.

Finishing

When the embroidery is completed, lay over a thick, soft pad and press carefully to avoid flattening the French knots. Mount the picture over the hardboard.

Home crochet/wallhanging

▲ *The wall hanging can be hung by either tacking directly to the wall or by mounting over a frame and then hanging as an ordinary picture*

Working in fabric strips can be swift and exciting. The simple patterns are based on circular or straight crochet, using traditional stitches in rounds or rows. The water lily hanging illustrated takes this a stage further, using the lines of the rows to create additional visual texture, and has the same impact as a brilliant modern painting. It

is worked in separate sections which are then sewn together. This pattern could be used to make an attractive throw rug.

Working in fabric strips

Either of two sizes of crochet hook are equally suitable for rag rugs, No.K and No. Jumbo ¾in. The choice depends on the final effect desired. The larger

hook will obviously create larger stitches and the work will grow quickly. The finer hook will naturally produce smaller stitches and it will take longer to work the same area. The work will also look finer. Use strips of not more than half an inch wide, the longer the better. Always join pieces in the center of a row by laying the two ends on top of the previous row and

working over them with the new piece. Start using a new strip on the last stage of a stitch (see Crochet Know-how 5 and 32).

Water lily hanging

Size

This will depend on the width and thickness of the strips, and also on the hook size used.

1714

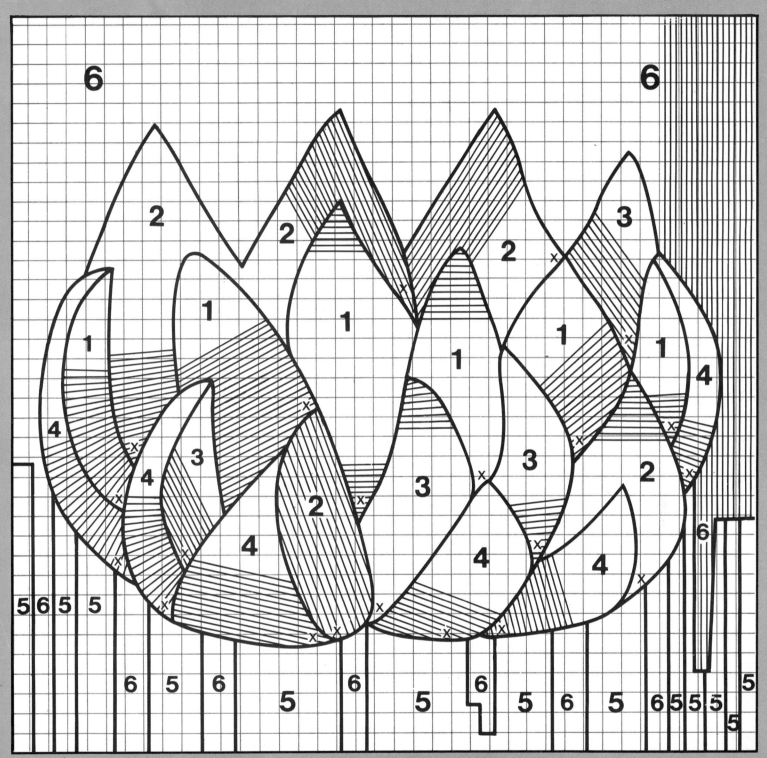

▲ *Each square represents one inch, but by taking them to represent a different measurement the design can be worked to any dimensions desired*

Materials

This also depends on the hook size used and the finished size desired, but the following is a rough guide:
One No. Jumbo ¾in crochet hook
3yds cream, 1
4yds pale beige, 2
4yds medium beige, 3
3yds dark beige, 4
5yds blue green, 5

7 yds yellow green, 6

Sections

Make actual size paper pattern pieces from the chart. Use single crochet throughout, working into the back loop of the stitch from right side of work and front loop from wrong side. Begin at the point marked X of

each section. Work each area separately, continually measuring against the paper shape and increasing and decreasing as needed to produce the finished shape. Check with the chart and the illustration in which direction the stitches lie. If a section curves work part of the row, turn and work back, then work the next row

across all stitches.

Finishing

Sew the sections together on WS with matching sewing thread. Roll the hanging in a damp towel and leave for two hours. Pin out flat, WS up, and press with a warm iron to obtain a flat surface. Dry thoroughly.

Tailoring five

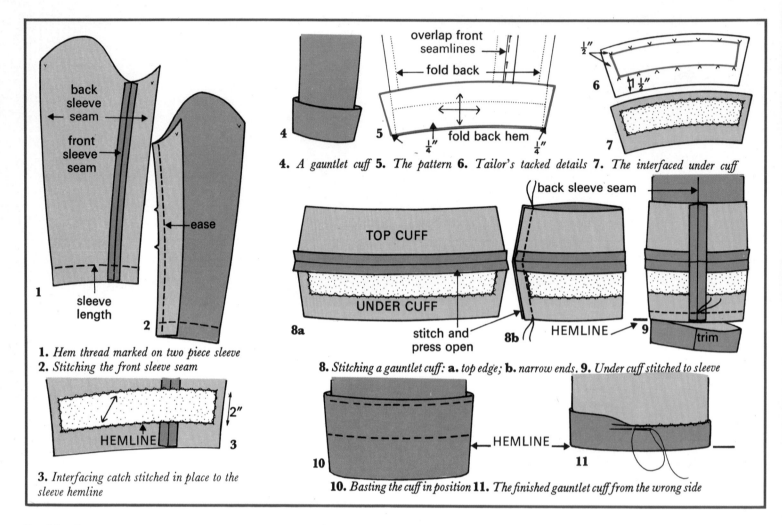

1. *Hem thread marked on two piece sleeve*
2. *Stitching the front sleeve seam*
3. *Interfacing catch stitched in place to the sleeve hemline*

4. *A gauntlet cuff* **5.** *The pattern* **6.** *Tailor's tacked details* **7.** *The interfaced under cuff*

8. *Stitching a gauntlet cuff:* **a.** *top edge;* **b.** *narrow ends.* **9.** *Under cuff stitched to sleeve*

10. *Basting the cuff in position* **11.** *The finished gauntlet cuff from the wrong side*

In this chapter

A. Plain tailored sleeve: stitching the sleeve; finishing the hem edge.
B. Gauntlet cuff: cutting the pattern; making the cuff.
C. Strap cuff: cutting the pattern; making the cuff.
D. Imitation vent opening on sleeve: the pattern; making the sleeve.
E. Two piece sleeve with vent opening.
F. Lining a sleeve: plain sleeve lining; sleeve with a vent.
*Terms and stitches.

A. Plain tailored sleeve

Coat sleeves must be well fitted and have a crisp finish at the hem. With a two-piece tailored sleeve there is usually ease at the elbow level and great care must be taken while basting and stitching to keep this in the correct place and so prevent the sleeve from twisting.

Stitching the sleeve

1. After fitting the sleeves rip the armhole basting. Thread mark the length. Mark any seam alterations. On a one-piece sleeve unbaste the sleeve seam. On a two-piece sleeve unbaste the back sleeve

seam only.
2. On a two-piece sleeve stitch the front sleeve seam and press open. If the sleeve has ease in it stitch carefully and press as for an eased seam.

Finishing the hem edge

Cut a strip of interfacing in the bias grain of the fabric to the width of the sleeve and two inches deep.
3. Baste to the wrong side of the sleeve just above the hemline and catch stitch.
Turn up the hem and press. Catch stitch to the interfacing.

B. Gauntlet cuff

4. For a gauntlet cuff it is not necessary to interface the sleeve hem as it would be too bulky.

Cutting the pattern

5. Place the two pieces of sleeve pattern together with the lower part of the front seamlines coinciding, and the hem and back seam allowances turned back. Cut the cuff pattern extending it ¼ inch each side at the hem edge and extending the top edge as style dictates. The cuff can be anything from 2 to 4 inches deep.

Making the cuff

6. Using this pattern cut two pieces of coat fabric for each cuff adding ½ inch seam allowance on the sides and top edge and 1½ inches at the hem edge. Tailor's tack all around pattern.
7. Cut interfacing exactly to pattern, without seam allowance, and catch stitch to the under cuff section as shown.
8a, b. Stitch the cuffs together along the top edge (**a**). Then fold and stitch narrow ends together as shown (**b**).
9. Place the right side of the faced under cuff section to the right side of the sleeve. The cuff stitching line should be ½ inch above the sleeve hemline and the cuff seam corresponding to the back sleeve seam as shown.
Stitch, trim seam allowance to ½ inch.
10. Fold the top cuff over and baste along the top through both cuff layers only. Baste at hem through all fabric layers.
11. Turn the sleeve to the wrong side and catch stitch the lower edge of the

Right: Vogue 2671, in green doeskin cloth, has a two-piece sleeve (because this fabric has a pile the coat was cut on the straight grain of the fabric). Far right: This Vogue pattern made in a home furnishing tapestry, has a cuffed sleeve.

1717

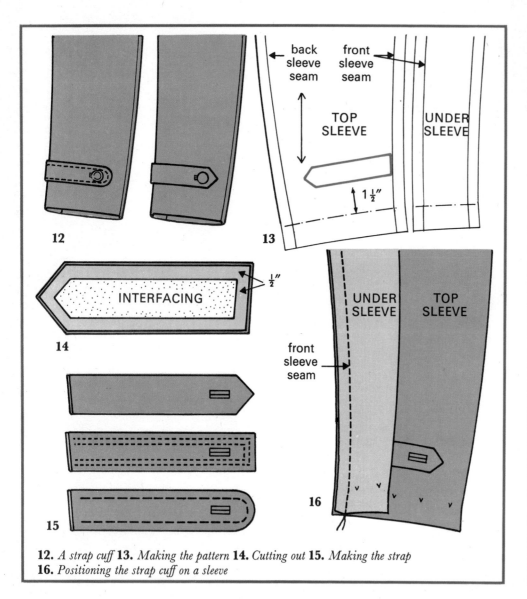

12. *A strap cuff* **13.** *Making the pattern* **14.** *Cutting out* **15.** *Making the strap*
16. *Positioning the strap cuff on a sleeve*

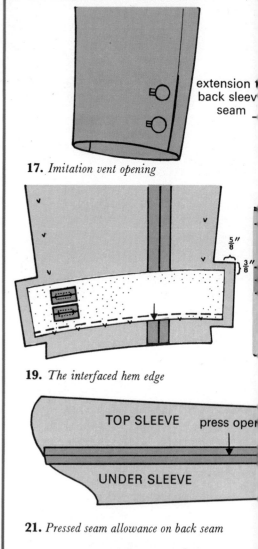

17. *Imitation vent opening*

19. *The interfaced hem edge*

21. *Pressed seam allowance on back seam*

cuff as shown, turning under the raw edge to make neat.

C. Strap cuff

12. A strap cuff usually lies from the front seam of a two piece sleeve to the back seam, across the top of the sleeve.

Cutting the pattern
13. Make a pattern for the strap, using the top sleeve pattern piece to give the correct angle. These straps usually end 1 inch from the back sleeve seam.
14. Cut the cuff from double fabric allowing ½ inch all around for seams.
For each strap cut one piece of interfacing to pattern without seam allowance.

Making the cuff
15. Make the cuff as for the ¼ belt in Tailoring 4.
16. Baste to the front sleeve seam before the seam is sewn up.
Finish as for a plain sleeve.

1718

D. Imitation vent opening on sleeve

17. Decide whether you would like this sleeve finish before you cut out the coat as additions have to be made to the back sleeve seam.

The pattern
18. Cut an extension to each side of the back sleeve seam as shown. The extension should be 1¼ inches wide by the depth of the vent plus ⅜ inch top and bottom for seam allowance.

Making the sleeve
19. Stitch the front sleeve seam and baste interfacing to hem as shown. Make buttonholes on upper sleeve if required.
20. Baste and stitch the back sleeve seam as shown.
21. Snip the seam allowance on the under sleeve to allow the vent to lie on top of the sleeve. Then press the sleeve seam open above and below the vent.

Press the lower vent seam up.
22. Press hem up to vent opening and catch stitch to interfacing.

E. Two piece sleeve with vent opening

23. Cut a strip of interfacing on the bias, wide enough to reach the top of the opening by the sleeve width, without seam allowance.
Make piped buttonholes to match the coat if required.
24a, b, c, d. The next step is to miter the corners. Cut away the corners ⅛ inch from the interfacing (**a**). Fold up the ⅛ inch and press (**b**). Turn hem up and sides in, snipping at top of opening (**c**). Catch stitch to canvas and draw stitch * mitered ends together (**d**).
25. Stitch the back sleeve seam.
Snip ¼ inch above vent then press seam open above snip and together below snip.
26. Baste vent in closed position and make a bar tack * at the top of the opening.

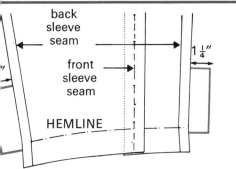

18. *Cutting extension on back sleeve seam*

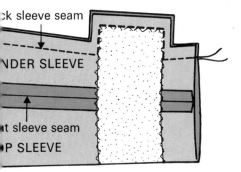

20. *Stitching the back sleeve seam*

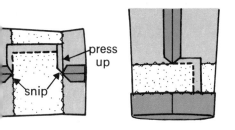

22. *The hem catch stitched in place*

Sleeve detail of plain cuff, Butterick 6518

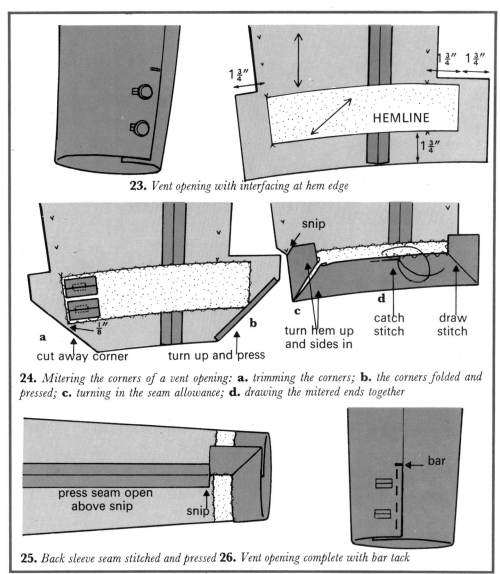

23. *Vent opening with interfacing at hem edge*

24. *Mitering the corners of a vent opening:* **a.** *trimming the corners;* **b.** *the corners folded and pressed;* **c.** *turning in the seam allowance;* **d.** *drawing the mitered ends together*

25. *Back sleeve seam stitched and pressed* **26.** *Vent opening complete with bar tack*

Sleeve detail of vent opening, Butterick 5925

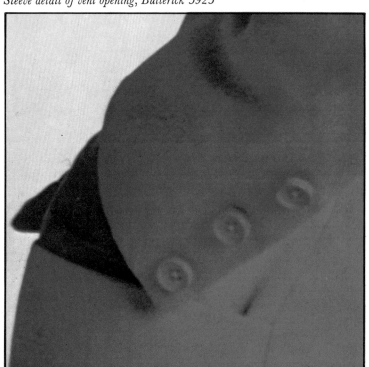

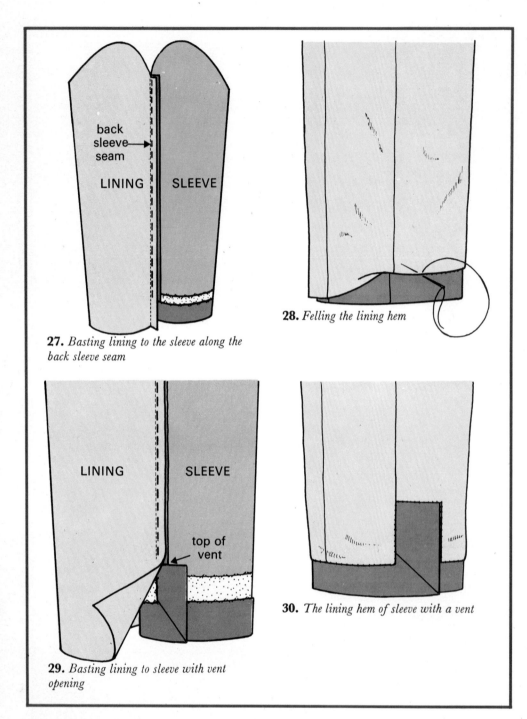

27. *Basting lining to the sleeve along the back sleeve seam*

28. *Felling the lining hem*

29. *Basting lining to sleeve with vent opening*

30. *The lining hem of sleeve with a vent*

F. Lining a sleeve

The sleeve lining is sewn in place before the sleeve is stitched to the coat. It is much easier to do this now without the whole weight of the coat to contend with.

Plain sleeve lining

The method used here is also applied to a sleeve with an imitation vent, cuff or strap finish.

Make the sleeve lining and press the seams open.

27. With wrong sides out, place the sleeve and lining side by side with back sleeve seams corresponding. Baste together along the seamline.

Turn the lining right side out over the sleeve.

28. Turn in the hem allowance of the lining and fell* to the sleeve.

Sleeve with a vent

Make the sleeve lining, leaving the appropriate seam open below the vent.

29. With wrong sides out, place the sleeve and lining side by side, with the back sleeve seams corresponding. Baste seams together above the vent.

Turn the lining right side out over the sleeve.

30. Turn the raw lining edges under as shown and baste. Fell* lining to the sleeve.

*Terms and stitches

Bar tack (31): used to strengthen the top of a pleat or opening, and can be decorative as well as functional.

Using matching thread make a bar of 4 long stitches. Oversew tightly along the length of the stitches.

Draw stitch (32): used to close two folds of material together. Slip the needle through the top fold for $\frac{1}{4}$ inch. Then, directly under the end of the first stitch, slip the needle through the lower fold for $\frac{1}{4}$ inch.

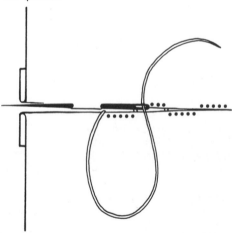

Felling (33): this is a firm form of hemming with a stitch at right angles to the hem or fold.

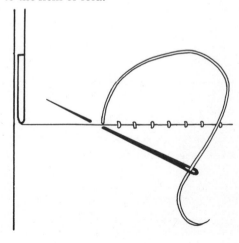

Crafts/suede and leathercraft

New approach to leathercraft

One of the oldest of crafts, leather work fell into obscurity at the end of the nineteen-thirties, when pride in craftsmanship gave way to mass production. Thonging, as a means of joining two pieces of leather, was out, and fashion demanded that craftsmanship did not show, and that the article bore as close a resemblance to the machine-made as was possible.

A gayer, livelier interpretation of the original craft has now developed, losing none of the old standards yet making use of modern techniques. The essence of current fashion is reflected in the choice of materials and colors, and the way in which designers are now using suede and leather shows an exciting awareness of the scope of natural fibers.

To be able to design and make exciting and luxurious looking garments and accessories in leather and suede, it is important to know a little about the different kinds of leather and the best uses for them.

Different kinds of leather

For most of the items a beginner will want to attempt, sheepskin is probably the best skin to use. It is supple, easily obtainable and falls into the medium price bracket. Sheepskin is dyed to a wide variety of colors as well as being finished in attractive natural tones, and can be used for leather garments and is ideal for accessories. Sheepskin suede is of a particularly good quality, soft and velvety, and is usually used for better quality fashion clothes.

Cowhide is a much heavier leather and comes in two or three different thicknesses, the central area of the hide being the thickest. This is used for shoe soles, suitcases and anything which needs to wear well. The sides of these hides are thinner and are suitable for heavier weight garments, such as skirts and jerkins and shoe uppers.

Cowhide is also sold in "splits", which means that the skin has been split through its thickness into two layers. Splits are the cheapest kind of leather to buy, but are not very strong and shouldn't be used for articles where there is likely to be a strain on the leather—such as across the shoulders of a garment. It's perfectly suitable for accessories and is easily obtainable.

Calfskin, the smooth, beautiful leather used for good handbags and shoes, is available in different weights and finishes and is more expensive than sheepskin.

Among the fancy leathers are pigskins, goatskins, lizard and snakeskin and but these are generally rather difficult to obtain.

Leather and suede is sold by the square foot unless one is buying offcuts or scrap pieces. Skins are of an irregular shape with the legs and neck of the animal sticking out from the "body", but these are calculated in the given measurement.

The basic tools

To make even quite simple things, a few basic tools are essential. The most important are a cutting board, a sharp leather knife and a good pair of scissors; ideally these should be leather shears but this isn't essential. A bone folder, which nowadays is sometimes made of plastic, is used for scoring lines on the leather and for smoothing and flattening edges. A skiving knife, available from craft shops, is invaluable where hems and turnings need to be as thin as possible. Useful adjuncts are an oilstone on which to keep the knife sharp, a leather punch for thonged articles, a stitch marking wheel and a stitch tool, which makes slits for the thread instead of holes. A steel ruler, a set square and a compass are necessary for accurate measuring.

Sewing leather and suede

Of the four basic methods of joining leather—glueing, lacing or thonging, machine-stitching and hand-sewing—the latter two are used most.

To sew leather by hand, both straight and curved needles, glover's needles (which have a sharp triangular point) and saddler's needles are used, depending on the item being stitched.

For sewing using a sewing machine, medium thick needles will be found to be the most satisfactory, and the size of stitch should be regulated to the thickness of the leather. For thick work, set the stitch large, and for fine leather the stitch can be relatively small. Suedes tend to drag when more than one thickness is going through the machine, and to correct this adjust the stitch to the next size up. The thread will sink into the suede anyway and the finished appearance should be satisfactory.

Threads for leathercraft

Choose a thread suitable for the job in hand, determining the gauge for both appearance and performance. Whichever thread is chosen however, it must be waxed with beeswax or paraffin wax before use to prevent fraying and breaking. Heavier kinds of cotton, silk and nylon threads can be used for hand-sewing and for machine-stitching, providing that the machine needle is the right size. Linen thread is both decorative and strong for hand-sewing and is ideal for thin, supple leathers and suedes. Buttonhole silk is appropriate for gloves and bags, while bookbinder's thread and carpet yarn, available in different gauges, are very strong and are suitable for most types of leather. Saddler's thread is good for heavy duty articles.

Preparing leather for joining.

Sewing leather by hand can be fairly hard work, and by piercing holes first the job is made much easier. For saddle stitch-

1722

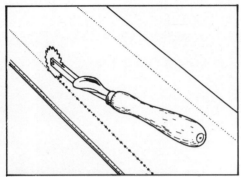

1. *Piercing with stitch marking wheel*

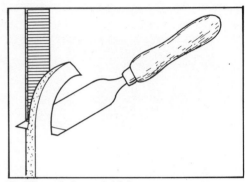

2. *The technique of skiving*

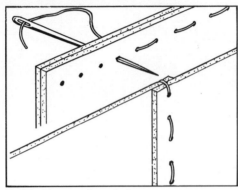

3. *Working running stitch*

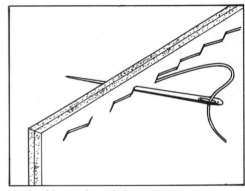

4. *Double running stitch*

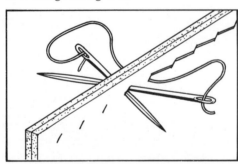

5. *Working saddle stitch*

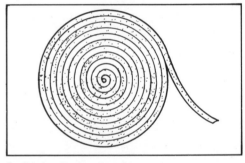

6. *Cutting leather thonging*

ing, pierce the holes with a sharp pointed awl but make sure that the holes are equidistant. Pierce along a ruler's edge or use a stitch marking wheel (diagram **1**).

For leathers and suedes which aren't too heavy, use the sewing machine without thread in the needle to pierce holes.

For lacing or thonging, holes are either punched or slit. Slit punches and pronged thonging tools can be purchased in craft shops; a plier-action punch is best for making round holes.

Skiving. Skiving is the term used for paring down the edges of leather and suede so that they can be more easily turned for glueing. Diagram **2** shows the technique. The knife is held at a very tight angle against the wrong side of the leather and guided toward the body and outward.

Stitching seams by hand

There are three methods of stitching seams by hand, these are:

Running stitch. This is used for joining ordinary seams and lapped seams. If thongs are being used for stitching, punch holes first in the leather. On lightweight leathers and suedes sew with a glover's needle. For heavier leathers, pierce holes and sew with a saddler's needle (diagram **3**).

Double running stitch. This gives a much stronger join and has something of the appearance of saddle stitching. Sew the seam once, using a gloving needle and a single running stitch. Then sew back the other way using an ordinary needle. The change of needles is necessary because if a gloving needle were used for the second stitching, the spear-like point would cut the first stitches (diagram **4**).

Saddle stitching. For this attractive finish, first wax the thread. Beeswax is used by professional workers but paraffin candle wax will do quite well. Pierce holes at a slight angle and then work as shown in diagram **5**. Two needles are used simultaneously to pull threads through and it is important to make uniform stitches.

▲ *This beautiful patent leather clutch bag can also be made in soft calf or suede*

Thonging and lacing
Leather thonging can be purchased but it is quite easy to cut one's own. Diagram **6** shows the method.

Glueing
There are good leather glues available from craft shops in both tubes and jars. Tubes are useful for edges and small areas; a jar with a brush is more satisfactory for larger areas. Rubber cement and latex based adhesives are good because they will rub off without leaving a stain.

Glueing is mostly used for attaching lining leathers to surface leathers and for putting on decorative leather edgings and bindings.

Making a clutch bag

Patent leather has been used to make the bag illustrated, but any kind of leather or suede can be used instead. The pattern is based on very simple principles and can be adapted to make a coin purse, a tobacco pouch or a simple brief case.

Copy the diagram onto squared paper. Decide whether you are going to skive the edges so that they can be turned in for the same finish as the bag illustrated. If you decide not to attempt this kind of finish, the edges can be left raw. The line for cutting leather for a raw edged finish is colored. This is also the cutting line for the lining.

When the pattern is outlined on the squared paper cut out the pieces, main bag and gussets, in heavy paper and take these with you to a leather supplier to choose a skin. Choose a lining skin, called a "skiver" at the same time.

Cutting out
Lay the pattern pieces on the skin so that the best area of leather is used for the flap. The paper pattern can be kept in position by stitcking it to the leather with one or two pieces of clear tape. Mark around the pattern carefully with a pencil using a ruler. It is worth stressing at this point that possible difficulties will be minimized if three rules are observed:
1. Cut out the paper pattern carefully.
2. Mark the pattern carefully on the skin.
3. Be really accurate in cutting out the leather.

Skive the edges of the leather at this point if this is the technique you are following.

Interlining and pocket
Cut three pieces of cardboard interlining to the measurements given on the diagram and glue them to the wrong side of the leather, making sure that the edges are absolutely parallel. This is important if the bag is to fold properly. If a fastening is being used, this is the point at which the plates of the fastening are inserted. Snap fasteners can be used instead if preferred. Turn the skived edges of the bag flap and front edge (A-B-C-D and F-G in the diagram). Snip into the turnings $\frac{1}{2}$ inch where the top edge of the gusset will lie (D-d and A-a). Turn in and stick down the top edges of the gusset pieces too. Leave to dry.

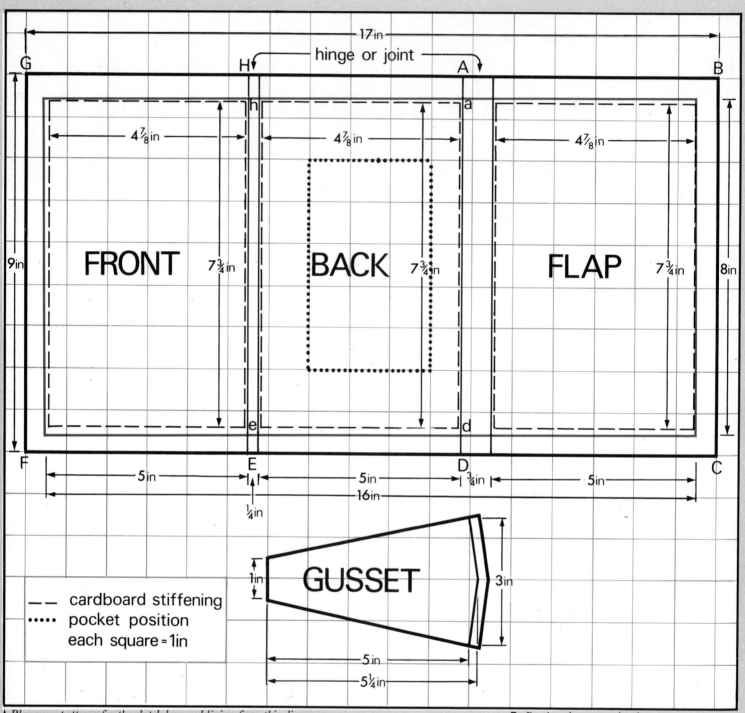

17 in
hinge or joint

G   H h   A a   B

4⅞ in   4⅞ in   4⅞ in

FRONT   7¾ in   BACK   7¾ in   FLAP   7¾ in

9 in   8 in

F   E e   D d   C
5 in   5 in   ¾ in   5 in
16 in
¼ in

1 in   GUSSET   3 in

— — cardboard stiffening
••••• pocket position
each square = 1 in

5 in
5¼ in

▲ *Plan your patterns for the clutch bag and lining from this diagram*

7. *Putting the gussets in place*

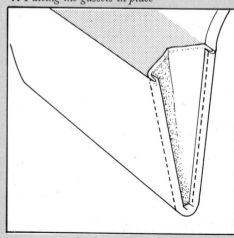

Fold the pocket piece in half as indicated and glue the two sides together to make a piece measuring 5 inches by 3 inches.

Meanwhile, cut out the bag lining from the lining fabric and lining for the gusset pieces, using the pattern.

When the pocket piece is dry, lightly stick it in position on the lining as indicated in the diagram and then machine stitch in position on three sides.

Attaching the lining

The lining is now glued to the outside leather, onto the surface of the cardboard interlining, and the gusset lining pieces are

also glued to the gusset pieces. Turn in the edges of lining as you work and smooth it down using the bone folder. When everything is dry, stitch the top edges of the two gusset pieces. Then machine stitch the top edge of the bag (G-F) and all around the flap (ABCD).

Turn the skived edges of the gusset pieces to the right side and turn the skived edges of the bag along lines GHA and FED to the wrong side. Snip at E-e and H-h. Glue and then stitch the gussets into place (diagram **7**). If it seems difficult to machine stitch the gussets, they can be sewn by hand.

▲ *A simple belt, a beautiful buckle*
▼ *Ways with bright suede*

▲ *Simple bag and belt in appliqué*
▼ *Belts and purses to make*

▲ *Make this gay patchwork jerkin in diamond shapes. Cut a template first and cut sufficient pieces from scraps of suede. Cut out the garment pieces from heavy cotton (use a commercial paper pattern for a jerkin). Lightly glue the diamond shapes in position, just touching. Use a latex adhesive. When the glue is dry, machine stitch the diamond shapes into position, using a zigzag stitch. Make the garment as instructed in the pattern.*

▼ *A quick belt to make in leather or suede. Cut out several shapes and link to waist measurement*

Fasten with buckle or thong.

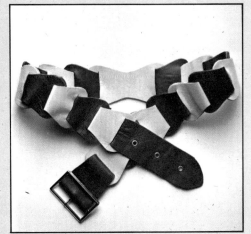

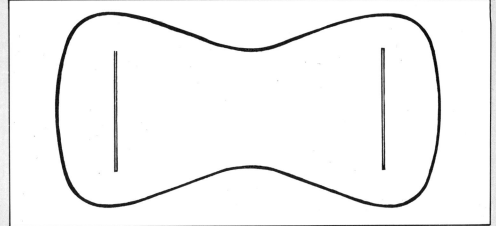

Knitting pattern/chevron stripes for children

This children's outfit has back and front panels of chevron stripes. The contrast color continues in the hat and mitten edges.

Sizes
Directions are for 24in chest. The figures in brackets [ ] refer to the 26, 28, and 30in sizes respectively.

Pullover. Length, 14[16½:19:21½]in.
Sleeve seam, 11[12½:14:15½]in.
Pants. Inside leg, 12[15:18:21]in.
Mittens. Length, 7[8½]in.
Hat. To fit average head.

Gauge
5 sts and 6½ rows to 1in over st st worked on No.7 needles.

Materials
Spinnerin Deluxe Knitting Worsted
Pullover. 3[3:4:4] skeins main color, navy, A
2 skeins contrast, orange, B
Pants. 3[3:3:4] skeins main color, A
Hat and mittens. 1[1:2:2] skeins main color, A
1 skein contrast, B
One pair No.5 needles
One pair No.7 needles
Waist length elastic for pants

Pullover back

First side
Using No.5 needles and A, cast on 69[73:81:85] sts.
1st row K1, *P1, K1, rep from * to end.
2nd row P1, *K1, P1, rep from * to end.
Rep these two rows for 1½in, ending with 1st row.
Next row *Rib 2[2:3:3], K up 1 (inc), rep from * 4 times more, rib to last 10[10:15:15] sts, **K up 1, rib 2[2:3:3], rep from ** 4 times more. 79[83:91:95] sts.
Change to No.7 needles.
Next row K17[19:21:23], turn and cast on one st.
Continue on these 18[20:22:24] sts in st st until work

measures 8½[10½:12½:14½]in from beg. End with a P row.

Shape armhole
At arm edge, bind off on every other row 5 sts; then 3 sts; then 2 sts.
At armhole edge, K2 tog on every other row twice.
Continue without shaping on rem 6[8:10:12] sts until armhole measures 5½[6:6½:7]in, ending with a P row.

Shape armholes
Bind off 3[4:5:6] sts at beg of next row.
P 1 row.
Bind off rem 3[4:5:6] sts.

Second side
Return to sts which were left and with RS facing, slip the first 45[45:49:49] sts onto a spare needle, attach yarn, cast on one st, K to end.
Continue on these 18[20:22:24] sts to correspond to first side, reversing shaping.

Center panel
Using No.7 needles and A, with RS facing, work over the center 45[45:49:49] sts as follows:
1st row Rib 4. Turn.
2nd row Rib 3, work into front, back, then front again of next st—called inc 2—.

3rd row Rib 10. Turn.
4th row Rib 9, inc 2.
5th row Rib 16. Turn.
6th row Rib 15, inc 2.
7th row Rib 22. Turn.
8th row Rib 21, inc 2.
9th row Rib 26. Turn.
10th row Rib 25, inc 2.
Break off yarn.
Slip all sts onto right-hand needle, attach yarn and with WS facing, beg at left side, rep 1st to 10th rows as above. Break off yarn and slip all sts back onto left-hand needle. 65[65:69:69] sts.
With RS facing and using B, continue as follows:
**1st row K.

1726

2nd row Inc 2, rib 28[28:30:30], K3 tog, P1, K3 tog tbl, rib 28[28:30:30], inc 2.

3rd row Rib.

Rep 2nd and 3rd rows 3 times more, then 2nd row once.**

Using A, rep from ** to **. Working alternately 10 rows B, 10 rows A, continue as before until work measures the same as side piece to beg of shoulder shaping, ending with 10th row of a stripe.

Next row With next color, K.

Next row Rib to 3 sts before center st, K3 tog, P1, K3 tog tbl, rib to end.

Next row Rib to end.

Rep last two rows 3 times. more, then first row once. 45[45:49:49]sts.***

Next row With next color, K.

Next row P2 tog, rib to 3 sts before center st, K3 tog, P1, K3 tog tbl, rib to last 2 sts, P2 tog.

Next row Rib.

Rep last two rows until 9[9:7:7] sts rem.

Next row K1[1:0:0], K3 tog, P1, K3 tog tbl, K1[1:0:0]. Bind off.

Front

Work as given for Back to ***. Bind off.

Sleeves

Using No.5 needles and A, cast on 35[37:39:41] sts and work in rib as on Back for 2[2¼:2¼:2½]in, ending with 2nd row, inc one st in center of last row and one st at each end. 38[40:42:44] sts.

Change to No.7 needles. Beg with a K row, continue in st st, inc one st at each end of 3rd and every following 8th row until there are 52[54:58:60] sts.

Continue without shaping until sleeve seam measures 11[12½:14:15½]in from beg, ending with a P row.

Shape cap

Bind off 5 sts at beg of next 2 rows.

K2 tog at each end of next and every other row until 26 sts rem.

Bind off 2 sts at beg of next 6 rows, then 3 sts at beg of next 2 rows.

Bind off rem 8 sts.

Neckband

Join side panels to center Front and Back panels. Join right shoulder seam.

Using No.5 needles and A, pick up and K71[75:79:83] sts around neck.

Beg with second rib row, work in rib as at beg of Back for 4[4½:4½:5]in. Bind off loosely in rib.

Pants right leg

Using No.5 needles and A, cast on 37[41:45:49] sts and work in rib as on Back of Pullover for 1¼in, ending with a second row.

Change to No.7 needles. Beg with a K row, continue in st st as follows:

1st row K9[10:11:12], sl 1, K17[19:21:23], sl 1, K9[10:11:12].

2nd row P.

Rep these two rows 2[3:4:5] times more.

Next row K2, *K up 1, K7[8:9:10], sl 1, K7[8:9:10], K up 1*, K3, rep from * to *, K2.

Keeping the continuity of the sl sts, work 5[7:9:11] rows.

Next row K2, *K up 1, K8[9:10:11], sl 1, K8[9:10:11], K up 1, *K3, rep from * to *, K2.

Continue inc in this way on every 6th[8th:10th:12th] rows until there are 77[81:85:89] sts.

Continue without shaping until work measures 12[15:18:21] in from beg, ending with a P row.

Shape crotch

Bind off 4 sts at beg of next 2 rows, then 3 sts at beg of next row.

P 1 row.

Next row K2, K2 tog, K to last 4 sts, K2 tog tbl, K2.

Continue dec in this way on following 4th row, then on every following 4th[4th:6th:6th] row until 58[60:62:64] sts rem.

Continue without shaping until work measures 7½[8:8½:9]in from beg of crotch shaping, ending with a K row.

Shape back

Next row P to last 32[32:36:36] sts, turn and K to end.

Next row P to last 36[36:40:40] sts, turn and K to end.

Continue working 4 sts less on every other row 3[3:4:4] times more.

Next row P across all sts, dec one st at end of row. 57[59:61:63] sts.

Change to No.5 needles. Continue in rib as at beg for 1¼in. Bind off in rib.

Left leg

Work as for right Leg, reversing all shaping.

Hat

Using No.5 needles and B, cast on 95[99:103:107] sts and work in rib as before for 1[1¼:1½:1¾]in, ending with a second row.

Change to No.7 needles and A.

Next row K5[2:4:6], * K up 1, K5, rep from * 16[18:18:18] times, K up 1, K5[2:4:6]. 113[119:123:127] sts.

Continue in rib until work measures 6½[7:7½:8]in from beg, ending with a WS row.

Next row K1, *K2 tog, rep from * to end. 57[60:62:64] sts.

Next row P.

Next row K1[0:0:0], *K2 tog, rep from * to end. 29[30:31:32] sts.

Break off yarn, thread through sts, draw up and fasten off securely.

Mittens

Using No.5 needles and B, cast on 46[55] sts.

1st row K1, *P2, K1, rep from * to end.

2nd row P1, *K2, P1, rep from * to end.

Rep these two rows for 1¾in, ending with a second row.

Next row K1, *P2 tog, K1, rep from * to end. 31[37] sts.

Continue in K1, P1 rib until work measures 2¾[3¼]in, ending with a WS row.

Break off B.

Change to No.7 needles and attach A.

Work 4 rows st st.

Next row K15[18], K up 1, K1, K up 1, K15[18].

Next row P.

Next row K15[18], K up 1, K3, K up 1, K15[18].

Continue inc in this way on every other row 3[5] times more, ending with a P row.

Next row K24[31], turn, cast on one st.

Next row P10[14], turn, cast on one st.

Next row K11[15], turn.

Continue on these sts for thumb for 1[1½]in, ending with a P row.

Next row K1, *K2 tog, rep from * to end.

Break off yarn, thread through sts, draw up and fasten off.

Join thumb seam.

Return to where work was left, attach yarn and K up 1 from base of thumb seam, K to end.

Continue on these 31[37] sts until work measures 6½[8]in from beg, ending with a P row.

Next row K1, *P1, K1, rep from * to end.

Next row P1, *K1, P1, rep from * to end.

Next row K1, *K2 tog, rep from * to end. 16[19] sts.

Next row P.

Next row K0[1], *K2 tog, rep from * to end. 8[10] sts.

Break off yarn, thread through sts, draw up and fasten off securely.

Finishing

Press work with a warm iron under a damp cloth, omitting ribbing.

Pullover. Join left shoulder seams and neckband. Sew in sleeves. Join side and sleeve seams. Press all seams.

Pants. Join center front and back seams. Join leg seams. Sew elastic inside waistband with casing-stitch. Press all seams.

Hat. Join and press seam. Make pompon in two colors and sew to top.

Mittens. Join and press seam.

Stitchery pattern/pattern for furnishings

The design for this richly decorated table runner is embroidered in two simple stitches using white yarn on a blue background to give a dramatic effect. This interesting design would also make a good inner and outer border decoration for a tablecloth, as a border on a curtain or worked in vertical bands. The design could be easily adapted for use on a pillow or to decorate a drum shaped lampshade.

To make this table runner measuring 14 inches wide by 50 inches long you will need:

- ☐ ½yd 59 inch wide even-weave linen with 21 threads to 1 inch, blue
- ☐ D.M.C. Pearl Cotton No.8, 3 balls
- ☐ Sewing thread to match linen
- ☐ Crewel needle No.16

Method

With basting stitches mark the center of the fabric vertically and horizontally following the grain of the fabric. Work the design from the chart over two threads of fabric each way. The main part of the design is worked in cross-stitch and the fine lines in Holbein or double running stitch. Work twenty-one complete repeats of the design down the center along the length of the cloth. Finish the edges of the runner with a 1 inch deep hem, mitering the corners neatly.

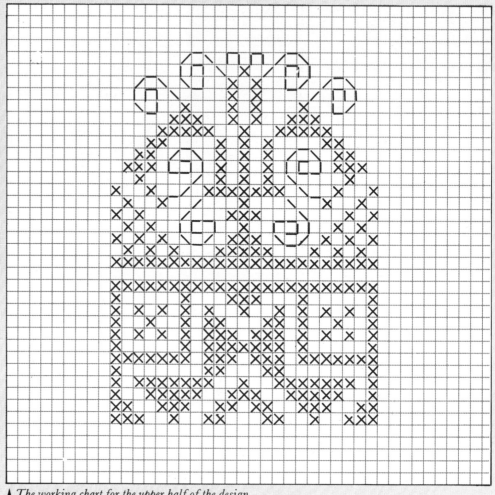

▲ *The working chart for the upper half of the design*
The table runner embroidered in cross-stitch and Holbein stitch ►   *Ways with the pattern*▼

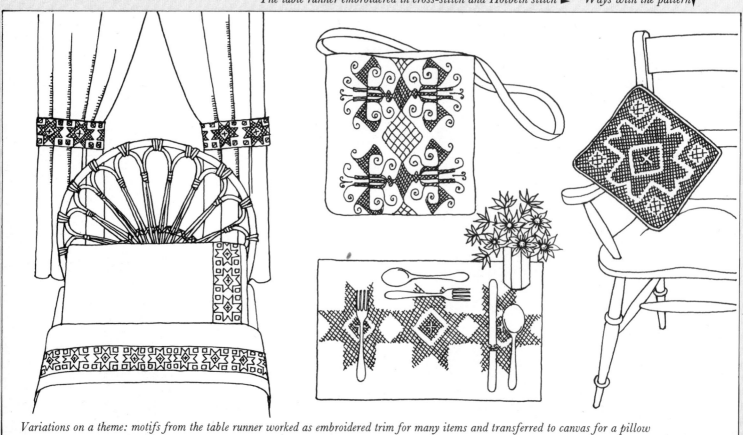

Variations on a theme: motifs from the table runner worked as embroidered trim for many items and transferred to canvas for a pillow

1728

1729

Stitchery design/metal thread embroidery

This chapter on metal thread embroidery illustrates some of the different effects which can be achieved by varying the threads and the techniques of applying them.

Although gold threads are rich and exciting to work with, silver and silver Lurex threads produce embroidery with a cool and exquisite look.

Uses

Metal thread embroidery is traditionally associated with ecclesiastical work as a decoration for copes, miters, altar frontals, pulpit falls and prayer book covers, but in modern embroidery it is used for wall panels, and as a decoration for lids of fabric jewelry boxes.

On fashion garments metal thread embroidery adds luxurious richness, and will not cause cleaning problems as a variety of washable Lurex yarns are available.

Fir cone

The background fabric is a cotton/synthetic mixture in dark brown. The applied fabrics are Japanese silk in bronze, gold kid in a variety of tones, and gloving leathers in browns. The metal threads used are Japanese gold, pearl purl, Lurex in antique gold and gold fingering knitting yarn. The Japanese silk was applied first, couched down with Japanese gold and Lurex. Shapes cut from leather and gold kid form cone seed detail. Couched gold threads and gold fingering knitting yarn are used for finer design lines.

Tree bark

The background fabric used here is natural colored burlap, and the applied fabric is gold orion cloth which resembles kid. The raised, padded sections were worked first. Several layers of felt in varying sizes were stitched in place beginning with the smallest and finishing with the largest, giving a smooth, rounded padding. The orion cloth was then stitched down over the padding. The textured stitchery is a combination of gold and lurex threads couched down in vertical flowing lines to form rhythm in the design.

Silver on blue

This sampler is worked on a slub textured home furnishing fabric, using a variety of materials in tones of silver. Narrow silver ribbon is crumpled in a random fashion and tiny matte, silver beads are stitched into the folds. Silver checkered purl, cut in lengths, is applied in small loops. Finer silver and Lurex threads and pure silk lightly scatter the background in the form of small star stitches and random crossed threads to contrast with the heavier textures. The circles of silver kid make interesting focal highlights.

▼ The design entitled "fir cone" worked in gold kid and leather   *"Tree bark" which uses padded areas▼*   *Silver on blue, cool and lovely ►*

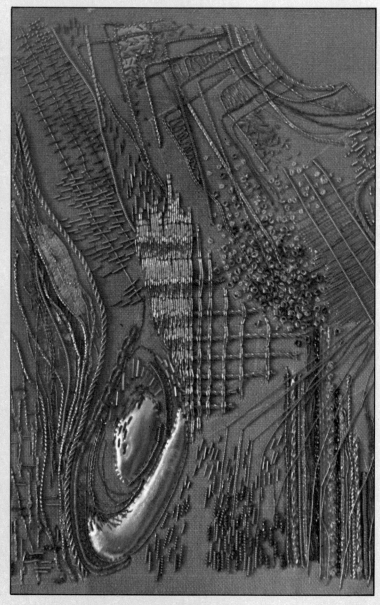

Home crochet/bedspread for an heirloom

Here is the pattern for a beautiful bedspread that you will be proud to hand on to your children's children! This pretty bedspread is crocheted in knitting cotton, and can be plain or colored as desired. Three sizes are given, but as the pattern consists of one easy-to-work motif repeated over and over again, the bedspread can be adapted to fit a bed of any dimensions.

Sizes

Single bed size. About 56in by 102in.
Double bed size. About 70in by 112in.
King bed size. About 77in by 116in.

The figures in brackets [ ] refer to the double bed and king bed sizes respectively.

Gauge
One motif measures 3½in.

Materials
Coats & Clark's O.N.T.
Speed-Cro-Sheen
39[54:60] balls
One No.D crochet hook

Motif

Using No.D hook, ch8, join with a ss into first ch to form ring.

1st round Work 24sc into ring, join with a ss into first sc.

2nd round *1sc into next sc, ch3, skip 1sc, rep from * 11 times more, join with a ss into first sc. 12 sps.

3rd round Ss into each of next 2ch, 1sc into sp, *ch5, 1sc into next sp, ch3, 1sc into next sp, rep from * 4 times more, ch5, 1sc into next sp, ch3, ss into first sc.

4th round Ss into next ch5 sp, ch4, 6tr into same sp, ch3, 1sc into next ch3 sp, *ch3, 7tr into next sp, ch3, 1sc into next sp, rep from * 4 times more, ch3, ss into 4th of 4ch.

5th round 1sc into same place as ss, 1sc into next tr, ch2, 1sc into each of next 3tr, ch2, 1sc into each of next 2tr, ch4, *1sc into each of next 2tr, ch2, 1sc into each of next 3tr, ch2, 1sc into each of next 2tr, ch4, rep from * 4 times more, join with a ss into first sc.

Second motif

Work rounds 1-4 as for first motif.

5th round Work as given for first motif until 5grs have been worked over, 1sc into each of next 2sc, ch1, insert hook into ch2 loop on first motif, yoh, pull yarn through, ch1, 1sc into each of next 3tr, ch1, insert hook into next ch2 loop on first motif, yoh and pull yarn through, ch1, 1sc into each of next 2tr, ch4, ss into first sc.

Finishing

1st row Join 16[20:22] motifs.
2nd row Using the same method join first group to first motif of previous row, second group to second motif of previous row. On all but the first motif, the sixth group is joined to the previous motif on the same row. In this way the second row is positioned alternately to the first. Continue in this way, joining by the same method on the required groups, until 29[32: 33] rows have been joined.

▼ *Close-up detail of a single motif from the bedspread illustrated left*

▼ *Various ways of using the motif in a bedroom scheme*

Home crochet/window filigree

Crochet window filigrees are a charming idea, popular in Scandinavia where they originated, probably inspired by the patterns of magnified snowflakes. This pretty design can be used in other ways around the home. It would make a beautiful table mat, with the edges left irregular. Alternatively, you could add an edge by working a chain instead of using a hoop, and working single crochet into each chain all around.

Size
About 16in diameter.

Gauge
7dc and 2 rows to 1in worked with No.D crochet hook.

Materials
American Thread Puritan Bedspread Cotton
1 ball
One No.D crochet hook
16in diameter metal or plastic hoop

Filigree

Ch4, join with a ss to form a ring.
1st round *Ch15, ss into ring, rep from * 3 times more.
2nd round Into each of the 4 loops just made work 30dc.
3rd round Ss over first 7dc of first loop, 1sc into next dc, *(ch7, skip 2dc, 1sc into next dc) 5 times, ch5, 1sc into 8th dc of next loop, rep from * 3 times more, ending last rep with ss into first sc of round.
4th round Ss over first 3ch, 1sc into loop, (ch7, 1sc into next ch7 loop) to end, ending with ch7, ss into first sc of round.
5th round Ss over first 3ch, 1sc into loop, *(ch9, 1sc into next loop) 3 times, ch3, 1sc into next loop, ch10, ss into last sc worked, 21dc into the ch10 loop just made, ss again into the same sc, ch3, 1sc into next loop, rep from * 3 times more, ending with ss into first sc.

6th round Ss over first 4ch, *6sc into loop, (6sc, ch2, 6sc) into next loop, 6sc into next loop, ch5, 1sc into 8th dc around ring, (ch5, skip 2dc, 1sc into next dc) twice, ch5, rep from * 3 times more, ending with ss into first sc.
7th round Ch9, *(1sc, ch2, 1sc) into ch2 loop, ch5, (1dc, ch3, 1dc) into last of 6sc in next loop, ch5, skip next loop, (1sc into next loop, ch5) twice, (1dc, ch3, 1dc) into first of 6sc, ch5, rep from * 3 times more, ending with 1dc into first st, ch3, ss into 4th of first 9ch.
8th round Ch5, *(1dc, ch3, 1dc) into ch2 loop, (1dc, ch5, 1dc) into next dc, ch3, 1dc into next dc, ch7, skip next loop, 1sc into next loop, ch7, 1dc into next dc, ch3, (1dc, ch5, 1dc) into next dc, rep from * 3 times more, ending with ch3, 1dc into first st, ch5, ss into 4th of 5ch.
9th round Ss into next ch5 loop, ch3, 4dc into this loop, **(ch3, 1dc into next loop) twice, ch3, 9dc into next loop, ch2, 9dc into next loop, (ch3, 1dc into next loop) twice, ch3, *5dc into next loop, rep from ** twice more, then rep from ** to *, ending with ss into 3rd of 3ch.
10th round Ch3, 1dc into each of next 4dc, **(ch3, 1dc into next dc) twice, ch3, 1dc into each of next 4dc, ch2, skip 1dc, 1dc into each of next 4dc, 4dc into ch2 sp, 1dc into each of next 4dc, ch2, skip 1dc, 1dc into each of next 4dc, (ch3, 1dc into next dc) twice, ch3*, 1dc into each of next 5dc, rep from ** twice more, then rep from ** to *, ss into 3rd of 3ch.
11th round Ch4, (1dc into next dc, ch1) 4 times, **ch2, (1dc into next dc, ch3) 3 times, (1dc, ch1) 4 times into ch2 sp, then 1dc into the same sp, skip 4dc, (1dc into next dc, ch1) 3 times, 1dc into next dc, (1dc, ch1) 4 times into ch2 sp, then 1dc into the same sp, ch3, skip 3dc, (1dc into next dc, ch3) 3 times*, (1dc into next dc, ch1) 5 times, rep from ** twice more, then rep from ** to *, ss into 3rd of 5ch.

12th round Ch5, (1dc into next dc, ch2) 4 times, **ch1, (1dc into next dc, ch3) 3 times, (1dc into next dc, ch2) 4 times, 1dc into each of next 2dc, ch2, (1dc into next dc, ch2) twice, 1dc into next 2dc, (ch2, 7dc into next dc) 4 times, ch3, (1dc into next dc, ch3) 3 times*, (1dc into next dc, ch2) 5 times, rep from ** twice more, then rep from ** to *, ss into 3rd of 5ch.
13th round Ss into next sp, ch3, 4dc into this sp, **ch2, skip 1sp, 1dc into next dc, ch2, skip 1sp, 5dc into next sp, (ch3, 1dc into next dc) 3 times, ch3, 5dc into ch2 sp, skip 1sp, (ch2, 1dc into next dc) twice, ch2, skip 1sp, 1dc between next 2dc, ch2, skip 1sp, 5dc into next sp, ch2, skip 1sp, 1dc between next 2dc, (ch2, 1dc into next dc) twice, ch2, skip 1sp, 5dc into next sp, (ch3, 1dc into next dc) 3 times, ch3*, 5dc into ch2 sp, rep from ** twice more, then rep from ** to *, ss into 3rd of 3ch.
14th round Ch5, **5dc into ch2 sp, ch2, 5dc into next sp, skip 4dc, (ch3, 1dc into next dc) 3 times, ch3, skip 1sp,* (5dc into next sp, ch2) twice, skip 1sp, 1dc into next dc, ch2, skip 1sp*, rep from * to * once more, 5dc into next sp, ch2, 5dc into next sp, ch3, skip 1sp, (1dc into next dc, ch3) 3 times, rep from ** 3 times more but ending last rep with (1dc into next dc, ch3) twice instead of 3 times, ss into 3rd of 5ch. Fasten off.

Finishing

Work in blanket stitch all around the metal hoop, covering it closely.
Pin out the filigree to size and press under a wet cloth using a hot iron. Leave to dry.
Sew the filigree to the hoop as illustrated.
Crochet a chain the required length and sew to hoop, forming a loop at one end to use for hanging.

The filigree stitched to a metal hoop to hang in a window ►

1735

Tailoring six

In this chapter
A. Making a step collar: the under collar; pressing the collar pieces; stitching the collar; attaching the collar to the coat.
B. Making a fitted collar
C. Making a mandarin collar
D. Setting in the sleeves: pinning in the sleeves; smooth fitted sleeve cap; gathered sleeve cap.
E. The third fitting
F. Stitching in the sleeves: sleeve cap padding.

A. Making a step collar

The collar of a coat should be smooth and well fitted, so great care must be taken not to distort it when stitching and pressing. The collar is sewn to the coat by hand to insure a perfect fit.

The under collar
Stitch the center back seam. Trim the seam allowance to ¼ inch and press open.
1. Working on the under collar canvas, trim the center back seam allowance to ¼ inch, overlap on sewing line and stitch.
2. Lay the canvas to the wrong side of the under collar with center backs matching. Pin along the crease line, then run a taut thread along the crease line in matching thread.
3. The crease line on the collar divides the stand from the fall.
4. Fold the under collar on the crease line with the canvas side up, and pad stitch the fall, keeping within the stitching lines all around. Work with the crease line away from you and work up and down in staggered lines.
5. Similarly, pad stitch the stand, again working with the crease line away from you.

Pressing the collar pieces
To fit the coat correctly the under and top collar pieces need to be pressed and molded before being stitched together.
6. Lay the under collar, right side down, on an ironing board. Using a damp cloth press the fall, gently pulling the outer edge of the collar slightly, just above the shoulder position. Always pull toward the center back as the center back must not be stretched. The edge should not be stretched more than ½ inch.
7. Repeat for the stand.
8. Turn the under collar right side up and lay it flat on an ironing board with the stand folded over on the crease line. Using a damp cloth press firmly without stretching.
9. While the under collar is still damp, curve it around a dessert mold, with the stand turned in, to dry into a curve.
1736

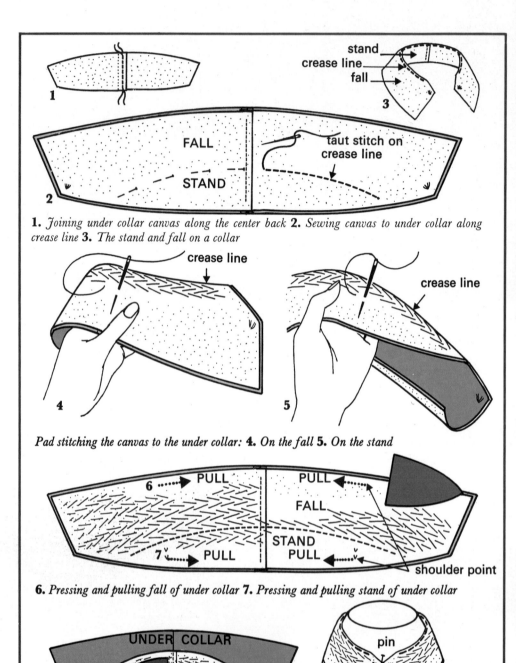

1. Joining under collar canvas along the center back 2. Sewing canvas to under collar along crease line 3. The stand and fall on a collar

Pad stitching the canvas to the under collar: 4. On the fall 5. On the stand

6. Pressing and pulling fall of under collar 7. Pressing and pulling stand of under collar

8. Pressing the under collar *9. Curving under collar around dessert mold*

Prepare the top collar similarly, but turning the stand under.

Stitching the collar
10. Working on the under collar, trim the canvas to just inside the stitching line.
11. Check that the under collar fits neatly into the neckline with the ends matching.
12. Place the top and under collar pieces together, with right sides facing. Baste along crease line and along outside and step edges.
13. Stitch, layer seams and snip corners.

14. Turn the collar to the right side and work the corners or curves into a good shape. Working on the underside, baste along the stitched edges keeping the seam rolled to the underside. Side stitch the seam edges to keep them in place.
15. Turn under the seam allowance on the neck edge of the under collar and baste. Snip into the neck edge seam allowance of the top collar at the shoulder points. Turn under the seam allowance from the front edges to the shoulder point as shown and baste.
Press the collar very carefully.

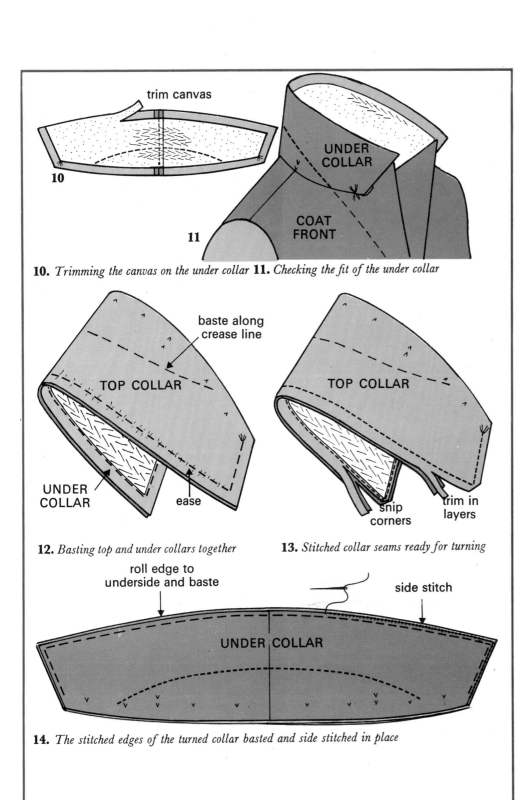

10. *Trimming the canvas on the under collar* **11.** *Checking the fit of the under collar*

trim canvas

UNDER COLLAR

COAT FRONT

baste along crease line

TOP COLLAR

UNDER COLLAR

ease

12. *Basting top and under collars together*

TOP COLLAR

snip corners

trim in layers

13. *Stitched collar seams ready for turning*

roll edge to underside and baste

side stitch

UNDER COLLAR

14. *The stitched edges of the turned collar basted and side stitched in place*

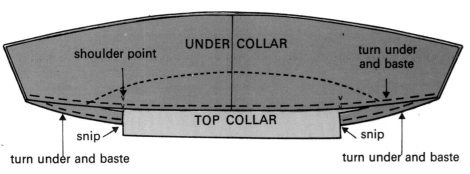

shoulder point

UNDER COLLAR

turn under and baste

snip

TOP COLLAR

snip

turn under and baste

turn under and baste

15. *Turning under and basting the neck edges of the collar ready for attaching to coat*

Coat with step collar, Butterick pattern 6462

Coat with fitted collar from Vogue Patterns
Coat with mandarin collar from Vogue Patterns

Attaching the collar to the coat

Lay the coat, right side up, over your knees with the neckline toward you.

16. Lay the under collar to the neck edge of the coat, right side up, with the folded edge of the undercollar meeting the sewing line of the coat neck edge. Carefully match the center backs, shoulder points and crease line. Pin along the neck edge distributing the ease evenly.

17. Fell the collar to the coat, starting at the center back and working to each end. Finish the ends off securely.

18 a, b. Still with the coat on your knees, turn the coat over to the wrong side. Pad stitch the end of the bridle firmly to the crease of the collar (**a**). Turn in the seam allowance of the facings along the neck edge in a smooth line and baste to coat (**b**).

19. Put the folded edges of the top collar to the folds of the facing. Using a draw stitch, draw the folds together making the stitches invisible (Tailoring 5).

20. The raw edge at the back of the top collar is herringboned down as shown. This is eventually covered by the lining. Press the neck seam carefully over a ham.

B. Making a fitted collar

21. A fitted collar is worked exactly as for the step collar. The crease line on a fitted collar runs from center front to center front as shown.

C. Making a mandarin collar

Like the step collar, the mandarin collar is also attached to the coat by hand.
22. Cut a strip of wool and hair canvas to the shape of the collar without seam allowance. Catch stitch to the inside collar piece.

23. Place the collar pieces together, with right sides facing. Baste and stitch, starting and ending at the neck seamline.

24. Layer the seams and snip corners. Fold the neck seam allowances to the wrong side and baste.

Turn the collar to the right side, working corners into a good shape. Baste and press.

25. Sew the mandarin collar to the coat as for the step collar (figures **16, 17, 18,** and **19**), in the position indicated on the pattern, remembering that the under collar is now facing inward.

D. Setting in the sleeves

The coat is now ready to have the sleeves set in.

Pinning in the sleeves

Make sure that the sleeves are put into

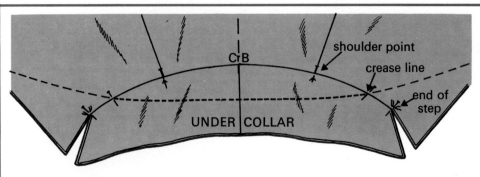

16. *Pinning the under collar to the coat neck edge*

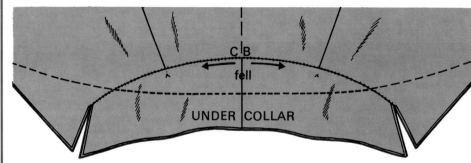

17. *Felling the under collar to the coat neck edge*

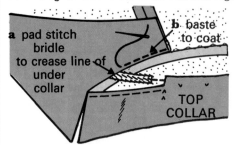

18a. *Stitching the bridle extension;* **b.** *turning in neck edge of front coat facing*

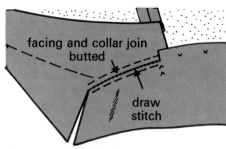

19. *Drawing the folds of the facing and top collar together invisibly*

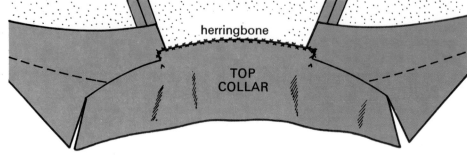

20. *The seam allowance at the back of the top collar herringboned to the coat*

their correct armholes. This might sound a silly thing to say but a mistake can easily be made.

26. Turn the coat wrong side out. Put the sleeve into the armhole with the right side of the sleeve facing right side of coat.
Working from inside the sleeve, pin all matching points as shown, incorporating any alterations made during the second fitting.

Smooth fitted sleeve cap

27. Hold the coat with the armhole seam rolled back over the fingers. Pin away the ease between the pins already in place. Baste with small stitches.

Gathered sleeve cap

28. Some fashion coats are being designed with a slight gather at the sleeve cap.
Run a gathering thread as shown in the pattern instructions. Pin in the sleeve as shown in figure **26**, then pull this thread until the sleeve cap fits the armhole.

29. Make sure that the gathers are even, then pin and baste with small stitches.

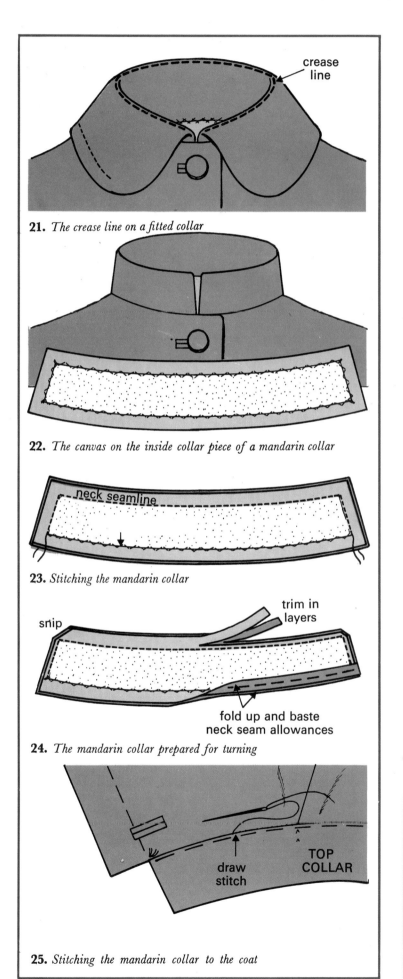

21. *The crease line on a fitted collar*

22. *The canvas on the inside collar piece of a mandarin collar*

23. *Stitching the mandarin collar*

24. *The mandarin collar prepared for turning*

25. *Stitching the mandarin collar to the coat*

crease line

neck seamline

snip

trim in layers

fold up and baste neck seam allowances

draw stitch

TOP COLLAR

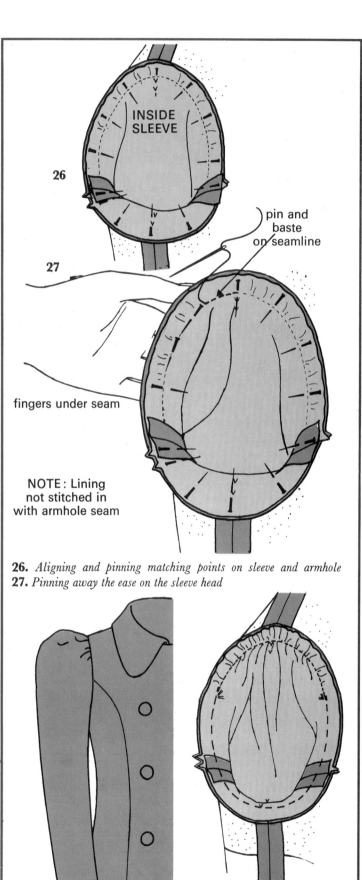

INSIDE SLEEVE

26

27

fingers under seam

pin and baste on seamline

NOTE: Lining not stitched in with armhole seam

26. *Aligning and pinning matching points on sleeve and armhole*
27. *Pinning away the ease on the sleeve head*

28. *Gathered sleeve head*

29. *Gathers evenly distributed and basted on gathered sleeve head*

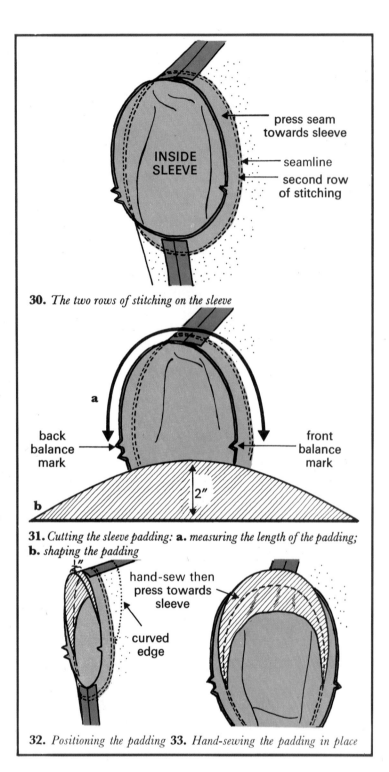

30. *The two rows of stitching on the sleeve*

31. *Cutting the sleeve padding:* **a.** *measuring the length of the padding;* **b.** *shaping the padding*

32. *Positioning the padding* **33.** *Hand-sewing the padding in place*

E. The third fitting

Position shoulder pads if needed and put on the coat to have a final look at the sleeves. Ask a friend to help you as the hang of the sleeves alters with movement and you need to be perfectly still to get the correct set.

Also check that there is enough ease across the back when you make natural movements, such as sitting in a driving position, pushing a baby carriage, etc.

It is a good idea to give the length a final check too.

1740

F. Stitching in the sleeves

The sleeves can be machine-stitched or hand-sewn in place with a backstitch. Always work from inside the sleeve as you can control the fullness this way.

30. Make a second row of stitching in the seam allowance $\frac{1}{8}$ inch outside the first row. Without trimming the seam press it toward the sleeve, shrinking the sleeve seam carefully at the top.

Sleeve cap padding

Padding the sleeve cap gives a slightly

rounded look to a smooth cap and will support the shape of a gathered one.

31a and **b.** Measure the length over the shoulder from the back balance mark to the front balance mark (**a**). Cut two pieces of tailor's wadding to that length and shape as shown (**b**).

32. Place the curved side to the sleeve so that the padding extends $\frac{1}{4}$ inch at the sleeve cap.

33. Using matching thread, hand-sew the pad firmly in place on the second line of stitches, working through all thicknesses of the fabric.

Crafts/dressing costume dolls

▲ *Note the detail of material and accessories in this Victorian dress.*

▲ *A copy of the costume worn by Dame Margot Fonteyn in "Firebird"*

Choosing a theme for costume dolls

Dressing costume dolls is an appealing craft for anyone who likes to work in miniature and finds enjoyment in improvising for detailed effects. A collection can be built up according to one's particular interest: historical costumes provide an opportunity for working with rich fabrics, sequins and beads, while national costumes offer scope for embroidery. Theatrical costumes are another idea for a collection, choosing clothes worn by famous actors and actresses, or one might decide to build a collection of twentieth-century fashion.

Selecting a suitable doll

It is important to choose dolls which can be obtained fairly easily, particularly when a collection is being started. Dolls with an adult look are essential—it is very difficult to make a baby doll look anything but a baby—and if special poses are required choose one with adjustable limbs. All the dressed dolls in this chapter are of one particular type, and it can be seen that they seem to take on different features once the costume is on them.

This particular make of doll is made in such a way that the arms, legs, and head can be easily removed to simplify dressing.

The Firebird is of the same make but with jointed limbs.

Fabrics and effects

It is very important to use fabrics in scale with the doll. Look for fabrics with this clearly in mind. Small prints and fine weaves will give a dressed doll a more realistic look, and if the desired print isn't available use a plain fabric and paint the design. The Tudor doll's skirt has been treated in this way and it looks very effective. Fabrics can be painted with gold, silver, poster paints or inks after they have been constructed. Alter-

▲ *A pretty Swedish folk-costume with blouse and vest.*   ▲ *A Regency outfit with a heavily trimmed hem.*

natively, felt pens or fabric paints can be used to paint the fabrics before they are made.

Short cuts can be used to achieve the final effect, such as glueing on details like sequins, jewels, feathers or trimmings, but use a good adhesive that will dry clear.

Search out and keep miniature trims of all kinds: broken necklaces for jewels, ribbon, lace edging, rouleau trimming and tiny buttons all help to build up the effect. Silver paper, foil, doilies in white, silver and gold, feathers, scraps of wool, pieces of tinsel, and even gift wrapping paper should be in your store of pieces.

Choose fabrics which do not fray easily wherever possible. Felt, of course, is good,

1742

and so is Pellon interfacing; the latter can be painted or sprayed and is very good for making hats and other accessories. Don't, however, reject velvet, silk and satin as fabrics simply because they fray—they do add tremendous richness to costumes. Instead, handle these materials carefully and don't cut seams too finely.

Ideas for costume and making patterns

Once the collective theme has been decided on, try to find color pictures or drawings to work from. Study the reference carefully and get the essential line of the dress firmly in mind. One characteristic of the garment will stand

out—in the Tudor doll's costume, for instance, it is the sleeves. Try to find out what the back of the costume looks like—this is fairly important.

Cut patterns for the garment pieces in newspaper, pinning them onto the doll for fit, but remember to allow for seams. Costume dolls are rarely undressed so it isn't necessary to consider openings and fastenings.

Once sewing has started, it is usually easier to sew sections directly onto the doll. The Tudor costume was constructed bodice first, then the skirt, the ruff, and finally the sleeves. A better fit is achieved in this way and if one section is wrong it can easily be removed.

Regency lady

The main characteristic of this period was the high waisted dress ending well above the ankles, heavily trimmed on the lower half of the skirt to emphasize the tubular look of the dress. It was slightly padded at the junction of the skirt and bodice at the back to make it stand away from the body.

Over the dress went either a dark colored Spencer jacket, as in our costume, or a coat that ended above the hemline. In summer, heavily fringed, patterned shawls were used indoors and out, and a high crowned hat or a turban was worn, usually richly trimmed. White or pink stockings and flat heelless slippers completed the outfit.

Draw the pattern pieces from the chart to make a paper pattern. Cut out the pieces. Choose a sprigged, dotted or plain pale cotton fabric for the main dress. Join the bodice at the side seams, and edge the neck and armholes by turning under a very small amount, slip stitching into place. Cut one skirt piece and join it at the back, leaving a one inch opening. Gather the skirt. Gather rows of fabric frills or lace or ribbon onto the skirt and hem the edge. Cut out the jacket sections in dark navy or black fabric, making the opening of the bodice in the front this time. Sew on thick embroidery thread or wool at the lines shown on the graph and lace at the lower cuff edge. Pin the sleeves into the bodice while it is flat, allowing the fullness to be at the top to get the delightful puffed effect.

Sew the sleeves in securely and then sew the side and underarm seam in one operation. The bottom band of the Spencer is put on like bias binding and slip stitched inside. The collar is made in the same way. Both garments can now be fastened onto the doll with small stitches using matching thread.

The bonnet is made from Pellon or felt. Join the crown back seam and stitch in the crown top, make small $\frac{1}{4}$ inch cuts $\frac{1}{2}$ inch apart on the bottom edge of the crown. This will allow it to sit on the brim without a clumsy seam. Stitch or glue in place. Sew lace around the brim and glue ribbon around the crown and brim junctions to cover the overlapping parts. Allow ends 3-4 inches long to tie under the chin. Glue feathers or flowers to the side of the bonnet.

Tudor lady

This costume is copied from a portrait in the National Portrait Gallery in London, England. The ruff is made of Pellon and

▲ *A Tudor costume taken from a portrait in the National Portrait Gallery, London, England*

the headdress is made of Pellon covered in ribbon. Lace trim is glued on afterward. It is difficult to get fabric to pleat well in miniature, so it was important for this costume to get a good representation of the general line.

Victorian lady

The fabric has to be constructed to scale for this costume and consists of lace ribbon over rayon. The skirt and blouse are made separately and joined on the doll. The jacket is a separately made garment and the brooch is a jet button. The hat is made of Pellon and the shoes have been painted with model paint.

The Firebird

This costume was inspired by one worn by Dame Margot Fonteyn in the ballet "The Firebird". The feathers are hen feathers dyed in ink and sewn to the dress bodice. It was necessary to sew the doll's hair into a different style for this costume, and stage make-up has been painted onto her face.

Swedish folk-costume

The blouse is made on the doll and the vest is separate. Motifs were cut from braid for the hat decoration. A crochet strip was worked for the hat.

▼CHART FOR REGENCY COSTUME

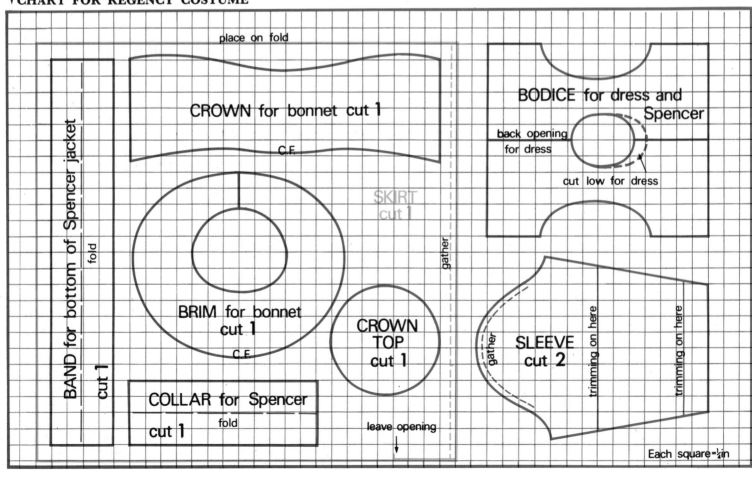

place on fold

BAND for bottom of Spencer jacket

fold

cut 1

CROWN for bonnet cut 1

C.F.

BODICE for dress and Spencer

back opening for dress

cut low for dress

SKIRT cut 1

gather

BRIM for bonnet cut 1

C.F.

CROWN TOP cut 1

gather

SLEEVE cut 2

trimming on here

trimming on here

COLLAR for Spencer

cut 1   fold

leave opening
↓

Each square=¼in

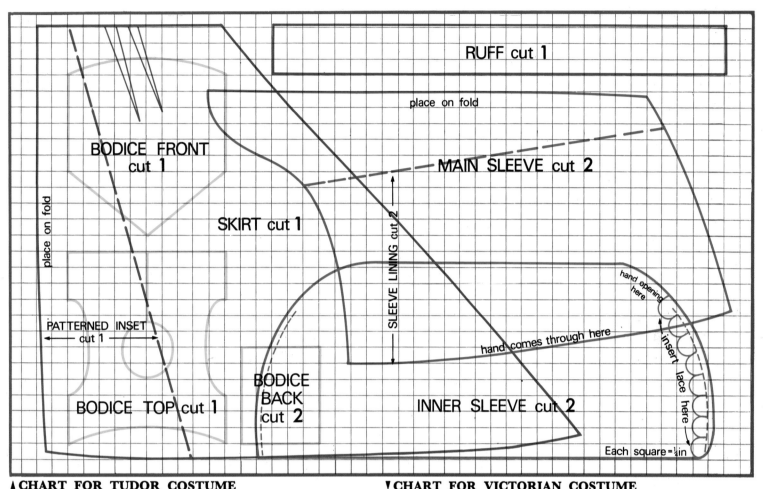

RUFF cut **1**

place on fold

BODICE FRONT
cut **1**

MAIN SLEEVE cut **2**

SKIRT cut **1**

SLEEVE LINING cut **2**

place on fold

hand opening here

insert lace here

PATTERNED INSET
cut **1**

hand comes through here

BODICE TOP cut **1**

BODICE
BACK
cut **2**

INNER SLEEVE cut **2**

Each square = ¼in

▲ CHART FOR TUDOR COSTUME   ▼ CHART FOR VICTORIAN COSTUME

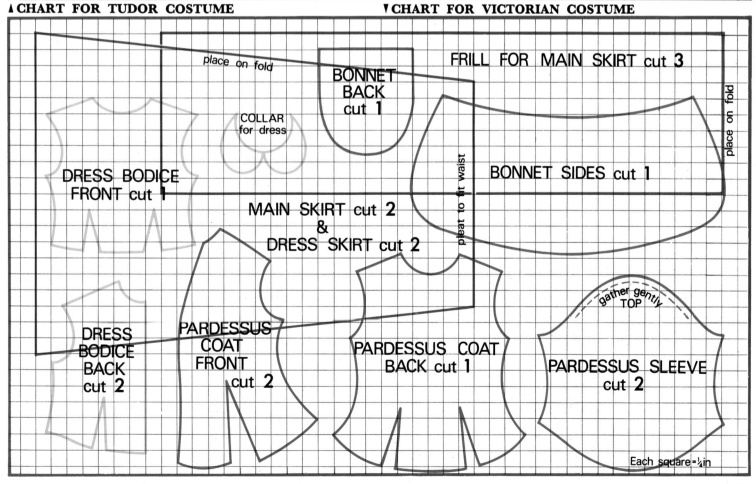

place on fold

BONNET
BACK
cut **1**

FRILL FOR MAIN SKIRT cut **3**

place on fold

COLLAR
for dress

BONNET SIDES cut **1**

DRESS BODICE
FRONT cut **1**

MAIN SKIRT cut **2**
&
DRESS SKIRT cut **2**

pleat to fit waist

gather gently
TOP

DRESS
BODICE
BACK
cut **2**

PARDESSUS
COAT
FRONT
cut **2**

PARDESSUS COAT
BACK cut **1**

PARDESSUS SLEEVE
cut **2**

Each square = ¼in

1745

1746

Knitting pattern/belted suit

The skirt of this elegant suit is knitted in stockinette stitch, and coordinates with a rib effect jacket that is three-quarter length.

Sizes
Directions are for 32in bust. The figures in brackets [] refer to the 34, 36, 38 and 40in sizes respectively.
Jacket. Length, 29[29½:30:30½:31]in.
Sleeve seam, 16½[17:17:17½:18]in.
Skirt. Length, 19[19½:20:20½:21]in.

Gauge
6 sts and 8 rows to 1in over st st on No.4 needles.

Materials
Unger Derby
Jacket. 24[25:27:28:29] balls
Skirt. 11[12:13:13:14] balls
One pair No.3 needles
One pair No.4 needles
8 buttons
One buckle
One 7in skirt zipper
Waist length elastic for skirt

Jacket back

Using No.3 needles, cast on 134[140:146:152:158] sts and K 10 rows.
Change to No.4 needles and continue in patt as follows:
1st row K.
2nd row P0[3:6:9:0], K2, *P10, K2, rep from *10[10:10 10:12] times more, P0[3:6:9:0].
These 2 rows form the patt and are rep throughout.
Continue in patt until work measures 2½in, ending with a WS row.
K2 tog at each end of next and every following 10th row until 104[110:116:122:128] sts rem.
Continue without shaping until work measures 22in from beg, ending with a WS row.

Shape armholes
Bind off 9[10:11:11:12] sts at beg of next 2 rows, then 2sts

◄ *Garter stitch stripes in stockinette stitch create wide rib effect*

at beg of next 2 rows.
K2 tog at each end of every other row 4[4:4:5:5] times. 74[78:82:86:90] sts.
Continue without shaping until armhole measures 7[7½:8:8½:9]in, ending with a WS row.

Shape shoulders
Bind off 7[7:8:8:8] sts at beg of next 4 rows, then 7[8:7:8:9] sts at beg of next 2 rows.
Bind off rem 32[34:36:38:40] sts.

Left front

Using No.3 needles, cast on 73[76:79:82:85] sts and K 10 rows.
Change to No.4 needles and continue in patt as follows:
1st row K.
2nd row K13, *P10, K2, rep from * 4[4:4:4:5] times, P0[3:6:9:0].
Rep the last 2 rows until work measures 2½in, ending with a WS row.
K2 tog at beg of next and every following 10th row until 58[61:64:67:70] sts rem.
Continue without shaping until work measures the same as Back to armholes, ending with a WS row.

Shape armhole
At armhole edge, bind off 9[10:11:11:12] sts every other row; then 2 sts.
At arm edge, dec one st every other row 4[4:4:5:5] times. 43[45:47:49:51] sts.
Continue without shaping until armhole measures 4½[5:5½:6:6]in, ending with a RS row.

Shape neck
At neck edge, bind off 14[15:16:17:18] sts, then 2 sts every other row 3 times.
K2 tog at neck edge every other row twice.
Continue without shaping until armhole measures the same as on Back, ending with a WS row.

Shape shoulder
At arm edge, bind off 7[7:8:8:8] sts every other row twice.

Work 1 row. Bind off rem 7[8:7:8:9] sts.
Mark position of buttons on front edge with pins as follows: Place first pin 2½in from beg, 2nd pin 3in below neck edge, then 6 more evenly spaced between these.

Right front

Work to correspond to left Front, reversing all shaping and working buttonholes to correspond to pin positions as follows:
Buttonhole row (RS) K5, bind off 3 sts, patt to end.
Next row Cast on 3 sts over the 3 sts bound-off.

Sleeves

Using No.3 needles, cast on 50[52:54:56:58] sts and K 10 rows.
Change to No.4 needles and continue in patt as follows:
1st row K.
2nd row P6[7:8:9:10], K2, *P10, K2, rep from * twice more, P6[7:8:9:10].
Continue in patt, inc one st at each end of every 8th row until there are 78[80:82:84:86] sts.
Continue without shaping until sleeve seam measures 16½[17:17:17½:18]in, ending with a WS row.

Shape cap
Bind off 5 sts at beg of next 2 rows.
K2 tog at each end of every other row 15[16:17:18:19] times.
Bind off 2 sts at beg of next 12 rows.
Bind off rem 14 sts.

Collar

Using No.3 needles, cast on 85[87:89:91:93] sts and work in garter st for 1¼in.
Next row K19[20:21:22:23], *K up 1, K2, K up 1, K3, rep from * 8 times more, K up 1, K2, K up 1, K19[20:21:22:23].
Continue in garter st for 2¾[2¾:3:3:3¼]in. Bind off.

Belt

Using No.3 needles, cast on

11 sts. Work in garter st for 30[32:34:36:38]in. Bind off.

Skirt front

Using No.3 needles, cast on 91[97:103:109:115] sts.
1st row K1, *P1, K1, rep from * to end.
2nd row P1, *K1, P1, rep from * to end.
Rep these 2 rows for 1½in, ending with a 2nd row.
Change to No.4 needles.
Beg with a K row, work 4 rows st st.
Next row K10, K up 1, K24[26:28:30:32], K up 1, K23[25:27:29:31], K up 1, K24[26:28:30:32], K up 1, K10.
Work 5 rows.
Next row K10, *K up 1, K25[27:29:31:33], rep from * twice more, K up 1, K10.
Work 5 rows.
Next row K10, K up 1, K26[28:30:32:34], K up 1, K27[29:31:33:35], K up 1, K26[28:30:32:34], K up 1, K10.
Continue inc in this manner every 6th row twice more, then on every 10th row 9 times.
Continue without shaping until work measures 18[18½:19 19½:20]in from beg, ending with a K row.
Change to No.3 needles and K 10 rows. Bind off.

Skirt back

Work as given for Front.

Finishing

Press under a damp cloth and using a warm iron.

Jacket
Join shoulder seams.
Sew in Sleeves. Join side and sleeve seams. Sew on Collar.
Press seams.
Sew on buttons. Make a loop on each side seam for belt, sew buckle to belt and thread through loops.

Skirt.
Join seams, leaving one open for zipper. Sew in zipper.
Press seams. Sew elastic inside waistband with casing-stitch.

Crafts/making fabric boxes

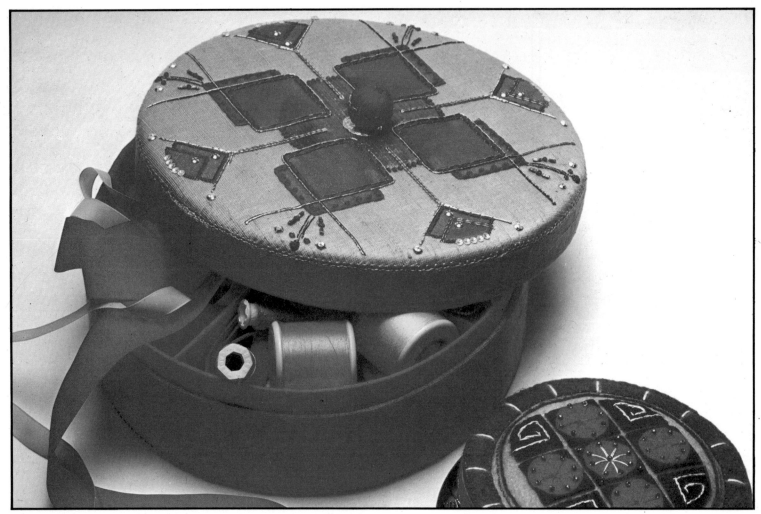

▲ *Make large boxes for sewing materials, jewelry, keepsakes; small boxes for pins and rings. Vary the fabric and decoration to suit yourself*

The forgotten craft

Making embroidered fabric boxes is in some ways a forgotten craft. Many people, keen embroiderers, never think of turning their stitchcraft into the production of boxes—yet an exquisitely made fabric box provides the maker with a tremendous sense of achievement. Embroidered fabric boxes make marvelous gifts—but having made one you'll find it difficult to part with it.

Boxes take time, patience and care to make and measurements must be absolutely accurate if they are to look professional. Cleanliness is essential for this craft. Work with a clean cloth over your lap, and wash your hands frequently while working. Remember that adhesive dropped onto fabric will often leave a permanent mark and vigilance is needed during the glueing stages.

Materials and equipment

Boxes are made of cardboard which is then padded and covered with fabric. Various weights of cardboard are used in box making and each of the projects in this chapter recommend the most suitable

weight of cardboard. Fabric adhesive is used for all glueing and it is best to use a narrow spatula for applying it.

Equipment needed for this craft is little more than you would need for any sewing craft, but you will also need a steel ruler, a good quality cutting knife, a set square and a piece of masonite for cutting on.

Fabrics and padding

Thin smooth fabrics are better than thick ones, and those without excessive stretch in them are best. Silk, satin, rayon, linen, cotton, velvet and felt are all suitable fabrics, and those with lurex finishes or rich-looking prints make superb jewel boxes. The top of the box can be left plain if desired, or can be decorated with appliqué, beadwork, goldwork or surface embroidery of almost any kind to produce the desired effect.

Initials make boxes individual and beads can be piled one on another with sequins added for a jeweled effect. All surface embroidery must be completed before starting to construct the box. If patterned

fabrics are used, boxes often look prettier unadorned.

Padding materials

The padding of the boxes which is placed immediately under the top fabric should be a plain fabric; cotton flannel or Pellon is recommended.

Planning a box

First of all draw out the box you intend to make as a rough perspective drawing (diagram 1), and then draw out each piece, marking the measurements. Lining pieces are made smaller because you must allow for the thickness of padding and the covering material. Be very careful with these measurements if lids are to fit properly and not be too loose or fall into the edges of the box.

As you cut out each piece of cardboard, mark it clearly on the wrong side for outer, and right side for linings, so that you know which part of the box it is and whether it is a lining piece or outer piece. The mark is made because you will be covering one side of the cardboard with fabric, and

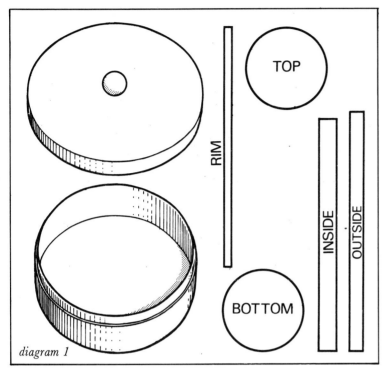

diagram 1

▲ *Rough perspective drawing of the box and opened up in sections*

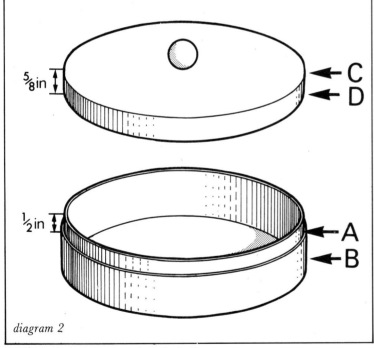

diagram 2

▲ *The various parts marked A, B, C, D*

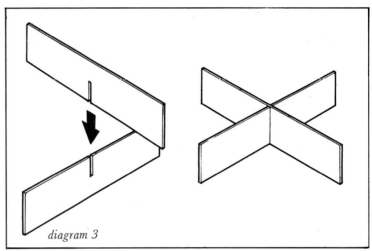

diagram 3

▲ *Making the dividing sections*

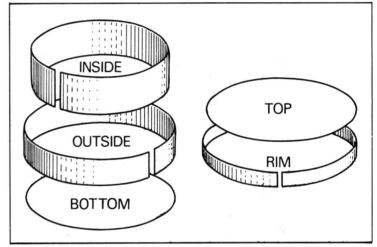

▲ *Drawing showing three sections of bottom of box*

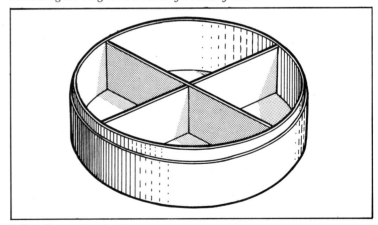

▲ *Showing sections in place*

pieces can easily lose their identity and become a bewildering muddle once you have begun to cover and pad.

Round box with overlapping lid

Ticket-weight cardboard is used for the sides and the lining of the box. Mat board is used for the top and base. The outside measurement is just over 3 times (3.14) the diameter of the box bottom.

Method

Cut the lining cardboard for the inside (marked A on diagram 2) so that it makes a circle ½ inch deeper than the outer box side (marked B on diagram 2).

Form the lining and outer strips into circles by butting the ends and sticking the join with transparent tape (do not overlap joins because this causes a bump). Remember that when these two circles are fitted inside one another the joins must be kept apart or they form an ugly bump.

Top

Cut out a circle from the mat board for the outside of the lid (C diagram 2). This should be exactly the diameter of the outside circle (B) just formed. Cut out the lining for the lid from the ticket-weight cardboard making it slightly smaller than the outside lid.

Rim of lid

Cut this in ticket cardboard so that it makes a circle exactly the same circum-

▲ *Carefully planned abstract designs, worked in beads, sequins and thread on a plain fabric, can make an unusual decoration for a box lid*
▼ *Open Cretan stitch, used to stitch sections of fabric together*   ▼ *Mitering and snipping for lining and covering fabrics*

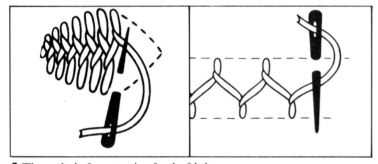

▼ *The method of construction for the felt box*

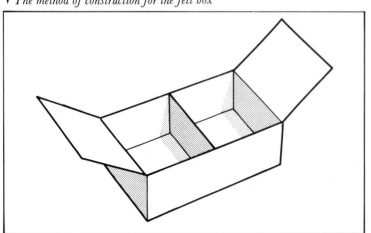

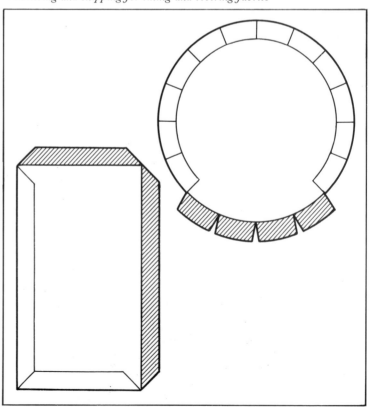

▲ Richly embroidered fabrics, although expensive, make beautiful boxes. A small piece can be used to cover a little box for rings and brooches

ference as the lid, and $\frac{5}{8}$ inch deep (D, diagram 2). Butt and join into a circle and stick with transparent tape.

Bottom
Cut mat board to exactly the same diameter circle as the top and then cut the lining slightly smaller.

Cutting the fabric
Cut fabrics for both outside of box and lining to the above sizes, allowing $\frac{1}{2}$ inch turnings. Allow $\frac{3}{4}$ inch extra when cutting the lining for (A) as it has to turn over the lip. Allow extra when cutting fabric for D as it has to turn under the rim.

Padding
Cut padding to same size as the board.

Applying padding
Padding sides of box. Glue two thicknesses of padding to the inside of the lining cardboard and to the outside of the outer cardboard, butting joins.
Padding the bottom. Cut two pieces of padding to the exact size of the bottom and two more pieces $\frac{1}{2}$ inch larger all

around. Using one same size and one larger size, glue the two thicknesses to the outside of the outer cardboard and two thicknesses to the inside of the lining cardboard. The bigger piece of padding is brought over the edge to round it off. Snip the edges for a smooth finish and glue down.
Padding the top. Glue two thicknesses of padding to the inside of the lining and at least three thicknesses of padding to the outside of the lid piece (C).

Stages of covering the box
Covering the sections. 1. Join the side pieces of both outer and lining fabrics into a circle and press seams flat (A and B pieces).
2. Join rim fabric into a circle and press. Cover the side pieces A and B with fabric, glueing it into position and when completely dry, slip piece A into piece B.
3. Cover rim piece D with fabric, over sewing the open, upper edges together.
4. Cover the outside of the bottom circle and the inside of the lining circle with fabric, taking turnings over the edges.
5. Cover the top circle with fabric and decide at this point if a knob or top

decoration is desired. If so, stitch the knob to the circle, stitching right through the cardboard.
6. Stitch the rim to the top (along oversewn edge of rim) using open Cretan stitch and six strands of thread.
7. Join bottom circle to sides, using open Cretan stitch. When stitching pieces together, stitches should go through fabric and padding but not through the cardboard. Keep stitches regularly spaced.
8. Decide at this point if box divisions are desired (see diagram 3). Cover cardboard without padding it and then stitch the divisions to the bottom lining circle.
9. Put adhesive on the inside of the bottom circle and carefully press the lining section down upon it.
Put adhesive on the inside of the lid and press lining section onto it.
Leave to dry.

Square boxes

Square boxes are made in exactly the same way as round boxes except that the four pieces of the lip and rim are sewn together at the joins.

1751

Stitchery design/pansy and anemone motifs

Ways with flower motifs

Motifs such as this simple pansy and anemone can be used for a wide variety of needlepoint items by enlarging or reducing them. Worked on large mesh canvas over more threads, they make squares for rugs or panels and pillows. Reduced, they can be used for curtain tie-back motifs and for stool tops. As petit point designs, they look pretty in miniature.

1752

Red flower square 12 inches by 11 inches
☐ 16in by 15in single-weave canvas with 10 threads to 1 inch
☐ Matte embroidery cotton in orange, red, white and green
☐ D.M.C. Pearl Cotton No.1 in scarlet
Purple flower square 12in by 13in
☐ 16in by 17in single-weave canvas with 10 threads to 1 inch
☐ Matte embroidery cotton in silver gray, purple, and white

☐ D.M.C. Pearl Cotton No.1 in bright pink and purple

To work the squares

Mark the center of the rectangle of canvas each way with lines of basting stitches. Work in cross-stitch over two threads of canvas each way, following the designs from the center of charts.

If both designs are to be incorporated in a piece of work, extend the background of the red flower to match the purple.

Floral motifs enlarged to make a rug, reduced to ornament a box lid, and used same size for a stool

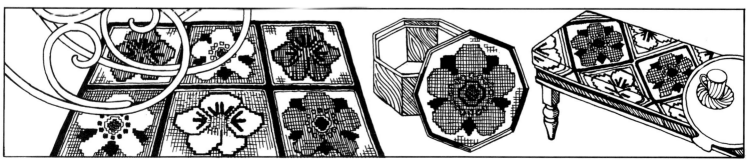

1753

Stitchery pattern/tablecloth in blackwork

This striking tablecloth in blackwork combines backstitch, cross-stitch and whipped backstitch. It is worked here on pale blue linen, but would be equally attractive on a white or strongly contrasting background.

To make this tablecloth you will need:
- [ ] 1⅝ yds 59 inch wide pale blue even-weave embroidery linen
- [ ] D.M.C. Pearl Cotton No.8, 5 balls black 0403
- [ ] Tapestry needle No.24

Method

Square the fabric and mark the center each way with lines of basting stitches. The photograph on the facing page gives one quarter of the design. The center is the upper left-hand corner of the photograph, and this should coincide with the basting stitches on the fabric. The number within the bracket indicates the number of threads between the center section of the design and the border. Note also from the photograph the arrangement of the stitches on the threads of the fabric. Commence the embroidery at the top of each central flower motif, 36 threads down from the crossed basting stitches, and work the center section and border section as given. Repeat in reverse from the left-hand edge of the photograph to complete one half of the design. Then turn the fabric and work the other half in the same way.

Press the embroidery on the wrong side. To finish, turn back a one inch hem on all the edges, miter the corners and then slip stitch.

center

120

Border
repeats
from here

1755

Tailoring seven

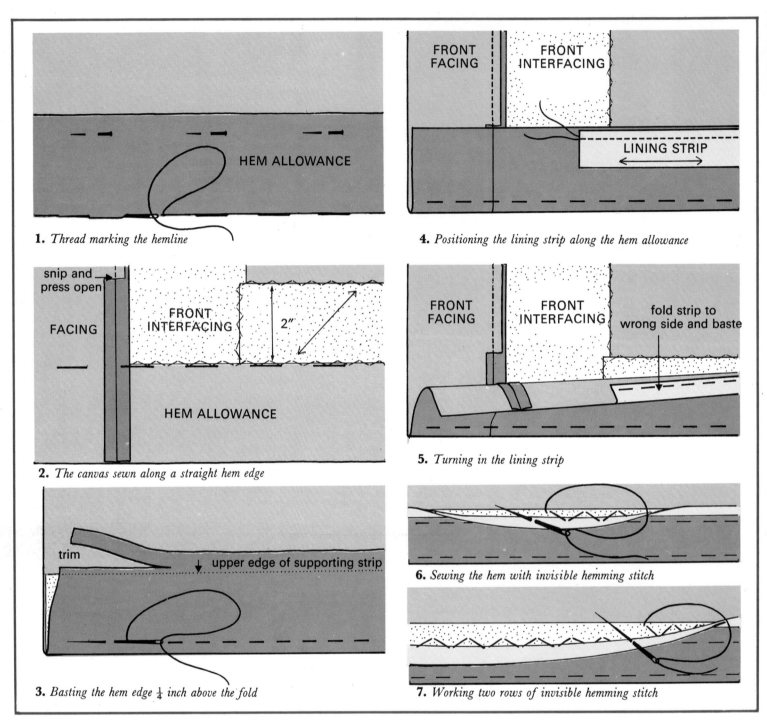

1. *Thread marking the hemline*

2. *The canvas sewn along a straight hem edge*

snip and press open

FACING

FRONT INTERFACING

2"

HEM ALLOWANCE

3. *Basting the hem edge ¼ inch above the fold*

trim

upper edge of supporting strip

HEM ALLOWANCE

4. *Positioning the lining strip along the hem allowance*

FRONT FACING

FRONT INTERFACING

LINING STRIP

5. *Turning in the lining strip*

FRONT FACING

FRONT INTERFACING

fold strip to wrong side and baste

6. *Sewing the hem with invisible hemming stitch*

7. *Working two rows of invisible hemming stitch*

A. Sewing the hem: straight hem; curved hem.

B. Finishing the facing

C. Finishing piped buttonholes

D. Hand-worked buttonholes: sham buttonholes.

E. The final press

F. Sewing on the buttons: making a shank; keeper button.

*Terms and stitches

A. Sewing the hem

Straight hem

These instructions are for a coat which

has a perfectly straight hem edge or is only very slightly curved.

1. Thread mark the fold of the hem then remove the pins.

2. To give the hem a good crisp finish, support the hem edge with strips of duck or canvas. Cut the strips 2 inches wide on the bias of the fabric and to the length of the coat hem edge, joining if necessary to make up the required length. Sew to the hem edge with catch stitch as shown.

3. Turn up the hem and baste flat ¼ inch above the fold. Press well, making sure that the iron does not impress the hem edge into the fabric.

Measure the hem depth to just above the supporting strips and trim.

To bind the seam allowance on the hem, cut 1 inch wide strips of coat lining fabric on the straight of grain. The selvage is useful for this.

4. Position the lining strip on the hem edge, but, to avoid bulk, do not continue the binding along the part of the hem which will be under the front facings. Stitch, taking ¼ inch seam allowance.

5. Fold the binding to the wrong side and baste. Press, making sure the hem lies away from the coat, otherwise impressions will be left on the coat fabric.

6. Baste the hem in place matching seams.

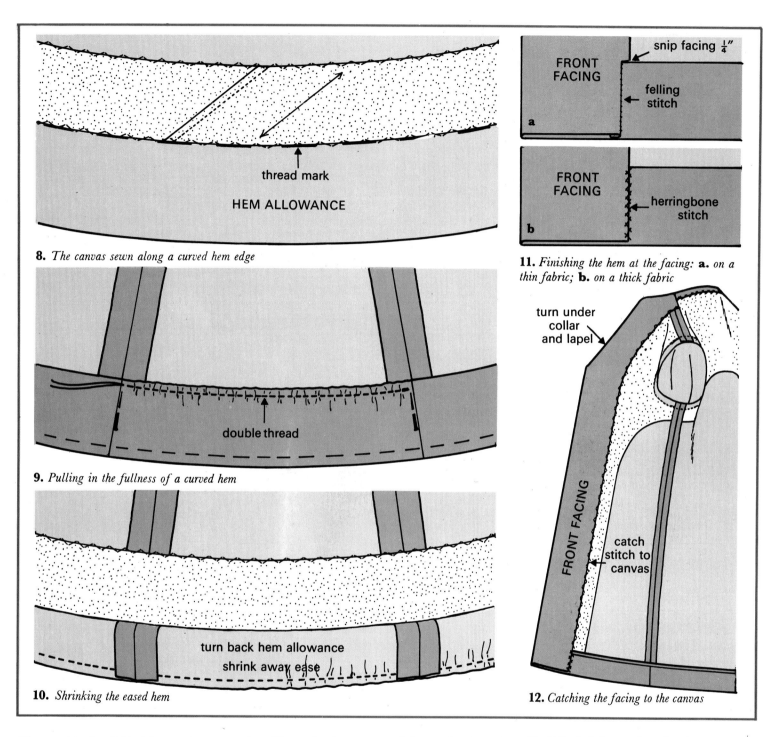

8. *The canvas sewn along a curved hem edge*

HEM ALLOWANCE

thread mark

9. *Pulling in the fullness of a curved hem*

double thread

10. *Shrinking the eased hem*

turn back hem allowance

shrink away ease

11. *Finishing the hem at the facing:* **a.** *on a thin fabric;* **b.** *on a thick fabric*

snip facing ¼"

FRONT FACING

felling stitch

FRONT FACING

herringbone stitch

turn under collar and lapel

FRONT FACING

catch stitch to canvas

12. *Catching the facing to the canvas*

Then, with the folded hem edge toward you, lift the hem slightly and sew neatly to the canvas with invisible hemming stitch*.

7. If the coat is very heavy, or you have left a deep hem as on a child's coat, sew two lines of invisible hemming stitch to hold the weight.

Curved hem

For a coat with a flare use this method of putting up the hem.

8. First work as for a straight hem edge in figures 1 and 2, gently easing the canvas into position around the curve of the coat hem.

Turn the hem up and baste flat ¼ inch above the fold, then trim the hem edge to just above the supporting strips as for the straight hem (figure **3**).

9. Matching center backs and fronts and seamlines, pin the hem as shown. Then run a double thread through each section, pulling up the fullness until the hem lies flat.

10. Lift the hem away from the coat and shrink away the ease.

To bind the seam allowance on the hem, cut 1 inch wide strips of coat lining fabric on the bias, then continue binding and sewing up the hem as for the straight hem as shown in figures **4, 5, 6** and **7**.

B. Finishing the facing

Place the coat on a flat surface and turn the facing to the inside. There are two ways of finishing off the hem edge.

11a, b. On thin fabrics, first snip into the facing seam allowance at the top of the hem. Then turn the facing under ¼ inch at the hem edge and fell firmly in place to the hem seam allowance (**a**). On thick fabrics do not turn under the raw edge to make neat, but simply herringbone the raw edge in position (**b**).

12. To finish off the facing, lay the coat flat, facing side up and lapel turned under. Catch stitch the facing to the canvas.

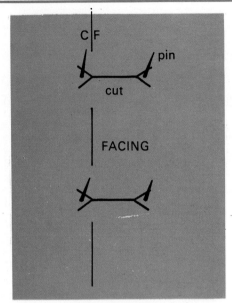

13. *Cutting the facing for the buttonholes*

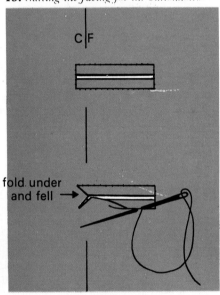

14. *Finishing the back of the buttonhole*

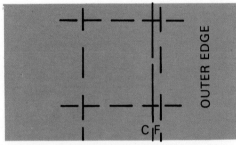

15. *Tram lines for hand-worked buttonholes*

16. *The outer edge of the hand-worked buttonhole:* **a.** *circle;* **b.** *a triangle*

17. *The cut buttonhole*

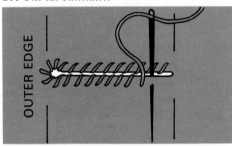

18. *Oversewing the buttonhole with single thread*

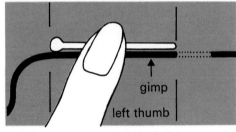

19. *Gimp laid along the buttonhole*

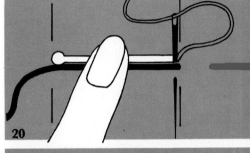
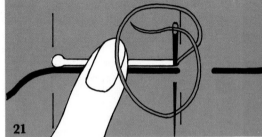
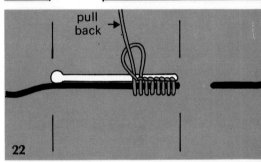
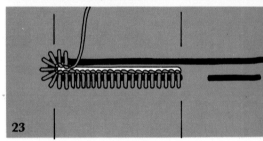

20 to 23. *Working the buttonhole*

C. Finishing piped buttonholes

With the facing now in its final position it is time to finish the back of the piped buttonholes.

Working from the right side, push a pin through to the wrong side at each end of the buttonhole to find the exact position of the slit on the facing.

13. Make a slit through the facing between the pins and miter the corners just beyond the pins.

14. Fold under the raw edges and fell securely in place.

Finally, press on the wrong side.

D. Hand-worked buttonholes

Tailored, hand-worked buttonholes are

beautiful when sewn evenly, so practice on a double-piece of the fabric with interfacing in between before starting on the garment itself.

The thread used is silk buttonhole twist and you will also need buttonhole gimp. An alternative to buttonhole gimp is two threads of buttonhole twist waxed together to prevent them from untwisting.

15. Prepare the buttonhole tram lines (see also Tailoring 3, figure 10).

16a, b. Using a stiletto, make a round hole at the outer edge of the buttonhole (**a**), or cut out a triangle (**b**).

17. Continuing from the hole, cut the length of the buttonhole. Cut very carefully as a jagged line shows up on the finished buttonhole.

18. Using a single strand of matching thread, oversew around the buttonhole

through all thicknesses.

19. Lay the gimp along the buttonhole as shown. The gimp is held in place with the thumb when working the buttonhole.

Thread the needle with a long length of buttonhole twist so that you will have enough to finish the buttonhole without joining.

20. Starting at the point shown and working with the right side of the coat facing you, insert the needle through the back of the buttonhole making sure that all layers of the fabric are caught.

21. Take the thread forward under the needle.

22. Pull the needle through and tighten the loop with the thread pulled back, so that the knot lies on the cut edge of the buttonhole.

23. At the circle or triangle, fan the stitches

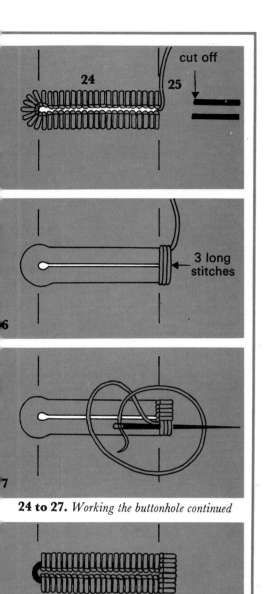

24 to 27. *Working the buttonhole continued*

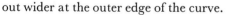

28. *A sham buttonhole*

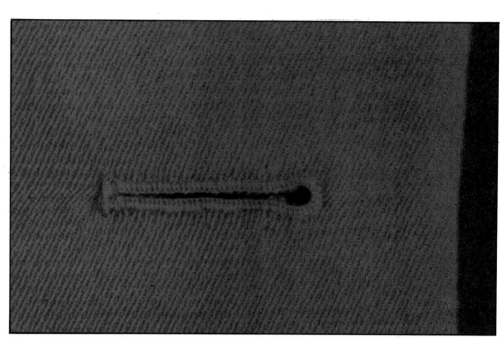

Above: *Enlarged hand-worked buttonhole; the button bar has not been sewn over with buttonhole stitch.*
Below: *A garment with hand-worked buttonholes (left) and a garment with piped buttonholes (right)*

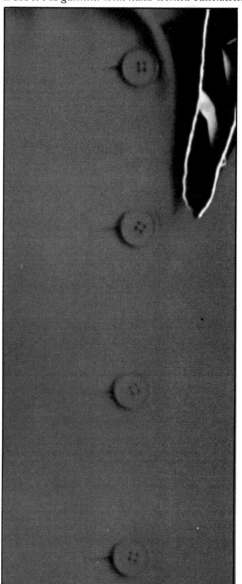
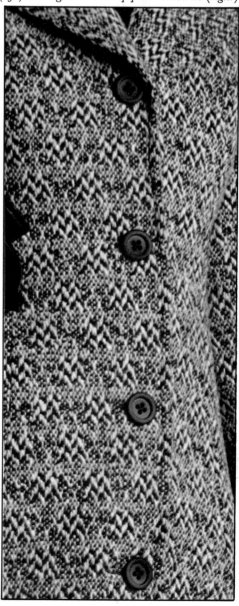

out wider at the outer edge of the curve.

24. Complete the other side of the buttonhole but do not cut off the thread yet.

25. Pull the gimp tight, thread between the layers of fabric and cut off.

26. To make the bar tack at the end of the buttonhole, work three long stitches as shown for the bar.

27. Work buttonhole stitch over the bar and through the fabric, bringing the knots to the top as shown.

Sham buttonholes

Sham buttonholes are sometimes made for vents.

28. Without cutting a slit, work buttonhole stitch along the buttonhole line. Make a bar tack at the end but omit the circle at the front end, as the button covers the lack of circle.

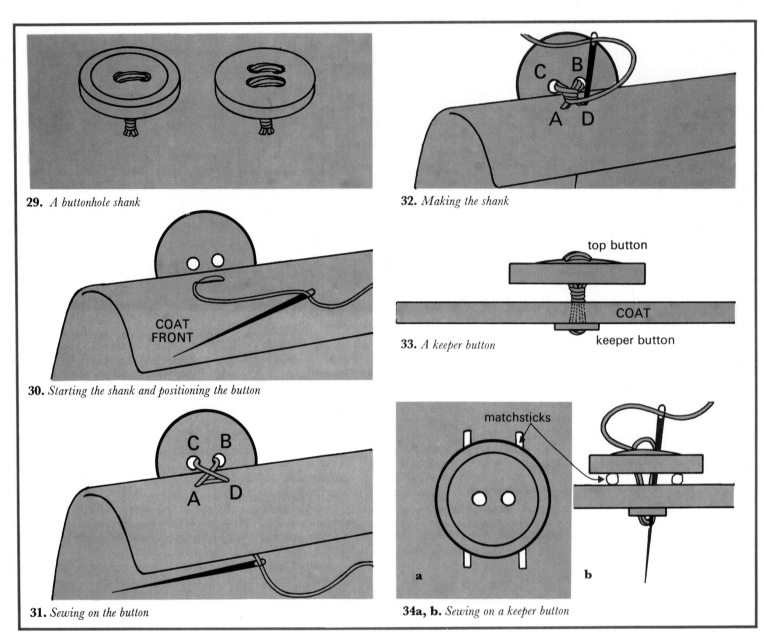

29. *A buttonhole shank*

30. *Starting the shank and positioning the button*

31. *Sewing on the button*

32. *Making the shank*

33. *A keeper button*

34a, b. *Sewing on a keeper button*

E. The final pressing

Lay the coat right side up on a board.
Using a wool pressing cloth under a slightly
damp cotton cloth, gently press all over
the coat, moving each section of the coat
so that it lies flat as you press it.

This process should be done with hardly
any pressure on the iron to avoid making
impressions on the coat.

Hang the coat to dry before lining.

F. Sewing on the buttons

Before the coat is lined the buttons should
be sewn on.

Making a shank

29. A flat button should be sewn on with a
shank so that the button does not distort
the buttonhole by being too close to the
fabric.

30. Using a strong buttonhole thread, take
a backstitch through the fabric at the
button position. Do not use a knot.
Fold the coat back and hold the button in
position as shown.

31. Take thread from A through holes B,
and then C, then back into fabric at D.
Repeat three or four times, and again if
the button has four holes. This gives
crossed threads which make a strong
foundation for the shank.

32. With the thread coming out from C,
wind it tightly around the shank. Take
the thread to the back and fasten off
securely to finish.

Keeper button

33. For added strength, a little keeper
button can be sewn onto the back of the
coat at the same time as the top button
is being sewn on.

The keeper button should be a tiny button with the same number of holes as the
top button.

34a, b. Lay the top button over two
matchsticks (**a**) and sew on the button, at
the same time sewing through the matching holes on the keeper button (**b**). Leave
the thread quite loose.

Remove the matchsticks and make a
shank (see figure 32).

*Terms and stitches

Invisible hemming stitch (35)

35

Original candles

Using simple equipment and a lot of imagination, an almost infinite variety of candle shapes can be made. Some of the ideas in this chapter are beautiful and some are astonishing — such as the water candles above.

Materials and equipment

Assemble the materials before starting work. A candlemakers supplier will stock most of them.

You will need:

☐ Paraffin wax
☐ Beeswax sheets (for beeswax candles)
☐ Stearin
☐ Wax dyes
☐ Candle perfumes (if perfumed candles are required)
☐ Wicks
☐ Candy thermometer
☐ Two large saucepans: one is for melting wax, the other for dissolving color
☐ Enamel pitcher with a lip for pouring molten wax

☐ Deep enamel pitcher for making dipped candles
☐ Mold seal (plasticine or clay)
☐ Ruler
☐ Wicking needle (to make holes for wicks)
☐ Deep receptacle for cold water
☐ Molds
☐ Spoons for ladling molten wax
☐ Sand, for sand casting, in a box

Paraffin wax. The types of paraffin wax available vary widely, but it is recommended that a fully refined wax with a melting point of 135°-140°F be used. This type of paraffin wax is available from candlemakers suppliers in solid blocks or in a powdered form, which may be more convenient.

Wicks. Candlewicks are made of bleached linen thread and these are woven and graded to burn a certain area of wax. Wicks are usually sold in packs and sized according to the diameter of the candle they will successfully burn. A 1 inch wick will burn a candle 1 inch in diameter, and it will also burn a 1 inch

hole in a larger candle. It is therefore essential to use the correct size of wick; a large candle with a small wick looks very nice when burning—until the wick drowns in a pool of wax.

Wax dyes. Candles can be left white or colored with dye—wax dyes are the best for the job. These are available in either powder or solid form. It is advisable to test dyes carefully, as too much dye will diminish the candle's glow. Test by taking a spoonful of the colored candle wax and putting it in cold water. As it sets you will get an idea of the final shade. For most colors a tiny pinch of powdered dye will color a pint of liquid wax.

Stearin. Dye is dissolved first in stearin— a white, flaky type of wax which allows the dye to dissolve readily and completely with perfect color suspension. The proportion added is 10 per cent stearin to wax.

Thermometer. A candy thermometer with readings up to a temperature of 400°F must be used, for although there is little danger of over-heating the wax to the point where it will burst into flames it is impossible to judge when the wax is at the correct temperature, and it is the temperature at which the wax is worked which gives many of the different effects.

Molds. Although craft shops sell ready-made molds of rubber, glass and metal, improvised molds work very well and can produce fascinating shapes. Some household containers can be used, as long as they are leakproof and do not collapse under the heat of the wax. Yogurt cartons, tin cans, cardboard milk cartons, plastic drainpipe, rubber balls, balloons, acetate and vinyl sheeting are some of the things which can be utilized for molds, but remember that the candle has to be removed when it has set, therefore the mold must either have a wide neck or be breakable.

Preparing the wax for colored candles

Measure out the powdered wax or break up block wax into pieces. Measure out the stearin, one part stearin to ten parts of wax. Melt the stearin in a saucepan and then add the dye. Stir until all the particles of dye are dissolved. Melt the paraffin wax slowly in the second saucepan and then add the stearin and dye mixture.

White candles can be covered with a final layer of color by dipping them into molten colored wax. Float a 2 inch layer of molten colored wax on hot water (heated at 82°C 180°F). Dip the white candle through the wax and into the water, then withdraw it so that it picks up color along its length. If the wax is too hot very little color will be picked up, and conversely, if the wax is too cool, the color will be flaky. This dipping process can be repeated for depth of color.

Candlemaking methods

Dipping

Dipping is one of the oldest methods of candlemaking and all that is required is wick, wax and an enamel pitcher, a little deeper than the desired length of candle. Attach a piece of wick to a small stick. Fill the pitcher with wax heated at 82°C, 180°F. Dip the wick into the wax. Remove it and hold it in the air for about half a minute, or until the coat of wax has hardened. Dip again and repeat until the candle is thick enough. As the wax in the pitcher cools, bubbles will appear on the surface of the wax or the candle. When this happens, reheat the wax to 180°F. When the candle is finished, hang it to harden. For an all white candle or for one colored throughout a good finishing shine can be given by giving a final dip
1762

▲ *Statue-made mold* ▼ *Rolled beeswax sheets*

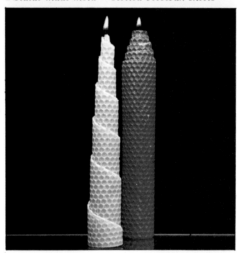

in wax heated to 200°F, 93°C, and then plunging the candle into cold water. If the pitcher is wide enough at the neck, several candles can be made by dipping simultaneously.

Ways with dipped candles

Molding dipped candles

Candles can be molded to shape by hand between dips. The pear shaped candles illustrated were made in this way.
Build up the candle to about ½ inch diameter, then start to dip or pour wax from halfway up; the lower part of the candle will begin to thicken. At this stage, between dips, roll the candle between the hands toward the shape you want.

Carved candles

By dipping a short length of wick in a succession of different colors, building them up to about ¼ inch thick, multicolored layers are formed and these can be carved back with a sharp knife to great effect. For this process the wax must be very strongly dyed, or the layers of color will show through each other.

▲ *Ready-made mold* ▼ *Carved dipped candle*

To save wax follow the method given for floating colored wax on hot water, but first make a center core at least 1 inch thick by the normal dipping method to prevent water from getting on the wick.

Twist and braids

A braid of three dipped candles in contrasting colors looks effective and these are easily made if someone else holds the ends while one braids. A twisted candle is made with a finished but still soft dipped candle. Lay it on a smooth clean surface and flatten it gently with a rolling pin. Square off the base and, taking the candle in both hands, twist top and bottom in opposite directions. Cool immediately in cold water.

Beeswax candles

Sheets of pure beeswax, honeycomb textured and smelling delightfully of honey, can be used to make simple candles. These sheets are available from candlemakers suppliers. Choose a suitable wick and cut it to the desired candle length plus a few more inches. Lay the wick along one edge of the sheet and fold the wax over to cover

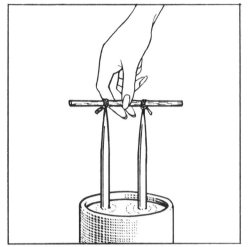

▲ *The technique of dipping candles*
▼ *The technique for layered candles*

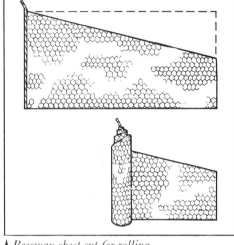

▲ *Beeswax sheet cut for rolling*
▼ *Candle mold suspended and filled*

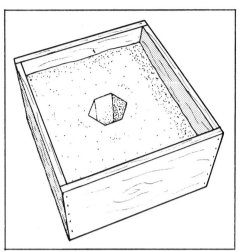

▲ *Damp sand prepared in a box*
▼ *The sand mold before carving*

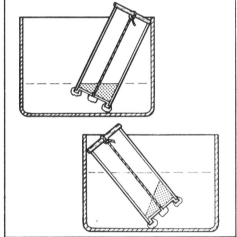

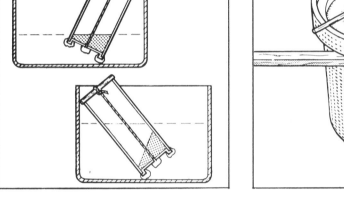

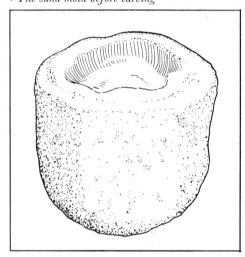

it. Roll up the candle, gently and evenly, making sure that the base is even. Trim the wick and dip it in molten beeswax. To make a pointed candle, cut the sheet of beeswax as shown in the diagram. Two contrasting tints of beeswax sheeting can be used together for variation.

Molded candles

Ready-made molds

Craft shops sell different kinds of ready-made candle molds made of both metal and flexible latex rubber. Decorative relief candles are made in these in one casting. Treat latex rubber molds with care, washing and drying them carefully after use. These molds have no wick holes, and this has to be made with a wick needle. Make sure that the same hole is used each time the mold is used. To wick-up a mold thread the wick through, tying the bottom end to a rod or a stick with the top end of the wick pulled tight. Seal the hole with mold seal. Support the mold by hanging it on an improvised rack (see diagram).

To make a candle, heat the wax to 180°F and pour it slowly into the mold. Tap the sides of the mold gently to release air bubbles. After a while a well will form around the wick as the cooling wax contracts. Prod the surface to break it and top up with wax heated to 180°F. Do this as often as necessary until the surface of the candle remains flat. If the candle seems to be misshapen, manipulate the mold with the hands while it is still soft. When the candle is completely cold and hardened, rub the surface of the mold with soapy hands, and peel back the mold, being careful around the wick area. Return the mold to its original shape, wash and dry it. Remove the wick rod from the candle and trim the base.

The candle surface can be polished with the hands or with a soft cloth. Add a small amount of beeswax to the paraffin wax for a better shine.

Relief work can be highlighted by coloring the surface of the candle with water-soluble paint mixed with a little soap. Paint the candle and rub the color off just before it dries, leaving some in the crevices. Do not over-do the color because water soluble paint does not burn, and may clog the wick if used to excess.

Making flexible molds

Molds for making candles are made from a molding liquid which is obtained from candlemakers suppliers. Choose an ornament, jar or statue made from wood, glass, plastic, stone, plaster or clay. Make sure it is free from dust or grease.

Heat the object gently in front of a fire and dip it into the molding liquid, covering it completely. Remove and hold the object until it stops dripping. The mold will set faster with a little heat, so hold the object in front of an electric heater until the whitish color changes to yellow. The first few dips will go almost transparent. Air bubbles must be blown off and you must be careful not to touch the setting mold. Continue to dip until a smooth, even coat of about one sixteenth of an inch thick or more has built up. Leave the mold to stand until the molding material has set. Trim uneven edges, and after rubbing the surface with liquid soap peel it away. Make a wick hole at the top of the mold and use it in exactly the same way as ready-made flexible molds.

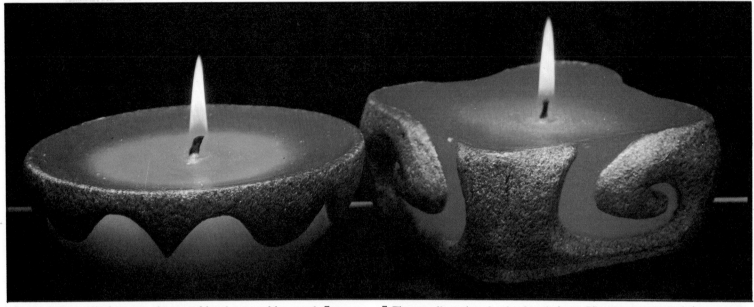

▲ *Sand candles made from an ashtray and bowl—carved into castles*▼

▼ *Two candles using the chunk technique. The square was made in a tea can*

Other candlemaking techniques

Sand candles. Fill a box with damp sand and smooth off the surface without packing it down. Dig a hole out of the center and push an article into the hole to make a shaped hole.

An ashtray, small bowl or the end of a bottle will do. Heat the wax to 250°F, and pour it into shape in the sand, being sure to pour into the center of the hole. The hotter the wax, the more sand is picked up; at 250°F, between $\frac{1}{2}$ inch and 1 inch is picked up. If a thicker sand wall is required, the wax should be hotter. Refill the hole as the level of the wax falls, keeping the temperature

of the wax high. Allow the sand candle to harden in a cold place for 1-2 hours. After this time, push the wicking needle down the center and leave it standing upright. Leave the candle overnight. Next day, dig the candle out, loosening the sand around it carefully and brushing away loose sand. Remove the needle and insert a wick which will leave an inch of wax unburned (for instance, if the candle is 3 inches in diameter put a 2 inch wick in). Top up with melted wax (220°F) and allow to set. Carve away areas of sand to make a design, taking care not to dig too deeply into the wax. If the right wick is chosen, the sand shell will remain intact after the candle has burned out and can be refilled.

Chunky candles. Arrange chunks of colored wax in a mold, pressing them to the sides and keeping them as far apart as possible. Pour molten wax (200°F) over these chunks. Allow the mold to stand for one minute, then place in a cooling bath. Push a wicking needle down the center. When set, take the mold from the bath, and place it in water just under boiling point. The outside of the wax will melt, and the colored chunks will also melt and blend with the new wax. Top up the wax at 180°F, covering the whole surface of the candle and allowing the wax to flow down the inside of the mold so that the whole surface is covered with molten wax. Place mold in a cooling bath again and allow to harden. Remove

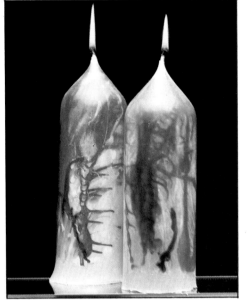
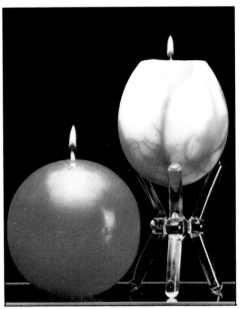

▼▲ Marbled effects on multilayered candles, and two from a ball and a balloon ▲

▼▲ Beeswax candles and water candles

candle, put in wick.

Marbled candles. Fix a wick in a warmed solid mold, and pour in a wax-stearin mixture at 190°F. Allow a minute for air bubbles to rise, then place in a cooling bath for 40 seconds. Pour the unset wax back into the pan, leaving a wax shell in the mold. Then, using pure dye, spoon a little into the mold, and quickly swirl it around and tip away the excess. Do this two or three times with different colors until a design has built up. Then pour in half a cup of candle wax (180°F), swirl it around quickly and empty the excess into a separate container (so that the wax will not contaminate white wax if it has picked up color). Do this seven or eight times to trap the color between

two layers of white wax. Then fill the mold with candle wax in the usual way. To achieve a well defined pattern it is essential that the mold be kept warm and that there is no waiting between processes.

Multilayered candles. These are made by pouring different colored waxes into a mold at 82°F, allowing each layer to partially set before adding the next color. By standing the mold at an angle in a cooling bath, layers can be built up diagonally.

Ball candles. Round candles are made using a rubber ball as a mold. Cut the ball in half and cut a hole in the top. Stick the two halves together again with adhesive tape.

Whipped cream candles. Whip cooling

wax with a fork to make a frothy mixture and use it to make candles in molds which wouldn't stand higher temperatures.

Water candles. These strange looking candles are intended to be used for table decorations but they can be burned. Put a small quantity of melted wax (210°F) into a saucer and, wearing rubber gloves, hold a plain candle upright, resting in the wax. Holding the saucer in one hand and the candle in the other, push the candle and saucer into a bucket of cold water with a swift, smooth movement. The wax will float upward, and practice will gradually make the formation less random. By twisting the saucer as it is immersed, the wax can be swirled around the candle.

Knitting pattern/twin set for children

This pretty twin set would delight any little girl. The sleeveless pullover is worked in an easy diagonal eyelet pattern with bands of this repeated on the stockinette stitch cardigan. Picot edges finish all hems, and the cardigan has raglan sleeves.

Sizes

Directions are for 26in chest. The figures in brackets [] refer to the 29 and 32in sizes respectively.
Pullover. Length at center back, 15[18½:21]in.
Cardigan. Length at center back, 16[19½:22]in.
Sleeve seam, 11[14:16]in.

Gauge

7 sts and 10 rows to 1in over st st worked on No.4 needles.

Materials

Bernat Pompadour
Pullover. 5[5:6] skeins
Cardigan. 8[8:9] skeins
One pair No.3 needles
One pair No.4 needles
5 buttons

Pullover back

Using No.3 needles, cast on 96[108:120] sts.
**Beg with a K row, work 8 rows st st.
Next row K1, *ytf, K2 tog, rep from * to last st, K1.
Beg with a P row, work 9 rows st st.**
Commence patt.
1st row K1, *ytf, K2 tog, K4, rep from * to last 5 sts, ytf, K2 tog, K3.
2nd and every other row P.
3rd row K2, *ytf, K2 tog, K4, rep from * to last 4 sts, ytf, K2 tog, K2.
5th row K3, *ytf, K2 tog, K4, rep from * to last 3 sts, ytf, K2 tog, K1.
7th row K4, *ytf, K2 tog, K4, rep from * to last 2 sts, ytf, K2 tog.
9th row K5, *ytf, K2 tog, K4, rep from * to last st, K1.
11th row K6, *ytf, K2 tog, K4, rep from * to end.
12th row P.

These 12 rows form patt and are rep throughout.
Continue until work measures 10½[13½:15½] from beg.

Shape armholes

Bind off 5 sts at beg of next 2 rows.
Dec one st at each end of every row until 72[80:88] sts rem.
Continue without shaping until armholes measure 5½[6:6½]in from beg, ending with a WS row.

Shape shoulders

Bind off 6 sts at beg of next 2 rows.
Bind off 3[5:7] sts at beg of next 2 rows.
Beg with a K row, work 8 rows st st on rem sts, dec one st at each end of every row.
Next row K1, *ytf, K2 tog, rep from * to last st, K1.
Beg with a P row, work 9 rows st st, inc one st at each end of every row.
Bind off loosely.

Pullover front

Using No.3 needles, cast on 96[108:120] sts.
Work as given for Back from ** to **.
Commence patt.
1st row K3, K2 tog through back loop (tbl),

▲ *A close-up detail showing the diagonal eyelet patterning*

ytf, * K4, K2 tog tbl, ytf, rep from * to last st, K1.
2nd and every other row P.
3rd row K2, K2 tog tbl, ytf, * K4, K2 tog tbl, ytf, rep from * to last 2 sts, K2.
5th row K1, K2 tog tbl, ytf, * K4, K2 tog tbl, ytf, rep from * to last 3 sts, K3.
7th row K2 tog tbl, ytf, *K4, K2 tog tbl, ytf, rep from * to last 4 sts, K4.

9th row K5, K2 tog tbl, ytf, * K4, K2 tog tbl, ytf, rep from * to last 5 sts, K5.
11th row *K4, K2 tog tbl, ytf, rep from * to last 6 sts, K6.
12th row P.
These 12 rows form patt.
Complete as given for Back.

Cardigan back

Using No.3 needles, cast on 102[114:126] sts.
Work as given from ** to ** for Pullover front.
Change to No.4 needles.
Beg with a K row, continue in st st until work measures 11[14:16]in from beg, ending with a P row.

Shape raglans

Next row K2, K3 tog, K to last 5 sts, K3 tog tbl, K2.
Next row P.
Rep these 2 rows 4 times more.
Next row K2, K2 tog, K to last 4 sts, K2 tog tbl, K2.
Next row P.
Rep last 2 rows until 34[38:42] sts rem.
Work 1 row. Bind off.

Cardigan left front

Using No.3 needles, cast on 56[62:68] sts.
Work from ** to ** as given for Pullover back.

Next row Patt 48[54:60] sts as given for Pullover front, K8, cast on 8 sts.
Next row P.
Continue in this way working 1[2:2] complete patts and 6 rows of the next patt on the first 48[54:60] sts and keeping the rem 16 sts in st st.
Change to No.4 needles.
Beg with a K row, continue in st st across all sts until work

measures 11[14:16]in from beg, ending with a P row.

Shape raglan and neck

Next row K2, K3 tog, K to last 18 sts, K2 tog, K16.
Next row P.
Rep these 2 rows 4 times more.
Next row K2, K2 tog, K to end.
Next row P.
Next row K2, K2 tog, K to last 18 sts, K2 tog, K16.
Next row P.
Rep these 4 rows until 22 sts rem, then rep first 2 rows only until 16 sts rem.
Beg with a K row continue in st st on these sts for 1½[1¾:2]in.
Bind off.

Cardigan right front

Using No.3 needles, cast on 56[62:68] sts.
Work from ** to ** as given for Pullover back.
Next row Cast on 8 sts, K16, patt rem 48[54:60] sts as given for Pullover back.
Complete as given for left Front, reversing all shaping and working 5 sets of buttonholes as follows, ending at center edge and working first set when work measures ¼in from the 8 cast-on sts.
Next row K2, bind off 3 sts, K6, bind off 3 sts, K2, patt to end.
Next row P to end, casting on 3 sts above those bound-off on previous row.
Work 4 more sets of buttonholes in this way at intervals of 2[2¾:3¼]in, measured from center of previous buttonholes.

Cardigan right sleeve

Using No.3 needles, cast on 48[54:60] sts.
Work from ** to ** as given for Pullover back.
Change to patt as given for Pullover back.
Work 1[2:2] complete patts and 6 rows of next patt.
Change to No.4 needles.
Beg with a K row, continue in st st, inc one st at each end of next and every following 5th row until there are 74[82:90] sts.

▲ *This useful twin set for a little girl has an attractive lacy pattern on the pullover which is repeated on the sleeve and lower edges of the cardigan*

Continue without shaping until sleeve measures 12[15:17] in from beg, ending with a P row.

Shape raglan cap
Next row K2, K3 tog, K to last 5 sts, K3 tog tbl, K2.
Next row P.
Rep these 2 rows once more.
Next row K2, K2 tog, K to last 4 sts, K2 tog tbl, K2.

Next row P.
Rep last 2 rows until 10 sts rem.
Work 1 row.
Next row Bind off 4 sts, K2, K2 tog tbl, K2.
Work 1 row. Bind off rem sts.

Cardigan left sleeve

Work as given for right Sleeve using the patt as given for

left Front and reversing shaping at cap of raglan.

Finishing

Press lightly.
Pullover. Join shoulder seams. Using No.3 needles and with WS facing, pick up and K 95[101:107] sts evenly around armholes. Work 6 rows in K1, P1 rib. Bind off in rib. Join side

seams. Fold picot hems in half and slip stitch to WS.
Cardigan. Join raglan, side and sleeve seams. Fold picot hems in half and slip stitch to WS. Join bound-off edges of borders together and oversew to back neck. Fold border in half to WS and slip stitch. Buttonhole-st around button-holes, working through both thicknesses. Sew on buttons.

1767

Here are the two final designs for the set of pillows featured on page 1670. An anemone and thistle flower have inspired stylized designs to be worked for pillows. For a bolder effect the designs could be worked in crewel wool on a background of fine, even-weave woolen fabric. The individual's choice of colors is dictated by the extent to which she wants to follow

1768

nature's lead or allow whimsy to be her guide.

To make each pillow measuring 15 inches square you will need:
- [ ] ½yd 36 inch wide even-weave linen
- [ ] Sewing thread to match linen
- [ ] 10 inch zipper
- [ ] 16 inches square pillow form
- [ ] D.M.C. 6-strand floss

Anemone pillow

D.M.C. 6-strand floss in the following colors: **1.** dark blue 336; **2.** medium blue 312; **3.** light blue 334; **4.** yellow/green 701; **5.** dirty green 890; **6.** green 986.

One skein of color 1, two skeins each of colors 4, 5 and 6, and three skeins each of colors 2 and 3.

Method

Using three strands of floss in the needle, work the design in long and short stitch. Start on the large flower using light blue color 3, then embroider with medium blue color 2. Finally, work the center of the flower and the streaks in dark blue color 1. Work the buds in the same order, stitching the dark blue streaks last.

Thistle flower pillow

D.M.C. 6-strand floss in the following colors and amounts: **2.** dark turquoise 517; **3.** light turquoise 807; **4.** gray/blue 806; **5.** olive green 987; **6.** yellow/green 988; **7.** dark green 986.
Color number **1.** navy blue crewel wool. Three skeins each of colors 1 and 2, and two skeins each of the remaining colors.

Method

For the flower centers use two strands of crewel wool in the needle. Some of the centers are worked in satin stitch and others filled with French knots. The rest of the embroidery is worked with three strands of floss in the needle. The flowers are worked in satin stitch, the leaves in long and short stitch and the stems in outline stitch.

1769

Tracing pattern for anemone

1770

Tracing pattern for thistle flower

1771

Home crochet/tablecloth in squares

This attractive tablecloth is made of one hundred and thirteen simple motifs. Fewer motifs can be used to make small mats, or a greater number for a larger tablecloth or even a bedspread.

Size
48in square.

Gauge
Each motif measures 4½in.

Materials
Coats & Clark's O.N.T.
Pearl Cotton
57 balls
One No.B crochet hook

First motif

Using No.B hook,
ch9, join with a ss to form a ring.
1st round *Ch2, 5tr into ring, ch2, 1sc into ring, rep from * 3 times more.
2nd round Ch9, *skip 2ch and 2tr, 1tr into next tr, ch6, 1tr into same tr, ch5, skip 2tr and 2ch, 1tr into next sc, ch5, rep from * twice more, skip 2ch and 2tr, 1tr into next tr, ch6, 1tr into same tr, ch5; join with a ss into 4th of first 9ch.
3rd round 2sc into sp, ch5, ss into first of these ch—called 1 picot —, 2sc into same sp, *2sc into next sp, 1 picot, 2sc into same sp, 1 picot, 2sc into same sp, (2sc into next sp, 1 picot, 2sc into same sp) twice, rep from * twice more, 2sc into next sp, 1 picot, 2sc into same sp, 1 picot, 2sc into same sp, 1 picot, 2sc into same sp, 2sc into next sp, 1 picot, 2sc into same sp, ss into first sc of round.
4th round Ch9, skip 2sc, 1 picot and 2sc, 1tr into first sc of corner sp, *ch5, 1tr into center picot on corner sp, ch6, 1tr into same picot, (ch5, skip 2sc, 1 picot and 2sc, 1tr into first sc of next sp) 3 times, rep from * twice more, ch5, 1tr into center picot on corner sp, ch6, 1tr into same picot, ch5, skip 2sc, 1 picot

and 2sc, 1tr into first sc of next sp, ch5, join with a ss into 4th of first 9ch.
5th round (2sc into next sp, 1 picot, 2sc into same sp) twice, *2sc into next sp, 1 picot, 2sc into same sp, 1 picot, 2sc into same sp, 1 picot, 2sc into same sp, (2sc into next sp, 1 picot, 2sc into same sp) 4 times, rep from * twice more, 2sc into next sp, 1 picot, 2sc into same sp, 1 picot, 2sc into same sp, 1 picot, 2sc into same sp, (2sc into next sp, 1 picot, 2sc into same sp) twice, join with a ss into first sc of round.
6th round Ch9, skip 2sc, 1 picot and 2sc, 1dc into first sc of next sp, ch6, skip 1sc, 1 picot and 2sc, 1dc into first sc of next sp, ch6, skip 1sc, 1 picot and 1sc, 1dc into next sc, *ch9, skip 1 picot and 1sc, 1dc into next sc, ch6, skip 1 picot and 2sc, 1dc into first sc of next sp, (ch6, skip 1sc, 1 picot and 2sc, 1dc into first sc of next sp) 4 times, ch6, skip 1sc, 1 picot and 1sc, 1dc into next sc, rep from * twice more, ch9, skip 1 picot and

1sc, 1dc into next sc, ch6 skip 1 picot and 2sc, 1dc into first sc of next sp, ch6, skip 1sc, 1 picot and 2sc, 1dc into first sc of next sp, ch6, join with a ss into 4th of first 9ch.

Second motif

Using No.B hook, ch9 and work as for first motif for first five rounds.
6th round Ch9, skip 2sc, 1 picot and 2sc, 1dc into first sc of next sp, ch6, skip 1sc, 1 picot and 2sc, 1dc into first sc of next sp, ch6, skip 1sc, 1 picot and 1sc, 1dc into next sc, ch5, ss into 5th of 9ch on corner of first motif, ch5, skip 1 picot and 1sc on second motif, 1dc into next sc, (ch3, ss into next ch loop of first motif, ch3, skip 1sc, 1 picot and 2sc of second motif, 1dc into first sc of next sp) 5 times, ch3, ss into next ch loop of first motif, ch3, skip 1sc, 1 picot and 1sc on second motif, 1dc into next sc, ch5, ss into 5th of 9ch on corner of first motif, ch5, complete motif as before.

Joining motifs

Continue joining motifs in this way, joining on as many sides as necessary. The cloth is formed from the points with one motif in the first line, three in the second line and so on, increasing by one motif at each end until there are fifteen, then decreasing two motifs on each line until only one remains.

Edging

Attach yarn at an inside corner, work 5sc into ch5 sp, (into next ch6 sp work 3sc, 1 picot and 3sc) 6 times, in corner sp work 3sc, 1 picot, 3sc, 1 picot, 3sc, 1 picot and 3sc, (into next ch6 sp work 3sc, 1 picot and 3sc) 6 times, 5sc into ch5 sp, continue around in this way, remembering that on the single motif line two outer corners will be worked consecutively.

Finishing

Press under a damp cloth with a hot iron until dry.

▼*Close-up detail of one square motif of the tablecloth which is illustrated on the facing page*

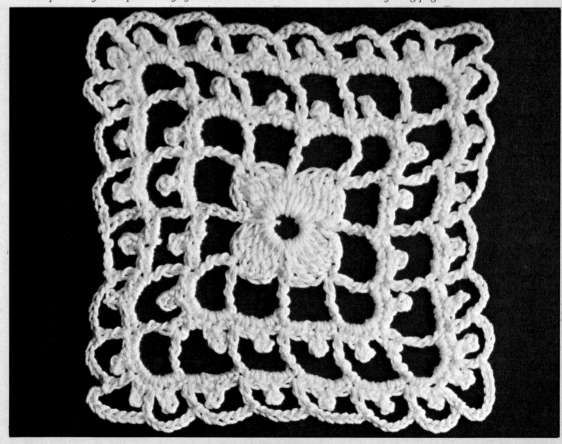

Costume design/dress up in Pellon

Most parents are asked at one time or another to make or supply "dress up" clothes for children. Ready-made ones are generally expensive and limited in size range.

Since play costumes should be quick to make and give an instant effect, Pellon is a good material to use. This non-woven interlining is well known to dressmakers and is useful for dress up clothes because it does not fray, dyes very well in hot or cold water dyes, and can be painted, crayoned or tie-dyed. Pellon can be used for decoration or for a whole outfit, and the thicker quality is better for garments that are likely to get a lot of strain. All the costumes in this chapter are designed to be made from Pellon, either colored before cutting out or spray-painted afterward. Other fabrics can be used instead for more lasting costumes.

The basic pattern given in this chapter will make a princess costume, a flower fairy, an elf, a jester and a pirate, but many more costume ideas can be easily adapted from it.

The pattern is designed to fit an eight year old, measuring 38 inches from shoulder to hem on the full length garment.

The princess
Cut two basic dress shapes from Pellon and cut out a square neck on both front and back. Sew up the shoulders and put in the sleeves. Sew bands of decorative ribbon on the cuffs. Sew up the sides and underarms in one operation. Sew on decorative bands at the hem. Cut out a Pellon train tapering the ends to fit the shoulders. Sew snap fasteners on the shoulders and the ends of the train. Cut out large silver or gold paper stars and glue them onto the dress and train. Alternatively, make a stencil from stiff cardboard and paint shapes on the dress with poster paint, mixed very dry, using a stiff brush. A crown in Pellon, painted gold, completes the princess outfit.

The flower fairy
A lighter weight Pellon can be tie-dyed in one or more colors for a lovely soft effect, or sprayed with diluted poster paints after the garment is finished.

First, cut out two basic dress shapes, sew up the shoulders and join the side seams from the armhole downward for 6 inches. At the point where the stitches stop sew braid or ribbon around the chest. Cut the rest of the skirt into strips from the hem to the ribbon line, pointing the bottom edges.

Make leaves from green Pellon and flowers from crepe paper, felt or tissue paper, attaching them to lengths of green yarn.

Stitch the flowery strings to the ribbon at chest line. Knot one short length for a crown to fit the child's head. Brightly colored tights are worn to complete the costume.

The elf

The basic pattern is cut to mid-thigh with a pointed hem. Emphasize the hem and the round neckline with a painted or ribbon border.

Sew up the sides and one shoulder. Sew a snap fastener onto the open shoulder. Sew ribbons to the shoulder seams so that they hang down over the arm. Choose ribbons to match and tone with the colors of the main outfit. The little elf illustrated is dressed in yellows and greens with yellow tights. Make a flower-shaped hat from five long, leaf-shaped pieces of Pellon joined halfway down each side. Make a stalk for the flower by rolling up a strip of Pellon.

The jester

The basic pattern is cut off at the same point as for the elf, but the hem points are cut longer and thinner. Put sleeves in after the shoulder seams are sewn up, leaving one shoulder seam partly unsewn for the head opening. The hood has a long point with a bobble sewn on the end. Cut the neck edge of the hood into points. Add matching tights and a stick with a bell on it and the jester is complete.

The pirate

The basic units for this outfit can be assembled from children's day to day clothes. Old pants are cut off at the knee, gathered with elastic and tucked into knee-high boots. A shirt is left open at the neck and pulled in at the waist using a bright scarf as a cummerbund. The Pellon vest is then cut from the basic pattern, open at the center front. It finishes at mid-thigh or even at the knee if preferred. When the shoulder and side seams have been closed, gold braid is sewn around the edges as shown in the drawing. A black Pellon hat is cut into two pieces which are joined along the top edge, and a white skull and cross bones and gold braid sewn or stuck on the top edge completes the outfit. A stuffed parrot on the shoulder, made of Pellon and painted in bright colors, would give the Long John Silver look.

Basic pattern for five children's costumes ▶
◀ *For some of the costumes shown, you will need to accessorize with garments from the child's own wardrobe. The flower fairy, jester and elf costumes require colored tights; the pirate needs old pants and boots.*

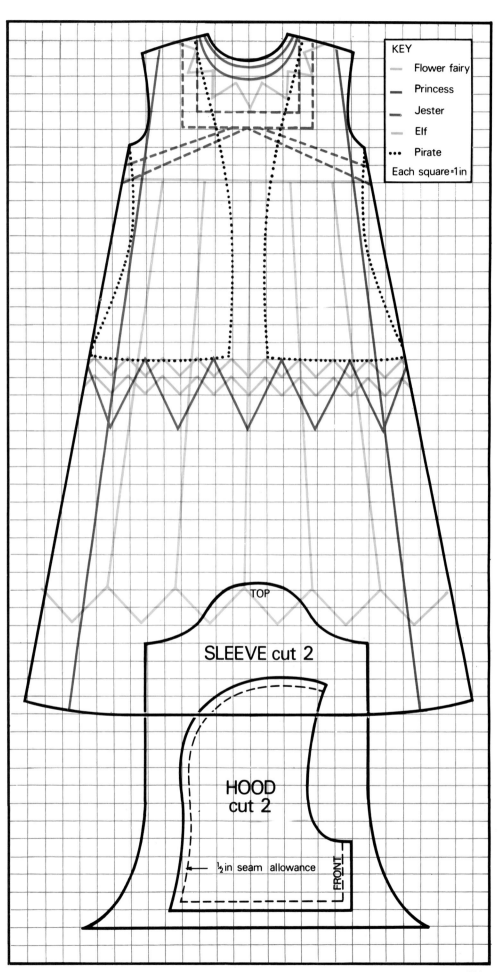

KEY
— Flower fairy
— Princess
— Jester
— Elf
··· Pirate
Each square = 1 in

TOP

SLEEVE cut 2

HOOD cut 2

½ in seam allowance

FRONT

A selection of coats from the wide range of coat paper patterns available, all of which the home dressmaker can now make herself. Selected from Vogue and Butterick patterns, they demonstrate some of the different effects which can be achieved by a change of fabric and style. **Above: A.** *Back-belted coat in gabardine.* **B.** *Classic step collar in wool tweed.* **C.** *Wraparound coat in plaid angora, and jacket in cashmere, both tie-belted.* **D.** *Country casual in tweed.* **E.** *Dress coat in a home furnishing fabric.* **F.** *Fun collar and front detail in a coat weight doeskin cloth. Right: one pattern and two moods. These coats, in yellow coating and a herringbone tweed are suitable for any occasion.*

pleat

turn under
collar and lapels

tuck in
sleeves

fasten
buttons

1. *The stitched lining*

turn
under ⅛"
and stitch

2. *Making the lining seam allowances neat*

3

3. *Positioning coat on a tailor's dummy*

4a

4a, b. *Pinning lining to coat (front and back)*

In this chapter
A. Lining a coat: cutting and stitching the lining; putting in the lining; french tack.
B. Lining a jacket

A. Lining a coat

The outside of the coat is now finished, and all that remains is for the coat to be lined. A lining covers the seams and prolongs the life of a coat and also makes

it easier to wear.

Cutting and stitching the lining
Cut the lining according to the pattern instructions, bearing in mind any alterations you have made to the coat.
1. Pin, baste and stitch any darts or pleats. Then pin, baste and stitch all seams except for the shoulder and armhole seams.
2. Make the seam allowances neat by turning under the edges for ⅛ inch and stitching as shown.
Iron the lining well, but be sure to test

the iron temperature first on a spare piece of lining fabric.

Putting in the lining
3. If you have a tailor's dummy, put the coat on it, wrong side out, tucking the sleeves flat to the sides. Fasten coat buttons and adjust coat to hang correctly.
If you do not have a dummy, lay the coat right side down on a table. As you work on a section lay it as flat as possible on the table.
4a, b. Pin the lining to the coat, wrong

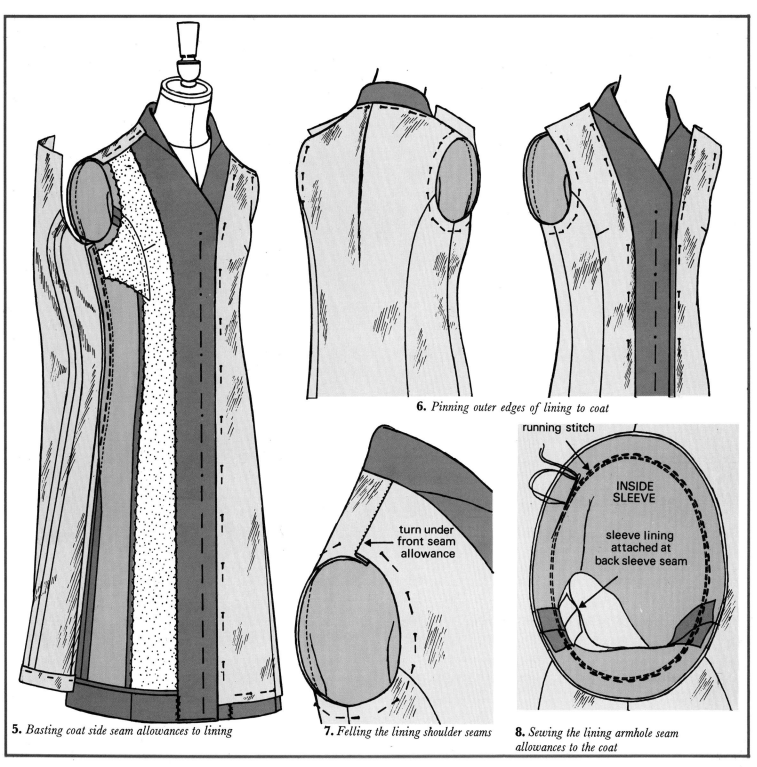

5. *Basting coat side seam allowances to lining*

6. *Pinning outer edges of lining to coat*

turn under
front seam
allowance

7. *Felling the lining shoulder seams*

running stitch

INSIDE
SLEEVE

sleeve lining
attached at
back sleeve seam

8. *Sewing the lining armhole seam
allowances to the coat*

sides together. Start at the center back of the neck and do not turn under the raw seam allowances at the edges of the lining. Pin in this order:

Around back neck, after pleating at the center back as shown in pattern instructions.

Down any style seams at the back.

The side seams.

The front style seams or darts.

Down the front.

Around the armholes. If the armholes have stretched during making do not cut the lining to match. Instead, ease the coat onto the lining to avoid distorting it.

Along the shoulder seams, overlapping the seams over any shoulder pads if used.

Down the center back pleat if there is one. Turn up the lining hem 1 inch above the coat hem, and pin.

Slip on the coat to see if the lining is pulling at any point. Once again it is better to have a friend help you.

5. Lift the lining, baste the side seam allowances of coat and lining together from underarm to hip level, unpinning where necessary to do so.

6. Turn under the seam allowances along the neck and front edges of the lining and repin to facing.

Turn up the hem and fell firmly.

7. On each shoulder turn under the front shoulder seam allowances on the lining and position over the back seam allowance. Fell as shown.

8. Working from inside the sleeves, sew the lining to the coat just outside the sleeve stitching line. Use a double thread and running stitch.

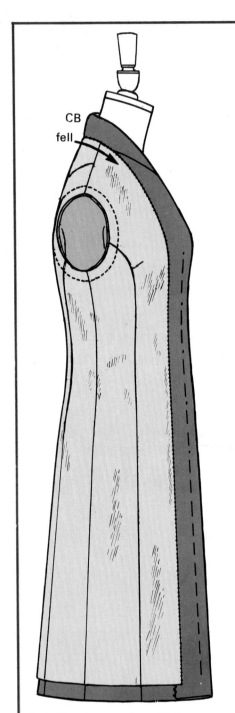

9. *Felling the outer edges of lining to coat*

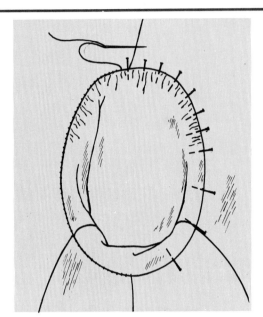

10. *Felling sleeve lining to armhole seam*

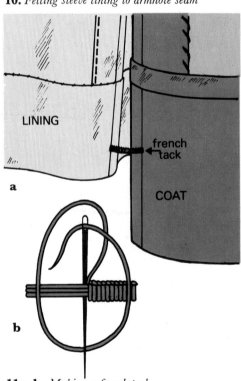

11a, b. *Making a french tack*

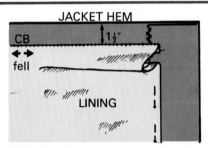

12. *Felling lining hem edge on a jacket*

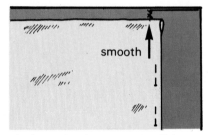

13. *Smoothing down the jacket lining*

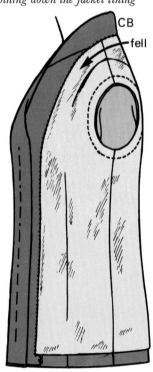

14. *Felling the lining to the jacket around the outer edges*

9. Working from the center back of the neck, fell the lining to the coat around the outer edges to the hemline.

10. It is now time to sew the lining armhole seams. To do this, bring the sleeve lining up and turn in the seam allowance. Pin over the coat lining taking the ease into small gathers.

Fell firmly to the coat lining.

Make french tacks at the hem ends of the side seams to hold the lining to the hem.

French tack

11a, b. To make a french tack, first sew

1780

3 to 4 long stitches anchored to coat and lining as shown (**a**). Then, with the same thread, work buttonhole stitch over the entire length of the long stitches (**b**).

B. Lining a jacket

A jacket lining is attached the same way as a coat lining except at the hem edge which is not left loose, and attached with a french tack as on a coat.

Follow figures **1** to **4,** but pin the lining hem to the same length as the jacket.

12. Follow figures **5** and **6** but lift the hem

edge of the lining up 1½ inches above the jacket edge. Fell to the jacket hem allowance along the entire length, as shown. Follow figures **7** and **8.**

13. Smooth the front lining down into a fold at the hem edge.

14. Starting at center back of the neck, fell the lining to the coat around the outer edges down to the fold at the hem. The extra length in the lining provided by the fold at the hem allows for movement when wearing the jacket.

Finally sew the lining armhole seam as shown in figure **10.**

Index

How to use this index

The index to Golden Hands has been designed to help you find your way to every aspect, every detail in the entire six volumes.

Page Numbers
To avoid confusion, page number references are given in all cases—use the table on this page to check which Volume each page is in.

Sections
Each section in Golden Hands has its own index and each section is entered in the order in which it appears in Golden Hands. Each section is identified by the key motif shown at the top of each chapter.

Alphabetical entries
Entries are made alphabetically and as many have been cross-referred as possible. However, you will find that in most cases we have grouped all stitches under 'Stitches', rather than spreading them through the entries as running stitch under R or Gobelin stitch under G. So if at first you don't find the item you are looking for, think of the group it belongs to.

You'll also find in many cases that garments have been grouped together so that you can look through the complete 'wardrobe' at a glance.

Key to symbols
Included in Basic Wardrobe are reference symbols which indicate whether a garment is knitted—(K), crocheted—(C) or machine knitted—(mK). Similarly, Pattern Library keys are indicative of Embroidery—(E), appliqué—(A), and needlepoint—(N).

Pattern Library

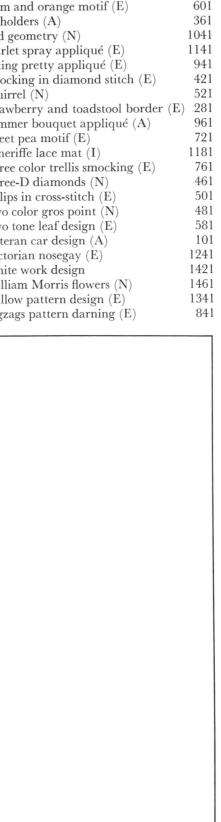

Knitting Know-how

Crochet Know-how

Basic Wardrobe

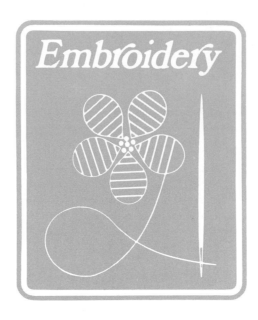

Embroidery

Needle-point

Collector's Piece

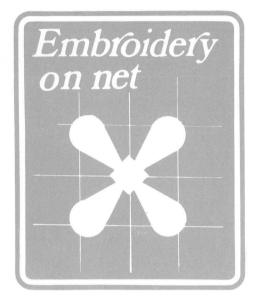

Embroidery on net

Embroidery on tulle

Netting

Macramé

Daisy work

Dress-making

Fashion Flair

1796

Volume Six

Crafts

Dictionary of Sewing Terms

Appliqué

A motif or design sewn or stuck to fabric or a garment.

Beading

Lace, embroidery or openwork trimming through which ribbon can be threaded.

Bonding

An adhesive process of joining two fabrics, which adds body and stability to knits, sheers, laces and other fragile fabrics.

Braid

Narrow binding or trimming fabric; can be round or tubular, but is usually woven or flat. Includes rickrack, soutache, military etc.

Calendering

A mechanical finishing process of pressing the fabric between a series of heated cylinders to produce a flat, glossy surface.

Carding

Process which separates fibers of cotton, brings them into line like a thin web, then compacts them into a continuous strand. It removes most impurities.

Crimp

Wrinkles or waviness in fabrics (natural or manufactured) which lends bulk and resilience.

Denier

Unit of weight indicating fineness or coarseness of a fiber filament. The higher the denier number, the coarser the yarn. Used also to denote weight of threads in nylon stockings.

Ecru

The color of unbleached cotton, wool or silk fabrics: light tan or beige.

Face

The side of a fabric which looks better because of weave or finish.

Filling

Crosswise yarn in a weave, sometimes called *weft* or *woof*. Also a term for sizing substances, which give body to a fabric.

Fulling

Finishing process of dampening then beating under heat, used on woolens. This shrinks the cloth, increasing its weight and obscuring the weave.

Gimp

Trimming composed of flat, open work strips of twisted strands of fiber, run through with metallic wire or coarse cord for body.

Gray goods

Fabric in an unbleached, undyed or unfinished state.

Hand

Feel, drape, or handling qualities of a fabric; refers to texture and quality.

Jacquard

A complex loom with a versatile, pattern-making mechanism which permits the weaving of very elaborate designs.

Laminated

Two or more layers of fabric joined together with glue, resin or other adhesives, or by heat. Also a face fabric backed in synthetic foam.

Lappet

A weaving process for small-figured cloths, such as dotted Swiss, in which the pattern is embroidered into the body of the fabric as the cloth is woven.

Leno

A weaving process in which the warp yarns are paired and twisted, giving the fabric strength and stability.

Marl

Yarns of two different colors or lusters twisted together for novelty effect.

Mercerize

To treat cotton yarn or cloth in a caustic soda solution, usually under tension. Increases strength, luster and affinity for dyes.

Mesh

An open-textured fabric with even spaces between the yarns. Can be knitted, knotted or woven, in fine or coarse threads or yarns.

Moiré

An irregular, wavy finish on corded or ribbed fabrics of silk, cotton and many of the man-made fibers. It is produced by engraved rollers, steam, heat or chemicals.

Momie weave

A weave in which the yarn is twisted, giving it a granite or pebble effect as in crash toweling.

Multiple fabric

Fabric composed of 2, 3, or even 4 layers bound together by the structure of the weave.

Nap

A soft, fuzzy finish raised on various fabrics, usually by brushing cloth against a cylinder covered with short, protruding wires. Gives fabric a soft hand and downy appearance, making it warmer and more durable.

Neps

Little knots or clusters in cotton or wool fibers formed either naturally or during processing.

Noil

The short fibers removed in the carding and combing process.

Nub yarn

A novelty yarn spun intentionally with slubs, knots etc.

Ombré

A rainbow colored effect in fabrics, either dyed or woven in, with colors graduated. Effect can be in varying shades of the same color, or a mixture of different colors.

Ondule

A wavy rippling pattern produced in fabrics by alternately spreading and converging a small group of warp threads.

Package dyeing

A method by which the dye solution is circulated through yarns wound around perforated tubes.

Panne

A finish for velvet or satin produced by pressure. It flattens the pile on velvet, giving it a lustrous sheen, also makes satin smoother and more lustrous.

Passementerie

A general French term referring to edgings and trimmings, usually made from gimp, cord, beads etc.

Pearl cotton

A mercerized cotton thread or yarn, used for embroidery and other needlework, as well as knitting and crocheting.

Pilling

Forming small tangles of fibers on the surface of a fabric as a result of abrasion. Considered a defect.

Pinwale

An edge or rib that is very narrow and found in fabric such as corduroy.

Plissé

Puckered stripes or pattern on cotton fabric. Achieved by weaving with yarns of different degrees of shrinkage or by chemical treatment.

Pyroxylin

A coating applied to cotton or rayon fabrics to make them waterproof and stain resistant.

Ratiné

A textured yarn made by twisting a thick and a thin fiber under uneven tension.

Reeling

Process of winding single silk filaments from unbroken cocoons into skeins.

Ret

To moisten cellulose fibers in order to loosen the fiber from the woody tissue. Used in processing flax and hemp.

Selvage

Narrow woven edge of fabric, which prevents fraying and supports tension in weaving.

Sizing

Compounds applied to yarn or fabrics, which give smoothness, luster or improved body.

Twill

A basic weave with a diagonal rib, or twill line, producing a strong, durable, firm fabric.

Wale

In woven fabric, a rib, cord or raised portion. In knitting, a series of loops lying lengthwise in the fabric.

Warp

The threads running lengthwise in a woven fabric, parallel to the selvage.

Weft

The threads running widthwise in a woven fabric, also known as *woof* or *filling*.

MANUFACTURERS' ADDRESSES

The following firms will accept written inquiries about mailing supplies:

D.M.C. Pearl Cotton from—
Merribee Needlecraft Co.
2904 W. Lancaster
Fort Worth, Texas 76107.

Embroidery and needlecraft materials

American Crewel Studios
P/O Box 1756
Point Pleasant Beach, New Jersey 08742.

Boutique Margot
26 W. 54th Street
New York, New York 10019.

In case of difficulty in obtaining any yarns featured in Golden Hands, please write directly to the following manufacturers' addresses to find the location of your nearest retailer

American Thread and **Dawn** yarns by
American Thread
High Ridge Park
Stamford, Connecticut 06905.

Bear Brand, Botany, Bucilla
and **Fleisher** yarns by—
Bernhard Ulmann Co.
Division of Indian Head
30-20 Thomson Avenue
Long Island City, New York 11101.

Bernat yarns by—
Emile Bernat & Sons Co.
Uxbridge, Massachusetts 01569.

Brunswick yarns by—
Brunswick Worsted Mills Inc.
Pickens, South Carolina 29671.

Coats & Clark's yarns by—
Coats & Clark's
430 Park Avenue
New York, New York 10022.

Columbia-Minerva yarns by—
Columbia-Minerva Corp.
295 Fifth Avenue
New York, New York 10016.

Reynolds yarns by—
Reynolds Yarns Inc.
215 Central Avenue
East Farmingdale, New York 11735.

Spinnerin yarns by—
Spinnerin Yarn Co. Inc.
230 Fifth Avenue
New York, New York 10001.

Unger yarns by—
William Unger & Co.
230 Fifth Avenue
New York, New York 10001.